Thomsen, Moritz.

The farm on the
river of Emeralds

DATE		

The Farm on the River of Emeralds

MORITZ THOMSEN

HOUGHTON MIFFLIN COMPANY BOSTON

1978

Library of Congress Cataloging in Publication Data
Thomsen, Moritz.
The farm on the river of Emeralds.
1. Farm life—Ecuador—Esmeraldas Valley. 2. Thomsen, Moritz. 3. Farmers—Ecuador—Esmeraldas Valley—Biography. I. Title.
S522.E2T36   986.6'3   [B]   78–6760
ISBN 0–395–26311–5

Printed in the United States of America

S 10 9 8 7 6 5 4 3 2 1

For Ramoncito and Martita

The inky sky over the Doldrums and the oppressive atmosphere are more than just an obvious sign of the nearness of the equator. They epitomize the moral climate in which two worlds have come face to face. This cheerless sea between them, and the calmness of the weather whose only purpose seems to be to allow evil forces to gather fresh strength, are the last mystical barriers between two regions so diametrically opposed to each other through their different conditions that the first people to become aware of the fact could not believe that they were equally human. A continent barely touched by man lay exposed to men whose greed could no longer be satisfied by their own continent. Everything would be called into question by this second sin: God, morality, and law. In simultaneous yet contradictory fashion, everything would be verified in practice and revoked in principal: the Garden of Eden, the Golden Age of antiquity, the Fountain of Youth, Atlantis, the Hesperides, the Islands of the Blessed, would be found to be true; but revelation, salvation, customs and law would be challenged by the spectacle of a purer, happier race of men (who, of course, were not really purer or happier, although a deep-seated remorse made them appear so). Never had humanity experienced such a harrowing test, and it will never experience such another, unless, some day, millions of miles from our own world, we discover some other globe, inhabited by thinking beings. We have at least the advantage of knowing that the distance can in theory be bridged, whereas the early navigators feared they might be venturing into the void.

LÉVI-STRAUSS, *Tristes Tropiques*

CONTENTS

AUTHOR'S NOTE

These pages cover the first four of the eight years I have so far spent as a farmer in Esmeraldas, that great coastal and jungle province of Ecuador which borders with Colombia on one side, the Pacific Ocean on another side, and whose other perimeters weaving through the Andes foothills are still being fought over from time to time in a legal and nicely Latin way with the province of Pichincha, that high sierran province whose jewels are Quito at 9500 feet and a whole string of some of the great South American volcanoes. This argument has been going on for about three hundred years, I believe, and has given gainful employment to hundreds of lawyers — maybe thousands — and, before it is finally settled, just possibly to thousands more.

The book is only vaguely chronological. So many things happened so fast and simultaneously that I had to handle the events and my heroes one by one. It may help the reader to know, for instance, though it is really not essential, that the story of Dalmiro takes almost the full four years to run its course. The same with Arcario and Jorge — and with Santo who is still on the farm and living with a nice old lady who makes few demands.

In telling Víctor's story and bringing it to an end I had to seriously distort the chronology. That is why Víctor, who has been banished from the farm in Part Two, reappears in Part Three, risen from the dead, to play his little final scene of burying his brother. The final conversation with Ramón at the very end of Part Two actually took place about two weeks after the ending of the book. Well, I'm sorry about that, but I couldn't figure out any other way to do it.

Part One

At the turn of Fortune's wheel,
   one is deposed,
another lifted on high
   to enjoy a brief felicity.
Uneasy sits the king —
   let him beware his ruin,
for beneath the axle of the wheel
   we read the name of Hecuba.

CARL ORFF, *Carmina Burana*

1

THE FARM AS JUNGLE

DOES ANYONE STILL REMEMBER that scene in what may have been Douglas Fairbanks's last movie — What was it called? Robinson Crusoe? — where, accepting a two thousand dollar bet (his skin as black as a Moor's, his dazzling teeth reflecting the dashing, exuberant freedom of his great soul), he rises into the air from a standing position in one unbelievable leap to the railing of a yacht and, before the eyes of his gasping and appalled friends, dives into the sea and swims toward a tropical islet topped with waving palms, circled by booming surf, to prove that he can throw off the trappings of his society to exist and flourish for six months in a natural and primitive world?

It has been almost thirty-five years since I sat in the front row of the Blue Mouse Theater madly stuffing popcorn into my pimpled face, the soul flying out of my body, absolutely stunned by the simplicity and purity of that stylish gesture. In those days I took serious things seriously: grace, nobility, courage — they killed me. In truth it was not Fairbanks at all who made that fearless leap into freedom. He was my agent, my double, showing me the way and plotting out a part of my life's scenario. For years after that I knew that someday, someday if life should ever become banal, I would know how to handle the situation, and I would find myself, naked to the waist, nattily executing a virile Australian crawl, moving toward those breakers, toward that jungled hill where lay, hidden in its shadowed depths, life and the mystery of life's beauty.

*

It is a morning of brilliant sun blazing in a cloudless sky, a furiously hot day in late November 1969. I am standing in the deep blue cooling shade of a great jungle tree on the banks of the Esmeraldas River, some twenty-five miles from the Pacific Ocean. The equator is out there someplace within a day's walk. Ramón is standing with me; he is my best friend now, that extra dividend that I have earned after four years as a Peace Corps volunteer, when I worked with him and his neighbors in a small coastal fishing village. I am a civilian again and I have come back to Ecuador to keep a promise: we are going to buy a farm together. My father has just died; I have ten thousand dollars in my pocket, and we have come to this spot for five days running, ostensibly to check out the property — take soil samples, walk the boundaries, search out areas of marsh or gravel, look for the hidden huts of poor *campesinos* who might be invading the land — although we have already made up our minds. It can't be done, any of it. Twelve-foot-high weeds and grass, covered with ticks, form an impassible wall on both sides of the gravel road that cuts through the property. It is impossible to move through the deserted fields, going back now to their original chaos of vines and grass and weeds and clumps of bamboo. We can see nothing. Still we are obsessed with the place and keep coming back to it, always ending up on the banks of the river at the end of the road and standing in the shade of that tremendous tree, from where we can look across the river to a half dozen grass huts that bravely confront a jungled hillside of intimidating tranquility.

We are in the heart of a rain forest area, and it is the dry season. The river is low, ambling, as blue as the sky, and we can see schools of fish suspended in its clearness. Raucous enchanting bird cries from across the river color the still morning air with flashes of hot color. Bugs buzz; butterflies flutter by. A pile of bananas rots in a collapsing shed roofed in tattered and yellowed leaves, and at the bottom of the path that leads from the shed to the river, three aging canoes carved out of tree trunks float at the beach's edge, caught like a mess of *pargo* on a single chain. Some small children must be watching us; they are hidden in the grass, but we can hear their sweet laughter as it blends with the high pitched droning of a million summer insects.

We are being set up; there is something aimed at our hearts. How could we resist this moment and the wish to prolong it for a lifetime? Or rather, how could we not wish to become a part of this eternity? Now, eight years later, I have figured it out. It was the tree that undid us, that spreading-branched tree in the middle of its enormous pool of blue shade, that gigantic tree with its buttressed roots and its soaring trunk that supported its colossal burden of deep green leaves, its nests of birds, its promise of peace and permanence. We would build the farm around it.

We found ourselves staring at one another and beginning to nod our heads as though we were answering each other's unasked question, and finally, knowing what his answer would be, I asked: "Well, what do you think? Shall we?"

Ramón grew pale and, trembling, squatted down among the dead leaves that covered the ground around the tree. He was a poor man who had never dreamed of owning much more than twenty acres; this piece of ground, though we had seen none of it yet, held something more than four hundred acres. Perhaps it was more than this farm's enormous size that troubled him and made him so weak in the knees that he had to sink to the earth; perhaps, subverted and made lustful for this land by the magic aura of the tree, he was still enough in command to question these rash emotions that were so unlike him when it came to money. Why did he want something so badly when he had never seen it? A full minute passed and I asked again, "Well, shall we?"

In a low voice, almost whispering, Ramón said, "Oh, my God, Martín, *yes;* let's get it." As though he were amazed at his own words, he blew out a great breath and shook his head violently. "But that's madness, isn't it? We can't afford it. *Can* we?"

"No," I said, "we can't afford it; it's way too much . . . But let's buy it; we'll think of something. A good down payment now, and the rest in a year. I think he'll go for that."

"Yes," Ramón said, "I bet he will." He got up quickly, raised both arms above his head and spun around a couple of times. He stopped and pointed across the road. "Look, over there just past the shed — we'll have to tear that damn thing down — that's where I want to build my house. And over there just past it on that little high ground we'll put the store."

"Oh, no, Ramón. No. That's not the way I see it. We must use this tree. Your house goes here in the shade, right here against the bank where you can look out over the river; and down there by that little gully we can put the store. Mornings the store will be in shade, too. Don't you think that's a much better idea?"

"Well . . ." Ramón said and shrugged his shoulders doubtfully.

A blaze of recognition flared in my head. Of course. Those fantasies of a fifteen-year-old were becoming real. Christ, what a stylish way to buy a farm. We had never done anything so stylish, nor would we ever again. It was as quick, as simple, as graceful as a flashing swan dive into a tropic sea.

I grab Ramón's black hand in mine and we rise together in one unbelievable leap to the railing of the yacht. We balance there for just a moment and fling our shirts away. Naked to the waist, teeth gleaming in dark skin, we turn, smile brilliantly into the camera's eye, and then soar, up and out and down toward the crystal waters and the coral beach and that jungled hill.

But I was still out there in the air when I realized that there was something terribly wrong with this scenario. That whole scene when Ramón dropped to the ground, trembling and pale, shook his head and flung his arms into the air, he had shamelessly up-staged me; I had had scarcely anything to do. For some reason I no longer felt like the hero of my life. I didn't have dazzling teeth, dusky skin, a stylish manner. I was about thirty years too late to star in this particular drama. Hell, I was fifty-three, half my teeth were gone or going, I could scarcely read a page without glasses, those damned cigarettes were rotting out my lungs.

Ramón soared up and out and down and cut the water like a knife. I stubbed my toe and bellyflopped behind him. Ramón, dashing dusky Ramón, with brave and virile motions moved swiftly toward the shore. Gagging on sea water, gasping for air, I dog paddled behind him. Somehow, I was still sitting in that front row seat, excited and watching intently but strangely uninvolved. I was too old for this particular caper, but it was too late to draw away now — nor would I back out if I could. Christ, Ramón was going to be the hero of the rest of my life.

*

And so we bought the farm, the whole negotiation being carried off with the most amazing cordiality. We had no idea at the time how desperate the owner was to be quit of the place. We offered a down payment of two thousand dollars, the balance in a year. Herr Schwager, wearing a mourning band of black upon his shirt sleeve, pretended to frown, pretended to find our offer quite ridiculous, but he couldn't bring it off; suddenly he jumped up from his chair, broadly smiling, and grabbed my hand, cinching the deal. About a week later, on a Monday morning, money and great piles of hand-written Ecuadorian contracts changed hands; that afternoon we moved out to the farm. There were four of us: Ramón, the hero; his pregnant wife, Ester; Martita, his young daughter; and I, that enthusiastic theatergoer. We came with beds and mattresses, pots and plates, twelve bottles of beer for snakebite, a sack of charcoal, a sack of rice, some tins of tuna fish.

Then everything became confusion as in no movie I had ever seen. Neighbors arrived to watch us unpack; they were all black, most of them in their twenties, many of them small children. The older people, observing the proprieties, politely waited until late afternoon to visit us. I was amazed that so many people were appearing out of this tranquil empty forest. Almost none of them was over forty. They were pleasant, handsome, lively people, dirt poor but wildly independent. We learned that they owned farms across the river or upstream from us. They were glad we had come; they hoped we would give them jobs. Several of them pointed out that while they were no longer day laborers they would gladly consider a foreman's job. They made quite a fuss over me but rather ignored Ramón, who was so obviously one of them, that black man with the large strong hands of a worker. They refused to believe the shocking rumor that was beginning to circulate: that Ramón was a partner, a half owner of the farm.

It took us a month to get settled; it was a month before I could say, "Hey, Ramón, don't you think it would be a rather smart idea if somehow we managed to walk through the farm and see what we have bought?" Temporarily we were going to live in some little shacks along the river. They were very small two-room disasters made out of rejected lumber and roofed in rusty and disintegrating corrugated iron. These cabins were the remnants of a sawmill that the former owner had established and then almost immediately abandoned. We had bought the farm thinking that there were only two shacks on the property, everything was so hidden in grass and *caña brava,* but every day, it seemed, we were discovering another one. The farm was a mystery; each day, as we wandered a few yards further into the grass of the river pasture, it began to seem as though we were creating our own farm. "It would be nice," I told Ramón one day, "if there were a little stream right here. You know, just in case we decide to buy some cattle." And fifteen minutes later, hacking our way through the grass, we came to the little stream we needed. Ramón loved to chew on great stalks of sugar cane; the very day he mentioned this and his desire to plant some in the front yard, one of our neighbors brought us some cuttings as a gift. The next morning all of us planted it together in a kind of rite — that first planting that made us the owners of the land.

We sent a message to Jorge Avila, the alcoholic carpenter in Rioverde, offering him steady work and wages of two dollars a day if he would come and build things for us. This was considerably more than he made in Rioverde, and shortly he arrived with his box of tools, his wife, and a couple of his alcoholic sons. First we put him to work straightening a large shed originally built to store freshly cut lumber. We had found this shed the second week, not thirty yards from Ramón's shack. It was beautiful, but though it was still quite new it had already begun to sag toward the north. We asked Jorge to jack it back into position and replace two of the rotting corner posts. We came back later that afternoon to find that he had jacked the whole thing so far that it had cracked and buckled and crashed flat to the south. We had, in a manner of speaking, been jacked off. We looked for Jorge and found him on the steps of his cabin. He was waiting for a new project, smiling drunkenly, giggling softly to himself, and fastidiously nibbling at a slice of papaya cut into the shape of a new moon.

"Jesus, Ramón, doesn't two dollars a day seem like pretty high wages to pay a man for wrecking everything on the farm? We're going backwards."

And Ramón, secretly furious with Jorge and feeling guilty because he had suggested that Jorge was the only decent carpenter on the coast, serenely said, "But this is a blessing of God. Don't you see? What if that shed had crashed down when it was full of chickens or pigs? It's absolutely the best thing that could have happened to us."

I began to get reacquainted with the Latin outlook.

As we settled down, we began to hire armies of men to help us. We sent Jorge to dig holes in that deep blue pool of shade beneath the tree for the hardwood posts that would support our new store, kitchen, and living area. It was going to be something out of Africa — five hexagon shapes nestled together like a beehive and roofed in palmetto.

We began to live our new life. It was good but not quite as I had imagined it. We hauled rust-colored water from the river for cooking, bathed along its muddy banks, used candles at night, and stepped out into the high grass to obey the calls of nature. There was no simplicity that seemed gross or unnatural.

We had a radio and a Datsun pickup; still we were pioneers and in a way existed in the past. The roughness of life around us — men hauling farm produce on scrawny tick-covered horses along muddy trails, women beating clothes on rocks along the river's edge, naked children playing in the small hacked-out hard-packed yards around their houses — all of it was, it seemed to me, like our own American West of a hundred and fifty years ago — a deprived life of brutish realities whose main objective was simply to keep existing. As we peered through the grass to see what a machete stroke may have revealed, we were always under the weight of the past, increasingly uncertain and confused about our roles in this place and about our relationship to this large prehistoric tract, still unseen, unknown, of which we were now the owners.

We knew that people were standing behind the wall of grass, watching us, and we began to get the feeling of being almost under siege. Ramón had brought with him that Latin distrust of strangers, and his suspicions of everyone were contagious. The people who lived along the river were still unknown to us; we had been warned in town that they were all thieves and would steal the very shirts off our backs. We had heard from half a dozen landowners in Esmeraldas that Herr Schwager, the former owner, had sold us the place out of fury because each time he had come to the farm to harvest his crop of *plátano* (a starchy tasteless banana-like fruit, the main ingredient of the coastal diet) he discovered that it had already been harvested. When, on about the tenth day, the radio was stolen out of the cabin where I slept, perhaps even while I slept, we began to affect a certain coldness toward our neighbors until they could begin to emerge as individuals whom we could trust or distrust. We moved Merdardo Luna out of the last of the huts and put him and his wife in a little cement house on the highway; he was paid to machete weeds during the day and to wander along the road looking for thieves at night. He reported one day that Alejandro, one of our workers, was stealing plátano. Ramón spoke to Alejandro, who confessed and swore on his sainted mother that he would never steal again. Two days later I caught him packing off a bunch of plátano, and we couldn't control him for another month, when we sent in a crew of men to cut down all the plátano on the farm.

About three months before we bought the farm, Herr Schwager had cleared thirty-five acres of ground with a bulldozer and planted it all with coconuts. Now we discovered that people were sneaking into the new planting, pulling up the young trees, and eating the seeds; others were taking out the trees to plant in their own farms. The coconuts along the highway were disappearing, and blank spaces were appearing all along a mile of fence line between us and our neighbor. We were in enemy territory. I try to remember what Frantz Fanon wrote when he was trying to explain why blacks are thieves; according to him it is almost their only way to revolt against an oppressive system that has kept them poor and which they detest. I can't buy this, since no one here on the coast has a political philosophy or is aware of being oppressed. If they are in revolt against something, why then do they steal from each other? Pigs, chickens, lines of drying clothes, blackened and dented pots hanging in an unguarded kitchen, these are the things that disappear along the river. But I am being twisted two ways. It was once illuminating to read a book about the psychological bases for theft among the blacks, especially when I read it in the heart of white America. But now I was living with blacks, and it was infuriating when they began to steal *my* coconuts. Hell,

I wasn't here as a white colonist to exploit and oppress blacks, was I? Was I?

At night, now, we tended to huddle together in the kitchen where Ester had already organized a refuge; even Jorge and his sons, in this strange territory, got in the habit of huddling with us. They sat outside on the steps or balanced on the windowsills, gravely smoking and dividing their attention between the food on the table and the enormous black night outside, which crouched over all the growing things and concealed some unspeakable menace. At eight o'clock when I walked through the grass to my shack everyone would stand outside with flashlights, lighting my way to the door. We had killed a half dozen coral snakes here, and as I walked through the darkness the skin on my ankles crept and twitched with anticipation. I rather enjoyed the terror; where else in my life had going from the dining-room table to the bedroom ever been a life and death adventure?

Sometimes at night, while I slept, and sometimes three or four nights in a row, a series of shuddering earth movements would rock the house, and I would half awaken to a growing feeling of being at sea, of rising and falling on long ocean swells. And now, because the jungle was beginning to take on a hostile form, I found in sleep thoughts that joined those rhythmic movements of the earth with the jungle, all of it confused but made profound by my new and increasing apprehension about having come to live in the wild heart of a black province. The rustle of rats in the rafters, the rustle of bats circling in the room, the outside night sounds, that incredible high-pitched whirring of a million insects — all were transformed into sea sounds — the flapping of sails or the slap of water against a hull or a brisk wind singing in the rigging — and then transformed again into some almost-grasped message about this farm, where we had come to live. Yes, I was learning about the history of the region, learning something cruel and hopeless. It emerged as a poor history of poverty and oppression, of man powerless against that destiny that was nature. One night I awoke thinking the words of Hemingway's dying Harry Morgan, "One man alone ain't got no fucking chance." But why? What profound thoughts one has in sleep — thoughts that dissolve at daybreak with one's inability to translate them. Although I didn't realize it then, I was already looking for some kind of a history to go with the farm.

At times the ground would roll and shudder in such frightening spasms that I would fully awaken. Across the river I could hear a woman scream; the books would tumble from the table, the half-rotten beams above me would crack, and the dry leaves in the coco palm outside the window would rattle wildly. Then for a time everything would be silent. Not a croak out of those millions of frogs in the darkness; the night birds, abashed, would sit silently on their branches; even the rats would hesitate and leave off their incessant investigations. The jungle crouched, humped in silence. All of us together were waiting for the end. Likely as not, the next day we would learn on the radio that thousands of Peruvians had perished under tons of falling mountain or that the color TV sets of all the people in the San Fernando Valley were on the blink. Here on the equator, at the middle of the world, we were all joined together for a time by a shuddering earth that communicated the tragedies of our brothers from Nome to Tierra del Fuego.

These times were strange and unreal but not at all unpleasant. Even lying in bed could be exciting in this exotic land. Nothing, I now decided as I hung on to the sides of my rolling cot, nothing opens life to new interpretations and loosens one's tenuous grasp on the stale realities more than having the earth itself heave and roll beneath you, transforming a bed into a boat, the clashing of palm fronds into salt-sea night wind moving through canvas, or the quaking movement itself into history. After a really good shaking up one sees the earth with new eyes, sees this little spinning ball of mud in all its vulnerable and trembling beauty.

Until some time in the 1950s the farm we bought had been part of a tremendous tract of land, almost completely uninhabited, that stretched from the ocean at Esmeraldas to Santo Domingo de los Colorados, a small village at the foot of the Andes, one hundred and fifty miles to the south. People moved into this area after the Second World War when the price of bananas began to boom, and in a colonization program sponsored by the government, about fifteen families took possession of what is now the farm. There was no highway in those days; the river, twisting for forty miles among low hills to the sea, was the road that one traveled to get here and the road one used to send the crops to market. What a terrible life it must have been. Those first settlers, incredibly tough, long-suffering, and enduring, would have impressed any of our early pioneers with their courage. When we compared our own efforts with theirs, we felt positively effete.

With the collapse of the banana export market, the price per stem fell from fifty cents to five cents to nothing, and the farmers here found themselves producing hundreds of tons of fruit that had no value except for hog feed. Some of the farmers hung on and changed from bananas to cattle; some of them just hung on, waiting, unable to believe that they didn't have a great future with the packing companies. But finally, out of desperation, they were forced off the land. Herr Schwager showed up. He offered them cash and offered to buy them all out at once. Hooray. They took the money and headed for the big city slums. Schwager built a small cement house on the highway for a caretaker, planted thirty-five acres of coconuts and fifty acres of pasture, and began to build a sawmill on the river. He named his new pride "Rancho Lolita" in honor of his wife. And then suddenly and cruelly she died. He sank into a long depression and lost all interest in the property.

Now we had it . . . Or it had us.

As we hacked out the grass and moved further on to the spot where we had decided to build the new *ramada* to replace the one that Jorge had pushed over, we began to get a glimpse of a hill behind us. It was covered with enormous trees and clumps of eighty-foot-high bamboo, through which at sunset we could see hundreds of parrots, neatly paired off in matrimonial felicity, heading for home on wildly beating wings that seemed too short to support their weight. They uttered horrendous squawks, shrieking incessantly at each other, as though either they could no longer bear the thought of flying beside their mate, or the idea of flying itself terrified them. Could that hill, those trees, those squawking parrots, things that suddenly existed for us within two hundred yards but were practically inaccessible, really be ours? What lay behind those trees? More trees, more hills, more streams?

We took our machetes one Sunday morning — we couldn't put it off any longer — and walked up the trail along the river to the southern boundary, where we intended to begin our explorations. In this corner of the farm we found that we were the owners of a public school, two small houses fighting for their lives against vines, and a *fútbol** field. Here we met Mercedes, a young farmer who lived on the land adjoining us with one of his several women and who had offered to take us through the farm all the way to the highway. We cut up from the river, through some almost obliterated plantings of cacao and coffee, into the abandoned banana plantings at the center of the farm where the big trees stood. It became very quiet.

We paused in this solemn place, feeling awe and resentment. This was no garden. It was just possibly the challenge that would kill us through the years as we sweated and hacked beneath this suffocating shade. The jungle for all its beauty was as forbidding as it was lovely, especially for us who had come with our civilizing instincts to try and tame it. It had an arrogance about it that made you want to see it brought down. There it stood, the jungle, silent and unmoving, but within it one was immediately diminished and made uncomfortably aware of some terrible generative power.

Unmoving? Is bamboo that grows a foot and a half a day unmoving? Or the *piquiua,* a vine that in one season climbs the trunks of all but the greatest trees and strangles them in an obscene fecundity of leaves and runners as strong as iron cables? Or the *matapalo,* the tree killer, a vine that starts out as tremblingly vulnerable as a lover's first kiss and ends by climbing a tree and simply absorbing it, growing around its trunk and choking it to death — that first kiss a prelude to thirty disastrous years of marriage with the wrong woman. One cuts down a matapalo not knowing what kind of a tree one will find embedded in its heart.

The land had been abandoned for only fifteen years or so, but already it had all but disappeared under the violent growth of balsa, laurél, *cedro, ceibo,* ebony, *juachapali, colorado,* bamboo, and the wild fruit trees — orange, lemon, avocado, *caimito,* guava. Under this shade of new growth the banana plants were stunted

* In South America soccer is called *fútbol.* — Ed.

and dying for lack of sun, their drooping leaves yellowed and torn with *sigatoca*. We stood beneath this double canopy of shade at ten o'clock on a Sunday morning in the sewer-smelling shade of night.

Silent? Off to the left a banana plant, its roots weakened by the rains or the *picudo negro* — or perhaps its will to keep struggling suddenly destroyed in some bananalike epiphany of illumination — crashed wetly to the ground with a sound of tearing leaves and with the utter submission of a human body violently shot through a hundred times with rifle bullets. The ground trembled. Ahead of us, a moment later, the same sound, the sound of a final defeat, came to us in the semidarkness.

I began to imagine this silent and unmoving jungle as it would look and sound if it were wired to record the terror of the plants and if it were filmed in those techniques that Walt Disney perfected to show in a few seconds the opening of a rosebud. And it seemed a real probability that the shrieks of dying plants and the snakelike lashing of a million vines — all at deadly war with one another in their writhing, choking, killing, as they strained and clawed toward the sun — would simply be too awful, too horrifying for a man to watch.

Still it was beautiful, in an inhuman way that reduced a man to some ultimate perspective of irrelevancy. It comforted one's conscience to be stunned and outraged by the naked obscene power of this jungle that we had come to cut down and destroy. I had the feeling that whatever ecological murder we were about to commit in the name of agricultural progress was only a childish attempt at domination — a mad flea crawling up an elephant's leg with rape in his heart. I was convinced that five years after we had died or left the place the jungle would once more proclaim its domination, healing the wounds of the plow, cutting little streamlets of water from the heavy winter rains across those deserted corn fields — the earth slowly disappearing once again under moss and fern, under *saboya*, elephant ear, orchid, balsa, matapalo, and giant one-hundred-foot-long philodendrons.

We moved on through the jungle without speaking until we reached the highway. Our shirts were soaked with sweat and an odor of death clung to our shoes. Warming ourselves in the sun,

we were once more slowly filled with a sense of our own importance. We had spent a couple of hours in the world on the fifth
day of creation, before man arrived to pollute and desecrate the
cycles of creation, of birth and death and rebirth from the faintly
stinking decomposition of the dead. Looking back into the shadows, into that chaos of growing profusion, I felt mocked, and I
seemed to live with the memory of derisive laughter. I noticed
something stunned in Ramón's eyes; it was also the first time he
had walked through jungle that he owned. He must have felt
something of the same thing, for suddenly he walked to the side of
the road and began to hack furiously at the grass; then he turned
to me and smiled. God, how we longed to get in there with our
crew of workers, with our swinging machetes and our axes, and
bring that whole arrogant thing crashing down around us.

Once you stop fighting and give in to it there is a special beguile-
ment about living in the tropics that lulls and disguises, that obliterates the passing of time. There are no seasons, no dead times, no
bursting weeks of spring renewal, no times like August's dead ripe-
ness with another year fulfilled in the bounty of peaches, grapes,
plums, and melons. Down here the months pass in a charmed and
unchanging way; there is no particular season for harvesting anything. December is identical to July; August, to April. There is
no sadness associated with the arrival of November, no sense of
coming to the end of a yearly cycle when one vaguely mourns the
passing of another year on the march to death or finds death's symbols in frozen earth or a dead bird or the dead stalk of a summer
flower broken and shuddering in the wind. In November we
planted corn. And in May. And in August. For the same reason
there is none of that wild exhilaration with the first greening of
trees in April or with the dead hills exploding in the overnight
miracle of spring grass. One feels that time has stopped and that
one has endlessly postponed, maybe even permanently defeated
the onslaught of old age and extinction.
    It is pleasant, but deadening and dangerous too. One glances at
a sunset blazing above the hills behind the pasture, the light on the
river as dramatic and charged as Shakespeare, the trees in the last
light glowing with an unearthly black varnished greenness that is

shot through with coldly blazing blues and deep violets, but there is no great impulse to leave one's beer, stand in the weeds by the river and become a part of this spectacle. It was the same last night; it will be the same tomorrow. And the tomorrows stretch away without end, uncounted tens of thousands of them. In their abundance they lose their value. The poetic impulse to grasp and dominate the moment, to freeze time, and for a moment to obliterate death is blunted in this static hothouse world. You don't grow old here; one day you simply die of old age. If the impulse to create art has any beginnings in man's awareness of his mortality, if art is a revolt against oblivion, this may explain why so little art has come out of the tropics.

Some years ago when I was a Peace Corps volunteer in Rioverde I visited old Bill Swanson one evening. I was getting ready to leave the place and wanted to say goodbye. Swanson was about seventy-seven years old then, a wreck of a man who drank a case of beer a day and who had just come back from a Guayaquil hospital with part of his stomach and most of his intestines snipped away. His whole body was shrinking and turning crepey and sexless, and a wild mat of exhausted white hair covered the upper part of his body, reminding me of that neurotic albino gorilla, Snowflake, who is incessantly being paraded through the pages of *National Geographic*. He was dressed in dirty unpressed ducks, laceless tennis shoes without socks, and his bare chest beneath the furze was splotched with an alcoholic rash and mildly infected fungus. His living quarters, an open veranda surrounding a single bedroom, were built on the second floor of an old balsa mill, one end of which was sinking and tilting into the mud at the river's edge. The whole scene was as squalid, as dramatically arranged as the last chapter of an early Conrad novel dealing with the final moral disintegration of a hero destroyed by his vices. He had lived in the old mill and in almost the same style for something like fifty years.

One didn't carry on a conversation with the old man anymore, he was so deaf. I sat, listening and nodding and drinking a warm beer that he had pulled from an almost empty case beside his chair. Tonight he was complaining; the operation hadn't been an entire success; they said he now had something called adhesions; the doctors had warned him to drink no more than one beer a day; to hell with the doctors, if he had to stop drinking beer he'd just as soon die. He wasn't afraid to die; it plainly said from dust you come and to dust you shall return, but Jesus Christ, boy, what if there *was* a heaven? If there was a heaven there was probably a hell to go along with it. Jesus, think about it. What if there *was* a hell? He still felt terrible, weak, couldn't ride a horse anymore. The *mayordomo* was short about thirty-five cows in the last count, a goddam thief. Where was it all going to end? I listened and nodded and found the situation ridiculous, for he was not a poor man; besides the ranch and almost a thousand cows, he owned a hundred thousand dollars in Standard Oil stock that he had picked up as a wild-catting roustabout in his youth.

So finally I began to scream at him. "What the hell are you doing here anyway? Why don't you go home to Oklahoma, see some good doctors, eat some good food, get fixed up?" He gazed at me tranquilly out of his rheumy washed-out blue eyes and sat there dressed like the last of the beachcombers with that disgraceful house crumbling and tilting around him. God, the whole thing was just unbelievable. "What are you doing here for God's sake?" I yelled into his deaf old ears, leaning right up into his face so that he would have to hear me. "Why are you here anyway?" And now hearing me he smiled a secret and superior smile, as though he knew something that I didn't, and croaked out in an old voice that was equal parts W. C. Fields and Edward G. Robinson, "It's the lure of the tropics, boy; it's the lure of the tropics." Oh shit, I thought, how corny can you get? He had obviously stolen the phrase from some third-rate book of wild adventures in the South Seas, some crummy volume read in his youth that had irrevocably poisoned his mind and pointed him toward this tawdry and final destiny.

For many years I remembered that evening and found it funny enough to laugh about. For many years he still hung on out there on the Rioverde beaches, drunk most of the time, sick much of the time, constantly robbed, once clubbed in his garden by someone intent on killing him, once tossed out of a canoe in the middle of the Esmeraldas River where he lost his grip on a little shaving kit full of 50,000 sucres. Lure of the tropics, indeed. But now I'm just beginning to understand what he meant, beginning to be entrapped in that super-romantic *ambiente* that the jungle holds. It is not the easy assenting dusky native girls, the lurid sunsets behind waving palms, not the languor of the air, the perfumes of scarlet blooms, not the booming of equatorial surfs against reefs of coral. No, it is simply this constantly held illusion that here at last one lives outside time, freed from death's milestones, the passing years.

I think it was Van Gogh who predicted, and probably before his friend Gauguin had even thought about moving to Tahiti, that the great artists of the future would come out of the tropics. How wrong he has been; one can be sure that Van Gogh had never seen a jungle. It is so opulent, so rich, in the final analysis so basically vulgar — like the over-orchestration of Richard Strauss — that no one I can think of, except Rousseau, has ever succeeded in capturing its million-textured, chaotic quality and transforming it into art. Writing about it, too, one soon discovers that to describe faithfully what one sees is to miss the mark. In the ultimate sense the jungle is not what one sees at all — that wall of trees at arm's length that encircles one in an endless variety of greens from yellow to blue and blue black. The jungle is behind that wall; it lives in the mind and in the feelings that grow out of what it is impossible to see.

Across the river from the house, the wall of jungle comes down to the river's very edge, except for downstream where I can just barely make out a long parklike stretch of grass. One gigantic tree, similar to an elm, with leaves of a perpetual spring green, stands in the water above a cave of black roots and leans out over the muddy rushing current. It is a chaos, this hill of a million trees, in which the eye is dumfounded by the sameness and the complexity of its textures. Hardly anything stands out except in certain lights, at dusk or at daybreak, when the sun glistens brightly on certain trees, and shadows form deep blue caverns in the gullies that transect the hill, giving it depths and places for the eye to come to rest. It is the river that opens up a landscape, so that one can see for almost half a mile in either direction. In the window behind me banana leaves brush against the screen; at noon it is too dark to read. From the window on the river side I can see across it to six houses in various stages of construction or disintegration. Around these bamboo houses roofed in yellowing leaves of *ranconcha,* palm trees like fountains spray their branches to the sky, and patches of bananas or plátano, explosions of nature at its most powerful and fecund, light the hill with their incredibly innocent green, the loveliest green in the world. How illustrative of that blindness that comes with familiarity, that I had to reread Tomlinson's *The Sea and the Jungle* to learn again how beautiful and symbolic a banana plant is; my senses had been blinded by constantly driving past one hundred million of them on the road between Quevedo and Santo Domingo.

Familiarity, that enemy of vision. Every morning the jungle is quite the same. After a few months I no longer feel the menace that I had so enjoyed before. I gaze or try to gaze deep into that space so crammed with leaves and stems and branches, mouthing the words — mysterious, ominous — and the jungle yawns in my face. I yawn back. I am beginning to regard the jungle as not much more than a super-efficient litter-producing machine. The path I cleared to my house the day I moved in has now been cleared another dozen times; in fact we have an old man, Dalmiro, who does little more than keep hacking out the eighty yards of trail that connect me with the rest of the world. Within the space of half a year delicate jungle plants that my mother, an obsessive worker, dug up and planted around the house on a month's visit to the farm turned into truly monstrous scaly creations with suppurating branches and leaves as gross as crocodiles. I fight my way upstairs to the main room, which overlooks the river through a mazy clump of ten-foot-long leaves shaped like double-edged swords. Each leaf has collected a quart of water in its heart, and by the fourth step I am drenched. How can I tear out or slash away at these swiftly spreading, tenderly planted mementos, so symbolic of a mother's love?

I enter the house, only to find birds fluttering against the window screens or bats circling in the dimness under the thatched roof. Spiders nest in the bookshelves, festoon the lamps, drag captured flies from here to there and from there to here. Butterflies sleep on the walls; how I would love to pin them there permanently, but the cockroaches would eat them in a day. Lines of ants, four abreast, file across the sills, and tiny ants called *locos* rush in clouds pell-mell over a spot on the desk where yesterday I left a shard of hard candy. Termites building enormous tumor-shaped houses tunnel up the outside walls to their chosen spot beneath the roof eaves. And from a dozen hair cracks in the walls new vines come crawling into the room, twining around the legs of the chairs and clawing at the screens, trying to get out, little Durantes singing, "Have you ever had the feeling you wanted to go, and at the same time had the feeling that you wanted to stay?" Each day each vine presents me with another foot of growth and two new shining heart-shaped leaves. Being inside is not a hell of a lot different from being outside.

At first it is infuriating to discover what is going on beneath your nose: the books rotted; the phonograph records green with mold, their jackets stuck together as though specially glued that way by an expert gluer; boots turning to penicillin; shirts, mold stained and smelling like sour bread, clammy across the back; prints by Gauguin hanging wetly across the walls turning into hallucinations by Max Ernst. Visions of old Bill Swanson flash across the mind as each day, more bereft, more naked, I begin to resemble him. ... But underneath this rage there is something else; I can feel a mystic and highly complicated — what? It is a kind of satisfaction, a kind of acceptance that I feel with the destruction of my possessions. It is much more than being faced with the simple challenge to find life good or bad in an ever more rapidly accelerating deprivation, to reach some Thoreauian rock-bottom level of essentiality and test oneself against pure nature. In some way I am like that desperate Russian on the frozen steppes who threw his luggage and then his wife and then one by one his children to the pursuing wolves to preserve himself. It is as though destiny has made a compact with me; I will be given extra years for the loss of my possessions. It's not a bad deal.

Nonetheless I feel lonely. It is the loneliness that grabs one when standing alone in an army chow line. I'm there ready to react, ready to communicate, but nobody gives a damn. Feeling like an alien and wondering why I feel it so strongly, I decide that perhaps it is because the jungle has no history; there is no sense of human continuity in the place. The little wasp-nest-colored huts timidly hugging the shore across the river are as impermanent as the clouds that move across the sky from the sea or come rushing up the river valley bringing the afternoon rains or hang fading in the trees like smoke at dawn. Those huts also live in a state of siege; for three or four years they shake their fists with bravado in the very face of the jungle and then crash down from the rotting of beams sieved by termites or slump and settle from the weight of vines. Gumercinda, who washes our clothes, lives directly across the river from me. In the last six months I have been watching her house disappear — first the front wall and the *pambil* steps, then the two side walls, and lastly the roof. Today Gumercinda and her little horde of abandoned grandchildren are living in a temporary lean-to, but my inclination to snort is tempered with the realization that my own house is disintegrating almost as rapidly; the two downstairs bedrooms have been for some time reserved for the termites and the rats.

The people, too, are as transient as the clouds. That land across the river, which now because I have never walked upon it is beginning to take on the mystery and glamour I have never found on this side, is largely free for the taking; but the squatters make so little money off their holdings that they move onto the rich haciendas a couple of times a year as day laborers to supplement the niggardly income that the jungle allots them. We get used to seeing the Cortez brothers lounging in front of their huts or fishing in the river or coming down a steep trail to the river's edge with sacks of charcoal. And then one day they are gone; they are working in the bananas up around Quinindé. A month after they have left their three little huts have disappeared in weeds and the front wall of Jorge's house has fallen out into the yard; and I am troubled by this violence because someone mentions that the mother has been left alone on the farm and is holding things together.

If only there were even an old ruin someplace on the land, some indication that someone had been here before us and that we were part of a human chain; but only stone would last in this steaming vat of organic dissolution, and there is no stone here except river gravel. In the midst of my longing for human continuity in those first days, I found a broken fragment of a plate three feet underground in a hole we were digging for the foundations of my new house. I experienced a moment of elation, of belonging, but it didn't last. On the back of the plate was inscribed "Turin, 1923." Analyzing this find I felt even more alienated than before. In God's name, what kind of a flood within the last forty years could have deposited three feet of sand on this spot along the river where I had decided to build. It had probably happened in one night. And wasn't it very possible that the same flooding river could take the house (and us) away in one night? The old-timers said no, it was impossible, the river never left its banks — and a month later the river rose thirty-five feet in seven hours, flooded all our pasture land, and stood five feet deep for ten hours in the new store we were in the process of building. Downstream from us whole villages were swept away, half a hundred people drowned, bridges disappeared, and for twenty-five miles to the south the hillsides melted into rivers of mud that buried the highway. Everything, it now appeared, was transient, even the earth itself. But that night, opposed to all this impermanence as I waded around ass deep in the rising water trying to jack up the pickup a little higher, the farm contributed its bit of human continuity: Ester was in the hospital in Esmeraldas while everything out here was dissolving or flooding away, and about midnight she gave birth to Ramón's first son, Ramoncito. If we couldn't be a part of history, we would make our own.

One day, out near our new ramada, Ramón dug up what appeared to be a bottle that had once held Spanish wine. It was a deep green pint-sized bottle shaped like an electric light bulb. Hooray! At last! Here was something one could cling to, this indication that a conquistador had ambled through the property. Immediately the imagination came alive to the possibility that Ramón and I were a part of the local history. Two months later, while disking our field of coconuts, I unearthed a two-inch fragment of an ancient clay jar. It was fired red like the millions of pre-Christian pieces one finds by the ton all along the Ecuadorian coast from Salinas to the Colombian border. Holding it in my hand I finally felt a true elation; I was being plunged into that bottomless well of the past. I asked my neighbors if they had ever found Indian fragments. Why, yes, of course. Sometimes after a heavy rain they found little figures, the heads of gods, or broken pieces of pottery in the banks of the intermittent winter streams that cut down through the land. "And just last week," Mercedes told me, "my neighbor says a friend of his found a great piece of gold hammered into the shape of a flying bird."

Now I could settle down to live here. It was becoming obvious that others had done it; why couldn't I? Calling on imagination, intuition, the gossip of neighbors, the laws of probability, Prescott's history, an electric-light-shaped wine bottle and a two-inch shard, I began to make a history for the farm.

2

THE FARM AS HISTORY

ARCHAEOLOGISTS AND ANTHROPOLOGISTS — for lack of the kind of
decisive proof they feel they need and in terror of their reputations
— are hesitant to declare that man has inhabited the South American continent for much more than twenty thousand years. What
cowardice, what timidity, simply because so far no one has found a
potsherd or a bone or a carved rock that can carbon date the oc-
cupancy of the continent back to the beginnings of human history.
The scientists say that man could only have come here from the
north after first hiking across the icebound Bering Strait. And yet
if man has existed on the earth for a million years (and Leakey
thinks it is closer to three million) it is simply mathematically impossible that in all that endless time a man and a woman capable
of bearing children and of founding a new race did not arrive to
claim this new, pristine, and tremendous land. There must have
been thousands of crossings. They arrived on wrecked ships, on
lost and ocean-tormented canoes, on great floating trees uprooted
in some hurricane and carried swiftly on the currents; they arrived
on non-sunken land bridges or on widely cruising oriental fishing
boats. The first Negro is supposed to have come to South America
in the early 1500s; how odd, then, to find four-thousand-year-old
statues of Negroes in the grave mounds of La Tola. Try throwing
beans at a narrow-necked bottle across the room from you; is it
likely that after throwing a million beans the bottle would still be
empty?

The history of any region has its own internal truth which lives
in the *ambiente* of the growing things and in the heaving of the

land and in the winds that move through the great trees that guard its ageless secrets. Man has possessed this continent far far longer than anyone has yet dared to imagine. Here on the farm in this mouldering jungle — where the afternoon rains arrive like clock-work and where early man's modest efforts to leave his mark of immortality in a carved stick or a mound of earth or a clay head must surely have been obliterated even before the man himself — why must we feel that there has been no history here simply because we are not slightly moved by those expanding ripples of a stone dropped by human hands into a still pool, half a million years ago? Is history only history when it is killing and when it has been notarized?

A couple of interesting things happened to me one week, during that first year on the farm, as I was scratching around in the earth trying to find a human history that would go with the place. I didn't want much, just a modest sip from the well of the past. But as I stretched to drink I fell into the well itself and plunged down to the first day of creation and then past it for at least another million years. If these revelations fail to stand up to the scientific method, well, so much the worse for science. How many more years will it take to prove Einstein's radiant and poetic revelations about time and space? On the other hand what great truth might be deduced by the discovery of a million-year-old G-string at the bottom of the hill where we planted pineapples? It would probably be as false and distorted as the deduction will be some fifty thou-sand years from now upon the discovery of some unatomized but still faintly radioactive Coca-Cola bottle, miraculously whole in a pile of unidentifiable rubble. Is it possible to resurrect a culture from a Coke bottle?

On Christmas Eve I had been invited to drink whiskey at my neighbor's farm. Those of us who gathered there were almost all expatriates: a Swiss banana buyer, a German agent for a shipping company who sent tons of balsa chunks to London, a German Jew who had lost his family at Dachau but had himself escaped to hack out a precarious living as a cotton farmer. A couple of Ecuadorian ranchers had also been invited, perhaps for local color. At any rate they were pretty much ignored, it was so pleasant not to have to talk Spanish in this international gathering. It must have been very late in the morning, for we had long since passed the Christmas carol singing stage when I found myself seated next to a Señor Alfonso León, who runs cattle on a piece of pasture not far down the road from us.

"I've just read," he told me derisively and rather out of the blue, "that they've recently discovered in Mesopotamia what is purported to be the oldest manmade art object. It's a four-inch-high figure of a female with a rather terrifyingly tremendous ass, and it has been dated to about 50,000 B.C. This kind of drivel sticks in my throat, especially as it attempts to pinpoint man's earliest origins."

This was elegant Spanish, the kind I never heard on the farm, and I was twelve words behind him trying to translate it. I smiled brightly and assured him that I, too, was convinced that the story of man's origins hadn't even begun to be told, if it ever could be.

"Absolutely," he agreed. "This utter claptrap, this complete fabrication about the migration of the peoples to the North and South American continents — it's particularly irritating to me. That a bunch of wandering Mongols, driven by what insane urges to keep going and keep going, fanned out across the great American deserts and the Dakotas and populated Mexico and Yucatán. And kept going and kept going. My God, why? Down across the Panamanian isthmus, through those hundreds of miles of impenetrable swamps, which to this day are almost impossible to get through? And then finally to burst upon the upland Andes Mountains, all ready to build the most sophisticated astronomical observatories? No, no, it's too outlandish, too impossible."

"Yes," I agreed, "they must have been terribly prolific and moving terribly fast to do the whole thing in twenty thousand years. But what's your theory then?"

"Oh, hombre," he said, looking at me intently over his glass of whiskey, with just the hint of a frown of disapproval for my stupidity, "hombre, hombre, but don't you see it? Look around you; open your eyes and look around you. What do you see and how can you deny it? Here was the Garden of Eden. It was here, right here on the Esmeraldas that the whole thing started. And it is this blessed land that has been lost to the people of the earth and which they search for now out of some dumb calling in the blood."

I sat there without speaking, impaled on the intensity of his vision, and he continued to study me intently and then said, as though having found no trace of ridicule in my face he could now clinch his argument, "But haven't you seen the mists, how they hang over the river in the mornings, and how they hang in the trees? It is the Garden, newly and perpetually created each day. Haven't you seen the sun, filmed in clouds, rise from behind the hills to bless the earth? Here on the river we are in on the creation. Haven't you seen the clouds in the late afternoon explode into the sky like atomic devices? Of course you have; that's why you're here. You've come back to the beginnings. Believe me, señor, there have probably been hundreds of migrations back and forth, back and forth across the oceans between the continents. But the *first* migration — and how many hundreds of thousands of years ago was it? — that first one was from here. It was from *here* that the great movement to populate the earth began."

God knows it was a delightful conceit, and I who had been looking for a history for my farm was more than willing to believe it. Yes, I had seen the river mists in that hour of dawn when the trees on the further bank mysteriously and shyly showed themselves. I had seen the hills, as though newly created, appearing out of the low-lying clouds as the sun rose and the trees burned and glistened. I found it much more sensible to believe that here indeed was some ageless Eden, at any rate one of them, rather than look for it in some barren Asiatic desert created by God of all earthly delights and beauties and compounded out of some sordid little oasis amid the sand dunes where a couple dozen camels, thirty mangy goats, and a hundred date palms symbolized earth's bounty.

We had been clearing land all that year since July, and now, on one of those days just before New Year's Eve, still waiting for the first winter rains, I found myself on some new land that we were clearing. I was picking up chunks of roots and logs and piling them for burning. All of our workers, dazed with the religious ecstasies produced by several dozen bottles of cane alcohol, were sleeping it off that week in their houses, preparing themselves for the really serious religious rites of New Year's Eve. I had already disked the ground once, but it was still much too trashy for planting, and the banana plants and the bird-of-paradise were already beginning to sprout again in a most violent, impressive, and irritating way.

Now suddenly this mysterious and unbelievable thing happened. I had been picking up and piling logs for about an hour, my mind completely empty, when, as I bent to lift a root that was in no way different from any other root that I had been handling, the hair on my head suddenly stood straight out, my arms broke into goose flesh, and I began to sweat in terror. From the deepest part of me, from that part that goes back ten million years to some shambling and hairy-bodied old grandfather, a voice spoke in my brain so clearly that I can almost remember its timbre. What it said was, "*Stop. Be careful. Coral.*" With absolute certainty, then, I very carefully moved the root with trembling hands and my body tensed to spring away, and there, coiled, banded black and yellow and scarlet, was the largest coral snake I had ever seen. Panting, sweating, grunting like an ape-man, I smashed it dead with a wood chunk.

What did it matter if from that moment on I got the same message a hundred times an hour — and it was always false? Somehow in that evolution that has made us fully human, or as human as we have dared to be, we have lost that secret unity with nature, with our ancestors, that preserved us in the past. I had heard that guttural scream of warning from out of a million years ago; it was as real and honest as the boots on my feet. And that voice had come complete with its own background. Unmistakably it came from the rain forest; perhaps from the jungles of some submerged and long-forgotten continent, perhaps from this clearing, this very spot upon which I stood — that first Eden, where man grew in innocence and joy. And which he owned and lost in his obsessive hunger for domination, separating himself from everything around him.

The oldest clay artifacts yet found in South America, the Valdivian pots of Salinas or La Libertad, were discovered about a hundred miles down the coast from my farm. I don't resent this discovery even though superficially it would seem to place the Esmeraldas area on the periphery of pot history. The weather conditions around here being what they are (as I write this I am almost deaf-

ened by torrents of rain beating like drums on the banana leaves
outside the house), it seems logical to insist that only in that
desert-like climate around Salinas, where it sometimes goes for
years without raining, could an object as delicate and perishable as
a clay pot be preserved through the thousands of years since it was
made. No, those pots may have been discovered in Valdivia, but
I'm convinced that they were formed and fired up there on the
level ground that we just recently cleared for peanuts.

Betty Meggers and her husband, Clifford Evans, both of the
Smithsonian Institution, advanced the theory some years ago that
these first pots had been made by shipwrecked Japanese who had
drifted to Ecuador by a great circle route of some eighty-five hundred miles on the natural ocean currents. For a time this theory
was held in contempt and labeled frivolous by more cautious and
timorous archaeologists, who apparently wanted to find "Made in
Osaka" stamped on the bottom of each pot. But now the theory is
pretty much accepted, and this is strange, for one hears funny
rumors in Ecuador that below that stratum where the Valdivian
pots were found there are still more levels of unsterile earth —
which Meggers refuses to investigate for fear of blowing a good
theory all to hell. At any rate, the comparisons of prehistoric
Japanese pottery with Ecuadorian pottery of the same era, some
seven thousand years ago, has established so many identical techniques of craft beyond the possibility of coincidence that the
theory is much less sensational than it first appeared to be.*

My own personal theories, grounded only in intuition and this
insane necessity to clothe my farm in the raiments of history (at
least panties and bra), is a bit more breathtaking. *Carajo mierda.
Of course,* some Japanese potters drifted to the Ecuadorian coast
some seven thousand years ago; it is inconceivable that that sea-
faring race with its tradition of fishing in the open sea did not dump

---

* Six years after writing the above, I am informed almost in secrecy by a
most reputable anthropologist that very soon the newspapers will be announcing a new discovery. Fantastic news. Some meters below the Valdivian level, which represented the oldest pot-making culture on the
continent, a new, completely different kind of pot has recently been discovered. If this pot has been correctly dated, in one stunning find pot-making will recede into the past another three thousand years, and a re-evalua-
tion of the Valdivian theory will perhaps be made necessary. — *August 1977.*

tens of thousands of Japanese onto this coast during the hundreds of thousands of years of their prehistory. Those potters who arrived in 5000 B.C. were the late-comers, the last-comers. When they beached their boats and rushed up into the clayey hills to start making those visible and enduring records of man's possession of the land — in other words, to begin making history — without a doubt they were greeted all up and down the coast by low bows and great steaming bowls of sukiyaki. Here they found hundreds of villages of Japanese who knew how to fish, but up until that time didn't know anything about throwing a pot. Can we deny the inevitability of this because no one yet has found any hundred-thousand-year-old fishing nets woven of cotton thread? More importantly, of course, those first potters encountered not only villages full of countrymen but also villages full of Turks, Mongols, Macedonians, and perhaps even a few Nordic types.

One thing is sure: from whatever place they started out, those early tourists, with their one-way tickets, would eventually have been brought by the ocean currents to within twenty-five miles of the farm. The Humboldt Current, that rushing stream of south polar water that washes the whole western coast of South America, begins to lose its force and swing out from the continent at Esmeraldas. But it still flows at one or two miles an hour; one goes in swimming *here* and comes out *there,* a hundred yards up the beach toward Colombia. From the north, from Panama and Acapulco, the Corriente del Niño gathers up all floating things, especially during the winter months of rains when the Humboldt Current veers away from the shore toward the Galapagos. Everything, everything loose in the Pacific, at one time or another floats past Esmeraldas or is caught on its immense stretches of imperceptibly sloping beach. This includes Greeks, Phoenicians, Polynesians, Jews, Sumerians, Mesopotamians — you name it. All of this is not history because once you wash up on the beach at Esmeraldas it's practically impossible to get away to write about it, like being flushed into some great continental toilet.

I have been in Ecuador so long now that I can scarcely differentiate and classify human faces by race, that most superficial way of identifying another human being. I didn't realize this until my friend Joe Haratani, the Peace Corps director, who came to visit

us on the farm a few years ago, drew me aside after our first lunch
to complain, "But why do you call Ramón a Negro? He's not a
Negro." I call him a Negro, because he calls himself one, though
his face is as Indian as it is black and as Spanish as it is Indian. He
has a pride in his blackness that makes him see himself as black,
and he has a mild contempt for a Spanish grandfather, a drunken
politician in Colombia, who left his mark and subtly corrupted the
purity of Ramón's blood. As for me Ramón is — well, he's just
Ramón. I hardly ever think of his color except in moments of rage
when all my worst prejudices come boiling to the surface, or in
moments of pride when I want to congratulate myself. "Your
partner, your best friend is a Negro," I tell myself in a kind of wild
disbelief, because although many of us have yearned to establish
deep and abiding relationships apart from any racial bias, how few
of us have been lucky enough to be able to do it.

So, while for the most part I am insensitive to racial characteristics, especially in this area of frantically proliferating intercourse between the races, I am still sometimes struck by the
Japanese cast to the faces of the Cayapas Indians, who infrequently
stop at the farm to buy salt or to offer to sell their hand-carved
canoes to us. When they are not smiling their faces hold a quality
that can only be described as oriental inscrutability. In Manabi, a
seacoast province to the south, where we sometimes go to look for
peanut seed or machinery for shelling peanuts, I am even more
aware of a strong oriental cast to the faces of the Manabitas, which
thousands of years of breeding with other races has not succeeded
in obliterating.

What about those great-beaked classic Manabi noses, which are
identical with the noses that are represented on the Incan and pre-
Incan figurines? Studying them carefully, eyeballs to nostrils, with
my whole scientific reputation in the balance, I can only say that
these are Arab or Phoenician or Egyptian or Jewish noses. Traveling in Manabi and under the spell of its gorgeous royal noses, one's
imagination is swept back in time many dozens of thousands of
years to when that first Japanese maiden, running and screaming
in anticipatory gusto, was ravished on the sandy beach of Esmeraldas by a fleeter-footed Phoenician, and the truly new, South
American race was put into the oven.

The fruit of that union is all around us here. The faces of the coastal people hold the history of their race, and the races of the world have come together in Manabi. This is much more conclusive than that cache of Valdivian pots, broken and twisted by the earth's pressures.

In 1527 as Pizarro sailed down the western coast of South America searching for the fabled land of Peru, the first solid intimation that there perhaps really did exist such a place occurred to him as he entered the shallow and treacherous harbor at Esmeraldas. Up until this moment he had encountered nothing but starving and terrified natives who fled into the jungles before him, and scattered and disintegrating villages of no more than half a dozen huts. Up until that time, for almost a year they had been unable to steal much more than a pound of gold. The sight of Esmeraldas must have jogged that old bastard into fits of new enthusiasm and crystallized the brutal directness with which so far he had surmounted and endured almost inhuman difficulties. At Esmeraldas and at Atacames, some ten miles further down the beach, he saw the first signs of an advanced civilization — towns with thousands of houses along streets, people adorned with golden and emerald jewelry and dressed in garments of finely woven wool or cotton, fields of rowed corn, groves of cacao, hillsides planted with peanuts, squash, and potatoes.

So says William Prescott in his classic study *The Conquest of Peru.* Well, it's not often that a nonhistorian of my caliber gets a chance to refute the words of a historian like Mr. Prescott and to challenge such inconsequential and nit-picking details as the kinds of crops that were raised in Esmeraldas in 1527. But if I'm going to get my farm into history, even through the cellar door, the attack has to be made.

Cacao grows on my farm, which is plunk in the middle of a rain-forest area twenty-five miles from the Pacific; cacao does not grow on the coast of Ecuador. In summer, between July and December, the Ecuadorian coast is almost as dry as the Peruvian deserts. In a narrow five-mile belt along the ocean, the pastures go dormant, the trees lose their leaves, all the smaller streams go dry, and the hillsides covered with small spiny desert-bush-like trees burst into a desperate bloom as though the trees in this drought were expecting death. To conceive of cacao growing in such a region, especially on those rather impoverished front hills that could be seen from Pizarro's boat, is pure fantasy; cacao, like balsa or rubber or banana, is a tree of the rain forest.

Hillsides planted with potatoes? Now, really. The potato is a cool-weather plant that thrives in the Ecuadorian highlands around Quito at nine thousand feet; it even originated there. But rowed potatoes in those hills around Esmeraldas, through which, give or take twenty miles, the equator runs? No. Pizarro might have seen yuca, peanuts, tomatoes, beans, corn, squash, or sweet potatoes (*camotes*), but it is impossible to imagine that he saw cacao or potatoes. Corn planted in rows? I doubt it. One gets the impression here that coastal agriculture has not changed from the earlier days. If this is so, what Pizarro saw is what you see today — nothing planted in rows, nothing planted in its own area, but everything scattered and mixed together in a kind of insane and exuberant confusion. Here a stalk of corn, next to it a bean or a tomato half smothered by a trailing vine of camote, each farmer's field a living half-smothered tossed green salad. Houses in rows? No, never, though perhaps, as today, there was a rough line of houses at the high-tide mark of the shoreline formed by the river.

While I'm at it, and simply to cinch my claim that Prescott drew too heavily on his romantic predilections and painted his canvas with colors too bright and fluorescent, let me quote part of the paragraph that follows that wild one about the cacao and the potatoes: "Here, too, was the fair river of Emeralds, so called from the quarries of the beautiful gem on its borders from which the Indian monarchs enriched their treasury." As any of us who live on the borders of the fair river of Esmeraldas knows, there are no mines, no quarries, and no emeralds; there never were. The very few emeralds that have been found here — planted within ancient ritual figures or found loose beneath grave mounds, with rough holes drilled through them so that they could be strung as pendants along with polished coral or carved clay beads — came from Colombia, along with much of the gold that one finds in decreasing amounts as one moves south from the border town of Tumaco. One feels pretty convinced that the River of Emeralds was so named in order to further enflame the lustful passion of the Spanish kings who so miserably financed the first expeditions of conquest. Or more probably still, the river was named for its banks covered with trees and grass and looping vines and bushes with leaves as big as jungle huts — all of cleanest, brightest, rain-washed emerald green. The nearest river to the north of any consequence, smaller in size but identical in the profusion of jungle life along its fair borders, is called Río Verde, Green River.

How difficult it is to reconstruct the past; history comes out like those police drawings of rapists whose qualities are described by ten victims none of whom can recognize the drawing of the man who violated them. One is tempted to write history, it seems so easy to simply invent. Let us return to Pizarro and involve him with my farm. According to Prescott, Don Francisco landed with his little band of heroes on the shore close to Esmeraldas, most probably at the sandy point near Las Palmas where today the fishing boats anchor or a little further south where the town's rich live in their modern houses behind locked gates and high steel fences. If he had landed on the other side of the river he would have been held up ten days by the Tachina mud flats. Even though I have an obsessional dislike for this feisty conniving conquistador, I still don't like to imagine him having to wade for a mile and a half, ass deep in sea slush. His story is slimy enough without that. I see him as a slightly madder Douglas MacArthur — vain, pompous, and insecure as only a pig herder elevated to a supreme command could be.

We now come to the crux of my thesis. Since Prescott, the great historian, has gone to the trouble of describing the cacao of the region, may we not assume that hot chocolate was served on that fateful day just before Prescott's ten thousand Indians changed their minds and decided to drive the Spanish back to their ships? Now where did that cup of hot chocolate come from?

It is my contention, and I can't think of a soul who would be threatened enough to contradict me, that the chocolate that Pizarro drank that morning came from the farm. Our land, some twenty-five miles inland from Pizarro's boats, lies just within the rain belt where cacao thrives. Cacao in those days was drunk only by royalty and was forbidden to the rabble, and drinking it on the sly must have been quite as much a thrill as smoking marijuana is today for the descendants of that earlier race. If there were really ten thousand warriors on the beach that day (which I doubt like hell), this makes my chocolate hypothesis even more probable. Ten thousand warriors is an awful lot of warriors for Esmeraldas; some of them must have come down from the upriver areas; some of them must have come from the farm, floating down on balsa rafts with a few black-market cacao beans or even tribute for the Quito Inca.

I like to think that the Indians from my farm came close to stopping Pizarro that day before he got started on his conquests. They would have stopped him cold, too, except that one of the Spanish soldiers fell off his horse, "which so astonished the barbarians," Prescott writes, referring to the Indians, "who were not prepared for this division of what seemed one and the same being into two, that, filled with consternation, they fell back, and left a way open for the Christians to regain their vessels." A drunken soldier falling off his horse. It is about the only equivalent to a fart or a tumble in a horse turd that takes place in that whole horrid conquest. And how it changed the history of South America. It might even explain that deep-green wine bottle that we found buried on the farm. It is the discovery of such detritus that anchors the past in irrefutable probabilities and moves this jungle Eden into the mainstream of history. Chocolate for Pizarro, the sow-suckled pig-faced assassin. Does anyone know another farmer in this day and age with his foot so firmly jammed into the portals of the inscrutable past?

The history of the region before the arrival of the Spanish is all misty possibilities and delightful ambiguities; the archaeologists have constructed five thousand years of history from a few bean-shaped hammered-gold nose pieces, some golden fishhooks, some Japanese pots, some painted figures whose heads are as subtle and noble as Egyptian carvings; it is a history of innocence, with all of man's lustful passions distilled out. The other kind of history, which can be dug up like the rotting corpse of some slaughtered animal and given authenticity by studying old records or the romanticized accounts of the fawning notaries assigned to the conquerors, began in Esmeraldas in 1527. It didn't last long. That first contact with the Spanish was so traumatic, so destructive, that within a decade Esmeraldas and Atacames, those centers of a great coastal civilization, had simply ceased to exist.

A Spanish colony, San Mateo, was ordered built at the farthest reach of the high-tide level on the Esmeraldas River; it was seven miles or so inland from the coastal beaches. It was a stupid place for a town; isolated from the cooling sea winds, on a narrow bench of land beneath oppressive hills, it was a pest hole for all the tropical fevers of the area. It lasted for a few years and was abandoned. Today, standing on the highway above the old site, one imagines that one can still see traces of this settlement in a few parallel lines of humped and sterile earth. In this rainy area where jungle plants fight to cover every available inch with something green, there is something ominous and prophetic about this barren piece of earth as clear of weeds as a football field. It was the first settlement of whites on the Pacific side of South America, and nothing has grown on this ground for almost four hundred and fifty years.

After 1527 the Indian population simply ceased to exist as a significant element in the coastal life. They died by the thousands in epidemics of measles, mumps, scarlet fever, and the common cold. Syphilis, which may have existed in a benign form, suddenly became virulent and fatal. The death rate climbed to 90 percent; villages disappeared in jungle vines, the roofs split open to the rains, and the untended fields went back to their original grandeur. The Spaniards, too, had passed on; they were busy further to the south, slaughtering the population, melting into ingots the golden art of the Incas, and bringing the message of Christ's mercy to the survivors.

And so it is easy to reconstruct the Esmeraldas of four hundred years ago; it was exactly like the Esmeraldas of the early 1900s — a few dozen cane houses leaning with the wind, a few canoes hacked out of trees drawn up on the beach, a single muddy street piled with refuse, and swarming with pigs, chickens, starving dogs. The population swung back and forth between about three hundred and five hundred; perhaps a dozen Spaniards gradually hybridized the race, the color of people gradually lightened until the Negroes came; they suffered with malaria, typhoid, yellow fever. The sounds of Esmeraldas: night birds and bats, frogs and cicadas above the perpetual murmuring of the sea; for a hundred years the plunking of Spanish guitars, the sad music of exile, and then gradually, as the blacks took possession of the land, that incredible African beat of bongos and marimbas so profound and true that, hearing it, it was impossible to believe it hadn't existed here always; in the early mornings the sound of a fisherman with pargos on a stick balanced over his shoulder chanting the good news to the housewives, "*Pescado fresco, pescado fresco*"; wind clashing the palm fronds dryly. Dominating all, the great river as it empties into the sea, staining it the color of chocolate, the sea itself breathing lightly in a charmed and perpetual tranquility; and over everything, hiding the curve of sky, a thin cloud cover that filters out and softens a furious tropical sun.

Up until fifteen years ago there was no road into the town; supplies arrived from Guayaquil by sail and later by small coastal steamers. The town was almost self-sufficient, and for centuries almost nothing came in; books, furniture, clothing immediately rotted in the climate, not that these were things that anybody needed. In the 1880s things like salt for preserving fish, beer for preserving people, and bolts of cheap cotton began to appear in the market, but for the most part Esmeraldas was as isolated and forgotten in 1940 as it was in 1540. The trip to Quito, which we now make in five hours over paved roads, used to take weeks, and only God knows what percentage of those foolhardy early travelers were drowned or murdered or brought low by disease on the interminable muddy trails down the Andes or further along, on the last lap, in the canoes that brought them down the river from Quinindé.

For hundreds of years the whole province was so isolated and so outside the possibility of being governed that entire towns of criminals were formed along the river; they were probably more honestly administered than the towns controlled by the Quito politicians. Towns of murderers, bankrupts, rapists, unfrocked priests, political eccentrics, horse thieves, grew and flourished, hidden and forgotten in the jungle between Santo Domingo and Esmeraldas and on the beaches to the north and south. They dominated the land until later when the Negro slaves began to escape in numbers and fled to this wild province where they could disappear. Ramón was born in a small Negro village half-way between Esmeraldas and the Colombian border; it is called Africa, and thirty years ago its entire population was composed of Colombian Negroes who had for one reason or another escaped their country. Some of them still think of themselves as Colombians in those rare moments when they consider their nationality.

On the farm we boast a sordid collection of bamboo houses; on the maps the place is called Male. For me the word has connotations of evil. "Where did the name come from?" I asked Mercedes, that young farmer whose main characteristic seems to be an obsession with being the leader of this squalid little town. "I'm not sure," he told me, "but I've heard that about a hundred years ago a Spaniard lived here with a whole bunch of wild and naked Negroes; they were doing something illegal or they had done something very bad, because they say that anyone who ever came near the place was murdered and thrown into the river." Judging by the number of corpses that float past the farm, I sometimes feel that the Spaniard or one of his grandsons is still upstream a ways guarding his privacy.

True or not Male is famous for its *maldad,* its badness. When Male invited Rioverde to come here one Sunday to play fútbol, the Rioverdenians accepted but arrived in a state of panic, for the reputation of the town for danger and treachery is famous up and down the coast. But Rioverde also has a dirty reputation; it is more isolated; it is the last outpost, the furthest refuge for an escaping killer. A dozen love affairs sprang up that Saturday night before the game when, drinking beer and *puro* and Pepsis, everyone discovered in a kind of ecstatic disbelief that they were all the same and that no more than the usual number were packing revolvers. It was a bucolic evening with only one fist fight — between two Male teenagers.

The province of Esmeraldas still lives in the minds of the ruling Quiteños as a wild and barbarous area. Of course it is; that is its principal charm. The old tales of robbery and murder, of smashed and overturned canoes, of muddy trails that lead to nowhere, simply refuse to die. But now these stories have been resurrected and twisted somehow to illustrate the bad blood of the Negroes. When I tell friends in Quito that I have a farm in

Esmeraldas they look at me with wide eyes as though they were
seeing me for the first time, "But that's a country of *monos,*
monkeys. Isn't it dangerous? As you know, they have absolutely
no respect for life." This is almost a personal jab; after so many
years on the coast I have absorbed many black sensibilities and almost all their prejudices. How we mock the lisping, effeminate
Spanish of the high sierra. The middle-class Ecuadorian insists
that he feels no racial discrimination, but this is a matter of
economic definition. An Indian who wears shoes is no longer an
Indian; in fact he would be insulted if you called him one. A
Negro's face suddenly loses its blackness when he puts money in
the bank or puts on a necktie. And that stupidity about "respect for
life"? I think of the *serrano* radio announcer in Santo Domingo
who reported a landslide on the Andes road which had buried
sixty-six workers. "We can give thanks to God that they weren't
human beings but just Indians," he said. I have begun to avoid
middle-class Ecuadorians, and if I can't I don't tell them that some
of my friends are murderers.

Chasing down the history of the blacks, I got into a conversation
with Ramón; it was something in which he had no interest but he
mentioned that he had a great great aunt in Africa, that small
coastal village, that she was 123 years old, and that if I wanted
to talk history why not take a fifty-mile stroll up the beach and
see what she had to say. She was still very sharp, very active,
Ramón said (who actually hadn't seen her for ten years). She had
the eyes and ears of a twenty-year-old; she smoked leaf tobacco
rolled into cigars, drank a couple shots of *aguardiente* every day
when she could afford it, washed clothes, hunted clams on the
low-tide beaches, cooked for herself, and at the village fiestas sat
erect as royalty in the place of honor, tapping her feet to the
rhythms of the marimba. She could still split open a coconut with
a sharp and educated slash of her machete; her teeth, worn to the
gums, were still all there, without a single cavity, like the ground
down teeth of an old horse; she still tore off chunks of sugar cane
with her teeth and sucked out the juice. She could still thread a
needle.

I didn't feel that I could cope with a monument of such dimensions, let alone walk fifty miles to see her, but I told Ramón that if he wanted to do it I would try to borrow a tape recorder. "That's a great idea," Ramón said. "I'll take her a bottle of Cayapa, some rice, and cooking oil and get her to talk into the machine."

So now like Ramón, who loves to make fantasies, I was carried away with enthusiasm; all through dinner we talked about his aunt and his visit and the kind of questions he must ask to spark some recollection of that time when she may well have lived as a slave. "Ah, yes, as a slave," Ramón said, his face taking on a hard and vacant look, a look he always got when I mentioned something that he didn't want to hear. He had told me once from what African tribe he had come; was it the Bantu? But that was years ago, and now he couldn't remember or didn't want to. I had showed him pictures of tribal Africans with their bodies painted or dancing naked or hunting with spears, and he couldn't accept the idea that his past was involved with these barbarities. Nor could he now face the fact that he was descended from slaves who had come to South America with their legs shackled to the boards upon which they had slept in their own excrement. Before dinner was over I knew that Ramón would never talk to his aunt about the past; this was something that he was in the process of rejecting.

Realistically considered there wasn't much history that she could tell us, and the plan died in its first half hour. In 1913 she had hidden Federico Lastre and cured his bullet wounds; he was the notorious black revolutionary who had killed so many Quito soldiers sent by the government to bring Esmeraldas into the national family. Her act had no political overtones; she had been moved to pity by the sight of a dying man who was being hunted through the jungle by troops of Indian soldiers so terrified by his name that they prayed never to catch him. This was her almost only contact with history, for she had spent her life in Africa, and in Africa there is no history to remember. The place is outside it, and the real history, the real truth of the place, is in the actuality of the woman herself and in the dignity and sacredness of her years. South American history is a squalid tale of stasis, betrayal, the abuses of tyrants, the empty and evil rhetoric of demagogues, the rape of the masses; this woman lives in spite of history, and it is this ideal that is transformed into the unconscious myth that can be written by nobody, only dreamed. It is a century-long story that has to do with the tides, with the wind in the cocos, and canoes drifting through patches of sunlight on clear-running streams. Her story is in the seasons and in the new moon and in those forty thousand dawns; in the growth and death of families; in the slowly dimming splendor of a crowded, man-polluted earth. And its meaning and grandeur are woven loosely through all the life fabric of the people who surrounded her and who didn't have a history either and never sought one. The political story of her era, the endless series of revolutions and grabs for power, the transience of identical corrupt governments who exist only to feed off the poor and legalize the exploitation of the rich — all this could have no meaning for her. Her name is Macaya Lopez. And she lived for a hundred years before she heard her first radio commercial.

Let us move on to a history more banal.

The only book that deals with the arrival of the Negro to Esmeraldas was written ten years ago by a black schoolteacher; it is innocent and arrogant and as racist as any book I've ever read. The author, you see, is not a *black* black but sort of a pale café au lait; he can boast of his black blood without ever running the risk of being taken for a Negro. The book is not really history but rather a tract aimed at the Quito politicians, in which the author bitches about their neglect of the Province. It must have worked; it turned a schoolteacher into a politician.

The book begins as a celebration of the Negro: his beauty and nobility, his generous and exuberant nature. But then the author gets carried away. The Negro has a magnificent enduring body built to last and suffer, and man, that dazzling smile will stop your heart. You ought to see him dance. He's a lazy drunken brute but he can dance; he's inexhaustible, stampin' them big black feet in the dust. Dancing, drinking, screwing, these specialities show off the Negro at his best. He's not too bright, of course, but not so dumb he'll kill himself working. It was fascinating and horrifying to read these words, written by a black man, which underlined the prejudices my father had bequeathed me. It seldom occurs to one while reading that the same description is as apt for a Negro as a Norwegian or a Turk or an Italian. I read on and came to the history.

Trying to be as factual as possible I confess that, out of the almost total absence of dependable data and my inability to decipher what little that there is, most of this black story is pure invention. I have never been one to be even slightly slowed down by total ignorance, a quality I seem to share with the author of my source material.

Well, then, in the year . . . My God, there are no dates in the book; the passing of centuries is scarcely indicated. A sentence may begin by describing the arrival of a Spanish brigantine and end with the breakdown of a diesel motor at the waterworks. Shall we start inventing?

O.K. In the year 1582 a merchant vessel loaded with groceries (it says here) and a cargo of men and women of color, bound south against the Humboldt Current to Peru from Panama, anchored in a small bay off the Esmeraldas coast. The exact location is unknown, but it was probably in the vicinity of "El cabo de San Francisco," possibly on the beach of Portete — in other words within thirty miles or so of the present site of Africa. The Negroes were not slaves but the servants of a grandee of Seville, Don Alonso Sebastian de Illescas. Whether he was on the boat or waiting for his help in Peru or sending them on ahead to make his bed is not indicated. The ship, being short of food and water, anchored out of desperation, and the blacks were sent ashore to round up vittles. A short time later, the wind beginning to rise, a boat was sent ashore to bring them back. As the boat approached the beach, Don Alonso's servants — seventeen men and seven women led by their chief, named Anton in honor of his boss (in discussing this first black leader the author of my source material uses the names Alonso and Anton indiscriminately; it's the emotion that is important) — moved slowly off into the high grass at the edge of the beach. When ordered to re-embark, Anton, famous for his bravery, fatness, and audacity, stuck his great smiling face out of a grass clump and joyfully yelled back against the rising wind the following message: "Get lost, mother fucker."

The captain of the ship, having received this message, lost his cool; he was, apparently, not much of an intellectual prodigy. He sent the entire crew ashore to round up the ungrateful wretches, and while the ship lay unguarded in the bay, the Negroes sneaked back aboard, stole what little food there was plus all the guns and ammunition, and, screeching with black laughter, once more and forever disappeared into the high grass. "It was thus that the first black contingent arrived and constituted itself to form the sure original origin of today's population," says my source . . . I think. This is hard to believe, for in the next paragraph the natives of the region, the Cayapas, furious with the Negroes for their rather excessive interest in rape, are killing them off like flies. And in the following paragraph, Anton-Alonso having been murdered, all the Negroes have begun to kill one another, in their plot to take his place as top banana. On one page Alonso ruled the area for sixty-seven years, on another, for one year. Since one year sounds truer, we turn it into history. After a year, then, seven men and three women still remained. This may well have been the first black contingent, but it is hard to believe, even taking into account their pure delight in rape, that they did anything definitive toward hybridizing a new race. What they did do, however — and it permanently crystallized the relations between the Cayapas and the Negroes — was earn the Indian's permanent suspicion and contempt.

Still no hard dates to go by, but sometime before 1600 the first absolute ruler of the Esmeraldas province — actually the ruler then of about 40 percent of the present Ecuadorian territory — suddenly appears, and disappears, from my source material. He was named Alonso (no last name), and he was noted for his bravery, his fatness, and his audacity. This Alonso ruled for an undisclosed time with great cruelty, murdering among many others another Alonso — this one Alonso Arrobe from Venezuela, who had jumped ship in Esmeraldas with his hot tamale, and before he was put to a slow and painful death had, if I have translated everything correctly, impregnated a good percentage of the local population. His fame rests in his horniness, which must have been phenomenal — the horniest macho in all that horny macho land. His crimes must have been political rather than sexual, for there is no indication that unusual sexual competence has ever been considered within the jurisdiction of the law in Esmeraldas.

The province apparently was always governed by blacks; apparently they were all named Alonso. It must have been a sad and interchangeable series of Papa Docs and Amins — three hundred years of blood and sadism and strutting pomp. They had one redeeming quality in common: a refusal to acknowledge outside sovereignty; no one from outside would make the rules. By the blatant misuse of their power they also taught the populace a great human truth: that the aim of almost all leaders is to diminish rather than expand human freedoms. It is hard to date the moment when the province of Esmeraldas finally recognized that it was a part of the Ecuadorian nation and subject to a national will; there are many who claim it hasn't happened yet, and on the far reaches of the rivers there are still people who claim no nationality at all; they are just human beings.

It wasn't until the middle of the eighteenth century that this enormous and uninhabited province began to fill with people; when it did, they were all black. The Jesuits in the Chota Valley, owners of a tremendous hacienda, imported and bred slaves in special breeding cages. Escaping down the river Chota, which turns into the Mira on the coast, the slaves populated all the southern jungle areas of Colombia and the rain forests of coastal Ecuador. They were hunters and gatherers of wild rubber and *tagua*. Much later the Quito-Guayaquil railroad was built by thousands of black freemen imported from Barbados who then migrated en masse to Esmeraldas. The freedom and wildness of the coastal jungles drew a steady flow of people, both legal and illegal, to this other Africa. Today the names of the present inhabitants still indicate the double quality of this movement; the descendants of slaves had the names of their parent's masters. They were Spanish names like García, Estupiñan, Prado, Gonzalez, Ramos. But those blacks who had never been slaves in Ecuador and who had cherished their original names were in the majority; they had names out of Africa, names like Cheme, Chere, Chichande, Chanchingre, Jama, Bone, Cagua, Angulo. And the villages they settled did also: Tapaila, Taripe, Tabule, Tacole, Tabiaza.

Perhaps in the whole world it was only in Esmeraldas that the institution of slavery was such a dismal failure and the Negroes won their freedom with such a minimum of violence. Slavery simply didn't work here. The land was so wild and enormous, so full of food, so similar to the African lands from which they had been stolen that there was no reason to be a slave unless one had been born with a fawning disposition or had grown addicted to Spanish dishes and Spanish wines as a house boy. The Negro chattels, imported from Africa, Trinidad, Jamaica, and Panama to clear the jungles for pasture or to work around the houses of the half dozen or so haciendas that gradually began to claim the borders of the territory, found upon their arrival here that in a sense they had come home. They took one look around them, had a few quiet words with the old-timers, and vanished into the jungle. In 1860 when slavery was abolished in Ecuador there were only one hundred and twenty slaves in the whole province, out of a total notarized population of around two thousand, most of whom were black. South American statistics have been described as pure poetry; in this case I would suspect that the figures were created out of pure emotion, for who could have counted the thousands of criminals who refused to show themselves for a census? There were still one hundred and twenty slaves in 1895, thirty-five years after they had been freed, since by law the government was pledged to recompense their owners and hadn't done it, lacking funds. Ecuadorian law is often as poetic as its statistics.

So here they came, floating down the river Mira to escape from the Chota Valley slavery of the Jesuits, and swarming down the beach from Colombia. They founded villages on all the streams from Tumaco to Atacames; they mutinied off the beaches and swam ashore, heading off for the great trees that marched across the horizon of the low hills; in the dead of night they deserted the farms of the Spanish landowners. They were made savage by the will to freedom; they populated the land with a living anarchy that still flourishes. Twenty armed invasions of Indian troops from Quito completely failed to tame and subdue them; the Negroes took the land and held it, or rather they were absorbed and lost into the land; like Johnson grass there was no way to root them out.

As late as 1930 villages of Africans were discovered on the middle reaches of the rivers Cayapas, Mate, and Verde, where no Spanish was understood, less was spoken, and a strange culture that had nothing to do with the Spanish heritage blossomed richly. Perhaps such places still exist, small tight groupings of bamboo huts steaming in the sun on some back river clearing at the foot of the Andes, where a man can have six wives and forty children, where a man can be king of the whole world, ruled by no one. But probably the good times are gone forever. Now no more than a handful of men have more than three women; the province is becoming effeminate. What finally destroyed those isolated paradises was the introduction of the portable radio; in twenty years it changed the province more drastically than the three hundred previous years had. Now it is only the Indians who will not speak Spanish, though the real country Negroes speak a Spanish that is so basic, so flawed with innocence, that it is almost another language. Now the youngsters in furthest isolation know that there is another world out there and that it is full of music and dancing and things to buy, medicines to make you beautiful and fragrant, clothes that will make you irresistible to others. They can hardly wait to get away.

The Esmeraldas blacks, with their love of freedom, were the first true liberals on the South American continent; ripped from their tribal cultures they made their own — anarchy. It was a philosophy that no one would have thought of putting into words; it was more profound than words; it flowed in the blood. When one asks what contribution the Negro made to benefit the national character, the two things that the country needed most spring immediately to mind: love of freedom and capacity for joy. The Indian of the sierra, plunged into the blackness of eternal sadness and resignation, is appalled by the wide open smile and the wild free laughter of the Negro.

And that's not all that appalled the Indian.

The last great military effort to bring the province of Esmeraldas into the national family began in 1913; it resulted, after some years, in an indecisive truce that has still not been completely resolved. It began when a Colonel Concha, one of the largest *hacendados,* defied the conservative politics and raised a black guerrilla army to resist the high-sierran tyranny and the fanaticism of the Catholic church. Whether Concha was a patriot or seeking personal advantage is still one of those undecided questions that one answers out of one's personal political philosophy. Those who would malign him say that he never left his ranch but directed the war from his office on the farm; he was more interested in breeding cows than in fighting against oppression. He had served in Belgium as a consul to the Ecuadorian government but had been forced to resign in disgrace over some shady business dealings. Whatever his part in the war, he soon lost control of it, and it turned into a bloody and violent purging of racial prejudices — black against Indian. There is hardly a village in the province that doesn't show traces of or have some bloody story to tell about that chaotic time. One can still see the bullet holes in a corrugated iron shed put up over a tomb in the Rioverde cemetery; Camarones boasts of a slaughter. There were ambushes and killings on this very farm, and on a narrow trail that skirts the western bank of the Esmeraldas River some three miles below us, the most frightening mass murder of the war took place.

The night before this battle a secret Conchista had invited several hundred Indian troops to drink aguardiente at his farm. The following morning, scarcely able to walk, this drunken army was ambushed by a small band of Negro *macheteros* who had hidden themselves along the trail. Early the following day hundreds of headless bodies began to float past the town of Esmeraldas; they were all Indians. And during this massacre something macabre happened, which has entered into the mythology of the war. Trying to escape, some of the soldiers jumped into the river and disturbed a tremendous bushmaster in the brush at the river's edge. According to Alfonso, one of our macheteros, this snake killed over three thousand Indian soldiers; that the snake sided with the Negroes proved that God was with them, a conviction that was reinforced a few minutes later when an Ecuadorian lieutenant on the other side of the river began lobbing artillery shells into a small group of his own troops who up until then had managed to escape.

With the arrival in Esmeraldas of so many dead bodies, a clearly marked Red Cross boat was sent up the river to investigate this outrage. Some time later this same boat, empty now, floated back past the town, surrounded by the usual tokens of the Negroes' rage — more headless corpses. Did those jungle Negroes know what that large red cross meant? If they did know, would it have made any difference? They had always refused to play by white rules. It was Federico Lastre who had commanded this massacre, and it was here and later that he became either a patriot or a sadistic monster. When the war moved to the coastal beaches, Lastre and a small band of men, skulking along parallel trails, followed the troops. They knew every trail and every short cut and every ideal spot for an ambush. They appeared — simultaneously, some said — at widely separated bivouacs. Twelve hours after slaughtering a squad of soldiers in Mate, they would appear some thirty miles away in those terrible hours before dawn. Ramón with pride recounts those stories that he heard as a child: how Lastre had turned killer after the Quito troops had raped and murdered his wife, how the soldiers would shriek in the night when they found themselves surrounded and their sentries dead, how they would kneel in terror and with praying hands beg for mercy, "Papacito, spare us; have mercy, papacito." Lastre had no mercy.

Concha's War. It was bloody enough to compete in the world press with that other war that was taking place in Belgium and in France. Esmeraldas became famous; it gained a reputation that it has still not lived down. No one with a decently long memory would dream of investing money in the place. To this day there is not one factory or one respectable business in the whole province. If the public has forgotten, the New York bankers haven't. A friend of mine, an ex–Peace Corps volunteer who stayed on in Ecuador to promote big deals, told me that in 1971 he had almost arranged a loan of a million dollars to buy the abandoned banana plantings of Folke Anderson, the province's deceased and only multimillionaire. "It sounds like a great opportunity," the bankers said. "Now tell us again exactly where it is." Esmeraldas. Their faces paled. "Not one cent," they said. "My God, that's communist territory; we wouldn't invest one cent in that barbarous place."

1910,1920,1930. Little random boomlets of prosperity blew lightly and intermittently across the coastal lands. The grave mounds at La Tola were uncovered and a small part of their archaeological treasures was sent away to the museums of the world. An Italian cattleman and an Arab shopkeeper bought up the priceless golden artwork of three thousand years ago and melted it down into ingots for the masks and ceremonial daggers, the golden needles, spoons, and fishhooks; the golden nose and ear plugs were considered national treasures and their exportation was prohibited. Until sometime in the 1920s the *tagua* nut was harvested where it grew wild and widely scattered through all the rain forest areas; it was shipped to Germany, England, and the United States and was used for making buttons. Hundreds of people had their standard of living further lowered when some jerk invented plastics.

For a time rubber was valuable, and the *tagua* harvesters turned into rubber hunters — until the price of wild rubber plummeted to zero between the wars. Old Bill Swanson, who has lived for fifty years on the Río Verde, tells with beery and senile gusto of how he continued to buy rubber long after it had become completely without value on the Esmeraldas market. There was always that chance, he thought, that the price would go up again — until some jerk invented plastic rubber. But even after that he kept on buying it out of a sense of pity for the Cayapas Indians who stubbornly continued to bring it down the river in their canoes at the Christmas and Easter fiestas, when they needed money. He paid a half a penny per pound and over the years filled up a great warehouse with the worthless stuff, and in 1941 he sold it for a 2000 percent profit. He had one small problem; when it came time to ship his rubber he found that it had all melted together into one solid mass, fifty feet long, thirty-five feet wide, and eighteen feet high; he had to dynamite the shed and then dynamite the rubber to break it up into manageable chunks.

The sudden arrival of foreign capital to a simple and innocent area is inevitably traumatic and corrupting. Hitler's invasion of Poland was the beginning of the modern era for Esmeraldas, catapulted in a single year from the seventeenth to the twentieth century. Rubber and balsa became critical war materials; farmers were promised enormous profits to plant *limoncillo,* a sweet-smelling grass used to make citronella; the price of coffee, cacao, and quinine soared to surreal levels. Wonderful and crazy things began to happen; teams of geologists mushed through the jungle muck looking for oil, tungsten, magnesium; CIA agents disguised as Spanish Loyalists or traveling gypsy peddlers blanketed the province as in one of those invasions of rabbits in Australia; a single Japanese spy ran up and down the northern beaches taking notes — until he walked on a stingray buried in the sand and died of gangrene. All the German and Italian immigrants were put on a blacklist of enemy aliens and jailed or deported. The poor people invaded the deserted farms and stole the cattle and harvested the crops; the rich hacendados claimed the land itself. It was a wonderful war with just enough redistribution of wealth to make everyone moderately happy. Gringo dollars sparkled in everyone's eyes. The war produced a hundred wealthy men and a million memories, among the still poor, of magical three-day drunks, of ravishing whores, and of so much money floating around that it simply couldn't be spent. Some of the more exuberant machos, when they couldn't screw any more and couldn't drink any more, were forced to buy beer and have the bartenders pour it over their heads, bottle after bottle. How else could a poor man display to his friends his greatness of spirit and the inexhaustibility of his resources? But it wasn't only the poor who squandered their chances; of those hundred wealthy men, ninety of them died in drunken shoot-outs or of alcoholic poisoning; some of them were murdered for the loose change in their pockets.

The Esmeraldas Negro, lavish and spendthrift, disdainful of to-morrow, spent his way back into poverty. The serrano shopkeepers who acted as middlemen in the transfer of jungle produce kept their heads; they sat in their stores with their crooked scales and robbed the country yokels with a shamelessness that was almost too blatant to be believed. They are with us still; they have ended up owning the province, and they call themselves *la buena gente,* the good people, as opposed to the sweating farmers whom they live off and rob and who produce the country's wealth. After the war, Esmeraldas for a time was once more left to its lonely iso-lation. The limoncillo farmers were all bankrupted when some jerk invented DDT. Another jerk synthesized quinine. Coffee and cacao became dirty words — there was so much of it on the world markets. The jungle began to flow back into the hacked out clearings. Stasis. About the only sound was the squeaking of softly swaying hammocks. It was an uneasy time, like that time between movements when the solo violinist tunes his instrument for some wild Bartokian climax. The people lived with a growing sense of expectancy; no one knew how it would come, but they felt that something bigger than the Second World War would arrive to sweep them up into the old deliriums of prosperity.

Around 1946 all hell exploded and the whole province saw its hopes more than fulfilled with the arrival of a mysterious gentleman from Sweden, Folke Anderson. Within five years Esmeraldas was up to its neck in the kind of prosperity that nobody in his most insane fantasies could have envisioned. Anderson, with brilliant clairvoyance, had foreseen a fantastic boom in bananas, and he had arrived with what seemed like unlimited capital to plant tens of thousands of *hectáreas* of the best and flattest jungle land. In fifteen years Ecuador was the world's largest exporter of bananas, and the whole coastal plain from Colombia to Peru was transformed into green and endlessly monotonous plantings. On the drier land, around Chone and south toward Guayaquil, the large fruit companies installed overhead sprinkling systems. Even Nelson Rockefeller was caught up in the madness; he bought several thousand hectáreas of land in the very heart of the banana belt. And then to everyone's amazement (did he have secret banana information?) instead of planting bananas he planted coffee. It was Robusto, a rather inferior type. Hardy, prolific but bitter tasting.

In Esmeraldas, where the land was bathed almost daily in afternoon showers, there was no need for irrigation; one simply stuck a banana *hijo* in the ground, kept down the weeds with an occasional *machetazo,* and in nine months began to harvest. For a mile or two on both sides of all the coastal rivers, acreages of plantings striped the land in sinuous bands. And now ton after ton of "green gold" began floating down the jungle highways on floats made of war excess P-52 ejectable gas tanks, on rafts of balsa or bamboo, in overloaded canoes. An endless stream of barges hauled the fruit to an endless stream of banana boats anchored in the shallow waters off the town. A moderately well-run banana farm earned profits of 100 percent a year; Anderson began making a couple of million dollars a year, help became scarce, and day laborers for the first time began to earn enough to live on.

It was Folke Anderson who now dominated the province with

his insatiable needs; he was the first and the last of the Esmeraldas financial geniuses. When he died it was rumored that he was worth some twenty-two-million dollars. If he had been able to control his empire and operate his business efficiently, he would probably have been worth three times as much, but everything happened so fast, the profits were so tremendous and so inevitable, his need for employees so great, that there was no possibility or necessity for good management. He was like a man standing in a rain of gold; he caught up what he could, but most of it disappeared. His underlings were rapacious and there was no way to control them. While firing everyone at Kilometer 200 for the blatancy of their thefts, he was robbed of a boatload of fruit in his absence from Timbre, and on another hacienda to the north he was robbed not only of the fruit but of the boat as well. Watching his employees must have been like watching a herd of fat hogs grunting and gorging in a trough of slop. Bookkeepers, bankers, banana buyers, foremen, *mayordomos,* watchmen, timekeepers, banana cutters, banana haulers, truck drivers, canoe-men, barge captains, inspectors, *macheteros* — they were all in there up to their bellies in the trough of slop. Thinking of those days when gold rained from the sky one realizes that sudden wealth is really a twisted blessing from God, that He is giving man a chance at self-knowledge, a chance to see himself as he is with all his capacity for hoggish gluttony and evil. Anderson filled a dozen warehouses with Jeeps, trucks, electrical generators, diesel engines, and tons of spare parts for the boats and barges and trucks that he used. And he might on any day find that a million sucres worth of equipment had been stolen while he slept. Toward the end he never had the slightest idea what his warehouses held; he only knew what should have been there. Today almost every middle-class middle-aged man in the province boasts of having worked for a time as Folke Anderson's trusted employee.

He was still alive in 1967 when I was a Peace Corps volunteer in Rioverde, but I never met him. I passed him once as he was eating dinner at a sidewalk restaurant, surrounded by half a dozen *pistoleros,* like a threatened sheriff in a Western movie. I don't remember what he looked like, but I still remember the emotions I felt upon glancing at him; it was more than just my natural resentment at seeing a mean-looking man of immense wealth. He gave off an aura of unhappiness, of isolation, of subtle unsavoriness. I think of a man dressed in shabby black, looking as though he needed a bath. I got the impression of a man who was just beginning to realize that he has wasted his life doing something unworthy of his talents. He was living out his last year; I think I noticed that too. Toward the end he lived alone in a perpetual black rage, a disgust for human beings dominated his life. He knew men too well; he knew what money did to them.

He was badly served by Esmeraldas in spite of the millions that he made; he built highways, presented the city with a concrete sports stadium; he established a half-decent minimum wage for the lowest stratum of the society; he had brought the province back out of lethargy and made it into a center of commerce. But he corrupted the people with his money and made thieves of everyone. This is the evil that lives after him.

Anderson was found one morning on the floor of his apartment in Guayaquil with his skull crushed in from a whiskey bottle and his body shot through with bullets; the room was a shambles of blood, scattered papers, overturned tables, chairs, and lamps; he had put up a ferocious struggle. Photographs of the body and the wrecked apartment appeared on the front pages of the nation's newspapers. The whole country was shocked, and Esmeraldas in particular was stunned and desolated. In Esmeraldas they talked of nothing else, and the local businessmen took an almost masochistic pleasure in blaming the whole coastal *ambiente* — as though this particular destiny had been inevitable. "This is what we do in Esmeraldas," they said. "When someone comes here and gives work to the whole province and makes everyone rich, what do we do? We kill him."

Who killed Anderson? To this day no one knows. Here are some of the theories that have floated around: His original money had been New York gangster money and he had been rubbed out by the Mafia. A provincial senator lusting after Anderson's properties had had him murdered. Someone high up in Social Security had stolen several hundred head of Anderson's cattle and, hearing that he was about to pay his back taxes, had murdered him out of panic. He was a homosexual who had picked up the wrong man on the streets of Guayaquil. He had been murdered by radical Negroes enflamed to violence by a communist labor union boss.

Ramón and I have a warm feeling of half-recognition about this last theory. Shortly after returning to Ecuador I was mistaken on the street in Esmeraldas for my friend John, who at that time was trying to promote a cartel to purchase Anderson's abandoned and invaded properties. I was suddenly accosted by an ugly drunken black, with eyeglasses about two inches thick, who blocked my way on the sidewalk and stood wavering before me, making slashing motions across his throat with his hands. I couldn't understand his drunken Spanish and asked Ramón what he was saying. "What he is saying," Ramón said, his face furious, "is, 'We killed that son of a bitch Anderson, and tomorrow we'll kill you.' I think he's a communist lawyer; anybody that ugly has to be a lawyer." I stood there immobilized with amazement, trying to think what I had done and ending up depressed and with a growing feeling of guilt, a vague and unidentifiable involvement in the racial oppressions of the place. I had been back just long enough to begin questioning the morality of my moving into black territory with my plans to mechanize its agriculture. A couple of weeks later I warned John and told him that he was next on the Anderson list; it was a joke by that time, but John didn't think it was very funny, and from that time on I seldom saw him in the province.

The corruption that grew out of Folke Anderson's involvement with the province was not confined to the middle class who fattened on his inefficiencies; the corruption that feasted on the easy money of those boom times contaminated the population on every level, down to the poorest day laborer. Pedro Lamilla, who worked as a machetero on the hacienda at Kilometer 200, twenty years later still talks about those hazy golden days when wages jumped from fifteen to forty sucres and the mayordomos were authorized to pay ten sucres for every poisonous snake that the workers brought into the farm headquarters. "Anderson was a great man," Pedro said. "He was generous with his money. We had our wives and children hunting snakes all over the province; we brought them in and were paid without a word. Naturally, every snake in Ecuador immediately became a deadly variety. We cut the big snakes in half and collected double on them. For a time we even cut them into three pieces. The bosses were stupid but not that stupid; they paid us for two and then billed Anderson for six. Ay, that poor señor, he must have paid for a million snakes. They were grand old times, and it really wasn't cheating, you know. He was a rich gringo and we were *pobres y humildes*."

My partner, Ramón, remembers the last years of the banana boom; his memories are not happy ones. He came to Esmeraldas at seventeen, lured to the city by its promise of high wages. But the city workers had formed a labor union, and they had long since refused to accept new members. They were paid 250 sucres a day to pack bunches of bananas from the barges into the holds of the banana boats. Out across a rough plank board, up the sides of the ship, and down steel ladders into the holds. The union men hated and feared the work, of course, and so they hired teenaged country boys to do the work for them. Ramón was lucky; he replaced one of his godfathers, and two or three times a week when the boats were in he earned 40 sucres a day (about two dollars) while his godfather, dead drunk, slept it off on the dock and made his 210 sucres. Ramón remembers him with bitterness and tells me with barely concealed satisfaction how some years later his godfather fell into the hold of a banana boat, landed on its steel plates, and broke his back. God's justice, *por fin*.

"Why did you do it?" I asked him. "Why did you accept that situation?"

"I had two choices," Ramón said. "I could take the work or I could become a thief."

Thinking about his alternatives, thinking of Ramón at seventeen, packing three hundred pounds of rice off the barges from Guayaquil, up to his neck in the sea, three sacks of rice laid across his shoulders; thinking of Ramón loading the banana boats until his back was bloody, until a doctor ordered him to quit or die, I feel in the deepest part of me that he made a strange, almost cowardly choice. Putting myself in his place I know that I would have gone the other way. I would have picked pockets, stolen chickens and the drying clothes off backyard clotheslines. I would have peddled marijuana, rolled drunks in dark alleys, cut snakes in half. I would have grinned and danced for the white bosses. I might even have tried to become a trusted employee of Folke Anderson. I would have become a thief.

3

RAMÓN

ABOUT ONCE A YEAR OR SO, when Ramón is feeling particularly nostalgic, he will ask me if I remember the day we first met. I don't have the vaguest memory of this meeting, but in the retelling it has taken on such an epic quality that I don't dare admit that that day was less important to me than to him.

"Remember?" Ramón asks. "You were sitting on a balsa log on the beach with a funny sad look, and I came walking up the beach with a paddle over my shoulder. You said, '*Buenos dias*' — my God, your Spanish was unbelievably bad in those first months — and I said, '*Buenos dias,*' and you said, 'To what place are you traveling with that wood?' and I said, '*What* wood?' and you pointed to the paddle and said, 'I don't know the word.' I told you *canalete* and you wrote the word down in a little book. I said I was going up the river to buy some lengths of bamboo and to sell some fish; you asked me my name and I told you, and you said you were in the Peace Corps and I was to let you know if you could help me in any way. Remember?"

"Sure," I lie. All I can truly remember is sitting on a log on the beach and staring at the ocean. That is what I did mostly for about three months as a newly arrived Peace Corps volunteer in Rioverde. A few months earlier I had been forced out of business after twenty years of farming in California; it was a terribly traumatic experience that had left me with little else but a conviction of my own failures. I had lost my identity and my excuse for being alive. When I arrived in Rioverde I was as close to being dead as I have ever been — with one exception, which I will get to later.

"About ten o'clock that night," Ramón goes on, emotion now beginning to creep into his voice, "I came back down the river — where it had been raining steadily all day — cold, tired, hungry, and you were in your house, with the door open, reading by a candle. I stopped in the doorway and said, '*Buenos noches,*' and you looked up at me and said, 'Did you get the bamboo pieces?' and I said 'No, I just ordered them, for they must be cut in the *menguante,* in the dark of the moon at the ebb tide, or the worms will eat them'; and the way you looked at me I knew you hadn't understood a word. You said, 'Will there be dinner for you when you get home?' and I said, 'I don't know if Ester has kept the fire going, for it is very late.' You went into the back room and came out with a chunk of bread, an orange, and a can of tuna fish, and I walked up the beach to my house really feeling good, walking on air, because I didn't know anybody in the world who would have thought of my hunger like that or given me food without my asking first, and I thought, 'Well, I've met my first gringo and it seems as though he likes me and that we are going to be great friends.' Remember? Remember?"

"*Claro,*" I say. "Sure, I remember." But I don't. I remember those black nights reading with a candle and the silent town as cold as a graveyard and the wind making a dry idiot scratching sound in the palms and the steady murmur of the sea like the faraway highway noises of big trucks and those screaming desperate roosters that crowed all night sending out their warnings and challenging that impenetrable darkness.

When I joined the Peace Corps, in 1965, I did it as an act of desperation and repudiation; circumstances had so closed in around me that it was almost the only open door. It was a decision as hopeless and unenthusiastic as suicide, as furious on another level as the rage of that character in the story by Edward Everett Hale who cries, "Damn the United States; may I never hear its name again." I would leave this country forever, this country where I had been ground as fine as dust, my assets dissipated, my instincts confused by an animal impulse to keep surviving, where almost every human relationship had become as empty as the wind, as pragmatic as a dentist's drill, and where, toward the end, lying in bed at night I could feel madness crackling in my head like cheap

panels of fuses shorting out. I would leave forever; I would throttle nostalgia. Still, until I was consumed by these vengeful emotions, I hung on.

By the end of 1964 I was probably the largest producer of fat
hogs in northern California; hell, I was probably the *only* hog
producer in northern California — a last ditch fanatic, with wild
terrified eyes, turning out ten million horseshoes and stirrups while
Henry Ford's Model T was sweeping the land. In those years it
cost eighteen cents a pound to produce a market hog. The price
fell to sixteen, to fourteen, to twelve cents a pound. It stayed
at twelve cents for months. I was losing about twelve dollars on
every hog I sold and selling about twelve hundred a year. I was
almost the last of the World War II veterans who had gone into
farming in 1945 and was still operating almost twenty years later;
everyone, all my friends, had given up in despair. They had faded
away with dignity, after all they had children to feed, but I felt
much luckier than them. I can't remember now why I didn't fade
away with dignity; I think it simply never occurred to me that I
should do anything besides farm or that, with the sacrifices I was
prepared to make, somehow I wouldn't be allowed to do it.

To hell with dignity. During the last few months I didn't own a
pair of Levis that didn't have butter-plate-sized holes at the knees
and at the ass. I lost my house and twenty acres of pasture where
I ran the dry sows, and moved onto the property where I had
built the farrowing pens in the middle of a pretty, abandoned olive
orchard. There was no house on this land so I put a bed and a
table in a little tool shed and installed the stove and the refrigerator
in one of the farrowing pens; it wasn't too bad except on the
coldest days, but it didn't take long to heat up a can of hash, which
is what I virtually lived on one winter. After it was all over, on
the day that I arrived in Montana to begin Peace Corps training, I
had twenty-three dollars in my pocket; this represented all my
capital, everything that I had accumulated in twenty years as a
California farmer.

There are certain days in life so packed with horror or revelation
that if you survive them your whole past stands rendered, the
essence so distilled and clarified that it is impossible to keep on
deluding yourself. In the revelation department one thinks of those
religious conversions that strike one down like lightning, turning

drunkards or thieves into missionaries. Days of revelation are the mileposts in life at which one makes ninety-degree turns or puts a bullet through one's head or murders one's wife or loops back violently, seeking again in the innocent past what had gradually faded away and made existence chaotic or meaningless. But in the horror department . . . I have been remembering a couple of those days now; they are separated by years but each has its little symbolic pool of blood in the foreground, and each helps to explain how at some fifty years of age I ended up on a jungle farm with Ramón as my partner. If it was twenty years of farming in California that almost killed me, it was Ramón who brought me back to life.

Early morning in California on a day in April of 1965. I was out in the farrowing house making coffee; it was chilly, and I was planning to take the coffee and crouch under one of the heat lamps with a bunch of newly hatched pigs when there was a furious skidding of wheels on gravel and my neighbor drove into the yard and began screaming at me. My dogs had been chasing his sheep again; he had warned me three times and he swore to God that the next time he would arrive with the sheriff and a warrant for my arrest.

Oh God. The dogs had been a real problem; there were six of them — the mother, Langendorf, and her five pups. I had spent months trying to give them away, without success; one afternoon I took all the dogs into the Vina grocery store and stayed there until closing time, begging anyone who came in to take a dog home. One of my friends, Marie, took one out of pity, but brought it back to me three days later because her other dog, a truly ancient and overfed spayed bitch, was neurotically jealous of the new dog. There was nothing special about that pack of dogs; they were sturdy country types with country manners who tried desperately to ingratiate themselves by leaping and licking. They had long noble tails like pampas grass. They ran all over the dry hills between Vina and Corning, and if they saw a bunch of sheep grazing on those worthless acres they would rush down to play with them. They were not killers; they were lovers. At night they would all crowd into the toolshed, where I lay on the bed watching TV, and sleep underneath the table. And slowly, very sneakily, one by one they would creep up onto the bed with me, so that in the morning I would be all but crushed by their weight or blown out through the door by all those wildly thrashing tails.

I had a young cat, too, who slept with me, always the same way, stretching her whole length out on my chest and putting her face as close to mine as she could. The cat and I were very close, very tender with one another. Aside from the six dogs, the cat, and about nine hundred and fifty pigs, I had very little contact with the world. I had become an embarrassment to the farm community as my assets faded away and my lifestyle turned brutal and ascetic; I was no longer an advertisement for the free enterprise system; if I was anything in those rag-picker's clothes I was the living contradiction to Hemingway's Old Man, who had decided that you could be destroyed but not defeated.

Until that day the destruction had scarcely touched me. But now that day had arrived, and now it was time to make another sacrifice, one so terrible that I had never imagined it and never prepared myself. I was about to be put in jail as a public menace to the United States sheep industry, and I was going to have to kill my dogs. I went out into the fattening pens and filled a couple of feeders, noticing that almost all the hog feed was gone and that I had to call the feed mill and tell them to get on the ball. I washed down the hog pens that were beginning to receive the sun, separated a couple of droopy pigs into the hospital area, and fed the sows in the farrowing house. Moisture condensing on the rafters had dripped down and burnt out a couple of the heat lamps; I replaced them. I went into the last farrowing pen, the kitchen, and drank more coffee, squatting outside in the sun in the gutter and looking into the branches of the olive trees, their leaves silver and glistening on this spring morning. It hadn't occurred to me, not once, that two months from now this whole place would be nailed up and deserted. When finally it was absolutely time to go, I walked down to the truck and sat behind the wheel with the door open, and the dogs, watching me and knowing that the open door meant that they were going for a ride, rushed into the front seat delirious with joy. They had never traveled all together like this and they were all half crazy with excitement, all of them fighting to stick their noses out through the partly opened windows . . .

After I had dropped off my dogs at the pound I drove on to Red Bluff and the slaughterhouse. A day before, I had sold forty fat hogs, and while Mr. Minch liked a couple of days notice, I had decided out of necessity to harass him for the money. I was a hog man and he knew that I was going down the drain and it was very seldom that he was blatantly rude to me when I arrived a day early looking for money. But first I called the feed mill in Ord Bend about my empty feed bins. I was immediately put through to the owner, who quite politely informed me that since I had a four-thousand-dollar feed bill, and with the new drop in hog prices, it seemed extremely unlikely that I could pay this obligation; the mill could send me no more feed on credit. It was stunning news, or rather, ordinarily it would have been stunning news to learn that I was being closed down, but I was already so numbed by the loss of my dogs that I could scarcely take it in. I continued on to the slaughterhouse. Mr. Minch, about six months away from the heart attack that would kill him, was rushing around in his office keeping everything going. He was provoked that I had not had the decency to wait another day but promised to make me out a check. "It's going to take a few minutes, though," he said. "While you're waiting why don't you go out in the cooling room and look at your hogs. I'm sorry I can't give you top price, but they have way too much back fat. I'm going to have to dock you."

I had never seen my pigs after they had been killed, and looking at them then — all strung up on iron hooks, split down the middle, as pink and smooth as babies, hanging in a long row in the semidarkness — it was hard to imagine them snuffling around my feet in the fattening pens and twirling and dancing with delight under the jet of water I used to play on them during the heat of the afternoons. Out of the hundreds that I had, there were a few with whom I had had rather friendly relations. We liked one another; we teased one another; they regarded me as an equal, and it was important to them to be touched and talked to and to be recognized. In the evenings while they rested, I used to play Shostakovich symphonies for them. I really did not want to look at my pigs with their lousy extra tenth of an inch of back fat and lined up and still and unbelievably dead in that dark cement room.

Beginning to stagger just a little, beginning to pant just a little, I left by the closest door — into another cement room, but one that was flooded with sunlight and crowded with men in white coats who were furiously cutting and hacking at the carcasses of cows.

No one will ever convince me that all this was simply coincidence and that that four-hour period was not organized and orchestrated to bring me crashing down. I had fallen under the malevolent eye of God, and He had more tricks up his sleeve. I didn't know if I could take any more that day, but I remember thinking, "It's coming, whether or not you can take anymore, and it's coming today," and the idea flashed through my head that by nine o'clock that night someone would come to the farm with a telegram announcing the death of someone that I loved and couldn't lose. But nothing that violent was needed now; all I needed was one more light tap on the head. It came in the next ten seconds.

I was going into deep shock, the blood vessels in my limbs so constricted that the blood felt like thickening honey; my hands and feet were ice, and in the fuse box of my head the connections were going dead or grounding out, and pinwheels of flaring light like strobes whirled and sputtered. Staggering, paralyzed, feeling as though I was losing my balance, I put out my hand to steady myself on the flank of an immense and placid cow who was standing at my side. As I touched her there was the crack of a rifle in my ear, and the cow, jerking and twitching, her eyes rolling wildly, dropped at my feet. In that space that a moment before she had occupied, standing on a little raised platform like a podium, was the largest Negro I have ever seen. He was bare to the waist and glistening with sweat, and he was looking deep into my face and laughing at me. A cold little thread of smoke rose from the gun he was holding.

I had an old television set in my shack which I had bought secondhand for fifteen dollars. That night the cat and I lay on the bed watching it. It was April but tonight it was icy cold in the shack, even under the covers. Sometime that evening I watched a minute-long spot advertisement for the Peace Corps. Their propaganda at that time was in one of its tell-it-as-it-is phases, and we lay there watching a young volunteer in the Ethiopian teaching program who was standing outside a miserable village of mud and sticks in bright sunshine, talking about how great it was to be involved with the lives of other people. Thousands of flies were crawling over her face as she spoke, gathering in her eyes like animals at a water hole, crawling into her mouth. I can't forget that girl; she radiated a kind of inner peace and joy and dignity. How I admired the Peace Corps for its honesty in putting something so essentially horrible on the screen to advertise what one might expect in their tight exclusive club. Later, with the television off, I lay in bed and listened to the pigs banging the tin doors on their empty feeders; they sounded like a mob of striking convicts pounding their plates on the table, and it helped me to focus my mind on the fact that I was out of business.

It was still a few days before I could climb out of my grave and begin to think of the future, and it was two weeks before I picked up a Peace Corps application at the post office and set it on the table and then walked around it warily for ten days as though it were a bomb ready to explode. I filled it out finally and sent it off air-mail, thinking, "I will leave this country forever, this country where I have been ground as fine as dust," etc. etc. And it took me years to realize that that day, which I had considered the worst day of my life and which had made me curse a god that until then I had scarcely believed in, had in reality been no more painful than the pangs of being born, and that far from being the worst day of my life, on the contrary, it had been the luckiest. Spewed out of that deadening rural life, screaming with rage and self-pity, as bloody and battered as a new born child, I was given another chance at a brand new kind of life.

But I didn't know any of this when I first went to Rioverde; I was still half dead from shock and, like a broken record, still endlessly obsessed with reliving my failures. It was Rioverde, it was Ramón, who brought me back to life.

Ramón was twenty-two-years old, just married, hopelessly poor. He made a few sucres by selling upriver the fish that he cadged from the shrimp boats, fish that were caught and killed in the nets and would only be thrown away. He used to paddle out two or three miles into the ocean when the shrimp boats passed the town at 4 A.M., and then at dawn he set out up the river, yelling out the news at each bamboo hut. He considered it demeaning work. To me he was just one of a group of fishermen who got in the habit of hanging around my house at night because there was nothing else to do in that town. Very gradually he began to emerge as an individual: the smartest, the handsomest, the funniest of all those smart, handsome, funny fishermen in Rioverde. He had completed three years of school, and he could read and write, but because there was little need for either skill in that isolated place, he did both painfully.

Ramón was bright, wholly alive, open, violent in his enthusiasms and his prejudices; he was like a high-tension wire whipping wildly in the streets and giving off shocks and sparks. He lived by his emotions and they were good; he trusted them. His instincts were noble — too fine, really, for that deprived place, where one stole to live and where in a moment of pity one could be undone. He was one of the few really poor people that I have ever known who had somehow escaped being brutalized by the life they were born into. He was sustained by a profound optimism that was grounded in his youth, in his health, and in an awareness of his innate intelligence. Twenty-four hours after having been robbed or cheated or wiped out by the sudden deaths of his animals or the breaking up of his canoe in a rough sea, he would be up there in the clouds again, dancing around with joy again, making bigger and grander plans. The intricacy and detail of his plans were stunning. A couple of times he talked me into lending him ten dollars to buy chocolate beans on the river to sell as contraband in Colombia; he had it figured out that he would double his money on the sale, and then double it again bringing back bolts of gabardine to sell in Esmeraldas; things never quite worked out, and each trip was so physically exhausting and dangerous that I finally talked him out of further trips. He always made some money though, and always ended up with a new pair of white duck pants, which made him as happy as if he had just discovered oil.

He lived out of an inexhaustible welling-up of joy, and because I had never met anyone like him before and because I was new to the culture of poverty which I found absolutely devastating, I was completely captivated by Ramón and his capacity to find life good. I imagined that in his place I would have found the quality of that life of poverty unbearable. He had strength, courage, the will to

endure; he was fiercely competitive and delighted with small vic-
tories; he was as alive as a poet. He had all those qualities that I
lacked and therefore, perhaps, regarded as the heroic qualities.

I spent four years in the Peace Corps, three of them in Rioverde,
and Ramón and I gradually became close friends. He was the
only Ecuadorian I ever met who trusted me completely and who
understood what we in the Peace Corps were trying to do, even
though we seldom did it and most of the projects in which he was
involved fizzled out in various degrees of disaster. I had brought
him the philosophy that being poor was more a matter of personal
choice than anything else, an inability to contemplate the alternatives and the disciplines they required, and he now believed this
and was determined to be poor no longer. He needed me to back
him up in this. And even more I needed Ramón, for through him
I had once more acquired a sense of my own dignity and once
more life seemed to hold some pattern, some purpose. I had never
had to throttle nostalgia; since coming to Rioverde the memories
of those twenty years as a farmer in California had become dim
and scattered. I didn't even hate my country anymore, and I
realized on another level that the opposite of love isn't hate, it is
boredom.

When it was finally time for me to leave Rioverde, both of us
were incapable of planning yet another life, one that would ex-
clude the other. At the same time I had developed a real terror
of that little town and its dedication to its own destruction. My
father was dying. I wanted to see him for the last time and put
whatever little bandages I could over the mortal wounds that we
had inflicted on each other; after years of silence he had begun to
write me pathetic letters full of guilt and remorse. I promised
Ramón, and I think he even believed me, that I would go home for
a few months, visit my father, see all the latest movies, eat a few
tons of tossed green salad, take a few hundred hot showers, and
come back, bringing him a pair of fine gringo boots. Ten months
later, a week after my father died, I came back to Ecuador, and
Ramón and I bought a farm together.

If we had thought in Rioverde that we knew each other, we were
now suddenly and violently disabused of this illusion. There, for
me, the relationship had been idyllic, very gratifying to the ego —

the relationship of a teacher to his pupil, a father to his son, a great white all-knowing daddy God to his innocent and deprived supplicant. Ramón had been the perfect sack of grain for the Peace Corps mill, the ideal subject that every volunteer is searching for and hardly ever finds, someone who is smart and eager and absolutely bored with being poor, someone who wants exactly what you want him to want — an undeprived life. His capacity for growth had been phenomenal; what I hadn't taken into account when I left him was the self-igniting quality of his capacity to change. When I came back in less than a year he was scarcely recognizable. He had proved himself without me, and he liked that feeling of independence which had grown with the awareness of his own potential. He no longer saw himself in the role of younger brother or dutiful son to my dominating ways. I had rather mixed emotions about the way he rejected some of my plans out of hand. Some of his early ideas, as naive as a child's building blocks, drove me right up the wall. One of our first and longest ranging conflicts was centered around just how, as a big rich hacendado, he should dress; he wanted to play his role right down to the smallest detail, and he asked me to look for a great black Stetson in Quito and a holstered revolver; the prancing stallion he would locate here. I talked him out of the hat and (for awhile) the horse, but I finally bought him a gun and a box of blank cartridges.

Very bravely, very naively we associated ourselves in that most intimate and delicate of relationships — a business partnership — and now the quality of our friendship began to change, to reverse itself.

Faced with the very practical problems of running a large tropical farm, I found to my embarrassment that not only did I not know where to begin but, since it would involve ordering around great masses of poor workers, I actually didn't much want to do it. A month after we moved onto the farm we were trying to track down twenty-three day laborers who either were or were not out there in the grass someplace making fierce hacking sounds with their machetes. Ramón had never ordered men around in his life; now he began to bloom as a great *patrón,* his secret fantasies of power suddenly made real.

How confusing it must have been for him, so recently inflamed

by my talk about the brotherhood of man, to be so rapidly disillusioned. Many of the people we began to hire, mostly small landowners along the river, had had their experiences with gringos
during the fat days of the banana boom. Being landowners themselves (the word totally misrepresents their economic status), they
felt not only that their brute work for us was demeaning, the kind
of work they themselves would have hired someone for could
they have afforded it, but naively that with their wide experience in
the outside world they had pierced through to the secret heart of
the white character. Whites were really pretty stupid; they required
only one thing: that they be set apart, above, to be treated with the
veneration of superior beings. You could dominate and fool a
gringo with a few simple tricks — elaborate and comical good
mornings, elegant little bows, doffings of the hat, great awed smiles,
hysterical laughter for the most pointless jokes — all those false
things that were simply contemptuous of one's intelligence or one's
simple ability to evaluate sincerity. While they grinned and bowed
their delighted-to-see-you good mornings, asking me how I had
slept and how I felt, there was a coldness and a rejection of me as a
person shining out of their eyes, which put me in the middle of a
rotten play whose lines I detested. Looking into those eyes —
which were as cold, blank, and appraising as a lizard's — and trying to smile back, I realized that of all the information I could give
them, nothing could bore them quite so much as to hear how I had
slept or how I felt. Mocking Ramón, they treated him the same
way, but their bows were more lavishly baroque, their great black
smiles travesties of joy, devotion, subjection. Brotherhood? What
bullshit. How can there be brotherhood between a man with a
five-thousand-dollar truck and a man who makes a dollar a day?

Some of this I saw and understood at the time; I thought it was
very interesting and rather comical. Ramón saw right into the
depths of the worker's jealousy, suspicion, and envy, and it terrified
him. By the end of six months, tense as a stretched wire, unable
to sleep, subject to fits of temper, he was informed by an Esmeraldas
doctor that he was well into a preulcerous stage. Until it became too
complicated, we tried to keep the refrigerator full of milk brought
in from town. How frightened and ashamed I felt to think that I
had made Ramón into a typical American executive-type so

quickly and that this adventure, this jungle game, was so deadly serious with him.

One afternoon, watching him stretch barbed wire with six men, I went out to show him how we did it in "God's country"; all those men rushing around like bugs, putting up three hundred feet of fence, struck me as madly redundant, but Ramón was so obnoxious with me, so arrogant, that I left him in disgust. That night at dinner he apologized, a thing he had done so rarely that I was touched by his sense of his own bad manners. "Look, Martín, you were right, and I'm sorry. I *don't* know a good way to build a fence; I've never built a fence in my life, and I'm just trying to learn. But I couldn't let all those men know that I wasn't sure of myself, could I?"

How desperately Ramón searched for his role and for the competence that would give him credibility. But who could he copy? The only bosses he had ever known, low-born *mestizos* hired by the rich to intimidate the workers, were rapacious, screaming, shameless animals. At the same time he rejected my philosophy as soft and romantic. In the face of a barely concealed contempt Ramón forged his own style, but for many months he was confused and uncertain and this wavering infected the workers and gave them hope. There wasn't one who didn't envy his friendship with a rich white man and who didn't dream of replacing him. They were sure that I had put him in his job as a buffer between them and me. He was just a foreman with a fancy name who could be brought crashing down. One night Ramón took the bus to Guayaquil with ten thousand sucres to buy weed killer for our peanuts, and while he slept someone picked his pocket. Three of the workers approached me about this and casually wondered aloud why I was so sure that Ramón had actually been robbed; wasn't it possible, wasn't it in fact quite likely that he had just *said* he was robbed? The idea of being ordered around by a Negro who was as plain and homespun as they were was unpleasant and demeaning; it offended their sense of dignity and self-respect; they would have preferred to be dominated by a Manabita dressed chicken-shit-style in a big white cowboy hat, packing a revolver, and touring the work on horseback; they would have known where they stood.

It wasn't only on the farm that Ramón was forced to reassemble

himself. In Esmeraldas, as soon as I had returned I began to meet
a weird bunch of men. I had known them before but very casually;
they hung around a little open-air café, the Brazil, where the big
shots, the banana shippers and the hacendados, gathered at mid-
morning to read the newly arrived newspapers from Quito or
Guayaquil and to drink small cups of very black bitter coffee or
bottles of Pepsi. They turned out to be middlemen who knew
everything and supplied the rich with contract labor or put them
in touch with men who had cattle or contraband medicines from
Colombia to sell. For a long time I thought they were pimps; later,
during a hot political campaign, I decided they were gunmen hired
by the politicians to shoot at their political opponents. No such
luck, nothing so romantic. They were there to give me what I
needed. Some cattle? A really first rate mayordomo? Another
piece of land, perhaps? They were all especially interested in
supplying us with cheap labor; this would give them a double
profit, but the way they talked, it would be practically free; they
knew of drought-struck areas where you could contract labor for
fifty cents a day. First, of course, you would have to feed them
rather well, for when they arrived they would be tottering, but
after a couple of weeks they could keep going on rice and plátano.

We didn't want to deal with these guys anyway; they were real
lizards, and we could already see, in fact for a time we were surrounded by, their work. Oil had been discovered in the Amazon
basin of Ecuador, and thousands of workers, whole tremendous
gangs of men supplied by those middlemen had flooded into that
area around our farm. They were employed to build the Texaco
pipeline, which would terminate at Esmeraldas. The pipeline
passed our farm a hundred yards or so behind the highway, and
the Williams Brothers Construction Company (most of the poor
farmers called it the Hermanos Brothers Construction Company
which, if you know Spanish, is sort of funny) had subcontracted all
the pick and shovel work to a group of tough unscrupulous na-
tionals, which isn't funny at all. For months the road was dotted
with men in tattered clothes; they had come to look for work, or
more likely, having worked for months, still destitute, they were
begging for rides to take them home again.

When the *contratistas* found they couldn't deal with me, they
began to seek out Ramón. Subtly insolent because they were talk-

ing to a Negro, a dozen men took Ramón aside, each secretly, and tried to involve him in deals that would enrich them both and help to bankrupt the gringo partner. Ramón was both stimulated and horrified by these proposals, and he told me about them in great detail. He was proud of his honesty but depressed also, for it was as though everyone took it for granted that Ramón had achieved the eminence of a great landowner by subterfuge and was now automatically being embraced as an equal into that shoddy club of *mestizos* who scrambled so desperately to butt their way into the lower levels of the middle class. One of my good friends was in the group; he explained very carefully to Ramón that now he had a chance to be a rich man if he played his cards right and that he, X, was prepared — for a reasonable percentage — to show him how to do it. "But we're friends," Ramón cried. "I'm not just in this for the money. We're friends; we're doing this together. I'm doing this for something that I feel here in my heart."

"*Friends,*" X said in disgust. "Holy shit. Don't talk like a child. Look, Prado, you'll never get another chance like this if you live a thousand years. Now listen to me, Prado, for the sake of Christ. You take a knife and slice open your breast and pull out your heart and hold it in your hand and try to sell it, no? How much do you think you can get for your fucking heart?"

"But how can I rob the farm," Ramón wailed, really depressed now, for both of us had always thought of him as being reasonably honest and having reasonably friendly feelings for us. "Don't you see? It's mine too; I'm an owner too. What do you want me to do, rob myself?"

From a practical viewpoint Ramón knew much more than I did about tropical agriculture, but he had grown up in that medieval world of ritualized poverty where out of absolute desperation a farmer goes into partnership with God. He prays instead of sprays. Ramón was also too proud and too anxious to prove himself to ever admit that he didn't know something. He had the verve and the passion to rush into new projects absolutely convinced that his santo, Jesucristo, was the third partner in our operation. He loved to rush things to some showy completion; if I had to leave the ranch for a few days to go to Quito, I would come back to find some weird new building spoiling the view or all my favorite trees cut down; how happy he was making independent decisions. He had fenced in fifty acres of pasture while I was still wondering and figuring out if cattle was a good business in Ecuador. I knew that Ramón and his six macheteros were doing something out there in the grass, but it didn't occur to me to ask *what* until he told me that he had ordered twenty rolls of barbed wire. After all the talk about the big black hat, the pistol, and the rearing charger, I should have known that we were destined to go into the cattle business.

It wasn't only Ramón who was confused. What were the planting seasons, if any, in this area where it rained almost every day between 2:15 and 6:30, when we sat down to eat dinner? What seed corn was best? How should we pay our workers, by the day or by contract? What crops should we plant? Would chocolate ever be worth anything again? Or coffee? Could we corner a market on pineapples in Esmeraldas? What was all the excitement about African palm and coconuts? How about oranges or grapefruit? What about tea or black pepper? There were a thousand such questions, some of them with no answers and some with two opposing ones. As time passed we began to agree on certain crops — oranges, pineapples, peanuts — but from the very first we began to pit our wills and our conceptions of farming against one another.

Both of us claimed to be trying to build our lives on a foundation of decent poverty; we claimed to be aiming at an existence reduced to essentials so its true shape would reveal itself; we wanted to live in some kind of balance with the rather primitive realities surrounding us and to have human relationships with our workers and the poor farmers who lived up and down the river. Our houses would have thatched roofs; if we had a refrigerator, part of it would be stocked with colas to be sold to our friends. But as time passed it became apparent that my idea of decent poverty didn't have much in common with Ramón's. Whole months might pass between harvests and the infrequent arrival of inadequate checks gleaned from my father's estate — months when we were reduced to high-class beggary and bought our groceries on credit. Three days of a rice and bean diet pretty much destroyed my philosophy of decent poverty; things were getting damned indecent. I would sulk and bitch, and Ramón, who for twenty years had eaten less well than we were eating now and who during certain periods of his life had gone days without eating anything at all, would grin at my displeasure and talk about the necessity of getting back from time to time to that life he had endured as a child.

"I don't ever want to forget how it is to be poor," Ramón would say emotionally, not really meaning it and stuffing a great gob of rice into his mouth.

"Let's not play games with poverty," I would answer. "You have every right to eat fried cow flops if that is what gives you pleasure, but as for me I would like to insist on something in the way of fresh vegetables. And I don't mean boiled cabbage which we have now had six days running." I felt that if we could buy rice on credit there was no reason why we couldn't also charge a pound of meat and a few ripe tomatoes. During these not infrequent times of culinary stress I began to resent a never-discussed possibility: that Ramón, God forbid, was trying to teach *me,* was trying to impress his values on mine. What the hell did he think he was, some kind of crazy Peace Corps volunteer?

My whole life had been a neurotic tightrope walk balanced over the abyss of financial insolvency, and I only felt really secure and happy when I had a few unclaimed dollars in my pocket to reinforce the inadequacies of my personality. I was happiest when I could go out and buy something stupid and expensive, something I didn't need, something that, when I owned it, sat forgotten in some closet. As we dipped deeper and more frequently into the rough seas of decent poverty and then into a condition more obscene, I became more vulnerable to depression and to the helpless feeling that I was a prisoner in a barbaric place with no control over my life. Ramón on the other hand became more and more exuberant as our money melted away, and when those days arrived when we didn't have a cent of cash on hand, he seemed to be driven into a wild excitement. Life had become 'normal again; it was something he could understand and handle. He found my ideas on poverty pompous and childish; now once more he could teach me values and show me to his delight that my fears were unmanly.

Perhaps I am putting this rather too strongly; for the most part we lived a simple and satisfactory kind of life; the really brutish things we wrote off as being only temporary. We were unaware of our deprivations until gringo guests would come to visit us, and then we would suddenly see our life through their astonished eyes and realize that life without a toilet or a shower or running water in the kitchen was actually rather inexcusably savage. We didn't think of ourselves as either rich or poor; rather, we accepted the judgments of our poorer neighbors who owned nothing, not even a future, and who considered us the richest people in the province. Well, they were right in a way; if we were not rich in money we were certainly rich in our thousands of young coconuts. More important we were rich in the present power that we had over their lives. Power, I now discovered as I watched Ramón beginning to manage the farm, was probably the greatest and most satisfying commodity that one could buy with money. In rejecting power for myself, I was perhaps rejecting on the most elemental level the necessity of being rich — but doing it in a neurotic and dishonest way.

After a year of cooking with charcoal, one day — at a time when we were absolutely strapped for cash — Ramón came back to the farm from Esmeraldas with a cheaply made four-hundred-dollar butane stove and oven, for which we were now pledged to pay in thirty-six strangling payments. I accepted this madness with a grace that surprised even me. Good, I thought, Ramón is screwed up, too, and has to go out from time to time and blow a great pile of money to feel secure. I liked him more now, feeling that he shared one of my flaws; though I must confess that as time went on and his passion for charging things swelled to manic proportions it became more difficult to share joyfully in this vice. When he bought the stove, however, I was heartened by the possibility that he needed more than just the exercise of power to give him satisfaction. He used his power well, he was very serious about it, but the joy it gave him made me nervous. I was troubled by the responsibility that I had refused and handed to Ramón as though it were possible to wash my hands so easily of the tremendous power that I now exercised, through my partner, over all the people of this area. Certainly we would use it in our own self-interest.

My friendship with Ramón was unlike anything out of that gringo world that I had chosen to leave behind and more complicated than any I had had before. The most complicating thing, but perhaps the least important, was that he was black and I was white, but I think that this was more important to him than to me. Until I came along he had never known a *blanco* who didn't represent a higher and unattainable economic stratum; until I came along he had never known a blanco that he could shove and bump and call an asshole. We had reached the point where we could shamelessly insult one another with a kind of granite security, with a proud conviction that we could say anything even in anger without threatening the bond that held us together. Each of us to the other was a trophy, a prize that neither of us particularly deserved but won in a bingo game that at first we scarcely knew we were playing. "Look what I've got," we wanted to yell to anyone who dared to listen. I suppose there was in this triumphal shout the implication that each of us had found something in the other that he never found in his own race — not because that something existed, but simply because out of some neurotic need or some predisposition to be engrossed with color we had taken the risk and the trouble to invent some quality that was ultimately not racial at all but simply human.

We had some terrible fights, fantastic encounters of complete bafflement and frustration, lizards trying to communicate with lemons. There we were, really furious, yelling at each other across a mile-wide abyss where nothing that either of us said could be understood and all that could be heard was an outraged tone of rage and isolation. How many dozens of times had each of us been ready to pack up and leave forever? Fed up; fed up. But how could it be any different? We were from different worlds, different cultures; we had been educated to different sensibilities. Actions that to him were perfectly normal struck me as completely irrational, the actions of an idiot. My nitpicking criticisms drove him to distraction.

"How you have changed," he cried. "When I think how awful you have become in your fifties, I dread to think how you will be when you are seventy. A monster; a monster."

"And you?" I yelled back. "If you don't start planning better you'll be back there on the Río Verde selling fish; that is if you still have the price of a dugout canoe."

·

I am crippled and restricted in South America by that puritan ethic that forces me to judge everything as either good or bad, that makes me uneasy with prolonged leisure or guiltless excesses, with procrastination and fatalism. I am nervous around emotion and unplanned joy. And Ramón? He is just as restricted and enslaved by his Latin heritage. We are both Pavlovian dogs who slaver on cue and react with the ringing of our own secret ethnic bells. Ramón is both sentimental and pragmatic almost beyond belief. He dreams ridiculous things that can never come to pass and then gets all confused between fantasy and reality. His solutions to the problems that I press upon him are so violent and destructive that they automatically create two problems instead of one. He has a staggering capacity to forget his mistakes; or no, rather, the inability to feel that he has ever made one. He has a deep faith in *mañana* and preaches the healing qualities of that tomorrow that never comes. Ramón is pure Latin and a much happier man than I am. While he is always dreaming of some crazy improbable future, he still takes wild pleasure in a present that to me is quite ordinary and only half realized. Ramón's god is Dionysius; mine, Apollo.

We first became friends probably out of an almost identical sense of pity for one another. Any American can, I suppose, imagine my pity for Ramón. It was grounded in the contemplation of an intelligent and ambitious youth chained by circumstances to crushing and lifelong poverty in a poor country that offered no future to its ineptly educated citizens. Ramón's pity for me was just as basic as he watched me moving about, confused and frightened in his strange world. I was unable to communicate with anyone about anything but the most animal needs of survival. Except for bananas, and I didn't know the Spanish word for them, I was unable to identify a single fruit or plant. I couldn't catch a fish or paddle a canoe or net a shrimp or weave a piece of rope out of a vine or find my way on a jungle trail or even walk on one for more than fifty feet without sinking up to my knees in mud. I couldn't machete out a patch of weeds or fix a leaking roof. I couldn't even cook a pot of rice that didn't come out like a great mass of glue. Jesus, I couldn't even walk a hundred feet without shoes. Ramón found my ignorance so overwhelming that he could hardly bear it; he was confused between tears, depression, and anger. Chances are when I macheted down a tree it would fall on me, hopelessly entangling me in its spiny branches; paddling across the river I was almost inevitably swept out into the rip tides where the ocean breakers crashed onto the sandbar. In the middle of all this, to hear me speak of my four years at university filled Ramón with an incredulous impatience, and about the third time I mentioned my educational qualifications for arriving to overturn his life, he asked me if, in view of my obvious ignorance of everything that he had taken for granted since he was three years old, I would please lay off the higher education bullshit. As I squatted sweating and swearing on the floor, trying to open a can of tuna fish, he grabbed the machete out of my hand and did it for me before I could slash my wrists and bleed to death.

I hope that Ramón is not still drawn to me for my ignorances, though by this time he must surely be aware of this ever-expanding field. I don't really know what qualities of mine he admires; he says that he feels something here in his heart for me, and he pounds his heart angrily and says he doesn't understand it, that he is bewitched, that when he is completely fed up and wants to leave that he can't do it because of this thing in his heart. He makes it sound like cancer. But he says he feels safe with me because I have never lied to him and because except out of petty anger I have never patronized him.

Telling lies is Ramón's most famous characteristic. I still remember, with slowly fading but still outraged disbelief, dozens of evenings in Rioverde when Ramón would head up the beach to eat dinner with his wife, promising to return immediately for a nice long conversation. Eighty percent of the time I never saw him again until the next day. I pinned him down finally, more out of curiosity than anger, for I had become resigned to his ghostly evening visits, and I had had the same experience with innumerable other Ecuadorians, to the point where I recognized this irritating need to fantasize as a national character trait.

"Tell me," I asked, "why do you keep lying about coming back after dinner? I don't give a damn if you come back or not; I'm just curious to understand what's going on in that fantastic little Latin head of yours."

"Lie to you?" Ramón said, honestly offended, honestly puzzled. "Why would I ever lie to you?"

"My God, Ramón, don't you know what a lie is? You lie to me every day when you leave here at six promising to come back at seven."

"Oh, *that,*" Ramón said. "That's not a lie; that's just good manners."

"*What?*" I asked, looking at him without understanding and feeling the Latin earth beginning to heave and lurch in its own special and irrational way.

"But I know you're lonesome evenings. Doesn't it make you feel good when I say I'm coming back? I just want to cheer you up and make you feel good."

I've realized by this time that what I call lies are to Ramón no more than statements of standards he'd like to maintain. So I don't understand why he is irritated when I don't take him seriously. And now it is depressing that he has more and higher standards than ever before, because this means that I am completely unable to find out with any certainty what we will be doing tomorrow, or even, if I naively feel that what we discussed together yesterday had a certain basic validity, what we are doing today. Workers who I thought were spraying cocos or hoeing peanuts turn up cleaning pasture, stretching barbed wire, or chasing cows. The things that are important to Ramón he never lies about — money, his dignity, his emotions. It is unthinkable that he would cheat me. Yet being a gringo I insist upon feeling cheated when he pulls the workers out of *my* cocos and scatters them out in *his* cow pastures to machete down bird-of-paradise or bananas, our two most stubborn weeds. Ramón, to sum him up in this regard, is the biggest liar I ever met. And the most honest man.

I don't know that Ramón was always so honest a man; his jealous brothers have told me stories about youthful escapades. I tend to think that at some point in our friendship, and this is the most impressive thing I can imagine about Ramón, he simply decided by an act of will that he would never steal again. And never did. Of all the changes that he underwent, and for which I might possibly claim some degree of credit, this change gives me the most joy.

Ramón was the fourth child born to Plinio Prado some thirty-four years ago, when Plinio was young and feisty and just getting steamed up and enthusiastic about the idea of founding his own private and poverty-stricken dynasty. In all the years that followed, except for a time when his first wife ran off with another man and Plinio wandered the trails in a daze looking for another mate, he never faltered in his aim to populate Esmeraldas with fine black sons who bore his name. He was much more interested in quantity than in quality, I'm afraid, for Ramón is the only one who is known all over the province as a fine and decent man and who has found a deep satisfaction in his reputation for honesty. It is his proudest possession. His brothers have rather tarnished names, if the truth be told. One of the most infuriating and humiliating things that can happen to Ramón is to be mistaken for his brother Orestes. While walking down the street in Esmeraldas, he will be confronted suddenly by a policeman with a drawn pistol or by some old woman, a victim of one of Orestes' shoddy deals, who will start cursing Ramón and screaming for the law.

"Ah, that Ramón," Evans told me one day. "He's a marvel, that man. If we had six more like him in the province we'd begin to move ahead." Evans runs the Timbre properties of God knows how many thousands of acres, and Ramón respects his opinion, especially this one, with which he is naturally in full accord.

"Ramón is one in twenty thousand," Manolo *el español,* one of our neighbors, tells me, and when I tell Ramón his eyes fill with tears and he asks me to repeat the story in a little more detail.

I wonder if Plinio — gray-haired and exhausted now, his capital of a few *criollo* cows inexorably turning into medicines for himself and his babies, his strength gone, and his organs riddled with worms — has ever coldly looked at this rabble of children that he has spawned, his heritage to an already overpopulated land. At dinner when I try to point out what he has done, mocking him for what I consider real criminal activity, he sits there half listening, smiling foolishly, blinking his eyes with satisfaction and giggling at my condemnation. Ramón's oldest sister is forty, his youngest brother, not quite a year. There is every reason to expect that Ramón is going to have a few more brothers before Plinio's fires die down. He is only fifty-five. Without counting a three-year-old son who died last year of pneumonia — the first of Plinio's children to die — Ramón has twenty brothers and sisters. I dared Ramón the other day to name them in their proper order, and he got a little over half way through the list and threw up his hands in defeat. He started out bravely, "Bolivia, Orestes, Luvia, Ramón, Elva, Nelly, Rufo, Mericia, Olga, Pedro, Wilson, Mariana..." The dead child? He doesn't remember ever having heard the name of his dead brother.

I don't know when Ramón first began to be ashamed of his father or when he first began resentfully to see himself as just one more piglet in an obscene and endless farrowing. Perhaps it was his contact with the timid, almost underground Peace Corps propaganda on family planning that helped him see his father from the outside. Ramón had been brainwashed. The main things he had been taught during his three years of school were, "*Es bello morir por la patria,*" and, "The most sacred and beautiful love in the world is that love between parents and their children." He had also memorized the first fifteen thousand words of the national anthem. He held on stubbornly to these things that his public education had given him, as though, along with a halting ability to read, they were the only foundation upon which he could build a special life. How hard it must have been for him finally to reject these concepts. It puzzled me that he could be so blind to what his parents had done to him. His mother had run away with a lover when Ramón was six; his father had been so busy breeding a reserve of cheap labor that hardly any of that first group of children had ever gone to school. One night as we drank beer together in Rioverde, Ramón, "confessing everything," told me about a pig he had stolen from an employer who had neglected to pay him his wages; and then, baring his soul absolutely naked, he admitted that actually in his heart he had never had much feeling for his mother. Some days later when I alluded to this remark he denied ever having made it. How could he have said such a thing? The whole world knew that between a mother and her child there existed a love that was as pure and profound as the love between God and man.

It was years before he could accept my conviction that it was not beautiful to die for one's country or for anything else and that it was not possible to love someone who was absolutely unlovable. It was more years before he could admit that perhaps I was right. I had always had ugly and catastrophic relations with my father, but Ramón would refuse to listen to me when, out of rage and frustration, I would begin to purge myself.

"Stop it; stop it," Ramón would cry in outrage. "How can you talk like that? How can you hate your own father? Don't you have any shame?"

"It's the father's job to love his children," I'd say, "but children don't have to love their fathers. Love is something that fathers earn; it's like interest on invested capital. If he raised me up and now thinks I'm a son of a bitch, then I'd say he invested badly. I am to some degree something that he made, you know; if he doesn't like what he's made, that's tough. I didn't ask to be born, you know."

"No, but you *were* born, raised up, cared for. You're alive in the world. Isn't that a debt you owe your father? Isn't it wonderful to be alive?"

"Do you want to debate *that?*"

"*Hermano,* you talk like a madman; I'm not going to listen to you anymore."

In high school I had thought of a cute question that I liked to ask people, and now I asked Ramón. "Look, let's say you have been found guilty of something and you have been condemned to spend the rest of your life waist deep in a great pool of shit. In a case like this would you rather know that it is shit and just stand there without moving and getting it all over your face and into your eyes and mouth, or would you rather be mistaken and think that you are standing in a great pile of flowers and, thinking that, dance around in it, flinging gobs of turds into the air?"

Ramón looked at me for a long time. "I would rather believe it was flowers," he said slowly. "I would rather dance."

"I would rather stand still," I said, and the memory flashed through my mind of a famous *Life* photograph of a furious monkey who had escaped from an island of his chattering peers to a small rock in the middle of a lake, where he sat immobile and isolated and glaring at the camera.

"Hermano," Ramón said softly, "we are not standing in shit."

"Hermano," I said, "I think you are right; for the first time in my life the question strikes me as stupid."

O.K., so it's not shit, but then, it's not flowers either. Thinking about this difference between us tended to diminish my own idea of myself as a man, and I felt that compared to Ramón I had been corrupted by my advantages and that I was spoiled, weak, and decadent. Ramón, born in a grass hut with only a *bruja* midwife in attendance, growing up on the beach as wild and undisciplined as an animal, naked until he was seven, barefoot until he was fifteen, without schooling, ignored by his father — Ramón found life to be enchanting, full of joys and joyous mysteries, full of obstacles to be confronted head-on and dominated. Life like a chunk of meat to be devoured, the bones cracked open and the last of the sweet marrow sucked out. Life was a dance, a celebration, an exhilaration of the senses, an ecstasy.

The doctor at *my* birth had been the most famous and sought after in all of California. He had cut out Will Rogers's gall bladder or something, perhaps circumcised Jackie Coogan, and attended Gloria Swanson, Joan Crawford, and Theda Bara when their flawless tummies gurgled. I had had everything in life that could be bought with money: nurses, tutors, private schools, a trip around the world, four years of college. I had studied under Whit Burnett and Oliver La Farge, had been friends with Mrs. Aldous Huxley, Patrick Hemingway, Wallace Stegner, Roy Harris. I had seen and heard Horowitz, Rachmaninoff, Marian Anderson. Hell, I had even knocked Toscanini down one night as I rushed out of Carnegie Hall trying to beat the crowd. I had lived in England for a year, in that magic British Columbia of Malcolm Lowry's for another year, and I had spent months in Mexico. Except as a soldier and a Peace Corps volunteer I had never had to work for anyone but myself. And yet in spite of these privileges I found life to be so full of peril, suffering, evil, and hypocrisy, so essentially insane, so essentially sad and meaningless that, like some two-bit Hamlet, I was immobilized much of the time by my conviction that whatever move I might make would be as absurd as any of the alternatives. Why did I try so obsessively to transfer my own dark feelings about life to Ramón, who saw everything through the bright shining colors of rainbows? Was I like some frightened father trying to prepare his son for a future when life once more would deal him low blows?

*

One of the more destructive things that happens to a poor man in the Latin culture is that as soon as he begins to move out of his poverty either by luck or by ability, all of his relations (and he now discovers that he has twice as many as before) will immediately crowd in on him to share his good fortune. I am cynical enough to believe that this is done not so much for the advantages that one can obtain by having a rich relation as it is a subconscious effort to destroy the man and bring him down to the common level. I was curious to see how Ramón would handle those dozens of brothers, uncles, and cousins who were now greeting him so effusively on the street and rejoicing over his new status as a great and wealthy landowner. And making plans to join us. Hand-delivered letters written in pencil on lined paper cut from the children's exercise books began arriving from the little jungle villages on the rivers north of Rioverde, towns like Las Naranjas, Las Piojas, Lagarto — Oranges, Lice, Alligator. They were illiterate letters, painfully executed by stiff fingers that possibly hadn't engaged in anything so challenging and delicate in years. Even Ramón's mother, who washed clothes in Guayaquil and whom Ramón hadn't seen in years, sent warmest greetings with one of her daughters. She wanted nothing for herself she said, she was used to the neglect of her children and had never expected appreciation for all the sacrifices she had made. But unfortunately she was forced to advise Ramón that his older brother, Orestes, who had had to leave Rioverde by foot and at night and five minutes ahead of the police, was now hiding out with her in Guayaquil. Frankly, she said, Orestes was the only son who seemed to really love her, though at times, of course, he was a little difficult with his, what you might call, drinking problem. She had given him all her savings, which he had spent, and now because of some ridiculous misunderstanding over the loss of ten *varas* of gabardine displayed in front of a store, Orestes was now also wanted by the Guayaquil police. Would Ramón as the only rich member of the family please immediately send one thousand sucres.

I used to watch Ramón, his lips moving, laboriously going through these one page notes line by line. In the first few months he received dozens of them. He had never learned the trick of jumping ahead when he came to a word that couldn't be made out and filling in its sense from what followed. He read a letter like a miner taking out coal from a narrow seam, each word in its proper order as he came to it. He would spend about fifteen minutes methodically working his way down to the signature; he never said much of anything, but his face would grow cold and stubborn. He never answered a single one of them, nor, until I urged him, did he bring any of his family to the farm to work.

Plinio came to visit us sometime during our first month on the farm; he was very delicate and only stayed one night. I hadn't seen him for over a year and it was sad to see how he had aged. He had lost weight, his hair was going white, and there was a film of vagueness spreading across his eyes like cataracts. When he got up from a chair or lowered himself carefully down into one, he groaned. He had bought a hundred-and-fifty-dollar house in Esmeraldas, leaving his farm and his fourteen cows in the care of a neighbor. He had about ten children of school age and his second wife insisted that they be educated in town. He was quiet at dinner, stunned into speechlessness, I found out later, by the magnificence of our farm, our new tractor, and the rows upon rows of young coconut trees that we were beginning to reveal with the disk. To Plinio, a man with a hundred coconuts was a rich man who had won through and had solved life's problems; we had almost two thousand and were talking about planting two thousand more.

After dinner I left father and son listening to the football news and went to bed — to be awakened at five o'clock the next morning by the sounds of someone prowling around outside my house. It was a five o'clock farce; Plinio had found that my untended front yard was bursting with certain wild plants of strong medicinal value. I watched him stuffing his pants with leaves and patting them against his kidneys. When I came over to the store at six, he was drinking a cup of herb tea, and the kitchen was piled with small bunches of different leaves and grasses.

"This farm of yours is better than the *clinica*," Plinio said. "Just look at the medicines I've found." He pointed to each pile in turn. "Nervousness, abortion, headaches, toothaches, *mal aire, mal de ojo,* kidneys, liver, fainting spells."

"Holy God," I said," I had no idea you were *that* sick. But you know, Plinio, this is all rubbish, this is all witchcraft."

"I have this terrible pain in my kidneys," Plinio said. He rubbed the small of his back and smiled, embarrassed, when his hand reminded him of the great pile of leaves, like a bale of wet hay, sticking out above his belt. "I suppose you would say this is witchcraft, too."

"Yes, of course it is. Pain is just a symptom for one of a dozen things. Stuffing your ass with leaves is about the craziest thing I ever heard of. Plinio, Plinio, go to a doctor, get an order to take a stool sample to the lab and find out what kind of animals are eating you up."

"You're right," Plinio said, but he turned away from me frowning slightly and closing the subject. I had harassed him for years in Rioverde about this, and it was something he would never do. There was something disgusting about walking through the streets of town with a bottle filled with filth.

He had slept on top of the store counter on a few sheets of newspaper, having refused Ramón's offer of a bed. He didn't like sinking into and being engulfed by a mattress. A mattress was a trap for forgetting; it was unmanly. He had lived his life on isolated farms or in small villages at the edge of the jungle, and he knew that night was a time of menace and that it was dangerous to sink into that deep obliterating sleep when one was helpless and vulnerable. One had to be alert and prepared always, but especially at night when thieves, murderers, dead men, and ghosts crouched waiting in the darkness underneath the big dripping leaves. No one would ever convince him that *muertos,* their faces green and phosphorescent, didn't wander the deserted nighttime trails; he had seen them. Months later when he came back and gradually moved in with us and planted a half acre of tobacco all mixed together with rice, tomatoes, squash, watermelons, and sweet red chilis, he continued to use the store counter as his bed, a loaded pistol in the pocket of those rolled-up work pants that were his pillow, and a lamp made of a coffee can and a rag, burning and smoking on a stool in the center of the store. As we grew familiar with his ways and benignly contemptuous of his country prejudices, we began secretly to laugh at him. It wasn't cruel laughter so much as simple amazement at his self-delusion and the simplicity of his feelings. He thought of himself, for instance, as a light sleeper attuned to the slightest unusual noise in that outside darkness. As a matter of fact he slept like a dead man. Banana trucks would arrive at midnight and load two hundred and fifty stems by candles and flashlights, with a half a dozen singing, cursing, chattering men working thirty feet from his sleeping head. In the morning Plinio would be amazed to find that all the bananas, which he had half thought of as being under his care, had disappeared.

Plinio wanted to help us. That first visit he had made had been for the express purpose of advising Ramón. "You will never get another chance like this; don't blow it. Work hard, be serious, don't steal. Don't steal *anything,* you hear."

Ramón didn't say anything but later commented on this conversation. "I don't know why he said those things. Does he know me less well than you do? Does he think I am like his other sons?"

But Plinio was very proud of Ramón, and gradually he spent more and more time with us. He felt no humiliation at working under his son as a laborer for a dollar a day; he wanted to teach Ramón everything he knew, and he planted two hectáreas of pasture for us in *elephante,* a gigantic grass that should have taken over the farm. He tried to get involved in our plans and our discussions. After dinner, over cups of herb teas, he told us how to catch thieves and what to do with them (kill them), how to keep the little rice birds from harvesting all the rice, how to grow tobacco and make it into four-pound rolls, how to stretch barbed wire, cure stomachaches, make banana preserves, kill the *jaulpa* in the coconuts. He sent us men from up the coast who he said were hard workers, serious types; he wanted to leave us with all the lore, all the tricks of farming that he had learned in his hard life.

Everything he told us and everything he did was a disaster. The pasture grass that he planted failed to root; all those swinging bottles and cans full of pebbles, which he had attached to hundreds of yards of string and which he rattled, failed to frighten away the rice birds and they ate his planting in a single day; his rolls of tobacco grew moldy while he held off selling them, waiting for a price rise; nobody wanted to eat his banana preserves, which looked like nothing so much as diarrhea wrapped and packed in leaves and smelling of wood smoke; nobody was interested in his crazy jungle medicines. If they were so wonderful, why was he each day a little weaker? Our neighbors robbed all his melons, his tomatoes, and his squash, and the baskets of red chili that he tried to sell in the Esmeraldas market suddenly had no value. He spent half his time in Esmeraldas trying to cure his and his children's coughs and fevers, and while he was gone the weeds and thieves moved in. Even the men he sent us turned out to be weird types who left us after a few days when they realized that Ramón would show them no special consideration.

I was a couple of years older than Plinio, but I thought of myself as being young in comparison to him. He was an antique, a holdover from another century with his magic cures and his goofy solutions. I also thought of him as older because he seemed much closer to death than I was; his life seemed to be over, he was rigid and seemed incapable of changing, he had no future, he was like an overripe fruit to which nothing new could happen. I liked him and liked having him in the house; there was something simple and noble about him at one particular time — when he sat by candle-light on the floor of the store at night, grading, oiling, weaving his tobacco into long ropes, the coil held between his toes to control its tension as his hands reached and selected and squeezed and enfolded the leaves; he worked with speed, grace, and economy, and it was always exciting to watch him. It was the only thing besides making babies that he did really well. The rest of the time he was almost outrageously incompetent, but a comfort to be around, this sadly smiling, aging clown who somehow failed at everything he put his hand to. It seldom occurred to me to wonder how Ramón was reacting to his father's increasing presence on the farm. Sometimes he seemed unnaturally tense and quiet when Plinio was telling us something for the fifteenth time; sometimes I saw little nervous grimaces of irritation flickering across his face, but he said nothing. The love of children for their parents is one of the greatest blah blah blah.

The second year Plinio planted almost a hectárea of rice plus all his other garden vegetables; the failure of the year before didn't seem to bother him. He had made a deal with us this time to share in the harvest, if any. I was to prepare the ground, buy the seed and the weed killer, and he would do the rest. But he had been sick off and on all winter, and it was about this time that the child who later died began to fade away. He brought Pedro and Wilson to the farm to help him, to hide in the weeds and pull the strings that would rattle the cans that would scare the birds. He was gone much of the time now, but when he was here he loved to walk through his rice with me and talk about the forty hundred-pound sacks we would be sharing. I estimated that he might with luck harvest six sacks, and I told him he could keep our share. When the rice headed out Plinio was laid up in bed and had to send his two young sons up the coast to check his cows; the birds arrived and in three days did their work. Our share of the rice that year was about eighty pounds; Plinio put it away for us in a shed and forgot to tell us it was ours. The rats ate it.

Pedro was seventeen, Wilson about fifteen, and they were both delightful kids except that they were at that awful age when all of us felt like stoning them to death at regular hourly intervals. They were typically late-blooming teenagers. They were absolutely useless; lazy languid dreamers. They had never had toys; in one sense they had never had a childhood, and now when one thought they were out helping Plinio one would find them down by the river playing with three-year-old Ramoncito's toy cars or Martita's dolls. They were so recently out of the Río Verde jungle, they were so innocent, that they didn't know that boys were not supposed to play with dolls. They seemed to be developing normally, however; Pedro, unobserved, liked to pull up the doll dresses and study those pink plastic sexless stomachs. They loved our wheelbarrow and spent hours hauling Ramón's children up and down the road in front of the house, and at night they would sit together on the tractor seat, turning the wheel and going "arhuum, arhuum, arhuum."

(I had special feelings for all of Ramón's brothers, even shameless disgraceful Orestes. Maybe even *especially* for Orestes, who most of the time was in hiding from the police while his children starved in Rioverde. Plinio had passed on to them not only a kind of identical, classic beauty but also some essence of sweetness and joy that radiated from him even in his old age. Meeting the brothers when Ramón was twenty-two, I knew exactly, through Rufo, what Ramón had been like at eighteen; through Pedro, what Ramón had been like at fourteen; through Wilson, what Ramón had been like at twelve. Those first years in Rioverde had been fantastic as I tried to understand Ramón and the culture that had produced him. I was surrounded by my best friend at ages four, six, eight, twelve, sixteen, twenty-two, and thirty.)

After Plinio lost the rice he put his sons to work in the tobacco; they built a lean-to of bamboo and leaves at the edge of the vegetable garden, which had once more begun to be robbed, and they cooked and slept there and gradually filled it with rows of drying tobacco strung out on lengths of rattan. When they ran out of food they would come down and hang around the house and Ester would feed them in the kitchen. Little by little, as Plinio's garden dried up or was robbed, we began giving Pedro and Wilson little jobs until finally they became steady workers, though this is hardly the proper word. Shortly before this, Ramón had accepted Plinio's suggestion that one of the girls come out and run the store, and shortly before *that* at my insistence we had hired Rufo back again, poor Rufo who was desperately in love with his pregnant girl, who desperately needed money, and whom we were always hiring and firing for the inane and uncontrolled regularity with which he kept sneaking into my house to remove the loose change from my trousers.

So gradually that we had scarcely noticed what was happening, we had turned into a Latin family. Ester was cooking regularly for a dozen people, and the house was bursting with Prados. They slept on the store counter, on the outside benches, underneath the dining-room table, on the kitchen floor. And Ramón's sister, though we didn't quite know it yet, was having a wild affair with Aladino (one of our macheteros) in the storeroom, about five feet from her father, that light-sleeping ever-watchful guardian.

Some years before all this I had worked for a while in Montana as a Peace Corps staff member in an experimental training program, a feature of which had been a timid exploration of personal encounter. Small groups met each afternoon; they were called T groups. T for what? Torture? We were supposed to be open, honest, and spontaneous with one another — for an hour a day. In other words we were expected to shed our natural reticence, forget everything we had ever learned about common courtesy, look for the cracks in our companions' defenses, and ruthlessly attack them. To our dishonor we rather enjoyed it; and if we could make someone weep, the psychologist in charge would dance around like Hitler in those old movies of him accepting the surrender of France. I don't remember that any of this planned cruelty did much good, though a couple of marriages that probably would have cracked up anyway were dissolved at the end of the training, and a couple of people dropped out of the program. I still carry a small scar from some remarks that Sarah Ashe directed my way; she saw certain hidden spots on my soul and in a few well chosen and troubled words stripped me naked before a dozen of my friends.

One night over dinner I told Ramón about this experience and tried to explain what enforced honesty was supposed to accomplish: the breaking down of suspicions and the building of trust between people. The whole concept struck Ramón as another example of Yankee ingenuity. He asked me to explain the whole thing again, and after I had done it he sat for a long time thinking. "It's a great idea," he said, finally. "You know what? I'm going to try it; from now on I'm going to tell the truth to everyone." That was as much of this idea as Ramón was ever able to understand. He never conceived of it as an exchange of honesties; he wasn't interested in hearing anyone else's truth. He had been changing so fast, his responsibilities had become so great, his sense of his own worth and dignity had so expanded, that he had felt suffocated as he searched for a new way to confront this new life that he planned to dominate. He could no longer operate out of that humility that a poor man affects to save himself from disaster. The hypocrisy of the false, ambiguous word, so necessary in a small town where hatred or disgust or distrust must be disguised from the neighbor with whom you must spend the rest of your life, was no longer a necessity. Speaking frankly was now a luxury that Ramón could afford; it was one of the rewards of power. Everything he had had to keep bottled up might now come pouring out; every insult he had had to accept might be avenged. Beneath the joy and the glad acceptance of life I began to glimpse a darker, more tortured and more neurotic personality. He had been wounded to his depths by things over which he had had no control: his poverty and his color. I was amazed to discover this, which was a measure of my stupidity. How could I have thought for so long that only Ramón out of all the poor would not have been twisted and deformed by the insults and deprivations of his position? It occurred to me that his early fascination with my whiteness had not been because he found it so beautiful; it was simply a reaction to some terrible self-hatred that year after year had been beaten into him. This was a chilling thought, for the word *self-hatred* or a word very much like it had been at the heart of that lightning bolt of revelation that Sarah Ashe had hurled at me in Peace Corps training. How could a friendship based on such weaknesses endure the strains we were putting on it?

Ramón changed overnight. Within a few months he had broken with two of his oldest friends from Rioverde, told a new friend, a schoolteacher, that he seemed to be much more interested in Ramón's money than in any of his qualities, refused on three separate occasions to bribe three different policemen who had stopped him for petty traffic violations, and made a scene in the Banco de Fomento when he burst into the manager's office, after waiting for over an hour to pay off a loan, and angrily told him that it was one hell of a way to run a bank. Once he was thrown in jail when his eloquence got out of control, and I bribed him out with two quarts of cheap Scotch. Instead of 10 sucres for bribes it cost us 260, but it was worth it to Ramón, for he had been locked in a cell with a dozen teenage thieves who to his astonishment had spent the entire afternoon and evening underneath a canvas tarpaulin experimenting with homosexuality. He made a mental list of all the storekeepers in town who had tried to cheat him or who had called him *zambo,** and he refused to patronize them.

It was while Ramón was high on truth that Plinio and his sons

* In South America the word *zambo* defines the offspring of a Negro with an Indian. As a term of address, in Ecuador at any rate, the word is derogatory and insulting, as insensitive to one's dignity as "nigger," which, in a sense, in Spanish it replaces. It may be more painful for a *costeño* to be thus addressed than for a *serrano* to use it: many middle-class Ecuadorians from Quito do not know its true meaning, defining a zambo as a person with tightly curled hair, using the term interchangeably with *muchacho,* "boy." This hybridization has created a race of men and women of extraordinary beauty and grace, but also a confused race still seeking its own identity.

gradually moved onto the farm like a slowly spreading stain and helped turn it into a surrealistic and disgraceful place. It was already, we thought, full to bursting. We had four dogs, a pet goat that I had bought for the children, from one to six cats, and a three-hundred-pound calf that we had raised up from the first day on buckets of milk. She insisted on coming into the dining room with us at meals, and she would lie down by my side at one end of the table and listen to us talk while she chewed her cud and burped grassily. Once we had accepted the idea that there wasn't much we could do about it, we were amused by all this outrageous mixture of man and nature. I had designed the store and the kitchen at ground level with everything open, and there was really no way to keep out anything that wanted to get in: the calf who ran in terror from the cows and hid in the dining room, the chickens who lined up at night on the window ledges and watched everything with their cold and disapproving eyes, endlessly discussing everything among themselves like a bunch of horrified dowagers; the goat who stole dishrags and underwear; the dogs who piled up at our feet beneath the table and snapped at scraps we dropped for them; our furious cats who regarded it all as madness and sulked on the highest shelf or on top of the refrigerator. It was an impossible way to live, of course, but we were out on the farm all day, and at night we had our own little houses to escape to, and actually, to spend an hour at dinner time in that wild confusion of people and animals was better than any circus. The Latin nuclear family. One part of me loved it; another part, out of ethnic arrogance, was trying to carry everything to its ridiculous extreme, to mock the country people who lived in such a close communion with their animals. I bought a half-grown toucan; it took up residence on the top rung of Plinio's chair and, during dinner, climbed up on his shoulder and stained his shirt, front and back, with wet papaya droppings. "What we need is a couple more goats and a baby hippopotamus," I said, and Ramón didn't answer but looked at me as though behind those newly troubled eyes an idea was knocking to escape. He had *really* been brainwashed. Now in the house we had almost more people than animals; the thought had never entered his mind that he could stand up to his father and feel resentment or irritation with this innocent and traditional invasion.

Behind the memory of those days, which in one way were as bucolic and moving as those in a certain Bethlehem stable, there is another memory of Ester cleaning up behind that careless horde of sphincterless goats and chickens, our noble, fearless toucan, and that arrogant calf; I best remember her now endlessly scooping up turds and sweeping away the stains with buckets of water. We were a Latin family; none of us ever raised a finger to help this Latin woman, nor, in all probability, would she have allowed it. In this whole earthy barnyard mix there was only one thing that really irritated me: Plinio's country habit of spitting on the floor. Mentioning this to Ramón with the request that he speak to his father about it was perhaps the first intimation that his father had qualities that might be judged. But he was reluctant. "You speak to him about it," Ramón said.

"I don't know how," I told him. "In Rioverde when I asked Orestes to please not spit all over my house he got insulted and told me I was as good as accusing him of having a communicable disease."

If Ramón did speak to his father about the spitting, nothing changed; fifty-five-year-old habits are hard to break. But now slightly put upon by this placid old man who sat at my side each evening with a crapping toucan perched on his head, once more I began digging at Plinio where I thought he must surely be most vulnerable: "Well, Plinio, there's one good thing about that family of yours; they'll never convict you of indecent exposure. When the judge counts your children he'll dismiss the charges and say, 'Hell, that's not indecent exposure; he just hasn't had time to button up his pants.'"

Everyone except Ramón was slightly shocked, but they laughed politely. Plinio chuckled, and in the darkness of the kitchen where his three sons were hunched over bowls of lentils, Pedro's teeth gleamed in the candlelight through the door. "We have a saying in Rioverde," Plinio said. *"Cada hijo nace con su propio pan.* Every child is born with its own bread."

"That must be a Spanish saying," I said. "First, there is hardly ever any bread in Rioverde and second, when there is, it is so awful it would kill anyone under the age of eighteen."

"Under the age of ten," Ramón said, suddenly. It was the first time he had ever become involved in a conversation of this kind aimed against his father. "I was ten years old before I ever tasted bread."

"Everytime I went to Esmeraldas I brought back bread for you children," Plinio said, hurt at Ramón's rebuke.

"Shit, papá, you couldn't pack that much bread on your back," Ramón said. He stared hard at his father and called into the kitchen, "Ester, will you please come in and take that damned bird off my father's head, and while you're at it wipe the shit off his neck."

"Ramón, *caramba*," Plinio said, "we do the best we can; we can't always do everything we'd like to do. *Asi es la vida de los pobres.*"

We ate in silence now, in tension. I glanced at Ramón; his eyes were flashing with anger. "Asi es la vida de los pobres," Plinio said again, finally, sighing. The old philosopher.

"Papá," Ramón said, "how could you have done it to us? In the name of Christ, Papá, how could you have done it to us? And I'm not talking about the bread. I'm talking about a whole family that can't write its own name. How could you have just kept on having us without thinking about our lives and what was going to happen to us? Like sending us to school, teaching us something, how to be a tailor or drive a truck or repair tires, or Christ, even be a barber."

"Ramón," I said, warning him. I was very proud of him in this moment but afraid of his anger that could grow stronger out of itself. "Ramón, *calma, paciencia, y fe.*" This was one of his pet expressions when I criticized the languid way our farm was managed; it always irritated the hell out of me.

"Aren't you ashamed, Papá?" Ramón went on, ignoring me. "Ninety percent of your sons can't read, and all your daughters are living with men who can't read. All of them, digging ditches or waiting on tables or doing dog work in the banana plantings. Thieves, *marijuaneros,* drunks, bums. All of them. Aren't you ashamed?"

As Ramón talked everyone in the kitchen got up very silently and filed out onto the front porch. They could still hear everything there without appearing to. "Well," I said, "if I'm going to Quito tomorrow — goodnight."

"Orestes has given me much pain," Plinio said. "You're right about him, and the boys *are* lazy, but I don't think any of them smokes marijuana, and Wilson knows how to read, and all the younger children will go to school. I've always done everything I could, son. No one ever taught me how to read; I taught myself."

"Someone stole one hundred sucres out of the store today," Ramón said. "This is something that I absolutely will not accept."

Plinio, staring at his empty plate, said nothing.

"I will not accept this; do you know what I mean?"

"Well," I said, "if I'm going to Quito tomorrow . . ."

As I left the store Pedro got up and followed me to the edge of the light on the path. "I didn't steal it," he said, making a cross with his thumb and first finger and kissing it. "I swear."

"I don't think it was you, Pedro. Don't worry. But you *are* awful lazy, you know. You'd better get serious around here. Tell me the truth, are you a marijuanero?"

"*Ni conozco la marijuana,*" Pedro said, passionately. It was the stock answer of all the young marijuaneros up and down the river, but this time it had the ring of truth. "He doesn't like us because we're poor; he's forgotten how it is to be poor; he has no sympathy with us anymore; he's getting hard."

"Don't you believe it," I said. "He wants to help you if you're worth it. He's going crazy trying to find a few people around here he can trust."

"He wasn't always *so* honest," Pedro said. "I remember when he used to steal cocos from Don Pablo in Rioverde."

"Oh, sure, so he stole coconuts when he was twelve years old. Go to bed, you jealous little bastard."

"If he wants to fire me, I don't care, I really don't. I'm not made for farm work. I want to join the army or go to Guayaquil; I want to buy a bicycle and a wrist watch."

"You've got a great future in Guayaquil," I said. "Get in with some gang and learn how to steal bicycles and watches. You'll love those slums."

"*Que va,*" Pedro said. "Come on now." I moved away and he called after me, "Bring me back a present from Quito, you hear?"

I drove to Quito the next morning expecting to be gone for one night. For two months I had been making almost weekly trips to the capital looking for a three-thousand-dollar check that some idiot banker in Seattle had sent me — apparently, to save postage, by mule-back via Acapulco and Tampico instead of by air-mail. We needed this money desperately to run the farm. Circumstances intervened; instead of one night I was gone for almost three months, two of them in a Quito hospital.

When I finally arrived back at the farm late one afternoon — the check received and already spent — driven by a friend in our brand new pickup because I was still too bruised and battered to manage it myself, everything had changed. Driving down the last little hill I could see that everything had changed. The store and the little buildings that had floated in the pool of shade around the great tree now stood naked and glaring in the sunshine. There was a tremendous pile, a raw tangle of dead leaves and shattered branches around an already rotting stump in that empty space where the tree had guarded us for so long. I had been very sick in Quito; now I felt sicker. As we drove into the yard Ramón, Ester, and the children were lined up waiting to welcome me back, but when Ester saw me tears spurted from her eyes, and Ramón, with a shocked look on his face, tried to lift me from the car as though I had already been embalmed. I pushed his hands away. "No, don't. I'm O.K.; I can walk. But what have you done here? What's happened?"

"Ester," Ramón called, "go fix the bed in Martín's house; immediately."

"What have you done, for Christ's sake?" We moved slowly toward the store which was unnaturally empty, and Ramona, our pet cow, hearing my voice, began to bawl with emotion and burst from the kitchen, where she had been resting, and rushed toward me with the sweet intention of knocking me down. She had put on another hundred pounds of weight, and the floor splintered and cracked beneath her hooves; all the floors in all the rooms had been destroyed, and I also noted that in my absence the thatched roof had begun to disintegrate at an ever-accelerating tempo and large patches of sky now lit up the dark corners in the store like tricky modern lighting. Ramón, interpreting the incredulous look on my face as rage instead of simple shock, began to talk.

"Martín, I had to cut that tree down; it was dangerous; go out and look at the stump, it's half rotted through. Right after you left, a big branch crashed down and almost hit the store. I cut it down while you were gone to spare you the pain. Don't feel bad; we'll plant coconuts in that space. You'll see; it will be beautiful . . . Now, about the new store. I've ordered lumber and thirty-two pieces of corrugated iron. No more thatched roofs on this farm; we'll put the store over there where I always wanted it. You'll see; with the cocos around it, it will be marvelous . . . Plinio? He's gone. I kicked the whole bunch out. Don't worry, I did it nicely. Rufo, Pedro, Wilson, Mericia, the whole lot. I let Aladino go too. Can you believe it? He was sneaking in here every night and screwing my bitch sister. I told her if she wanted to whore to do it in Esmeraldas and not dishonor my name here on the farm. Aladino said he wanted to marry her. I just laughed. "You're much too black for my sister," I told him. *'Cada negro en su puesto.'* "

Ramón's voice went on and on, and I half-listened to him. It was wonderful to be back again; everything he said was curious, outrageous, and fascinating. But behind all the words I was now aware of something grander: I no longer dominated the farm; Ramón had taken over. Maybe when I was stronger I would do something about it, but at the moment I just simply didn't give a damn.

I will come to what had happened; but first, some background.

A year before the expulsion of Ramón's family from the farm, one of our workers, Esmundo, mentioned in a dramatically casual way that he had overheard Celso Corea, a neighbor across the highway, telling someone how that Negro Ramón seemed to be the type who would inevitably screw things up on our farm. Who ever heard of a black who could manage anything. It was the kind of vicious small talk that hick-town people love to make and that hick-town people love to pass on for its power to wound and cause destructive and interesting breaches in the peace. Celso at that time was almost completely dependent on us to stay in business; how could he have been so stupid? Celso raised chickens, and we had been trying to help him by grinding his corn and hauling it out to the highway for him. It was not always convenient, his chickens would run out of feed at the weirdest times, but we did it as a public service since we had the only mill for miles around.

Ramón especially had been considerate to the man; he was a poor serrano who had bravely come to the coast and was trying to make a life for himself in this land of greater opportunity. He was middle-aged, hard working, honest, and reasonably sober; he had bought a cheap piece of ground that was several hundred yards from the highway and was usually flooded from the heavy rains. The change from the mountain freshness of ten thousand feet to the humid coastal plain jungles had really altered his metabolism. He had the drawn and pallid face of a man with some chronic and unidentified fever. One of the common bits of news around here is that once more Don Celso, *muy grave,* has been slung in a hammock between two men and hauled out to the highway babbling crazy disconnected things. Ramón liked him, a proof, it seemed to me, of Ramón's capacity to grow, for Celso was not a Negro. In Rioverde Ramón, like every other citizen of the town, had regarded anyone from the high mountain country as a semihostile. "Ugly, treacherous, scheming animals, those lisping Indians," Ramón used to say, automatically damning 50 percent of his countrymen. But Ramón had buried his prejudices; he and Celso hit it off. They visited each other's chicken houses and exchanged barbaric chicken lore; sometimes in the evenings Celso, would walk a couple of miles to our store to drink coffee with Ramón and talk about the mill he hoped one day to install; they even got drunk together once on a bottle of expensive Scotch which I thought I had cleverly hidden.

To hear now that Celso thought he was a shit was like a knife in Ramón's heart; no wonder he had never trusted anyone's truth but his own. For a couple of days he brooded sadly about the cruelty and injustice of Celso's words. He wondered if they might not be true. When he realized that they weren't, a cold fury began to obsess him. Now Ramón let me know, with all his new capacity for laying it on the line, that if I wanted to keep grinding corn for Celso, that was O.K. with him, but that from this moment on he wouldn't raise a finger to help me. Celso no longer existed.

I talked to Celso about this one morning when I was disking

coconuts out by the road; I told him he had been a fool with his loose mouth and that he must now be prepared to endure Ramón's vengeance. Celso was stunned. The next morning, very early, he walked into the farm and, standing in a light mist of rain outside the store, denied in a very loud voice that was almost a scream that he had ever maligned Ramón; he swore this on his mother's sacred honor, he loved Ramón like a brother, and he broke into tears when Ramón refused to accept his story. Esmundo was standing with a group of workers out of the rain and Ramón called him over and asked him in front of Celso if the story were true. "Absolutely," Esmundo said, a black man scoring off an Indian, and a rich one to boot. "Why would I lie? I heard him say it."

Celso denied it, weeping, "No, Don Ramón. No, no."

"Look," Ramón said, "I'm not mad at you, at least not anymore. But I don't trust you anymore, and the truth is I don't want anything more to do with you. You're not my friend; you're not my enemy. You're just nothing . . . But why did you have to say that? You, who hardly knew me yet, and in the face of the goodness we had shown you . . . To talk about me behind my back as though I were your enemy or some ignorant black zambo who would just take it with a big, wide, black, stupid, country smile."

"No, Don Ramón, as God is my judge, Don Ramón."

Ramón abruptly left him and disappeared into the high grass where the sows pastured, and Celso, deserted by all of us, stood in the road for about ten minutes, alone and frightened. Finally, still talking to himself about his mother's sacred honor, he wandered away.

So now it wasn't only Celso who suffered Ramón's implacable vengeance; I still felt obligated to grind corn and did it for another year until Celso bought his own mill. But I drew the line at packing two-hundred-pound bags into the truck, opening a half dozen gates, and delivering it to him. Except for a few emergencies when his chickens were starving for feed, I insisted that he pick up the corn at our *bodega*. For over a year he had to haul his ground corn on horseback, one or two bags at a time, that couple of miles to his chicken houses. This situation gave Ramón and me fuel for many heated discussions. At first I pointed out that while it might give him a great deal of pleasure to force suffering on Celso, I didn't quite see why I had to suffer along with him. "Well, it really is your problem, isn't it," Ramón said. "You really can't feel that I'm forcing you to grind corn for Corea, can you?"

Since I couldn't move him to pity me, I began to expound Christian ethics, at the heart of which lies the forgiveness of one's enemies. "You don't especially do it for your enemy," I said, "but for your own peace of mind. It really puts you one up on the poor bastard, confuses the hell out of him, makes him think he's losing his mind. And you'll feel better in your heart."

"Shit," Ramón said, smiling coldly, "I couldn't feel better. I feel just fine. When I drive to Esmeraldas in the morning, there he is in his damn rags, standing out on the road waiting for a ride into town, and he makes this little timid movement with his hand like he's half afraid to wave good morning, and I drive right by the son of a bitch as though he weren't there. Now what could I do that would make me feel better than that?"

I was getting sick of grinding corn, and after a few weeks of solid Christian ethics, I went a little further and brought Jesus into the conversation; Jesus has always been Ramón's particular santo, the one who solved his problems. I found the passage in the Spanish New Testament about turning the other cheek; Ramón was aghast. "Let me see that," he said. "I don't believe it." He read the words slowly, shaking his head. "Is this Jesus saying that if some *cojudo* hits me on one side I'm supposed to twist my head around so he can crack me on the other?" He sat there thinking, shaking his head and snorting with laughter. "I'm a Christian not a *maricón*. Any son of a bitch hits me on one cheek I'll break his damn jaw for him . . . No, Martín, lay off pressuring me, will you?" He made a cross with his fingers and kissed them and said, "I swear to God, Corea does not exist for me; I'll never speak to the man again."

Before the complication of grinding Celso's corn took over all my free time, there had been the complication of the pickup truck. Ramón didn't know how to drive. This meant that while we were getting established I had to make almost weekly trips to Quito and almost daily trips to Esmeraldas. Whenever there was any spare time I gave Ramón driving lessons, but he was a slow learner and I didn't at first have much faith that he would ever learn how to shift gears without first taking his eyes off the road, intently studying the gear shift, and ultimately running into a ditch as he tried to use only the forward gears when going forward. Finally, he caught on, and one day without warning I asked him if he would run into Esmeraldas and buy groceries. Ramón shook his head. In a way it was like the system my father had used to teach me how to swim; he had picked me up at age four and tossed me into eight feet of water. I still remember that slow and final descent into blue depths full of peace and promise. It was a paternal condemnation to die that, not knowing why, I was still convinced I deserved. It never occurred to me to use my hands; that would have been breaking the rules.

Ester, who heard us talking and perhaps noted some uncertainty in Ramón's voice, came running out of the kitchen. "No," she said, laughing nervously, "don't send Ramón in alone. He'll never make it; he'll kill himself for sure."

Women's talk gave Ramón courage, and he took off bravely. Ester and I spent four nervous hours waiting for the fatal news, but just before nightfall Ramón arrived, bounding over the ruts, twisting the chassis, and breaking springs. He was triumphant and giddy with joy. "I went up every one way street the wrong way; I went through every red light. But now I can handle this beast; I'll never be scared again."

Ramón turned into an excellent driver; he managed the pickup with ten times the skill that I can manage a canoe. He made three or four trips a week to Esmeraldas, and at first I think he even invented reasons to go to town. Despite his competence I never did feel completely at ease when he was gone. I still don't. If he leaves at two o'clock I expect him back at six, and if he is thirty minutes late I am outside pacing in the darkness or staring up the hill where his arrival will announce itself by the flashing of the headlights on the banana leaves while the truck is still half a mile away. Ramón is one of the people that I can't afford to lose, and I regard this dependency as a challenge to heaven that must be taken up one day just to prove who is boss. After Ramón learned how to drive I had to confront this fear. In spite of all our fights I had never been so happy or so aware of being happy. Since I had never conceived of a life that could hold conscious happiness,

I lived in a state of apprehension and guilt, as though I had stolen something that must be taken from me. I felt this very strongly and even wrote about it to friends, saying: Things are going along too well down here; Ecuador is fantastic; I'm too happy; God is never going to stand for it; every time Ramón goes to town I sit here waiting to hear that a banana truck has crushed him like a bug.

It was a surprise to us then, and especially to me, that after all this worry and apprehension over Ramón, I was the one who was finally squashed like a bug, not by one banana truck but by two. For years I had watched with trembling fury those lines of monsters careening down the middle of the narrow Ecuadorian roads at full speed and just barely under control. There is an anticipatory wall of air that blasts at you just before the truck screams past, full of ten tons of bananas, torn and wind-whipped banana leaves, and half naked and exhausted Negroes. Gazing high up, you can just make out through a mud-spattered windshield the evil and unshaven face of a drunken driver, both hands off the wheel as he lights a cigarette, or visiting with the six or seven companions who have crowded into the front seat with him; they are all laughing with the demented abandon of lunatics or shaking their fists at you because you have not driven off the road to let them pass. Whoosh. Gone. The roadbed trembles; the branches of the trees beside the road whip wildly in the wind; clouds of dust boil up behind them even on paved roads or on roads that are soaked with rain.

I have rarely gone to Quito without passing at least one banana truck lying upside down beside the highway, its pure green cargo streaming out behind it like entrails; or a truck, out of control, that has taken off through the countryside, cutting a swath through the banana plantings like some crippled and maddened tyrannosaur. On certain great days, when national or religious events are being observed by seeing how much alcohol can be consumed, it is not uncommon to pass three or four broken and tipped up trucks in the sixty-mile stretch between Quinindé and Santo Domingo. The road looks like a combat zone that has been strafed. No one ever sees the drivers; they crash and flip-flop and nose-dive and lazy-eight, landing in pieces or upside down, and fifteen seconds later the chauffeur and all his drunken cousins have grabbed their bottles of aguardiente and faded into the jungle. Three weeks later, with his teeth bared in an animal snarl and his senses once more blunted with cane alcohol, this same homicidal maniac is established behind the wheel of another *bananero* and is rolling from side to side down the highway looking for something else to destroy.

Two trucks roared around a curve in the fog as I crawled up the Toachi River canyon at the top of the Andes pass. Both of the trucks were racing; one driver was trying to pass the other; the other was doing everything he could to prevent it. I don't remember the crash, but I remember, sometime later, crouching on my hands and knees over a pool of my own blood contemplating my own death with relief. Blind, I had never seen things so clearly. I understood for the first time that life was simply an intricate and complicated arrangement of tensions supporting one another like a modern architectural edifice. Now all the tensions were relaxing, one by one; I was going loose, as though I were nothing so much as a little machine made of rubber bands and springs and cables that were now breaking apart or slackening up and releasing me. I had the impression that I had an unlimited amount of time to think about this and to appraise my life and to decide whether to live or die; I remember very leisurely checking off a list of things that seemed to make up my life and that I would no longer have to confront. They were all little things, hundreds of little irritations, banalities, silly challenges, hypocrisies, self-delusions, inanities. How could I consider for a moment that it would be worthwhile to reconstruct and connect and tighten these springs and cables that were going slack, especially when I contemplated the alternative with such joy, my own sweet, peaceful dissolution. My God, how wonderful to live free of those enslaving tensions, how wonderful to die. I checked down the list, "No, I won't miss that — nor that — nor that." And finally came to Ramón, and hesitated. Well, what about Ramón? Was he ready yet to run the farm alone? Probably not. Would my death now destroy his chances? Possibly not. It would be hard, there would be tears, but he would get over it; he was tough. To hell with Ramón. I was engaged in something much more important.

Someone said, "Do you have friends in Quito?" and I began to

laugh and said, "No, no, I don't know anyone," and I was laughing because I had lots of friends in Quito and I was playing a
good joke on them. I didn't want them messing with me, complicating everything, trying to prevent me from taking this final and
beautiful step into the infinite. Just before I slipped once more
into unconsciousness I felt someone taking the wallet out of my
pocket and saying something about the Peace Corps.

The Peace Corps office in Quito, which had hired an ambulance
to get me to the hospital, also called Esmeraldas and asked one
of the local volunteers if he would please take a bus out to the
farm and tell Ramón that his partner was *muy grave*. Ramón
scarcely remembers this moment, it came with such suddenness
and force. About twenty minutes later he discovered himself up
on the highway waiting for the Quito bus. He had grabbed a jacket
against the cold but had forgotten to change out of his work
clothes. The idea that I was dead or dying terrified him. He began to blame himself because he had let me go with faulty brakes.
He began to pray to Jesu Cristo, and it was at this moment that
he glanced down the road and noticed Celso Corea, who was waiting for a bus that would take him the other way. He was half
hidden in the high grass where he had stepped to avoid being ignored by Ramón. He waved timidly, and Ramón, out of some
urge to placate God or to do something that he knew I wanted
him to do, or maybe simply out of some necessity to hear a kind
word, rushed up to Celso with his eyes brimming with tears and
told him I was dying. There they were, the two of them hugging
and crying in the middle of the road, another of that tough-playing
inscrutable Creator's miracles. All He had had to do to bring
those two together again was to break my skull, crack my ribs,
and stick their jagged ends into my lungs.

This was the first positive thing that resulted from the accident.
The second developed more slowly. When I came back to the
farm and found everything in ruins, I was in a somewhat passive
and philosophical state and ready at last to submit with some degree of grace to Ramón's domination. That domination had begun in the hospital when I had swum out of unconsciousness to
find Ramón bending over me and saying over and over with
clenched teeth, "Don't die; don't die." I had never seen his face

so serious and so angry. I understood him immediately. He wasn't begging or pleading; he was giving me orders that he expected to be obeyed. It was uncanny, for it seemed as if he had seen through me to my secret intentions. I had learned something profound and comforting out there on the highway the day before, but now Ramón was bending over me, fighting with me, forcing me against my inclinations to keep supporting him. I lay there thinking, and finally said reluctantly and resentfully, "O.K., O.K., Ramón; don't worry, Ramón, I'm not going to die."

And I knew immediately that it was true. I was struck with another fantastic intuition about death: that in some way it was optional, that you had power over it, and that it came only when you really wanted it.

4

THE BLACK PAWNS ADVANCE

IN THE BEGINNING we were much more absorbed with the land and the plans we were making for it than with the workers we were hiring. Our workers were more like pawns in this battle with nature that we were planning without understanding. Somewhat later I would sometimes still see them as pawns, but pawns as big as queens, enemy pawns, stolid and motionless, blocking the brilliant lightning attacks we planned at night around the dinner table, frustrating our moves without even knowing that a furious game was being played and that they had become a part of the opposition.

At first we analyzed our problem as being a simple confrontation with the forces of nature. Using our heads we would win. We would bed down with science and technology; we would study the text books; our farm would become an enlightened model for all the farmers in the Esmeraldas area who, watching our clever tricks, would realize that in this rich land it was pure stubbornness to keep on being poor. One of the gringo old-timers told me, "If you want to leave Ecuador with a small fortune, arrive here with a large one," and I laughed about this; it didn't seem applicable in any sense. I had no plans to leave the country, and that inevitable fortune that we would make would be only an incidental dividend in the fascinating battle with the jungle that would wholly engage us in its intrinsic delights and challenges.

It took us several months to make a plan for the farm and over a year to build all the sheds and bodegas, the chicken houses, the fences for the pig pastures, the farrowing stalls, the drying floors for corn and cacao, roofed boxes for cattle salt, sheds for the cows to sleep in out of the rain, storerooms for bottles, ropes, and insecticides, houses for ourselves and the people we hoped would come to visit us. I was the architect, Ramón selected and hauled in the building materials, Jorge, our drunken carpenter from Rioverde, nailed everything together. We could barely keep ahead of the tropic's impulse to dissolve anything organic. Since we didn't know what we could plant with the expectations of making a profit, we decided to try a little of everything, hoping that the good crops would cancel out the bad ones, but even the simplest plans become insanely complicated in Ecuador. It wasn't just nature opposing us. Before we could plant peanuts, for example, we had to drive around the country for six days looking for peanut seed. To finance our cows we spent six months making almost daily trips to the Banco de Fomento to fill out stupid forms, always needing to return because so and so hadn't approved the third solicitation because of a death in the family or because someone had lost such and such a paper. Our list of enemies began to grow.

We planted corn and filled our chicken houses with about seven hundred hybrid fryers from an incubator in Guayaquil — and then discovered that it was impossible to find a dependable source of supplemental concentrate to mix with the corn. The dealers in Esmeraldas were incompetent; they promised us supplies that, more likely than not, took three weeks to make the ten hour truck trip from Guayaquil. Or the bus drivers were all on strike, the roads were barricaded at Santo Domingo with angry workers, and the police were tear-gassing the populace. The feed mills couldn't find the prime ingredients; the dispatchers apparently couldn't read. We would order chick feed and be sent laying mash. We spent a good deal of our time and all our potential profit driving around the country searching out a sack or two of concentrate to keep us going for another few days. Our schedule with the hatchery collapsed. On certain Tuesdays and Saturdays we were to receive boxes of day-old chicks; we would drive fifty kilometers to meet the plane, which arrived at any time between ten in the morning and three in the afternoon, only to find a good percentage of the time that the chicks had not been sent. The president of Ecuador at this time was a man with a slight drinking problem;

the rumors say that he either pissed in the punch bowl at an American Embassy party or pissed in the fireplace in front of one hundred and fifty guests; at any rate this political statement, which was not particularly pro-American, resulted in his being removed from office. For some strange reason this affected the supplies of fishmeal that were imported into the country from Peru; for six months there was no fishmeal in the country, no concentrate for chickens. And then the price of corn went from 60 sucres to 130 sucres. But by that time we didn't give a damn; we had given up in despair and our empty chicken houses quietly disintegrated and disappeared in the vines and grass.

Our only real emotional connection with those first years when we tried to raise chickens was Anita, a monstrous white hen with a soiled behind and great swollen arthritic feet as large and menacing as a condor's, who lived in the house with us and ran things. When Ramón was selecting the first group of chickens to be sold in the market, Anita, unlike the others, who were rushing around the cage hysterically, simply stood on a perch and stared at Ramón. It was a look so full of outrage, incredulity, and heartbreak that Ramón brought her to the house. "She knew exactly what I had in mind," he said. "I couldn't take it. What a look she gave me; what dignity, such disbelief; it was like looking into my mother's face; I want her to be one of the family and stay with us always."

For about three years, until she grew hidebound and crotchety, she was one of our best friends; then she grew old and inscrutable. She became too fat to leap up into the special box we built for her in the front of the store. Every evening for over a year we had to lift her up to her bedroom. Then she got too fat even to leap down in the mornings, and we had to take her down as well. We forgot her a few times, and this preyed on her mind. She couldn't forgive us; she moved out into the rain and slept on top of a movable tin roof we had built over a floor to dry corn and cacao; it was a place she could get to on her own — to hell with being dependent. For a time at first, when our friendship threatened to grow into passion, she used to lay eggs in my lap. This was a highly emotional moment for both of us and an act of love that I wanted to share with my mother when she came to visit.

"Now watch this," I said as Anita snuggled into me, half opened her wings and her mouth, and her eyes became glazed and abstracted. As the egg dropped, enormous and glistening, and Anita gave a little squawk of painful fulfillment, my mother's eyes turned cold, enormous, and horrified.

"My *God,*" she said, "that is absolutely the most *disgusting* thing I have ever seen in all my life." This was my own mother, who had never once been jealous of my wife and who had in fact usually sided with her against me. How odd of mother to be jealous of a chicken.

About the same time that we were raising chickens, we were also bringing our talents into focus with pigs; I had plans to dazzle the rural types with my twentieth-century savvy, but a few months after we sold our last chicken I was beginning to hope that hog cholera would arrive and wipe out the last pig, too. We bought ten pure-bred Hampshire gilts and a handsome boar from the Peace Corps farm in Santo Domingo with the idea of selling high-quality gilts and boars to the local farmers for breeding. Every farmer in Ecuador has one or two scrawny inbred pigs; on the coast they run wild through the banana plantings spreading that most fatal plague Panama disease and rooting up the neighbors' gardens, and in the mountains they are roped and staked in the short grass beside the highways, razorbacked and hairy as sheep dogs. It takes about two years to fatten an Ecuadorian hog for market — if it survives the mortality of cholera, banana trucks, and the wandering bands of *rateros* who live by stealing. Our pigs weighed two hundred pounds in six or seven months; part of this was due to a balanced diet, part to good breeding.

But we filled no great need. We sold purebred fifty-pound weaners for twenty dollars; but no one could afford them but the rich farmers from Quevedo who wanted to turn them loose in their abandoned banana plantations. The poor farmers who came to negotiate with us — some of them arriving by canoe, some of them having traveled for hours on the local buses — were appalled at our high prices. We ended up with a complicated and dishonest system of selling. If the buyer arrived in a pickup or a Land-Rover or if he wore shoes or if he had the face of a Manabita, we quoted and stuck to the five hundred sucre figure. If the buyer was black, barefoot, and frightened, if he arrived with all his family for this most important of negotiations, we sold him a pig for whatever he could pay. But it was a sad business; rich and poor, no one was interested in proper nutrition. On the coast, bugs and bananas formed the principal ingredients of a pig's diet; in the sierra, it was grass and human excrement. It got so I hated to sell pigs when I visualized how they would be treated; and when a neighbor arrived who wanted to trade cows for hogs, we made a deal and went out of the hog business.

Ramón had always wanted cattle. After fussing with the bank for months trying to arrange a loan, I exploded one night and said I would waste not one minute more in that hateful and disgraceful place. If Ramón wanted cows *he* would have to go through the humiliations of getting the money from the bank. He agreed and practically lived in town for four months as the negotiations went on and on until we were given permission to buy forty cows. Ramón, who hasn't seen too many cowboy movies in his life, not half as many as he'd like to see but more apparently than he was able to handle, was inflamed by that little band of feisty dun-colored cows with their spreading horns and their crazy nervous outlook. If he could have had his way it would have been pure hoofs and horns and cow shit and hi-ho silver twenty-four hours a day. Within three months Ramón began talking to the bank again, and a year later we received permission to buy another forty head. I used to like to sit on the corral fence when Ramón and his crew were spraying cattle for ticks and watch the cows suddenly soar over those twelve-foot fences, but most of the time I left the cows to Ramón. I was in the tropics and wanted to raise romantic tropical things like coconuts and pineapples. Not only that. I wasn't convinced that cattle was a good business to be in. I had never met an Ecuadorian cattleman who thought that it paid to raise cattle in this country where prices are controlled and where 90 percent of the population is too poor to buy meat.

We planted and lost varying degrees of money on corn, watermelons, tomatoes, cucumbers, soybeans, sesame, and peanuts. The only crops that seemed attractive were the ones we hadn't tried yet; there was considerable bliss in ignorance. In the first four years on the farm, we planted practically every damn tropical crop that seemed to have the slightest chance of being sold for more money than it cost to raise it. And out of necessity we gradually moved away from those ninety-day plantings with their built in traps, those plantings that needed good seed and fertilizers, sprays and constant weedings, a perfectly prepared seed bed, a tractor that always had fuel in its tank, crews of workers at the precise moment, and most importantly, a dependable market. We could never bring all of these factors together in the proper order. Science and technology in the tropics are whores. We began to plant more coconuts, more pasture, more pineapples; we planted a few acres of oranges, grapefruit, cacao. We liked the long-term crops that took years to prove themselves and postponed the moment of disillusion. And we liked the long-term loans that the bank was giving on those slowly maturing crops. We never stopped fighting with the jungle. How could we? We were hopelessly entwined in its green coils, but we tried to keep our tempers with it. *Calma, paciencia, fe,* Ramón kept telling me. Take it easy; there is always mañana — that word which, since I had come back from the hospital practically lobotomized, had begun to take on wisely profound meanings.

But if you take the passion out of farming what is there left but drudgery? I had wanted to stun the province with the twentieth-century technology that I had picked up in California, that modern system of farming that uses fifteen times more energy per acre than a farmer in an undeveloped country. I wanted to raise three tons of corn to the acre instead of Ecuador's normal six sacks. It was mighty frustrating (mighty embarrassing, too — what puzzled looks Ramón gave me) — after all the disking, the smoothing, the machine planting, the fertilizers, insecticides, and herbicides — to finally harvest, oh, say ten sacks and end up $150 per acre in the hole. We went back to thirteenth-century techniques, but not knowing which saint to pray to I felt somewhat superfluous, and after planting corn for a couple of days with a sharp stick I was as bored as I had ever been in my life.

The bugs and the weeds, the rains and the thieves, these were things we couldn't do much about. But what about the people? Could they be changed for the good of the farm? Ramón, who was wiser, never played with the possibility that we could make first-class workers out of our raw material. Years before, driven crackers by some concept that I had been trying to hammer into his head (did he think that *he* was the only bored one?), he had told me that the Peace Corps would never accomplish a thing in the way of change until it began to work exclusively with the youngest of the nation's children; by the time a boy was twelve he was set in his ways for life. In the face of the Peace Corps's failure, which would prove him right, I wanted to disbelieve him. More importantly, I had time on my hands; I wanted to confront *something* and, as each day I became more engulfed by the black presence, more engrossed, enchanted, and appalled by that black cunning, which was sometimes as subtle as Einstein's theory of relativity and sometimes as blatant and innocent as a good sharp boot in the ass, it became easier and easier to change the focus of my interests.

We shifted our tactics. We decided that the real battle was with the black pawns, and that we must try to immobilize them. No, more than that, we must try to bring them over to our side and make them know that our interests were identical, that they would suffer from our failure, that they would benefit from our success.

Part Two

At the end of the small hours, this nondescript beach for wrecks, the exacerbated odor of corruption, the monstrous sodomies of the host and the slaughter, the unscalable ship's prow of prejudice and stupidity, the prostitutions, hypocrisies, lusts, betrayals, lies, swindles, concussions — the breathlessness of petty cowardice, the wheeze of gushing enthusiasms, the greeds, hysterias, perversions, the harlequinades of misery, cripplings, itches, rashes, the luke-warm hammocks of degeneration. This is the pageant of comic scrofulous swellings, of festers begun by the strangest microbes, of poisons without known antidote, of pus from old wounds, of unforeseen fermentations in rotting bodies.

AIMÉ CÉSAIRE, *Return to My Native Land*

5

THE PEOPLE OF MALE

I LEFT THE COAST once some years ago, when I was a Peace Corps volunteer, to be seriously ill with hepatitis in a Quito pension. I spent a month in the high sierra listening to Quito Spanish, a curious language full of extra soft sounds and hisses — "lips pwes," whatever that means — coming out at two-second intervals and mixed wetly with everything else that was meaningless. Cured finally and on my way back to Esmeraldas, I stopped overnight in Santo Domingo and got a room in a cheap hotel overlooking the plaza. I ate something, went to a movie, and then to bed. I had been lonely for the coast without realizing the extent of my sadness until at four o'clock that morning I woke up in that crummy damp bed with the tears simply gushing out of my eyes with joy and the whole weight of that oppressive month behind me and forgotten. What was happening? I lay there filled with joy and wondering why, and then heard it again, awake now, the sound of voices in the street. When I rushed out on the balcony and looked down I saw only what I had expected to see: three strange Esmeraldas blacks standing huddled together in that predawn darkness. It was the sound of their voices that had awakened me; it was the sound of their voices — wild, extravagant, delighted, obscene, crazy, beautiful, full of life and freedom — that had released me from the sadness of Quito and told me that I was coming home, that I was almost there.

Buying the farm had confused my real feelings. Carried away with the novelty of owning exotic tropical land and the fascination of trying to dominate it I had forgotten for a time that people are

always more interesting than scenery. It was only after I had
realized this for the first time, four years before, that I had begun
to function more like a volunteer than a tourist, and it was only
after I had begun to understand the people a little that I began to
understand the landscape in which they operated.

Almost from the first day, Esmundo and Pedro and a half dozen
others had been our steady workers. It seems they had all been
included but not mentioned in the bill of sale, along with ten sheets
of corrugated iron (stolen) and the unharvested corn. They were
no worse than any of the other workers we ever had, but as we
grew to know them we became entrapped in our own pity for them.
Ignoring the labor laws — which gave them a tremendous power
over us after three months — we kept them on, most of them for
over a year. They mistook our pity for weakness, or perhaps they
thought we were so stupid that we found them indispensable.

We began to hear rumors that they were forming a secret labor
union, a *sindicato,* and that when they had organized everyone,
either Esmundo or Pedro (we could never quite pin down who was
leading this confused pack) would shut down the farm until we
agreed to pay everyone full wages for those national and religious
holidays when the *salones* burst into music and the people
danced.* There are about two hundred twenty such days per year;
this poor nonproducing country, corrupted by the church and by
cheap cane alcohol, had no better way to dull the peons into accepting their destiny. Well, Esmundo's or Pedro's scheme was
quite insane, so insane that we ignored it, but it was depressing to
realize what idiots they thought we were. We kept them on for

---

* There is no English equivalent for the word *salón* (pl. *salones*), which
describes a unique institution. A salón is not a bar, a beer hall, a saloon, or
a dance hall, though it may fulfill all of these functions. In the country, a
salón may be no more than a row of benches built around the walls of a
poor man's living room, where it is understood that people may enter without knocking and where the man's wife will serve little shot glasses of
aguardiente or bottles of warm beer. A salón may be two small tables with
benches set out under a shading tree or a ten-foot-square thatched hut built
at the edge of a stream and open on all sides to the subtle movement of air.
Because of its intimate nature and its blending into the village landscape, the
salón intimidates no one and offers solace and companionship to the poorest man.

different reasons: Pedro, earning about thirty dollars a month, was sending his children through high-school in Esmeraldas — we found this heroic; Esmundo made us laugh; Jorge Cortez was beautiful and had a great inner tranquility; Carlos and Heriberto Angulo? I don't remember. We just liked them and in fact had set one of them up in the chicken business and loaned him money to build a house and clear two hectáreas on the highway for corn.

Pedro was as slim and tiny as a half-grown teenager; Esmundo was big and ugly with protruding eyes, dramatic muscles in unlikely places, and a dapper moustache that made him look rather evil because it was identical to Hitler's. He was a big man and strongly built, but he was a rapacious eater, and his stomach bulged like the potbelly of a young child heavily infested with worms. He was one of the few men we ever hired who didn't mind working alone.

Esmundo had a wild sense of humor and was always mimicking his friends or acting out fantastic dramas. Listening to Esmundo one could believe that his life was a constant confrontation with enormous snakes, rabid tigers, man-eating whores, or desperate thieves. No fool, Esmundo; he always conquered. He carried a small, woman's pistol in a back pocket, but thank God he never used it; it was so old that it would inevitably have exploded in his hand. He liked to make people laugh and, when he was with a group of workers, liked to be at the center of their raucous delight. When he had everyone laughing uncontrollably his face would get sleepy and sullen, almost contemptuous, as though he were disappointed in them at being so easily manipulated.

How he would sweat and heave and grunt when he thought that he was being watched as he worked. He would roll logs across the field to the fires, tug great stumps out of the ground, wildly reduce whole trees to toothpicks — all the while groaning, moaning, shaking his head and flinging the sweat in all directions like a spring shower. The closer I got to him, the wilder his actions became, and I tried to keep my distance, convinced that if I came too close he would drop dead with a burst heart or that his guts would spill out in some bright, climactic hernia. By watching him furtively from the tractor, pretending to be studying a band of parrots flying across the clearing or that sudden wall of rain flowing up over the hills from the ocean, I probably saved his life. When I was out of his sight he would be languidly hacking at tree branches, eating a ten-pound hand of bananas, or crouching in the shade of a stump smoking cigarettes. I called him Actor; the name delighted him and inspired him to further ridiculous histrionic excesses.

Along with these steady workers, who in time became a kind of family nucleus, we hired another, more migrant, more shameless group of older men; and as we studied them and tried to appraise their workmenlike qualities, Ramón began to see himself as a great psychologist. He claimed to be developing the power to analyze character, evaluate motives, sift grain from chaff by the openness or guardedness of a face or a gesture. An eye that happened to blink at an odd time might put someone on the questionable list. We took turns checking on our crew and made a game of comparing our impressions. How still it would be out there when, walking as silently as I could, I went out to see what was happening. I hardly knew where to look for them until one of them would spy me and the jungle would ring with a peculiar bird cry and everything would come alive to the furious sounds of slashing axes and machetes. Coming closer I would find some of the men practically knee deep in banana and orange peels; I almost walked on a couple of them as they slept, curled up like exotic animals in nests of freshly cut leaves. Ramón's and my observations were almost identical, and finally we began firing the men and replacing them with their sons. Talk about leaping out of the frying pan . . .

With a few exceptions we kept the sons of our hired workers for almost as long as they wanted to stay. We liked them in spite of the quality of their work. They had been contaminated through their fathers by the presence of Folke Anderson and hated the idea of working up a sweat, but they stood in the winds of change; they weren't *lambones,* that Spanish word for kiss-ass; they didn't dance in the morning, at least not for us; they didn't bow and doff their hats. On the contrary they carried themselves with a refreshing kind of pride that was just short of arrogance. They had chic. They walked with a strutting elegance, high-stepping, swinging their shoulders wildly, their eyes alive and flashing with delight;

they were enraptured with themselves, with that vision of themselves in the first full flowering of their black virility. Most of them smoked marijuana, and they aped the movements and the slurred, cool language of the Guayaquil marijuaneros. In the depths of their trances they moved in new degrees of languidness, like dancers in a ballet with music by Debussy or Delius, a stylized dance charged with nostalgia and ritual. Yet, watching, I began to grieve for them, for they were still under the illusion of their power to direct their own lives, lost in the magnificence of the newly awakened awareness of their manhood, lost in their dreams of how they would conquer life. How modest their expectations and, in this brutal land, how impossible to fulfill. I knew they had no future; they lacked the opportunities and the inner discipline to do anything but end up like their fathers. Have you ever watched a little herd of lambs as they frisk and play in the slaughterhouse corral?

Monday through Friday these youngsters were infuriating; but on Saturdays they turned into beautiful tigers. God had made them to prowl the jungle trails and appear silently like omens, sun-dappled and silently half-seen, beneath the shade of the great trees. It was some sort of a crime against their true natures to put them sweating in the sun with machetes. We watched them with a new confusion, watched that unbelievably swift change that takes place in children as they are caught up and violently twisted in the furnace of adolescence. The fourteen- and fifteen-year-olds with the bland, pure, tranquil faces of deer came to us begging for work, and we turned them away because they were still tender and unformed. A few months later they were back, but now almost unrecognizable; their faces were marked by the mysterious suffering that had transformed them from deer to tigers; their thin reedlike necks were swollen in potency and their faces, their children's faces, had changed into likenesses of their fathers' — coarser, stronger, vaguely corrupted by life, somehow diminished.

Our young workers had the kind of smartness that wasn't hidden beneath even the most tattered and stinking work clothes. During the week these princes went disguised as beggars; on Saturday afternoon and Sunday, when they sat around the store all washed, oiled, and perfumed, all ablaze in their new shirts, six-dollar shirts of the finest material in clean bright colors of blue, orange, pink, scarlet, purple (each color was in style for a few months), they shed over the whole farm an aura of grandeur that we didn't deserve. They hung around the store all weekend telling stories, buying cigarettes one or two at a time, drinking cheap bottles of soda as brilliantly colored as the shirts they wore. They swung machetes at one another or played grab-ass or bounced a ball or played rummy with a pack of filthy cards or teased Ramón's children, Martita and Ramoncito ("Moncho"), teaching them all the dirty words. Five year old Martita could cuss like the most degenerate muleskinner. How bored and desperate the youngsters were for something to happen. Watching them, one forgave them everything — they were so trapped, so doomed. On the weekends it seemed relatively unimportant that they were impossibly lousy workers.

My feelings for all the workers were becoming schizophrenic; I was torn and tossed in a classically elemental love-hate relationship — placid and admiring on weekends, crossly critical Monday through Friday. I was being assaulted on all sides by this culture of poverty which I had so naively decided to embrace, and I was getting to the point where I didn't know what I felt about things anymore — or even what I was supposed to feel. Morality, it now became apparent, was simply something constructed around the cultural *ambiente* of any particular place. One had better not use middle-class North American standards on *this* farm. How contemptuous I had always felt of the thief, the kiss-ass, the liar, the vagabond worker who collected wages for sleeping the morning through in his hidden nest of leaves or managing each day to have a three-hour bowel movement. If I continued to detest, to judge, to condemn these things, would I not end up alone with Ramón, completely isolated from our community, from this world of desperate deprivation where all man's impulses are directed at simple animal survival and morality is a luxury that no one can afford? On the other hand could we survive as a business if we accepted the local standards of behavior? And if we didn't accept these things, would that mean that we were dirty capitalist pigs trying to exploit a downtrodden peasantry?

O.K., so the worker doesn't work very well because he eats so badly. O.K., so out of desperation a man steals. Now it gets complicated and confusing. How can this poor worker who suffers so from malnutrition, dance for twelve hours straight or, on Sunday afternoons, play fútbol with such fierce sustained enthusiasm? Why does the thief as like as not end up in the local salón, dead drunk from the sale of your radio or his neighbor's chickens? Should a poor man not play fútbol, not dance, not drug his boredom with aguardiente? Were these things, perhaps, just as important as bread? And now that worst and most delicate of questions, which made the head reel, Wasn't it possible that the man who stole your radio actually regarded you as his friend?

One day in April I went out to help Ramón on a ten-acre piece of ground that we were clearing of stumps and preparing for the disk. I had been out there alone the day before, hacking at limbs and piling them for burning, and when I had left I had forgotten my machete in the weeds. Ramón and a couple of men were working with the tractor and a long chain, and another half-dozen men were working by themselves, piling up small stumps and branches. When I came up to Ramón he jumped off the tractor and took me aside. "Don't look at the men over there," he said. "Just work with me here until two o'clock without looking at the men."

"What's happening?"

"It's Esmundo. He found your machete and he's hidden it in the grass. It looks like he's going to try and steal it, and now I guess the time has come to start breaking up the sindicate."

I worked beside Ramón for about an hour, until the one o'clock bus from Esmeraldas passed the farm; this meant that it was almost two. "Don't look; don't look," Ramón kept whispering, but head down, squinting through hair, I sneaked peeks along with Ramón and saw Pedro and Jorge and Carlos and Heriberto forming a little circle around Esmundo, who was packing off something wrapped in banana leaves. The bastards; they were all in on it. Ramón, watching them, began to tremble. When the men reached the gravel road and started down it toward the river, he yelled across the field and Esmundo came back toward us without his machete or mine. I moved away about thirty feet, took my place in the audience, and continued to pick up sticks with an intent, preoccupied expression — the brave landowner who wanted justice done but always left the dirty details to Ramón.

"Do you know what I want to see you about?" Ramón called.

"No, *jefe*," Esmundo said sulkily, staring at the ground.

"It's about the machete you just stole," Ramón said, still trembling.

"Oh, *that*," Esmundo said, smiling brightly. "I was just taking it down to the store to leave with the Señora Ester."

"All nicely wrapped up in leaves?" Ramón said. "Who are you trying to shit?"

Esmundo studied Ramón's face for a long moment and finally said, "Well, you're right; that story *is* a little hard to believe, isn't it?"

"Yes," Ramón said.

They stood staring at one another in the most brutal kind of confrontation, and what hung in the air between them was the whole question of who would dominate the farm — labor or management. We waited and Esmundo's glance faltered and the sindicato crumbled to dust. Ramón said, "Well, Mundo, that's all. Go on home. You understand that from now on we can't work with you anymore, don't you?"

"What?" Esmundo asked in a loud, incredulous, and threatening voice, making one last effort. "What did you say?"

"That I don't want to work with you anymore," Ramón said. "*Mejor dicho,* you're fired. Come on back this afternoon, and we'll settle up with you."

A little later when we were alone, sitting in the pickup, Ramón asked me, "Well, what do you think we ought to do about Esmundo?"

"I think we should demonstrate to everybody that we're not clowns," I said. "I think we should be hard and vengeful."

"Do you want him thrown into jail?"

"No, I want to cheat him out of his *desaucio,* all that extra money he has coming. Or part of it, anyway. We already gave him five hundred sucres extra at Christmas."

"All right," Ramón said. "This will be a pleasure. Next Saturday I'm going to fire Pedro Lamilla, and the Saturday after that, if we can afford it, I'm going to fire Carlos. Now, do you want to talk some more about turning the other cheek and about forgiving your enemies?"

"Fuck my enemies," I said in English because I don't know how to say it in castellano.

The destruction of the black pawn's sindicato was as clear, as understandable as a blow across the face. Watching two men trying to stare one another down is elemental drama. But usually things are not so simple for me; there is almost always something going on around here that I don't understand. I have to call on Ramón.

"Did you hear that drumming last night? My God, it was the worst I've ever heard — everybody just howling and screeching. It was different from the drumming they do for a dead child."

"Yes," Ramón explains, "It's for the sixth of January. This is a solemn religious festival, and the people celebrate it by drinking and drumming."

"And what's religious about the sixth of January?"

"Oh, I don't know; nobody knows except maybe the priest. Everybody just automatically gets drunk on the sixth of January; we are a very Catholic people."

This is Ramón's country; he has lived here all his life and he understands the people — their customs, their ways of thinking, the pressures that twist them, the drives that consume them, the things they want, and the things that make them proud or ashamed. Ramón understands all this so much better than I will ever be able to that most of the time I simply take Ramón's judgment as my own. Ramón is my eyes and ears; he is a patient translator who explains the truth behind appearance. He has even entered into that secret part of my heart that tells me to love so-and-so because he is a good and serious type or to reject so-and-so because he's not. Ramón likes Pablo and trusts him; so I like Pablo and trust him; in a small way I am enriched by sharing their common memories when they lived on the beach at Rioverde. Ramón decides that Gupián is a thief from the pregnant-looking way he walks down the road past our store, his innocent face ten times more innocent than we have ever seen it. Someone has reported to Ramón that Gupián has been seen loitering near our plantings of pineapples; he confesses that he picked two, two very small, wormy ones, and Ramón lifts Gupián's shirt and removes two eight-pound beauties. Immediately my whole feeling about Gupián changes with Ramón, and I greet him coldly or walk past him without speaking as though for me he no longer existed.

Ramón's judgment has not been infallible, but it has been much better than mine; certainly it has been more realistic and cynical, for he knows in his life's blood how poverty corrupts man's impulses. We live in an area where almost everyone is unbelievably beautiful, and I have lived my whole life like a fool, convinced that an outward beauty is the reflection of some inner goodness. Twelve-year-old Lenny with the shatteringly beautiful face of a black angel gets caught stealing pennies out of the box beneath the store counter. My God, *Lenny?* The news staggers me; I can't reconcile the two things.

At night after dinner Ramón and I sit at the table and above the croaking of the frogs or the steady pounding of rain on the thatched roof we talk about the people and some of the insane things that are going on around here. Much of what he tells me makes me feel stupid and blind, like Plinio asleep on the store counter while his daughter was being seduced on the other side of a bamboo wall. Much of what he tells me is fantastically funny and outrageous, much of it, before I can filter it through Ramón's *criollo* morality, tragic and sordid. He has helped me to accept and understand the quality of the life here without making too many gringo judgments. The culture of poverty is devastating and unbelievably ugly; that is the gringo speaking. Ramón helped me move away from the unfortunate tendency to label everything either good or bad and helped me to discover the vital life force that pulses in black lives and the element of grandeur that lies hidden in their heroic will to endure.

It wasn't hard to accept Ramón's sense of delight with the quality of life on the river; what was difficult was to see it as something that existed outside the usual morality. I had always been in a state of rather constant amazement with the coastal people. They were so wildly free, so irrational, so unpredictable, that I could never take them for granted. Perhaps I was even more renewed and freed from time's tyranny by my contact with their pure passion and joy in being alive than by that false feeling of

immortality that I got from the unchanging seasons. Their exis-
tential feeling for life lies at the heart of the black mystery. With
whomever you were speaking, of whatever age, there was always
the sense of speaking with someone young and alive. On the farm,
of course, it was almost always true in fact.

In Ecuador the average life expectancy is something under forty-
five years; I would imagine it to be much less on the coast, considering the prevalence of malaria, tetanus, typhoid, and a few
other deadly tropical diseases. Mortality soars when sickness is
combined with the average coastal doctor's incompetence. He
treats each sickness with the identical prescriptions: injections of
penicillin, vitamin tablets, and worm medicine. In addition to the
high mortality achieved by being diagnosed and treated for something you don't have, there are those wolf-pack banana trucks
prowling and killing on the coastal roads. And then there is the
deadliest thing of all: a swinging machete clutched in drunken
hands.

The average farm worker in the coastal areas is a very special
kind of man, a kind of hero, actually. In the traumatic break that
occurs when he has decided to move away from the domination of
his family and make his own way, he has, in choosing to be a
machetero, made a tremendous decision; the other alternative was
to be a thief. Very broadly speaking these represent the two alternatives that offer themselves to a young man with no more than
three or four years of schooling, trained to do nothing but paddle
a canoe or slash at weeds, and faced with a bleak future. It is a
thankless life; a machetero is the national garbage, the lowest form
of human life. And he is the man who produces the national
wealth. No one chooses to be a machetero on a permanent basis.
Any young man who finds himself trapped into this life, if he has
any intelligence at all, any imagination, any dreams of raising a
family that he can educate, will with fanatic obsessiveness try to
figure out a way to make a change. The average, bright young
machetero lasts about three years; he makes a wage that scarcely
pays for the food he eats to give him the strength to keep working.
If there is some little something left over he drinks and dances it
away on Saturday night. Why not? When he needs a new shirt or
a pair of pants he makes elaborate plans, floats loans, eats a little

less food for a couple of weeks. To buy a radio he will pay 40 percent interest on a three-year contract if he can find an employer who will guarantee his honesty, but this rarely happens.

The coastal machetero is forced by the labor laws of Ecuador, passed to protect his interests but achieving just the opposite, into the animal life of a migrant worker. The law states that after three months on any farm the worker is entitled to certain rights and benefits, extra pay which amounts to fifteen months of pay for twelve months of work. The only practical result of such a law is that after three months the worker is fired. And sadder still, from the employer's viewpoint, at the end of *two* months, knowing that he's going to be fired at any moment, the average machetero turns into a gold brick.

There is, of course, a certain percentage of young guys who can never break away; they're not sharp enough or they're too innocent to cope with urban life or they just live from day to day. Maybe, like some of us, they are gulled into inaction by the lure of the tropics; they accept the life of a machetero because it's out in the woods, *muy tranquilo*. . . . And you're doing work that is so stupid and automatic that you don't have to think about it; the mind is free to soar where it will, and so while you're bent over in the hot sun swinging at weeds, you're *really* sitting at a table, drinking beer with this absolutely gorgeous girl who has a room upstairs, while a tango is playing on the *rockola* — "Light of my life, my lips on yours, I'll never be content until you say you're mine" — and you're dressed in tight black gabardines and black shined shoes with enormous macho heels and one of those American shirts that costs a week's wages, your pocket full of hundred-sucre bills.

But if you're a sharp one — they're usually a little older — you're thinking all the time of how to get out of this life. You've gone through those dreams; you know that that gorgeous girl has gonorrhea and that her bed is swarming with crab lice. Those fancy shoes are made of cardboard; those American shirts are rejects from Colombia. You've been working in jungles now for a couple of years, and there are times when you can hardly crawl off your mat in the morning you're so weak and tired; an intermittent fever warmly flushes the skin on your legs, your face is hot and flushed, your arms scarred and infected with open wounds from the ticks; some part of you is slowly healing from the bite of your machete. By the time you're twenty-four or twenty-five you have reached some moment of revulsion when you definitely renounce the life of a day laborer. You'd rather die; no more, never again; *nunca, jamás.* You join the army as a recruit or get a job as an *ayudante* on the big trucks hauling logs to the plywood factories in Quito or bananas to Guayaquil. You dream of learning how to drive some day, having a license, sitting there behind the wheel, barrel-assing down the road, wow, a hundred kilometers an hour, taking those curves without slowing down, blasting on the horn, scattering people and pigs before you like scraps of paper, with chicken feathers slowly drifting down to mark your passage. Or you have dreamed up some little business for yourself; you're self-employed and independent, finally, with some little deal where you have a kind of self-respect — buying lemons or avocados or guavas from the farmers and selling them in town. If you can stick with it maybe in time you don't have to peddle your stuff in the street, crying it out from house to house; you have your own little kiosk or a storefront with a blanket stretched across it, and behind it your woman is nursing a child or cooking something in a box of charcoal. Maybe with luck, *si Dios quiere,* or if you can gain a reputation for being honest and serious, the butchers will give you money to buy pigs for them from the jungle farms, and if you're really lucky you can act as an agent for the big *comerciantes,* buying corn or coffee or cacao on commission. You're a capitalist, working your own hours, developing a clientele; maybe making as much as two dollars a day, your own man, taking shit from nobody.

Some of the bravest and most serious of the macheteros are planning their upward mobility in a more respectable and traditional way. Peddling lemons or stale fish on the streets is — well, it's humiliating; haggling shamelessly with some shameless housewife over a penny for fifteen minutes is not exactly their idea of the good life; many of their friends who do it, they feel, are slightly suspect, tainted, compromised — hot air artists involved in a sharp business where you have to be more or less dishonest to survive and where you're always balanced on the edge of disaster, all your capital tied up in something that, if you're not careful, will show up tomorrow rotting in its baskets. There's a kind of hairline division between the comerciante, that desperate man trying to get rid of his slightly tainted fish, and the thief who sneaks into some yard and steals shirts off the clothesline. There is something corrupting about the city.

The ones who spurn this life, the brave and old-fashioned ones who want to live in the tradition of their fathers, dream of having their own farms. There are thousands of hectáreas of jungle a few miles back from the main road and all along the other side of the river; it is almost free for the taking — government land, with twenty years to pay. But moving out into the jungle without capital, without tools except a machete, and with nothing in the way of food reserves but a few pounds of rice and a few pounds of paper-thin dried fish — my God, what an existence. And what a difference between the dream of independence, the beckoning urge that lives in the blood — to own your own land, to recapture your dignity and once again find meaning in your life — and the actualities of living out there a mile from your nearest neighbor in a patch of clearing that shrinks each day as the jungle obliterates your work. It takes heroism to make that move and then a kind of dedication that verges on fanaticism to survive the impossible problems that inevitably arrive to shatter the most modest of expectations: the *tigrillos* that carry off all your chickens, the smiling neighbor who steals your pig, the sickness of your children; the breaking up of your family when they reach school age. A careless swing with a machete and you are out there, five miles from a bus that will take you to a doctor, with an artery spurting blood or the flesh on your leg opened to the bone. Or you look down at a stab of pain, the terror already building in you at what you know you're going to find, and see an *equis,* a bushmaster, chewing on your foot.

Crop failures, months of rain out of season, the growing depression that comes with isolation, the growing feeling that you have been singled out, the starchy diet of plátano, yucca, rice, day after day, if you're lucky. Finally, after months, there is the simple, uncomprehended economics of transportation. How far can you afford to haul a bunch of plátano to sell when it's worth only fifty cents once you've gotten it to a place where a truck will pick it up?

How many bunches can a man haul in a day over muddy trails and across rivers? There are a hundred For Sale signs, crudely painted on slabs of balsa or on the backs of soapboxes, hanging along the road between Esmeraldas and Santo Domingo — SE VENDE ESTA FINCA — in most cases selling not the land itself but only the improvements: a bamboo shack worth twenty dollars, a hundred little coffee plants, a half acre of plátano, maybe four or five acres hacked out and planted to grass, a useless pasture without cows, unfenced, already going back to jungle. What happened? "We have to get the kids to town where there's a decent school"; or, "The high water took out all the cacao plantings"; or, "The cogollero killed the corn"; or, "Did you hear about Don Manuel? Standing there by the house making plans to clean a little patch of weeds and he just dropped dead."

Still there are some who survive in their isolation and hack out some kind of a life that satisfies them. Sitting in the house I can look across the river and see eight little farms. I have never been over there into that wilder land, but it seems infinitely inviting in its simplicity. From here it is just trees and huts, thin blue lines of smoke rising above the kitchens in the morning, women squatting in the sand along the river washing clothes, kids fishing or swimming, the single metallic cry of a rooster echoing out over the water. The people seem to be carved out of a finer harder material; their vices seem to be more monumental. We should have bought our farm on the other side; there is a truth over there that eludes us here.

As I watch, Esmundo gets into a canoe and crosses to our side. Esmundo comes into the store almost every week and buys a few pounds of rice, a pack or two of Full Speed, the cheapest cigarette, and perhaps a half pound of lard. It's not very much for a man like Esmundo whose vice is eating and whose thoughts seem to be always centered around his hunger. He doesn't work for us now, but when he did he was driven almost mad by the smell of frying bacon from our kitchen. Finally he asked me to buy him three pounds of the stuff in Quito and hang the cost; how could he die without having tasted bacon. Three pounds of bacon, five days wages. He kept it hidden under his bed and locked in the suitcase along with his revolver. He hunts *guatín* and *guanta* and the miniature deer that browse over there on the wilder land; sometimes he brings in a grubby looking tigrillo skin, which he then sells in Quinindé for ten or twelve dollars. He lives by burning hardwood and making charcoal, which he sacks and floats on balsa rafts to Esmeraldas every month or so, a hundred sacks at a time at fifty cents a sack.

The Cortez brothers. They work for us from time to time, but now they're over there planting pasture and cutting balsa and hand-sawing planks of amarillo and laurél. They live near a deserted farm which is owned by the bank, and they steal bananas along with everybody else and bring them across when a truck comes in looking for fruit to sell in Quito.

Roque and Gumercinda, his mother, live just across from us; they are almost as handsome as Lenny, Roque's son. Gumercinda is over six feet tall and thinks of herself as a great dancer; at the dances I am the only one who may dance with her without first buying her a Pepsi. Roque, we hardly know; he is a strange man living a mysterious life, too proud to work for us as a day laborer. He has two houses over there and can't seem to decide if he lives with his wife or his mother. Each house is filled with his children from two different women. We see him no more than once or twice a year, and when he does cross over he seems nervous and displeased by the workers who are always hanging around the store. He came to the last party we gave, to celebrate the end of the peanut harvest; Gumercinda had been in charge of the women, and he came not because he wanted to but because his wife and mother insisted. He spent the whole evening sitting on a bench, the only man who didn't dance or drink, sitting there crowded together with everyone but isolated from them, enclosed in a private cloud of anxiety. He kept watching his wife as she danced and danced, danced desperately, we thought, as though six months over there on the other side in that absolute unchanging tranquility had affected her a little. Ramón thinks he is jealous and afraid he is going to lose his wife as he lost Mari, the first one, who walked out on him one day and moved in with another richer farmer on the other side of the river.

Without wanting to I think about Dalmiro, and almost in this same instant, he appears stumbling down the trail to the river loaded like a mule with sacks of charcoal, his shirt blackened and torn. I feel as though I have conjured him up out of my own bad feelings about him. We fired him one night at a peanut party when he stood in the door screaming at Ramón that his mother was a whore, those ritual Latin words that invite death. But Ramón didn't kill him; he simply broke two of his ribs, picked him up over his head and tossed him out into the weeds. I had heard that he was over on the other side now, sleeping on the floor of Esmundo's house and helping him make charcoal. Someone, it is probably Ascensión, yells angrily at Dalmiro: "Come on; come on; move." And Dalmiro, slipping and lurching in the mud, his black body dulled and further blackened with smears of charcoal, staggers up to a tethered raft at the river's edge.

Out there is a young guy, more Indian than Negro, who lives alone, now here, now there. I think Marcelo and Ulderico are his brothers. The concept of private property is beyond him; he makes his living harvesting wild rubber, traveling a route through a hundred miles of uninhabited jungle. He has a name, of course, but we don't know it; we call him the wild *cauchero,* the rubber man; his clothes are stained black and thickened with rubber. He is in his twenties, shatteringly innocent and shy like a wild animal. He can't speak to anyone without breaking into a sweat and stuttering. His mother, they say, crossed the river last year to stay with him for a time, but he couldn't handle the crowd. Her presence in the house was too disturbing, too complicating, and he finally asked her to leave. He was at the peanut party too, though God knows why; none of us had invited him. How could we, even if we'd wanted to, when he sleeps each night in a different place? He was the drunkest man at the party, out of his head with good feelings and love for everybody, his arms around everyone, stuttering wildly and spraying spit into everyone's face in an ecstasy of good will. It was the first party he had ever been to in his life, and, if he doesn't learn how to control that spraying, possibly the last.

In a way I was caught up in the middle of all this swirling vigorous life; in a way, outside it. A certain role had been thrust upon me, and it was almost impossible to transcend my part. Not that I wanted to especially. We hauled sick people to the doctor, dead people to the cemetery, taped up macheted hands, preached the necessity of tetanus shots; we loaned money to the workers (who paid us back) and the neighbors (who didn't) when their mothers died or their children came down with *colorín;* we brought in the police from time to time when the workers in the salones began to get serious about their celebrating by breaking up all the chairs and tables, or when some little domestic crisis threatened to turn deadly. We didn't prevent as many murders as we would have liked. We handed out pills (stolen from the Peace Corps office) that suppress the symptoms of malaria; Ramón learned how to give injections. But these were just the basic courtesies, the basic obligations that were thrust upon us by our roles as the big landowning patrones of the area. Ramón became our locally practicing Peace Corps volunteer; he had advice for everyone, most of it pretty good, all of it unheard. I was an educated Peace Corps ghost who had learned what arrogance lay hidden in those easy words. Still, I was looking for another Ramón all the time, someone with the intelligence and discipline and the desire to break out of his infinitely complicated cycle of deprivation. And still, like an old record caught in a groove, I continued to yell at the mothers with their sick children: "Boil your drinking water; boil your drinking water." It was stupid advice, for now I knew that, being poor, they had no extra pots for boiling and storing water and that their children must die.

And now I knew that the death of children here is a kind of obscene blessing, a manifestation of God's inscrutable goodness. No wonder the whole village gathers for a night around those shoe-box coffins — dancing, drinking, singing, drumming, celebrating with joy the divine solution to an impossible situation. Long outside of the Peace Corps, squashed like a bug and made passive by those two banana trucks, I had lost the urgency to get involved in other people's lives and try to change them. There is a kind of madness or arrogance or naiveté in getting involved which, unless you are as fanatical as a priest or as insensitive as a missionary, can only drive you to despair. I had learned what the people had always known: that their situation was really impossible to solve by any methods yet devised. A few years ago such an admission of my inability to merge myself into this black life would have carried all kinds of bitter overtones, but now I realized that this separation was no great thing. It was my style to stand apart, it was something I had done all my life — moved off the stage and into the front row seats whenever I felt threatened.

Still there were good reasons more pressing than cowardice for going through the motions of uninvolvement. I had gone the other route once and almost died for my pains. My Peace Corps career came to a shattering and surrealist climax at three o'clock one morning in Rioverde when I found myself standing between two Ramóns, each intent on murdering the other. I saw myself as a peacemaker, but I was more involved in that terrible confrontation than I realized. When I had got the machete away from my friend Ramón and had tossed it over the top of the door into a locked bodega, the *other* Ramón stood before me with his raised blade. I saw the blade start down and put my arm up and the blade stopped and he backed away from me, giggling drunkenly, "*Chiste, chiste, chiste.*" Joke, joke, joke. But he hadn't been fooling; he had been drunk enough to want to kill me but not quite drunk enough to do it. He wasn't the only one, I imagine. I had got involved in that town, oh God, I had got involved in that damn town and aroused such feelings and such confusions in everyone that toward the end none of us could handle it.

6

DALMIRO

DALMIRO CAME TO WORK for us about four months after we had bought the farm. He was an old man from Rioverde, a landless day laborer who had spent his whole life as a machetero working for the poorest farmers on the coast. He cleaned their jungled hillsides at the end of the dry season, piling up the trash to burn, or he cleaned their very small plantings of corn or tobacco or plátano after the first rains when the weeds exploded out of the ground. He was an easy man to fool, and the poor farmers liked to hire him because they could make complicated arrangements — deducting certain amounts for food or promising him a hat or a pair of pants instead of wages. He was incapable of doing anything but clearing weeds; in all his life he had never done any kind of work besides stooping over until his head was only a foot above the ground and swinging a machete through the weeds. When he was sleeping in our chicken house we spent three hours once trying to teach him how to use a key in a padlock, but the fundamentals of this operation eluded him; it was new and complicated knowledge that he felt he didn't need in his already confused mind.

Dalmiro spoke a lisping and toothless Spanish that not even his oldest companions could easily understand, and he had probably never made more than fifty cents a day in his life. Much of the year he didn't make that much, and in the dry months between crops he often worked simply for the food that would keep him alive. In his younger days he had worked all up and down the coast, staying in the houses of poor farmers and eating with the family and sleeping on the floor of the kitchen; he would stay about six months in one place; it took him about that long to figure out that he was being cheated. Now he was getting old; he had reached the point where the work he could do in a day was no longer worth the food he ate, and it was harder and harder to find work. He had never learned how to count money nor how to distinguish the different values of the Ecuadorian notes, in spite of the fact that the fives, tens, and twenties are red, blue, and yellow respectively. This was another of those things he couldn't bother his head with; all he really expected out of a Saturday payday was that little handful of five-sucre bills that would get him drunk.

He had never stood out for me in Rioverde when I lived there; I had tended to avoid him as I tended to avoid all the disgracefully drunk people who staggered and wept in the single sandy street of the town. I remember him most vividly there as I had seen him one Sunday morning as he lurched drunkenly up the street past my house. All the children had gathered to torment him, circling around him like a flock of molting and tattered birds, one by one darting in with a scream to smear his face and clothes with handfuls of mud. He swung at them furiously with a stick, falling to his knees from time to time, and the kids were wild with the joy of it and only left him after he was completely covered with filth. Watching this little drama of small-town life was like opening a medieval book with woodcuts of barbarisms; watching it I thought of the millions of fools through history who had been treated the same way. Fools and animals.

Ramón left the farm one Friday and went to Rioverde to finish up some business in the town that he had recently abandoned. When he came back late the next day he told me that he had brought Dalmiro with him and that he was going to work for us. I struggled for a moment trying to remember who Dalmiro was and then, remembering, didn't believe Ramón. Laughing at his joke, for Dalmiro was the last man we needed on the farm, I stepped over to the window and looked out; it was true.

An old white-haired, toothless, barefoot, wrinkled, wreck of a man was standing in the back of the pickup trying to figure out how to get down. He had aged ten years in the year since I had seen him. We went out and lifted him down finally, and his face broke out in a great catastrophe of joy when he saw me. His face was all misplaced wrinkles, he had a great black gaping hole of a mouth, sunken stubbled cheeks, and eyes that were curiously filmed over, as if blind.

"*Cuñado,*" he said. "Ah, mi cuñado." He pronounced it "cuñao." Out of desperation he was adopting himself into my family. He was calling me his brother-in-law, and now if I would acknowledge the relationship, his future security would be guaranteed.

"*Bienvenido,* cuñado," I replied.

Ramón showed him where he would sleep and cook, pointing to a large new shed we were building, half full of bamboo-stripped chicken coops; we were surrounding it with an eight-foot fence of pointed stakes of pambil, against the expected arrival of the *rateros,* the sneak thieves of the night. Dalmiro moved in, carrying his possessions in a small paper bag: his pipe, a half-pound roll of tightly twisted leaf tobacco, a butcher knife, a pair of work pants; nothing more. He staggered with trembling uncertainty as though he were drunk or in the very last stages of syphilis.

"No," Ramón said. "I know he isn't drunk, and it can't be syphilis because in all his life he has never slept with a woman."

"Nor sat on a toilet seat?" I asked.

"That goes without saying," Ramón said. "He's from Rioverde; he has never seen a toilet and would probably flush himself out through the sewers if he tried to dominate one."

I wasn't too happy about the arrival of Dalmiro; guaranteeing his security for the rest of his life seemed to be something that Ramón and I should have talked about beforehand, inconsequential as his needs must necessarily prove to be. We had been hiring a lot of people from Rioverde, and I was uncertain about the wisdom of replacing the local people and so creating resentments among our neighbors.

"Well, what should I have done?" Ramón asked. "Left him in Rioverde to starve to death? He thinks of us as his saviors, his last hope. Look, Martín, I didn't know what to do. He was on the dock when I got to Rioverde, as if someone had sent up smoke signals that I was coming, and when he saw me he began to cry because I had promised to take him away two months ago and hadn't. 'I'm going with you,' he kept saying. 'I'm dying here, cuñado; take me with you, cuñado!' And I didn't say anything, and he followed me all day and all night and when I woke up in the morning in Pancho's house, he had been sleeping outside in the weeds with that damn paper bag all packed with everything in the world he owns, except for one cow to pay for burying him. And I still hadn't said yes or no and he followed me all day and finally without a word he followed me across the river and climbed into the truck, and when I started to say no, I looked at him and couldn't say it."

"O.K.," I said. "I guess you couldn't have; still it would be nice if we could plan things together and a little ahead of time."

"Well," Ramón said, "you didn't have to call him cuñado the first second you saw him, you know." Which meant, of course, in the good old Ecuadorian way, that it was now all my fault.

Dalmiro soon became a part of the background of the farm; we were happiest when we didn't notice him at all. He cleaned the ground around the houses where we lived, and when we moved to our new buildings and the new store, we put him to work there in the jungle garden we were planning. The area covered more than an acre, and due to the heavy daily rains, by the time he had macheted it clean it was time to begin again, The work took him about three weeks, and so for a few days in every lunar cycle we could see the river from our houses, winding down swiftly through the jungle, a sparkling openness of air, space, sunlight, seen beyond the clumps of bananas, coconuts, avocados, mangoes, and oranges that we were planting. And for a few days I would have to beat my way to the house at night through waist-high weeds, only partially convinced, when clouds obscured the stars, that I was heading roughly in the right direction.

Here comes Dalmiro at seven o'clock each morning dressed in his work clothes: pants and shirt so ripped and torn, so caked with dirt and sweat that he looks like some grotesque scarecrow or some new and exotic type of "thing," half human, half vegetable, whose essence could only be understood after peeling and peeling away that tattered outer skin, that rotting husk. In one hand he carries his machete, a honing stone in an old gunny sack, and a small gourd full of water to wet the stone. In his other hand, a pipe and a smoking piece of wood. Lighting his pipe is a perpetual process that is never really satisfactorily accomplished and that takes up about 80 percent of his working day. He staggers past the screened-in room where we sit drinking coffee, leers in to see that we are all alive, says "Buenos dias, cuñados," and lurching, disappears into the weeds, where from time to time the sounds of hacking — furious little bursts of energy that last about three minutes and then die out — can occasionally be heard. A long silence. Dalmiro is lighting his pipe or sharpening his machete.

One Saturday at noon when he came into the dining room, taking his turn at being paid, I asked him how old he was. He went into a kind of dance, slapping his sides with his hands, and laughing wildly because the idea lives in his head that everything I say is extravagantly funny. Ramón, watching him with cold disapproval as he moved in intricate dance steps across the floor, sternly repeated the question. "You don't even know, do you?"

"But, of course, cuñado, I'm thirty-two years old."

"You look more like a hundred and thirty-two years old," Ramón said, speaking the hard truth. "How do you know?"

"Because when I was seven years old I remember running with the people and hiding in the high grass with my mother when the soldiers came in looking for Lastre, shooting in the streets and firing into the houses and stealing everything out of the stores."

Ramón and I both figured back on our fingers. Concha's War and the battle of Rioverde took place in 1913. Ramón with a disgusted look handed Dalmiro a part of his pay. "These red ones are worth five sucres; there are five of them, enough to get drunk on. I'm deducting your store bill and giving the rest to Ester to take care of for you — for pants and shirts and shoes. And listen, cuñado, you're sixty-seven years old, not thirty-two. Take it easy, *viejo,* you hear? Watch yourself, viejo."

Dalmiro began to scowl and snapped his lips together; no sound came out; something too deep for words seemed to be troubling him.

"Why did you warn him?" I asked after Dalmiro had left. "And why are you holding back his wages again? Doesn't he have a whole box full of new shirts and pants?"

"Just wait," Ramón said. "You'll see; I think he's falling in love again."

He had come to us half starved; now after less than a year he had gained a good fifteen pounds and at Ramón's insistence had bought several complete changes of clothes and a mosquito net under which he slept; we had given him an old mattress. But falling in love? Dalmiro? There was something indecent in the idea, and I hadn't been able to imagine such a development, though I should have, remembering something that had happened shortly after he arrived.

For a couple of months we had employed another old man to take care of the pigs. He slept and cooked in the chicken house with Dalmiro, but he drank so much that we had to let him go after a few weeks. But in that short time he had conned Dalmiro out of almost a hundred sucres with the story that one of his best friends was a *brujo,* a sorcerer, who could give Dalmiro whatever he wished for. What Dalmiro wished, to make one of his lonely fantasies real, was for Florinda, an older woman from Rioverde, to come to our farm in Male. Dalmiro, it seemed, was passionately but secretly in love with Florinda. On the day we fired the old man, Alcide Segura, he said to Dalmiro, "Listen, amigo, give me another twenty sucres; I'll talk to my very good friend, the brujo, and within two weeks he will send Florinda to the farm. That's all he can do, you understand; the rest is up to you." Dalmiro paid.

Two weeks later to the day, the Rioverde fútbol team and half the town besides suddenly appeared, walking down the little hill behind the store; they came upon us like a flash of lightning, materializing through a deep cut in the road which had grown up into almost a tunnel of caña brava, bird-of-paradise, tangled morning-glories, and twelve-foot-tall elephante. It was always damp there in that deep shade, and a thousand butterflies, resting by the pools of water in the road, now exploded into the sunshine before the advancing futbolistas. Leading the parade, flanked by flags and banners, with a three-inch-wide scarlet ribbon sweeping across her ample bosom, was the team's *madrina* — holy God in heaven, Florinda!

We stood there with our mouths open, simply astounded. Everyone had been brutally kidding Dalmiro his passion for Florinda for the last two weeks, and now here she was; the contract with the brujo had been honored to the letter; *cancelado.* We were all dumfounded except for Dalmiro, who had dressed in his best clothes and had waited expectantly on one of the store's benches. But her actual arrival must have been too shattering, too much like the Second Coming with all those flags and the choral singing, the bands of massed angels and that spectacular celebration of butterflies, for Dalmiro panicked at the last second and rushed into the bushes. From time to time his head appeared between the grass clumps, along with a pair of hysterically fluttering hands trying to light a pipe.

The brujo had done his part, but Florinda refused to cooperate. Later that afternoon Dalmiro slipped up behind her as she watched the fútbol game and, perhaps feeling like a pawn in the inexorable destiny that was sweeping them together, whispered, giggling, in her ear, "Buenas tardes, mi amor." Florinda turned, observed him coldly for a long time, cleared her throat, and then quite thoughtfully directed a great gob of spit at a point about an inch from the tip of Dalmiro's toes.

Now Dalmiro was falling in love again; he had become enchanted with Míriam, the fifteen-year-old daughter of Melquisedes, a farmer up the river who had inherited a piece of ground 30 feet wide and 3500 feet long, one of three farms that cut through our property and made it almost U-shaped. Míriam was a constant visitor to our store, and in the short time that we had known her, she had changed from a little country girl into a kind of pre-prostitute. You could tell what was on her mind, though I would guess that when Dalmiro knew her she was still more or less virginal; she had begun plucking her eyebrows in incredibly narrow arching lines and smearing her dark face with rouge, and she had bought a number of very tight-fitting T-shirts. They were always slightly soiled and had the word AMOR spread across her youthful blooming breasts — breasts as delectable as cocktail canapes. She had a tough, arrogant little face, the face of a street fighter.

All through his very short "affair" with Míriam, Dalmiro probably never once spoke to her; he was much too timid for that. He was simply obsessed by her beauty and loved to be near her, where he could watch her moving about. Every evening now he went to visit in the house of Melquisedes, sat silent in the main room, and gazed with drugged and hypnotized eyes at his bouncy teenybopper lover. I didn't even know what was going on until Ramón's disapproval of the situation made everything apparent. Ramón was really ticked off; what was happening was that Dalmiro had begun to give his weekly wages to Míriam, or he would come to the store when Ramón was gone and charge sacks of rice or sugar or beans against his wages, all to be hauled up the trail and presented to the Melquisedes household.

"But, Ramón," I said, "it's his money; this really isn't any business of ours. He has the right to be a fool and screw up his life if he wants to."

"Oh, no, he doesn't," Ramón said. "Every August he goes to the big fiesta of the fifth in Rioverde. I want him to go there in new clothes and a good hat, with shoes, to be fat and healthy, and to have money to buy all his old friends drinks. If not, well, you know how those gossiping *pendejos* are in Rioverde; they'll say we are working him to death and not paying him and cheating him out of his wages — like *they*'ve been doing to him all their lives. No, he can screw up his own life if he wants to, but he's not going to screw up ours. I want to throw Dalmiro in their faces with finer clothes than any of them has ever seen."

Dalmiro's passion for Míriam was interrupted for a few nights by another, more enduring passion that had grown in his mind in the last years. He was in love with the idea of his own death. When he found out that he was sixty-seven and not thirty-two, that in one shattering moment of truth he had jumped from young maturity to incipient senility, he immediately became preoccupied with the mechanics of his funeral; it was *much* later than he thought. For about a week he came to the store every evening and had long talks with Ramón about just exactly what was going to happen when he died. He had lived on the coast near Rioverde where he knew everyone, knew how they died and how they were buried; he was uncomfortable now in this strange zone where, for all he knew, we would toss him into the river the morning that he woke up dead. He had decided that Ramón should bring his cow from Montalvo to our farm, where we could care for it and have it handy for sale at the moment of his passing. The discussions ground on for a week; Ramón finally promised, making the sign of the cross and kissing it, that the moment Dalmiro died he would be rushed up the beach to Rioverde, and that he would probably arrive there even before he had fully cooled if the tides were right. Ramón would bring with him twelve bottles of aguardiente and thirty large-sized candles for a decent wake. He would pay the necessary forty cents for a dignified announcement on the radio. He would, if it were necessary, dig the hole in the cemetery with his own hands. He would commission Jorge Avila, the town carpenter, to make a cement crypt crowned by a great cement cross. Dalmiro loved to hear the details; he looked ahead to the grandeur of his wake and the drunkenness of his friends and the many candles that would burn all night, and the whole scene was enchantment. He was a little troubled by the thirty candles which, in case of an offshore breeze, would burn down very quickly.

"Don't worry," Ramón said. "Other people will bring candles; there will probably be hundreds of candles."

"Who else will bring candles?" Dalmiro asked furiously.

Ramón thought and thought and finally said, lamely, "Well, my father for one. And Don Julio; he's good for a package. Florinda?"

"Oh, shit," Dalmiro said, "*Florinda?* But that's O.K. as long as there's lots of cement. Lots of cement, you hear, cuñado?" He sighed, seeing the dignity with which he would lie entombed as a dignity he had never had alive. "Lots of cement. Lots of cement."

But finally this endless discussion of death was drained of its possibilities, and Dalmiro was once more drawn to the house of Míriam. For about a month he insisted each Saturday on receiving his wages in full, which he immediately presented to Melquisedes. Ramón, in a fit of anger and frustration, finally fired Dalmiro, told him that there was no more work and that he had better go back to Rioverde.

He had been with us for over a year, and during that time, if he hadn't eaten well, at least he had eaten better than at any time in his life; he was no longer timid and frightened of people; he had in fact grown increasingly objectionable and feisty. All through his life, being an extremely simple man, he had taken a great deal of ribbing. He had accepted it all — sometimes with a great gaping grin and sometimes with pouts and snapping lips. But now he had begun to fight back. He had gotten in the habit, on Saturday nights when he felt particularly insulted and when he was at the height of his drunkenness, of sneaking into the cabins where our workers slept and urinating on them. Dalmiro had a real talent for this; and because the sleeping man who had insulted him was usually drunk, too, the victim was almost always completely drenched from head to foot by the time he struggled out of his catastrophic sleep.

The last moments of these smelly dramas were always the same. Santo or Pablo or Aladino would wake up warmly flooded to find Dalmiro, like some black apparition out of hell, looming over him, buttoning his pants, and going "hee hee hee" in a paroxysm of glee. Santo or Pablo or Aladino would get up, smash his fist into Dalmiro's face, kick him a couple of times where he had fallen, and then throw him outside into the mud. None of this violence bothered Dalmiro; he had, like a dog, put his mark upon the object of his contempt and so dominated it.

But Ramón slept behind a locked door, and the Saturday he was fired, Dalmiro had to be satisfied with pissing on the steps and standing underneath the window in the moonlight yelling insults at Ramón. "You're bad, bad just like your father. You treat me like an animal; she loves me, you understand? And you're jealous."

"Let's see how much she loves you next week when the money stops rolling in," Ramón yelled back. "Now get to your bed, you crazy old fool, or we'll throw you off the property."

In less than two weeks Melquisedes asked Dalmiro to please stay away from the house and not bother them anymore; he didn't want a scandal and the people were talking. Dalmiro went out and hid in the bushes for a day, and that night — humbled, hungry, humiliated, and tired of living on bananas — he came to Ramón and begged his forgiveness. Ramón let him sweat for the rest of the week and then told him that he would give him another chance.

Dalmiro paid about twenty cents a month for pasturage to Ramón's father, who owned a small farm in Montalvo, up the coast from Rioverde; this is where he kept the cow that was to be sold at the time of Dalmiro's death to pay for his funeral expenses. In addition to the pasturage fees, Don Plinio automatically became the owner of any offspring, as is customary in such arrangements.

Like most life insurance and burial insurance it was barbarously expensive. After the dust from his fiasco with Míriam had settled, Dalmiro's thoughts seemed to turn away from romance once more and settled on his approaching death. We were all relieved since this obsession seemed more fitting and decent than his ludicrous attachment to a teenage girl. Ramón was very patient with the old man, and several times a week the two of them would sit out on the store's benches and review the burial arrangements that Ramón had promised to make. In the first days of August, as he always did, Dalmiro went to Rioverde for the big Independencia fiesta, but this year, before beginning to drink, he took a day to walk that ten-mile jungle trail to Montalvo to pay his pasture bill and to check out the health of his cow; he owed for three years. While he was gone Ramón told me that actually this cow was not the first that Dalmiro had owned, and that actually Dalmiro's love of death went back almost ten years. It was no new development.

When he was about fifty-five years old he had bought his first cow. Shortly afterward he had fallen in love with a widow from Rocafuerte. News gets around, and when the widow heard of his passion for her, she sent out word that she was wild to eat some meat, and in fact that she was so consumed with this desire that if Dalmiro would give her the meat from his animal she would agree to marry him. It was the first time in his life that a woman had ever shown the slightest interest in him; what a coincidence that it was the first time in his life he had ever owned anything that a woman might want. Dalmiro, out of his mind with fantasies of marital bliss, killed his cow and arrived at the widow's house with the two hind quarters.

"The contract is for the whole cow," the widow said.

"Yes," Dalmiro said.

"Now it wasn't a great big cow, you understand," Ramón explained. "It was a runty criolla creature, the kind owned by a poor man who wants to be buried with dignity. But after all it was a cow. And the widow sat in her house for ten days eating that meat, and every day Dalmiro would bring her more, some of it cut into strips and sun dried, some of it salted. And that damn woman ate that cow, everything but the asshole. The day Dalmiro arrived to bring her to his shack, there was nothing in her house but a pile of bones. She had packed up and left in the night, and nobody has seen her since."

"Has he always been so simple-minded?" I asked.

"Always," Ramón said. "If anyone even smiled at him he'd fall in love. No, it was worse than that; if anyone just didn't insult him he'd fall in love. He worked for my father for years when I was growing up and he was always the same way. He's sixty-eight years old now, and he's never had a woman; that's getting pretty simple, don't you agree?"

The other cow? After he had been jilted, Dalmiro continued working and saving his money; five years later he bought another cow . . . and within six months another woman, promising to marry him if he would sell the cow and give her the money, had robbed Dalmiro of five years' savings and his latest fantasies. She had also disappeared down the coast on her wedding day.

When Dalmiro came back to the farm from the Rioverde fiesta he brought with him the most monumental hangover of his life. He had never enjoyed a fiesta so much, he insisted; he had bought drinks for everybody, but he was tired and, oh, how his head and all his bones ached; now he was going to settle down and act his age. He kissed the cross made with his fingers, a sacred oath showing that he was serious.

Within two weeks he had fallen in love with Mari.

Mari lived alone in a small house up the river, a ten-minute walk from the store; she had three or four children by three or four different men and, out of desperation to feed and clothe them, had been engaging in shorter and shorter liaisons. She had spent two years with Roque across the river, a year with a small farmer some miles downstream from us, a couple of months with Mercedes, a couple of weeks with Francisco's foreman at the sawmill. She had even gone to Esmeraldas for a time, trying to make it as a prostitute, but she had been unable to pay for the card that would label her as a professional and put her under the care of the health authorities. She had worked on the street, out of a small private house that she rented with a couple of her friends, but she lived in constant terror of the police. She never made it as a whore. The Esmeraldas whores, with their frizzled hair, their tight silk dresses, their brightly painted faces, and their cold rapacious eyes, are immediately identifiable. Not Mari. Mari came from good, strong country stock; she had broad shoulders and a plain pleasant face with friendly eyes that really looked at you; she walked with the proud natural dignity of a woman, without coquetry; her voice was a little too loud and direct. I'm sure it never occurred to her that she was expected to dress in the deforming manner of a vamp, over-emphasizing her breasts and her ass; she could never have learned how to simper, giggle, flutter her eyes, feign passion or helplessness. She never made it, and after a couple of unsuccessful months she came back to Male.

I had always liked Mari; from time to time she worked for us, hoeing weeds in the peanuts or helping in the corn harvest, and I liked watching the aggressive way she handled a hoe and the perfectly natural way she handled all of our workers who were drawn to her and held to the proper distance by her dignity. She washed clothes for some of the bachelors and cooked meals. Ramón had developed a hostile attitude toward her. As a typical Latin, with his country-boy prejudices, he was turned off by Mari. "She gets too much pleasure out of screwing," Ramón said. The sexual rules of conduct are well laid out in the small coastal towns. A woman who out of necessity to eat or care for her children has intercourse with a man on a one time basis is scarcely condemned. But it must be a relationship without passion, without kisses or caresses. In a very large sense it is accomplished almost without physical contact. A woman who seems to be enjoying any sexual relationship that is not more or less permanent immediately gets a bad name. Out of hunger a woman may give herself in a casual way, but, by God, she will see that there is a minimum of pleasure transmitted in the act; even in the act of being ravished there is in her bored disdain, a core of incorruptibility, as though actually she were not even there. So it is that in the culture of poverty, where hunger as an ever present possibility dominates and corrupts, even the act of love, the poor man's only real possibility of joy and fulfillment, is twisted and poisoned, turned into a mechanical and cold-blooded purging of physiological pressures, about as satisfying as a good bowel movement.

Mari was cooking for the sawmill crew. Dalmiro, bored with

his own cooking, began to take his meals there too. Lightning struck in the same place; Dalmiro shivered with ecstasy under the blow. He began hauling water up to Mari's house; this was work so demeaning to a man that everyone was too shocked to even kid him about it. He sneaked out into a neighbor's weed-infested patch of plátano and stole bunches of the fruit for the sawmill workers' table. He began bringing his entire week's wages to Mari, and at night he would sit on the steps of his cabin and hum and moan love songs.

This time it was Aladino who shattered Dalmiro's dreams; lucky he did, because Ramón was getting ready to fire Dalmiro again. Why couldn't he learn? Why couldn't he realize that he was too old, too distasteful for even a whore to take him into her bed. Aladino had come to work for us from Rioverde. In the three years since I had seen him there he had changed from a pleasant-faced adolescent into a black Adonis, a man of spectacular beauty. He ate with a family on the farm, but one Saturday when they had gone to Esmeraldas he was left without a cook. Dalmiro invited him to Mari's house to eat. Perhaps Ramón was right in thinking that Mari was a little too eager; she had never seen Aldino before until he climbed into her house and lit it all up with that great dazzling smile of his. She had never seen anyone so beautiful, and after dinner, as he was leaving, Mari drew him aside and suggested that he come back later. She wanted to cook him a special little something.

At eight, when Dalmiro was walking back to the farm, he passed Aladino in the darkness on the river trail, heading back to Mari's house. A terrible suspicion flared up in the old man's mind. Trembling with jealousy, he crept back up the trail, hid for a time in the bushes, and watched the moon rise across the river. The sound of conversation and laughter faded away and died, and finally, very quietly, Dalmiro climbed up the ladder and peered into the single room. There in the moonlight, there, bright and shining and shameless in the moonlight, before his eyes — betrayed. He began to pant and sob; tears streamed down his face; he tried to climb into the doorway, lost his footing, and fell six feet to the ground. Mari and Aladino scarcely heard him, until he began bawling at them, raging at this traitorous friend whom he had invited for dinner and who had stolen all. "That's right, that's right, do it; go on, do it. Go on, do it; do it, do it."

That was the night, come to think of it, that Dalmiro at two o'clock in the morning, just a little drunker than usual if such a thing is possible, crept into Aladino's bachelor shack and urinated on him as he slept.

My God, how bored we were with Dalmiro, that shriveled, stinking, staggering old man who hacked out weeds around our houses. We had taken him in out of *lástima,* out of pity, so that he could have a place of security until he died. But he refused to die; instead, every few months he fell in love. What a mess. After every romance had exploded in his face he would go on a tremendous drunken bender. The little kids out on the highway would come down to the store and announce with laughter that Dalmiro was out on the main road crawling up and down on his hands and knees and baying like a dog; tourists from Quito were parking along the shoulders of the road to watch him. The first few times we went out and brought him back; he would spit at us when we threw him into the back of the pickup; and as we bounced down the road past the coconuts, if he were able to stand up, he would piss against the back window and cackle. Finally, we just left him out on the highway to crawl and bay; maybe with luck a truck would get him. How awful that we had so little feeling for him. His life had been an endless series of insults, humiliations, betrayals, deprivations; still, he endured, kept alive day after day by that insane dream of his, by that glowing half-realized promise in his soul, that someday he would find someone who would love him.

We were kept awake one night by the sounds of drums and chanting from one of the houses upstream from us. It was an all night festival of bongos announcing to us the death of another child and alerting God to the imminent arrival of an innocent. From its nearness I was sure that it was one of Merdardo Luna's babies. It was about time for one of Luna's babies to die. Almost as soon as they were born, his wife, with the most appalling negligence, would allow her children to sicken and die. This happened about once a year, and it was a regular event a day or two before the bongos to see them both standing on the highway waiting for the bus, both of them chain-smoking cigarettes and the señora holding with bored distaste something that looked like a bundle of dirty rags. Like most poor people they invariably waited until it was too late to get to a doctor. But the next morning Ramón told me that it was Theresa's baby who had died and that they had had the fiesta in Luna's house. He was all set up with his own bongos — a wise investment, we decided, since his principal production was dead babies.

Theresa? I had never heard of her, and Ramón told me the little that was common knowledge. She was Colombian, a stranger to the area, an eighteen-year-old girl who one day had simply appeared in Male. Maybe one of the truck drivers from the sawmill had brought her out to sleep with him for one night. She was from a small Negro fishing village on the ocean, near Tumaco. No one knew why she had left or why she was wandering the country alone and without friends. She had come with a baby, had been offered shelter in the house of Elsa, Mari's sister, and now the baby was dead. She was already, Ramón told me, quite definitely pregnant again.

The funeral procession that morning, unlike the usual celebration in which the whole village participates, consisted of Merdardo Luna and Silvano. They reminded me of caterers; they walked briskly up the road toward Viche and the cemetery, one of them carrying a small cardboard box wrapped in white tissue paper, the other a shovel. There were no women present, not even the mother. We watched them as they climbed the little hill behind the store; clouds of butterflies erupted around them just before they disappeared from view, thousands of yellow butterflies whirling around that paper coffin in the still cool air of early morning.

I didn't see Theresa for some time, until one day she came to the store to buy a candle and a box of matches. She was the classic example of a really small-time, isolated village girl, a country bumpkin on a grand scale — shapeless, loosely shambling, poorly dressed in stained clothing, self-effacing. Her face was not unpleasant, only disconcerting, for it mirrored little that one ordinarily associates with the human condition. Perhaps it was because she was pregnant and was lost and turned inward toward the mystery of her own condition. She bought what she had come to buy, and as she shambled off I watched her in a kind of awe, thinking that if she were to die, she, too, could be drummed into heaven with the bongos, she was that unaware and innocent.

To stay alive she hung around the main *salón* in Male where the sawmill workers sometimes spent their evenings sipping *tragos* and listening to the music; from time to time she would disappear with one of them into the bushes. She tried to better herself; she spent a week across the river in Cantante's house and another week with Chango. Cantante and Chango, the Singer and the Blackbird.

And now Dalmiro, who hadn't been in love with anyone for almost three months, fell under the spell of Theresa's charms and brooded away his days as he hacked out the weeds around our houses. He came to Ramón late one evening, after I had left the store and gone to bed, and confessed that he was in love, that this time it wasn't just adolescent infatuation but really love. "Cuñado, help me," he begged. "I talked to her that I truly love her and that I want her to be my woman, to live with me here and cook for me. That we will eat well; that I will buy her pretty dresses. She doesn't laugh at me; she just says *quizás,* perhaps, but she can't make up her mind."

"But what can I do?" Ramón asked.

"I think she would love me if she knew I was making as much as the others. Raise my wages; pay me twenty-five sucres a day and I'll work until four o'clock."

"Well, Ramón said, "you're not worth a dollar a day, but all right. And what else?"

"Talk to her," Dalmiro said. "You know how to talk. Tell her I am a sincere and serious type. That I will make her happy. Tell her who I am, *quien soy yo.* Just don't tell her that I have a cow in Montalvo."

Ramón sat staring at Dalmiro for a long time. "Why not?" he must have thought. In a way they were the perfect pair, the absolute bottom in the pecking order — a senile and simple-minded machetero who was half dead, and an abandoned and friendless eighteen-year-old girl, the refuse of the town, who whored for a dish of rice. Nor did the wider ramifications of arranging such a romance escape Ramón. It would make him famous; the news that Dalmiro had a woman would explode like a hydrogen bomb in Rioverde. Ramón could visualize the people shaken to their very cores by this insane news. He could see them shouting it up and down the street. Cheering, hysterical laughter, screams of disbelief, rage, dismay, stunned silence. Sunday morning Ramón took some money and walked up the trail to Male; he passed out twenty-sucre bills among the people. "Talk to the girl," he said. "Try to convince her that it would be a good thing for her, that she will be eating much better." That afternoon his friends came by to report that they had talked with Theresa, that they were putting pressure on her, but that she was still undecided. Ramón gave Mercedes another twenty sucres and sent him to her with the promise that Dalmiro would buy her a pair of shoes, for he had heard that Theresa was talking wildly in the town and saying that all of the innumerable men she had slept with had promised her shoes; but she was still barefoot.

Much later Mercedes returned grinning. "I think it can be arranged," he said. "Does Dalmiro agree absolutely — in the name of Jesus Christ and all the saints — to buy her shoes?"

"Absolutely," Ramón said. "*I* guarantee it on my honor."

I didn't know about any of this until the next afternoon when I came in from disking coconuts and heard Ramón and Ester talking together delightedly. We had gone out of the chicken business some time before; Dalmiro had moved into a small hut, but now he was moving into a larger cabin, the one I had lived in when we first arrived. He came by to borrow a broom, and he was glassy eyed and speechless in a kind of catatonic disbelief. The whole shoddy deal was depressing, when Ramón explained it to me, and I exploded with anger. "My God, how do you dare to do such things? Why are you playing God with Dalmiro? Why are you getting involved in filthy things that are none of your business and can only end badly? Listen to me, call it off, this is going to end badly for everyone."

But Ramón couldn't even hear me. "Don't be like that," he said. "Somebody has to be his friend. Don't you have some final advice for cuñado?" He grinned the smile of a great architect.

"Yes," I said, "tell the old son of a bitch to take a bath."

"Oh, hell," Ramón said. "And who's going to tell the girl to take a bath? *She's* the one who needs it."

"But they've both taken baths," Ester said. "They've both been to the river; Dalmiro even bought *jabón de rosas*. You never saw such suds. Mountains of suds; he almost covered the river in suds."

Dalmiro came to work the morning after he moved in with Theresa; he walked with a new dignity, his caved in chest thrown out and his eyes alive with a light that we had never seen before. He was a living negation of the *post coitus triste* — though we found out later that he had had a premature ejaculation. It was a measure of his passion, which must have been intense considering his age.

They stayed together for about four months. The initial problems, those little conflicts between newlyweds, seemed to have worked themselves out. The main problem apparently was the question of food. Dalmiro would come in from work and seat himself on the floor, ready to dig into that mountain of rice and plátano that Theresa was preparing. But when everything was cooked Theresa would pick up all the pots of food and carry them up the trail to Elsa's house. The two women along with Elsa's children ate it all. Dalmiro didn't want to complain; maybe this was the way things were supposed to be. He began cooking in the old chicken shed, which was now almost totally collapsed, until Ramón saw him there one day, found out what was happening, and spoke a few brisk words to Theresa.

One day toward the end of their alliance I was disking down the weeds in a little grove of coconuts that we had planted around the workers' houses. I broke through an eight-foot-high wall of pigweed and saboya and almost ran down Theresa, who had been kneeling at the edge of the weeds planting some sticks of yuca. The way the weeds had come down before the tractor, like a curtain opening on a brightly lighted stage, made me stop for a moment and study the set. I was in Dalmiro's front yard. Theresa had planted things around the house — peanuts, yuca, pineapples, bush beans, and plátano. Dalmiro, bare to the waist, stood in the door of the cabin smoking his pipe and watching Theresa with firm approval. Some visiting babies played in the yard. Observed in his own setting, Dalmiro had a certain dignity and the whole scene had an air of permanence and respectability — almost an air of grandeur.

I didn't like talking to Ramón about Dalmiro anymore; his outrageousness no longer amused me, and I thought Ramón had done something wicked and irresponsible. I was full of resentment when I thought of how he had played with Dalmiro and of how he had manipulated Theresa. But surprising them at home on the tractor had made me wonder; they looked so exactly like any other family.

"Is it *possible* that those two are going to stick together?" I asked Ramón that night.

"Is anything permanent?" Ramón asked shortly. He too was resentful that I had criticized him; he was never able to handle my anger. He couldn't understand why I was distressed about what was happening to a Colombian whore and a crazy old man who, when you made him angry enough, tried to piss on you.

"I notice that Theresa is still barefoot."

"*¿Y eso?*" Ramón said. So what?

"Didn't you guarantee her a pair of shoes?"

"Hombre," Ramón said, "do women believe everything that men say?"

We sat at the table staring at one another coldly and without speaking until Ester came in with coffee. She had been listening to us from the kitchen. "Three days ago she began to weep and scream in Elsa's house. That he's always rubbing her at night when she's trying to sleep, that it's driving her crazy, that she can't stand those cold hands, those cold snakes that grope and grab." Ester shuddered.

"Two times," Ramón said. "For Christ's sake, two times in four months. That is if you want to count the first time, when he didn't do anything. Is that so awful? Is that so much to pay for four months of the kind of eating she's never had in her life before?"

"It's his hands," Ester said weakly, going back into the kitchen.

Young Chango, who had taken Theresa across the river to live with him for a week, still felt a proprietary interest in the girl. Except for one time when he had gone to a whore house in Esmeraldas with Arcario, Theresa was the only girl he had ever slept with. As time passed he began to idealize that time when they had been alone together. He was about seventeen and still lived with his parents, but that week they had gone someplace to visit, and Chango had had the house to himself. He was a disreputable kid with a gnomelike, twisted old man's face that by the time he was thirty would be truly frightening; he was already beginning to look like his mother. The curse of the Micoltas. He walked crookedly; he smiled crookedly. One leg was shorter than the other because of a constantly suppurating wound in the calf of his leg which refused to heal. He had been very badly cared for, and his soul was crooked, too. He had worked for us for a time, and we had planned to take him to a good doctor in Quito; then we caught him stealing money out of the store and booted him off the farm. Later when Ramón became the inspector general for the zone, a more or less honorary job with few obligations, he had had to throw Chango in jail for a few days for trying to wreck one of the drinking places in the village.

The Saturday after I had crashed through that wall of grass into Dalmiro's front yard, Chango came across the river to drink in the new salón that Victor, one of our workers, had just opened. It was a grand opening with lots of brand new phonograph records and everyone was there. As Chango got drunk he began to draw into himself; he stood alone watching Theresa, who sat at a table with Dalmiro and a couple of other workers. When the music started and everyone began to dance, Chango went over to Theresa's table and held his arms out.

"You know something," he said when they were dancing in that dimly lit room, "you're still my woman."

"No," Theresa said. "No, Chango, I'm not anybody's woman."

"Now you listen to me," Chango said. "You're *mine*." He put one hand on her neck and began to squeeze it very hard, and she broke away and went back to the table and sat there staring at her hands. Much later, much drunker, Chango got her alone again, and as they danced he twisted one of her arms up behind her back and put pressure on it.

"Don't," she said. "That hurts."

"Are you my woman?"

"Chango, *don't* . . . *Chango,* you're breaking my arm."

"Say that you're my woman," Chango said. "Go on, I want to hear you say it." She didn't say anything, but struggled to get away. "Lay off," he said. "You want a good punch in the stomach?"

"Be careful of the child . . . *Chango!*"

"Are you my woman?" He jabbed his thumb hard into her stomach and then moved his face away from hers a little and smiled. "Are you?"

"Yes," she said. "Whatever you say."

"O.K." Chango said, letting her go. "I'll see you later tonight; leave the door open."

She locked the door, but his drunken pounding frightened her and she opened it almost immediately. He came into her cabin that morning at three o'clock with three of his friends — Adolfo, Carlos, who else? Gupián? — and while Dalmiro was sleeping in the back room all four of them took turns with Theresa on top of the kitchen table. Chango charged each of them ten sucres and, like a perfect gentleman, agreed to be last. They were so occupied that none of them knew when Dalmiro had first come into the room, disturbed out of his drunken sleep by their laughter. Nor did his presence in the doorway, when they finally noticed him, cause anything but a moment's mild alarm. Adolfo was embarrassed and tried to withdraw, but Chango put his hand against Adolfo's ass and said, "Hold it, hombre; don't waste all that work. And don't worry about the old man; she's my woman now." Dalmiro didn't say a word; he just stood there watching them as though it were something happening in a dream. Adolfo, drained and dreamy, not even bothering to button himself, sat down against the wall and plunked out chords on the guitar that he always carried with him to dances, and Chango replaced him at the kitchen table. The room was lit by a single candle, and Dalmiro was very drunk, but from the sounds alone he would have known what was happening. No one noticed when Dalmiro left the room, but he was gone from the doorway a few minutes later when they left the house, and the sounds of Adolfo's guitar faded away down the trail.

Sunday morning Dalmiro consulted with Ramón, Mercedes, Santo, Aladino, and whomever else was lounging around the store, and it was unanimously agreed that Theresa should be thrown out of the house as a shameless whore. Dalmiro, trembling, staggering, panting, returned to his shack and told Theresa he was through with her, that she was filth beneath his feet, that he never wanted to see her again. Without a word she gathered up her little pile of clothes, stuffed them into a paper bag, perhaps glanced longingly at a couple of Dalmiro's new pots, which she would have liked to take with her, shrugged, and left the house. And that should have been the end of it, but a couple of minutes later Dalmiro had a change of heart; lurching and falling he rushed up the trail behind her, up through the high grass and into the trees along the river. "My life, my soul," he bawled. "Come back. Come back, my love." But barefoot Theresa didn't turn around. She kept going, and I don't know where she went, and I guess no one knows where she went. I never heard her name mentioned again by anyone up or down the river, not even by Chango.

We had a party to celebrate the completion of the peanut harvest about three weeks later; it was then that Dalmiro, as drunk as we had ever seen him, began throwing handfuls of balled mud through the windows at the guests. Ramón and the *policia rural,* whom we had invited to the party for his restraining influence, went outside and told Dalmiro that if he didn't quiet down they would chain him to a tree like a dog. Dalmiro staggered off into the bushes, groaning. Five minutes later he stood in the doorway of the little packing shed, where everyone was dancing, and began pissing on the dance floor and screaming at Ramón that his mother was a whore. He had a little trouble breathing when Ramón got through with him; I think he landed on a pile of wood chunks lying in the grass, and he must have cracked a couple of ribs. I didn't see him after the party, but I heard that he was lying alone in his cabin and that he couldn't walk. I was terrified for Ramón that he might have killed him and begged him to take Dalmiro to a doctor, but Ramón furiously refused to even consider it. Someone finally called in one of the local brujos, who cured him with poultices of steaming leaves. He couldn't work, of course, and about ten days after the party he went to live with Esmundo across the river. Esmundo had offered him food and lodging if he would help him make charcoal. He was there for some months, but finally, deciding that he was being cheated, he began pissing on Esmundo and his wife as they slept, and Esmundo threw him out of the house for being a disgraceful incontinent lunatic and told him to get his ass back across the river. He had used up his chances in Male, and he went back to Rioverde.

7

THE BROTHERS CORTEZ

WHEN ESMUNDO WALKED AWAY from work with my machete that day, it served our purposes to believe that all the men who had walked out of the field with him knew what was happening, and that by surrounding him and hiding him from our eyes they approved of the theft and were proclaiming their real loyalties, which sure as hell weren't to us. It was dishonest reasoning since we were only looking for an excuse to fire them anyway. Now, without even mentioning the theft (we had pledged ourselves to silence), we proceeded to deconstruct and scatter the workers' sindicato. Thinking of them all as accomplices helped us to harden our hearts against them. That Saturday we let Pedro Lamilla go; we were getting caught up in our work, we said, and running out of money besides. The following Saturday we fired the Angulo brothers, Carlos and Heriberto. They had, and not entirely without reason, considered themselves as special pets of the farm, for we had given Carlos ten acres of land, money to build a house, and enough chickens and chicken concentrate to turn him almost overnight into an instant alcoholic. Heriberto, the other brother, also had special claims on us, and at the infrequent parties that we gave for the workers he would sit only with me, explain very carefully that he was not a Catholic but a Protestant and very ostentatiously would not get drunk with everybody else. They didn't want to be fired; they fought with everything they had: tears, threats, screams of rage, the dry heaving sulks. Carlos, if such a thing were possible, stayed even drunker than usual, his bloodshot eyes now redder than ever, burning like coals. We stood up to

them, compromising only to the extent of turning them from workers paid a daily wage to contract laborers paid so much per hectárea to cut down trees; they could have made more under the
new system, but they had lost the habit of working, and they
didn't have the discipline to plan out a daily schedule for themselves. Carlos took the separation money that we paid him, invested it in a salón, and drank up all his capital; Heriberto went
to work for a plywood company in Esmeraldas.

Now to be fair we would have to fire Jorge Cortez. So Jorge,
anticipating his turn and wanting to keep a little steady money
coming in for the family farm, brought his younger brothers across
the river, hoping that we would replace one Cortez with at least
one other. Or maybe he was smarter than we thought and realized
that it would take the two younger ones to do the same amount
of work that he had been doing alone. We thought there were
only three brothers, but now the oldest, José, suddenly appeared
from out of the Colombian jungles, where he had been in hiding
for seven years because of an unplanned murder he had committed. One morning when I came over to the store for coffee, all
four brothers were sitting in a row on the store's bench, all of them
dressed identically in torn and patched baby-blue work pants,
enormous and shapeless straw hats, and bare chests and feet. It
was almost too much to take so early in the morning. I had already been shaken to know three men who looked so much alike.
Now to be confronted, unprepared and vulnerable, by yet another
identical Cortez almost gave me an aesthetic shock that, in the
predawn dimness and before the couple of coffees that fortify one
against the day's blows, closely resembled the shock of seeing for
the first time — something absolutely overwhelming, like one of
those twenty-foot-long paintings of waterlilies by Monet.

Taken as a quartet the Cortez brothers were a spectacle; they
were so identical in appearance that they reinforced each other's
beauty, like the subtly developed and repeated motif of some
musical theme in a Beethoven sonata. There was something grand
and mysterious about the repetition of their large docile eyes, their
straight, thin classical noses, the intense blackness of their skin;
they were all about the same height, tall and slim, and they had
the delicate wrists and the long sensitive fingers that one associates

with the artistic temperament. When they first saw me, somebody pulled a switch and I was assaulted by four great identical smiles, miles of gleaming teeth. It even seemed that they had identical senses of humor: they had all let their hair grow and then proceeded to carve out of those tightly woven black naps exotic boat-prowed or duck-beaked hair stylings that were in sharp contrast to the conformist style of almost all the people on the river. They didn't copy anybody's style, they made their own, or rather, I found out later, Jorge had his own sense of style which the others copied. It is impressive enough to consider the miraculous power of nature to mass produce identical roses or white-banded Hampshire piglets, but when nature begins stamping out identical human beings one staggers under the grandeur and stability of the genes and gets a hint of some underlying and divine plan.

When we first got to know them all together, they were seventeen, eighteen, twenty, and twenty-two years old. José, Jorge, Arcario, Amado. They had their father's face without really resembling him. Out of age, poverty, and sickness, he had taken on the ascetic, fanatic look of an East Indian priest; still he had transmitted in quadruplet something strong and subtle from an African past — a sense of dignity, royalty, some inner tranquility of spirit compounded by independence and self-respect that identically illuminated their faces. (Except for José, the murderer, within whose eyes one could see that death constantly reenacted.) When we got to know them all well, we tended to confuse and minimize their individual failings because we thought of them en masse — a four-part profoundly unified work of art, a symphony. To some extent at least, I think this is how they saw themselves.

Here they were then that morning, all together, Beethoven's Seventh with José representing the slow movement, the funeral march.

"Buenos dias," Jorge said. "I'd like to present my brother, José, who is now back with us on the farm."

"*Mucho gusto*," I said, shaking hands. "And how can I serve you?"

"Well, we're waiting to talk to Don Ramón. About work. I thought it was possible that you might need some exceptionally talented men."

"*Claro*," I said. "Sure thing; no problem. We have to burn those ten acres of stumps before the arrival of the rains."

"José is the oldest, the strongest; he knows how to use the ax."

"I was thinking of using all of you," I said, anticipating Ramón's displeasure at my moving into his area and hiring men. I knew that he wasn't too impressed with Amado Cortez as a machetero.

"All of us?" Jorge asked in surprise. He had been waiting for three weeks to be fired, and now in one moment the family's income was being quadrupled. "But what will Don Ramón say?"

"Well, that's my problem. I'm an owner of this damn farm, too."

"Oh, claro, claro," Jorge said, but without too much conviction. "Shall we all start together on Monday?"

I nodded. As I studied the four of them together that first morning, it had seemed obvious that I was looking at a package deal and that it would have been aesthetically immoral to have separated them — like scissoring out and framing two blossoms from a bouquet of Van Gogh sunflowers.

Even before the Cortez brothers put on their short-lived but dramatic feature performance on the farm, the father had begun to fade away from even the fringes of the river's communal life. I've never been able to find out what ultimately happened to him or even if anything in the ultimate sense even got around to happening. There was no reluctance to talk about it; it was only that nobody knew or cared. He had gone through all of man's cycles, including that of the respected elder statesman, including even, perhaps, that of the still slightly respected but slightly senile sage. Everyone was bored with him; he was too old to work; it was time to stop lingering on the stage; he had long since used up all his lines. I think he lost his mind and began to walk the roads, because for some months I used to see him standing on the main highway at widely separated spots. He had the blank resigned face of a holy man who has decided to go out and actively seek his own death, and then, having moved out, forgets his mission. On Monday driving to Quito I might see him wandering vaguely along the road, miles from the nearest shack; on Wednesday coming back I might find him thirty miles up the road, standing isolated at the edge of a group of people or sitting by himself at the top of some high road-cut where he could look out over the tops of the trees toward the setting sun. Back at the farm I might mention to Jorge or Amado that I had seen his father wandering like a ghost some sixty miles from Male. And they would shrug, unable to say anything sensible in response to my observation.

(This lack of concern for the old man puzzled me. Until the day the grandmother died I thought of the Cortez brothers as being rather heartless, disunited, and lacking in those family ties that are so essential when one lives at the very heart of poverty. In truth, as I found out later, though they were ultimately to be blown and scattered to the winds, there was more unity in that family than in any of the others. The day the grandmother died they all came to me willingly and secretly, one after the other, and between them borrowed almost a thousand sucres; they planned and executed with great style the social event of the season, a wake with hired drummers, roast pig, bottles of aguardiente, free cigarettes, and hundreds of candles. She had been four days trying to die, but something in her had refused to let go until she could look into the eyes of a priest and receive his permission to pass on. And it had taken her grandsons four days to find a priest who was willing to drive to the farm and take a canoe across the river and climb that muddy trail up through the tangle of growth to the hut where she lay. Twenty minutes after the priest left she was dead. Later when Arcario told me about it I was awed and shaken by that old lady's dignity and by the beauty of her passing. I had seldom heard of such perfect faith, and it reinforced my own recently acquired conviction, when I knuckled under to Ramón's anger and went on living, that we only die when we are ready to.)

We never got to know José very well; he wasn't with us that long. In a drunken brawl at fifteen, he had killed a friend — a cousin of Carlos Angulo's — with a machete; under the law he was liable to as much as sixteen years in prison, but to come back into society middle-aged, morally dead, sexually brutalized, and incurably criminal is something that no one here accepts without first trying to run away. José fled the country and disappeared into the jungles of Colombia. When he came back with a wife and children, I suppose he imagined that he had suffered enough loneliness in his exile and that he had paid his debt. He wanted to put down his roots where he belonged, but this was not to be allowed him. A month after his return he came to work one Monday morning with his lower lip almost chewed off and enormous pieces of flesh gnawed out of one of his arms; he had been in a terrible fight at Carlos Angulo's salón.

"My God," I said when I saw him, "they just don't hardly kiss like that no more."

"It was Carlos Angulo," José said. He covered his face with one hand as though he were ashamed to be marked with the passion of a rage that so resembled lust.

"I think in your position I'd stay away from the salones and never, never get so drunk that someone could jump me when I couldn't defend myself."

"I wasn't very drunk," José said. "But you're right. I'll have to stay on the other side of the river."

But he wasn't safe on either side, and he wasn't safe drunk or sober. We heard now that there were cousins and brothers who had sworn revenge and that when they were drunk and brave they waited on the trails at night or floated past José's house in canoes yelling insults and threats into the darkness, unfamiliar voices full of rage and menace. He finally cracked. About three months after he came back to Male he disappeared again one day, and we haven't seen him since. He left with his wife and children, or at any rate, they all disappeared together, a kind of indirect reassurance that he hadn't been gutted and tossed into the river.

We had liked José, though there was nothing outstanding about him as a worker except that he came regularly and worked where we put him without whining; one place was as good as another. He was a shattered man who seemed to have lost his enthusiasm and capacity to plan his life. He was sad and passive. There was something terrible in his eyes, a kind of deadness, the kind of stunned and desolate look of someone who has just had a two-by-four brought crashing down on his head. He was in a final and permanent shock that had put out a light. I didn't connect this with the murder of his friend until a year later when we hired a watchman to guard our pineapples, which were being stolen by the hundreds. He was a young man from Manabi — one of the *bad*

Manabitas, the Negroes said, one of the yellow-colored Manabitas. He, too, had that dazed expressionless look in his eyes; in a way it was terrifying to look deeply into his face, for it was a face that was quite inhuman. He had lost some vital ingredient. Hope? Some capacity for surprise and delight? The necessity of communicating with another human being? It is sad enough to find those eyes in the faces of the aged, like Dalmiro — burned out sockets holding nothing but some faint residue of an old despair. But such eyes in the faces of the young fill one with an anger against life. Who could have looked into the face of Lazarus still half wrapped in his shroud, moving off his bier and into the sun, without cursing God? Ramón casually mentioned at dinner one night that thank God we would never have any labor problems with the Manabita; he was wanted in Puerto Viejo for murder. But, of course. I knew immediately that it was true, for I had already connected the Manabita with José; one couldn't think of either one of them without also thinking of the other.

So now the quartet became a trio, with Jorge beating time. Every morning he paddled his two younger brothers across the river, and though at that early hour they were sedate enough, I always had the impression that with their arrival the clowns and tumblers had entered the ring. They radiated good humor; they moved together easily, each of them reinforcing the other. They were always in touch, at times talking to each other about things in the most minute detail in a lazy country Spanish that was so slurred and soft that I could hardly understand a word; at other times they communicated the most subtle opinions with an imperceptibly raised eyebrow, a sudden opening wide of the eyes, a tiny shrug of the shoulder, a certain kind of sigh, an opening of the hands. What did they see in this torpid jungle that so delighted them and impelled them to such constant and intimate communication? Didn't they all display a kind of genius in being able to discuss for twenty minutes with shrieks and screams of laughter the fact that while one of them had been squatting out behind the house a frog had leaped with the clammy fingers of death onto his naked ass? The best thing about them was their capacity to enjoy one another. I never heard them quarrel; I never heard one criticize the other, though sometimes for five and six days at a time they would be engaged in complex wrestling matches or mock machete fights. One week they asked for a contract to replant a couple hectáreas of pasture; they spent so much time chasing each other through the grass, yelling their terrible curses, that instead of making the fourteen dollars apiece they might have earned, we paid each of them less than four dollars. A year later, the family now scattered and dispersed, Arcario thought of that disastrous week, smiled with nostalgia, and spoke of it as a real gas, one of the great funny times of his life. Even yawning and stretching at dawn they reflected their deepest feelings about life; they found themselves at the center of and in harmony with everything. Life flooded into them through their skins, and they hadn't come across anything yet that they couldn't handle. Not yet.

Just as before I had transferred my despair with Esmundo, Pedro, Uldarico, and some of the other *bandidos* who lived on the other side of the river to that land itself, now I began to transfer some of my delight with the Cortez brothers to that wild and mysterious place where I had never been and which, therefore, I was allowed in my mind to construct as a freer and more innocent world. I saw in their unity some quality of strength and purity which they had absorbed from the land, and it seemed then that, almost for the first time, I was observing qualities that could be admired in this otherwise screwed up culture that was all anarchy and self destruction. How nicely they had gone into debt to bury their grandmother in a traditional and more than honorable way. How sweetly they worked together on those twenty acres of worthless hillside across from us. They seemed so strong, so invulnerable.

The Cortez brothers all dreamed of one day having a little cattle spread. Their plan made sense; the land they owned was good for nothing but pasture. It was all steep hillside cut every which way by ravines, and its topsoil had washed away, leaving heavy clay mixed with rock. Years before we arrived they (or maybe it was their father) had begun to cut down the trees on the first hill above the river and haul canoe-loads of saboya grass roots to plant on those steep slopes. They claimed sixty meters of river frontage and God knows how many thousands of meters into the jungle; it was a wavering ribbon, dangerously intertwined with the land of

Roque and Gumercinda on one side and with Uldarico, Cantante and Julián, Esmundo and Pedro Lamilla on the other. We promised to loan them money to buy barbed wire and to guarantee their credit at the bank for a cattle loan when they had planted a few more acres of pasture, but this never came to anything because it turned out that they were squatters on government land, had never gone through the complicated ritual of surveying their property lines, and therefore had no title that could be used as security at the bank.

Now in four days everything changed. Ramón's sister-in-law, Margarita, with four children and married to a very wealthy and corrupt public accountant, was thrown out of her house in Guayaquil and replaced by a younger girl. What Margarita ended up with after twelve years of marriage was a herd of nine cows; she kept them in Quinindé on one of several farms that her husband owned, and her husband told her to get them off the property. She hired a truck and brought them to us and asked us to pasture them for her. But we had no extra grass, and so Ramón arranged to put them under Jorge's responsibility on the Cortez property. As payment for caring for them Jorge would receive half the calf crop. We bought him a hundred-pound roll of barbed wire for a start.

This whole arrangement, which had been suddenly and rapidly consummated, was like a benediction from heaven. It was the kind of dramatic and open-handed gesture that Ramón loved to make, and this one was especially gratifying since he was risking nothing of his own. All three of the brothers were electrified into violent action; their luck had changed. They strung three strands of new fence up the hill, cut down trees and burned new ground for planting, planted another patch of plátano around their mother's house, and even cleared a nice little area on a sandy bench of good land above the river where they then planted several hundred pineapples that we gave them. Arcario asked for extra work in the afternoon, some special little contract cleaning weeds, so that he could buy a horse. Even their mother, whom we had scarcely ever seen, came to the house and asked for work. She was prematurely aged, toothless and half blind, and she had a punched in kind of nose, almost no nose at all but for the flaring nostrils like two black holes. She was timid and dazed by her trip across the river and by the crowds of people (five or six) who moved around the store. We put her out with the other women hoeing peanuts. We were proud of her and scarcely resented that in two months she never learned how to distinguish between a peanut plant and a weed; really it didn't matter. She never learned how to use the hoe either, regarding it apparently as a new kind of hammer with which one beat the weeds to death. The whole family was filled with a new elation as they saw themselves moving up close to that ultimate goal, one which until now had seemed years away. They had heard, as had everyone here, about Pedro Tello, who sixty years ago had started out with one cow and before he died had the greatest fortune in the province. Well, of course, they had no plans like that, but it didn't seem unrealistic to dream of building, little by little, a herd of maybe thirty cows and never, never again having to hire themselves out as day laborers.

They were a perfect communist family, held together by the equal contributions that they made and dominated by Jorge, the eldest, who it now turned out was fatally flawed. He had been not too secretly in love with a second woman for some time, and he usually spent his weekends in another little village down the road. But now he was going to be rich, everything was going his way, and there was no reason to wait any longer. Flushed and confused he brought Adelina to his house and installed her as his second wife. Three months after the Cortez brothers had swum the cows across the river — the cows' heads roped to the sides of a large borrowed canoe — the whole intricate structure of their communal life began to crumble. Well, so even clowns can fall in love, and clowns can keep on making jokes while their hearts are being torn to pieces.

We suspected nothing for some time, gulled into security by the mask of Jorge's unchanging affability. We knew about the new girl, of course. He had brought her down the road one Sunday and showed her off briefly at the store. She was just a child, very beautiful, very clean and prim with her Indian hair tightly woven into two shoulder-length pigtails. Meeting her I was shocked at the idea of their coupling. She was so young and tiny, her face still bland and without character, Jorge so tall and overpowering beside her. It seemed like an outrage against nature, impossible and perverse, somehow incestuous. She didn't speak or look at anyone. She was, apparently, a well-trained country girl. She carried her clothes in a small bundle wrapped in leaves, and she crossed over to the other side looking small and helpless, only her head visible as she squatted in the bottom of the canoe that Jorge paddled, standing tall and triumphant in the stern. Things were quiet for about a month and then one day we heard that Jorge had lost control of himself the night before and had smashed his fist into his first wife's face and broken her nose. The family was breaking up; they had been quarreling over the ownership of eight chickens and two cooking pots. The same day that we heard the news on our side of the river she left her house, passed by the store with her swollen face and frightened eyes, and went back to wherever she had come from. Jorge kept two of the children, and the youngest, who was still nursing, went with her mother. Another two months passed quietly. There was no change in Jorge's smiling face and placid manner when he came across the river each morning, nothing to hint that, in the destruction of his family and in the installation of that shy girl as the head of his house — that shy girl who completely understood her power over him and who was now using it with all the spiteful and obsessive insistence of a spoiled child — his life was no longer tranquil and had in fact become a torment.

And now he fell sick, perhaps with some terrible and confusing combination of love, guilt, regret, and malaria. He tried to keep on working, because now more than ever he needed money for new dresses and golden earrings, but at times he could scarcely walk to work, let alone do anything when he got there. Some days he sent word across with Amado and Arcario that he simply didn't have the strength to get out of bed, and we half believed him but thought that he probably wanted to stay on the other side to take care of his animals.

From the house, in the late afternoons, I could look across the river and see the cows pasted bright as cutouts against the slowly fading green of the hillside; from time to time, as the river lowered with the dry season and sandy beaches and gravel bars edged the stream, I would watch the cows heading languidly upstream, pausing to mouth the water and to gaze out placidly at the river glittering in the sun. They would disappear in the high grass that hid Ascensión's or Pedro's plátano, shortly to be driven out, feigning terror, by furious shouts. The neighbors were jealous and resentful of the Cortez luck; they didn't like the idea of living poor beside this family that was now in the process of shaming them all with its new barbed-wire fences, plantings of pineapples, herds of cattle, and a brand new, two-room chicken house of split bamboo built above the ground. The news came back one day that someone had macheted off one of the cow's tails and slashed open a great wound on her hip. Ramón, at Arcario's request, crossed over with medicine to kill the maggots breeding in the putrefying flesh; he was angry at the way things were turning out since he was ultimately responsible to his sister-in-law for the care of her animals. Jorge was sitting in bright sunshine in the doorway of his house with a bedspread tightly wrapped around him; he was soaked in sweat.

"How are you feeling?" Ramón asked.

"*Tres cuartos regular,*" Jorge said, trying to smile. "About three quarters so-so."

"Are you taking Aralen?"

"Not yet. I was planning to send Arcario on Saturday to buy medicine for me and the cow; we are both in a sad way."

"Well, I'll tell you frankly," Ramón said, "I'm not too enchanted being sent across the river to cure animals that you're supposed to be curing." Jorge didn't say anything. "Who did it?" Ramón asked.

"How can one tell in a place like this," Jorge said. "We're surrounded by evil people."

"Somebody said something about Marcelo."

"Yes, why not?" Jorge said. "He's just like his brother Uldarico. Perfectly capable of macheteing a poor innocent creature. But who can say for sure?"

"But why Marcelo?" Ramón asked. "Have the cows wandered upstream that far?"

"It's turning into a very dry summer, Don Ramón; the grass is suffering for some sweet hard rains. And besides, Marcelo and Socrates are claiming the abandoned Tierra Nueva pastures for their horses."

"My God," Ramón said, appalled, "you're running out of feed."

"Have you ever seen it so dry?"

"Oh, my God," Ramón said, "you're going to blow it. You're going to blow the whole thing."

"Don *Ramón,*" Jorge said, gently rebuking his hard words.

"Arcario says you're out of salt."

"Yes, the cows are very anxious about that."

"More anxious than you, apparently," Ramón said sarcastically. "*Carajo,* you're letting a cow die with maggots, you can't keep your cows on your property, you haven't even got any feed for them. Couldn't you make a great effort, one of the three of you, and give them a little salt?"

"They had salt, Ramón," Jorge said. "We're just out of it for the moment."

"Yes," Ramón said, "the ten pounds I loaned you four months ago. Let me congratulate you, Jorge; you're quite a cowboy."

He left abruptly and, with the coiled rope hanging over one shoulder, climbed up the almost bare hill to where the cows were standing against the fence, contemplating the neighbor's greener pastures. They were large tame animals who had once been milked, and the wounded cow stood there quietly as Ramón roped and treated her. When he had finished he was too angry even to speak to Jorge, and he cut down away from the house to the river and the canoe. The cows were covered with ticks and *nuches,* those worms that knotted the sides of the animals and burst finally into great, bloody, spreading sores. It was apparent that no one had bathed the cows with Neguvon for months. That night he instructed Ester to write a note to her sister telling her what was happening and asking her to please make other arrangements.

In the next four days the family was dispersed and brought down brutally, as in some Bible story. The very next morning before work Arcario got me alone outside the store, told me he realized it wasn't Saturday yet, but could I please pay him off. He was leaving. He had a brother-in-law with a farm up the road about forty kilometers toward Quinindé, and he wanted to hop on the bus today and see if he could get a job planting pasture.

"Nobody's planting pasture now," I said. "Have you lost your mind?" Arcario shrugged his shoulders and, smiling sadly, stared at the ground. "But *why,*" I cried. "What the hell's wrong with you, the whole bunch of you?" Arcario shrugged again, spread his hands out in front of him, popped open his eyes, and arched his eyebrows. He was explaining everything, but I was too stupid to understand.

"Tell me, Arcario," I said. "What's happening around here?"

"*Nalga,*" Arcario said. The word means buttock and is a kind of funny play on the word *nada* used when things threaten to get too serious.

"What about the cows? Don't you want them? Why have you created this total disaster? You're not stupid, Arcario."

He stared at me very hard for a moment and then looked around to see that we were still alone. He lowered his voice. "This is just between the two of us." Then he stopped talking and stared at the ground again. "No," he said finally, "I'd better not."

"For God's sake, Arcario."

"Oh, *shit,*" he said after a very long pause. "It's the girl. Please, don't tell anyone. She's making up to me."

"What girl? What are you talking about?"

"Adelina," Arcario said. "Jorge's woman, that *bitch*. She's screwing everything up."

"Is she in love with you?"

"She's not in love with anybody; she just likes to play with Jorge to make him jealous; she's got him half crazy, and I don't know where it's going to end. But you're not to talk about this to anyone — you hear? Not even to Ramón. Anyway, I'm getting out."

"Jorge beat up the wrong woman," I said.

By the time Arcario got back two days later with the promise of a job and packed his things and his wife, Susana, up to the highway and left again for good, Jorge out of some desperation that was never explained to us had once more lost control and had beaten up Adelina, his second woman. She left him and went back to live with her family. A few days later, not even trying to smile anymore and with the beginnings of a dead and disoriented look in his eyes, Jorge went chasing after her. While he was gone the abandoned cows wandered up to Tierra Nueva and two more of them got slashed across the hips with a machete. We rounded up Margarita's cows and swam them across the river and put them to grazing with ours. After a time Jorge came back with Adelina, but things were different now. She hated that great brooding boring jungle on the other side, where no one ever danced or had fun or had music to listen to or interesting people to visit with; she would never cross the river again into that mess of in-laws. If Jorge really loved her and wanted her back he would get a job on a farm near the highway where there was life, music, people, a little excitement that one could look forward to. She wasn't ever going back to squatting in a jungle hut all day, taking care of someone else's babies with no one to talk to but herself and where nothing ever happened and where by ten o'clock in the morning you were holding yourself back, fighting with yourself not to start tearing out your hair and screaming, screaming with boredom.

So Jorge quit us, too. He got a job as a cowboy on Umberto Bone's farm a mile up the river, and they both went up there to live. Until it was stolen Bone had a phonograph, and, on Saturday nights, as long as people bought drinks he would play music for them. Jorge had been with us for a long time and we owed him several thousand sucres in severance pay. We deducted the roll of barbed wire, a thing he didn't like very much because he had promised to buy Adelina a three-band radio with the extra money that we owed him. Soon after that he took the fence down and from time to time sold us cut up pieces when he needed a little extra cash; there was a good deal of bad feeling between Jorge and Ramón, and I don't imagine we paid him much. The hillside and the pineapples went back to weeds, the chicken house rotted, for by this time even Amado had found himself a woman and had moved away to Ube, up the river two hours on the trail.

Amado the Beloved. He was the youngest brother and the dumbest of the four, and maybe being caressed all day long every day for eighteen years with a name like Beloved, his whole life took on the qualities of a mild hallucination. In his own mind he lived with the conviction that he *was* beloved, that he had been chosen out of everybody else to be cherished, and that everyone was interested in protecting him from life's blows. I guess that to the extent that any of us on the river was capable of a pure disinterested love his ideas about himself were true; at least no one took the trouble to gain that little moment of pleasure by disillusioning him. There was something soft, endearing, and cuddly about him. He had no forehead; a great pile of curls cascaded down, almost obscuring his eyes, and when someone spoke his name, Beloved, his eyes behind long girlish curling lashes would go all soft and yielding as though he had been touched and squeezed with loving hands. He was Male's baby panda, its teddy bear, this extremely simple kid who expected nothing petty or evil of people and, who, it seemed to me, by demanding affection received a little less crap than the rest of us.

Had he been given his share of brains? Possibly not. It was hard to figure out Amado. He had grown up behind the insulating wall of his protective brothers. He had never had to make those morally difficult decisions that would have compromised his ideals or diminished his humanity or made him question his own good- ness. He wasn't scarred by anything that he had ever done. In a sense you could say that, untouched by life, he had no character at all. He believed completely in his brothers. He believed, for in- stance, that it was bad for your lungs to masturbate, that it made you weak and ultimately crazy. I'm pretty sure, without of course being able to prove it, that he had decided to be just like his brothers and never to succumb to this childish vice; in those months, much later than most, when his sexual needs exploded and dominated his life, it must have been a difficult time for him. He talked about masturbation obsessively, boring everyone with his incessant tales of tuberculosis and madness. He must have been under terrible pressure, because four months after Arcario, at eighteen, took Susana as his woman, Amado in a burst of il- lumination, realizing that once again his brothers had shown him the way and that he didn't have to suffer any more, got himself a woman too, and ran off with her. He was seventeen and she was almost thirty, what Kinsey would regard as a perfect combination, these two hot people at the peak of their capacities. Well, Amado cheerfully sang his songs of love and ambled behind his brothers, who charted the way, cleared the trails, knocked the snakes aside, and cut down the looping vines and spiny branches that might have brushed his face. He was the beloved baby brother for whom nice things were done. Perhaps growing up before one has to is the real stupidity; maybe he was the smartest one of all. I don't know; it was hard to tell about Amado.

Almost every time I decided that he was kind of dumb and cloddish he would do or say something that would force me completely to reconstruct him in my imagination. For example: until someone pushed it out a window at one of Ramón's triannual birthday parties, we had a cheap battery-run phonograph. For about a month while the Cortez brothers were all together on the farm (we had put Amado to taking care of the pigs) I tried to make a music-lover out of Ramón, and at dinner I would play and replay certain records that I felt, with repetition, he might learn to enjoy. For a week we listened to Bartók's "Miraculous Mandarin." We were at that period deeply troubled by Dalmiro, and the terrible drive and beat of that barbaric music about a man who couldn't die because of love reminded me of Dalmiro's insane and unquenchable searching. Connecting that music with Dalmiro was a mistake; it offended Ramón's poetic sensibilities; he hated the music; it was all endless, squalid, brutal noise that pained his ears. For a few evenings I played him the last scene of Poulenc's opera *Dialogues des Carmélites*. This was one of the few records I had had in Rioverde and it was therefore doubly traumatic for me to listen to now. Hearing it I would be swept back to those desperate years in that disintegrating ocean village, and I relived those nights when — completely isolated from the world, crouched over a tiny phonograph, the windows tightly shut so that the wind would not blow out the single candle that lit the room, that lit the whole town — I listened, unbearably moved by this unbearably intense and tragic music that literally paralyzed me and seemed to crystallize my deepest feelings about man's hopeless condition. In time, I think, Ramón rather enjoyed the music. He shuddered with delight at the sound of the guillotine as it cut down the singers one by one, that coldly slicing sound that cut off an ecstatic song in the very middle of a note.

But I couldn't handle this music every night. It was too personal, and I had been programmed to overreact to its power. I felt foolish in front of Ramón when my eyes filled with tears and my throat so tightened and choked that I couldn't speak — like the only man in a crowded theater who suddenly breaks into loud and heart-rending sobs while everyone else is mildly enjoying a piquant scene of sadism. I thought we might get someplace with Falla's *El Amor Brujo,* and so for a week we played it at dinner each night. No luck. Ramón liked parts of it, but he was embarrassed by the quality of a highly trained human voice. This was pretentiousness. The soaring notes of a woman's voice hurt his ears and reminded him of nothing so much as a hog being slaughtered. But this music, which to me was the very soul of Spain and the very essence of Spanish art, completely captivated Amado, who had first heard it on the store bench and who after that every evening would crouch in the bushes outside the dining room where he could better hear it and who finally, when we had passed on to something else or maybe given the idea up entirely, came to me and asked me if I would play that wonderful music again for it was the most beautiful music he had ever heard and made him want to cry; it had made, he said with amazement — as though for the first time in his life he had been devastated and transfigured by the power of art — the hair stand up all over his body with goose flesh.

Was he dumb or not? I guess not. He certainly knew how to handle us; he was one of the most inept workers we ever had, yet we never once seriously considered firing him. He had worked us into a corner by making us feel that he regarded us more as friends than employers and that as friends we would never be gross enough to terminate a relationship that gave all of us such satisfaction. Isn't it one of our nicest qualities as human beings that we so often give in to that impulse to do what is expected of us?

When he left us finally and ran away with that woman, who down here would have been old enough to have been his mother, even this act which in another would have seemed almost irrational took on a kind of grandeur that filled all of us with admiration. He hadn't just stolen any woman or any man's woman; he had stolen Pedro Nazareno's woman, one of the local beauties, the object of everyone's lust and the wife of the biggest, most virile, most respected man in the whole area. It was as if Cheta, the monkey, had wooed and won Jane away from Tarzan or as if Woody Allen had stolen away Burton's Taylor. Amado, Male's very own teddy bear, Male's very own beloved Grizzly. The king of the mountain.

If Amado only had a four-month period of suffering between boyhood and marriage, it was Arcario who did Amado's suffering for him. They were both what the shrinks would call extremely late bloomers; almost all the way through their teens they had believed that those little dangling teeter-weeters were there simply to tee-tee out of. They were both from that innocent side of the river where, until they came across to work for us and became a part of those tiger packs of youths who prowled the trails on weekends and desolately hung around those salones of split bamboo that stank of urine and vomit, they had lived like two Huck Finns, a part of the river's life, where they fished and swam, and the jungle, where they roamed all day hunting for *guantas* with their dogs. Arcario joined the pack, learned how to drink up to three bottles of beer without passing out, learned how to ask a girl to dance and how to ply her with little pieces of hard mint candies or bottles of Pepsi. He felt nervous and tormented but he didn't know just why, and then after some months he had an experience that shook him to his depths and, until he straightened it all out in his mind, filled him with a kind of lovely horror made up of everything: yearning, revulsion, wonder, and resentment.

Arcario and four other boys, half drunk and giggling, had followed behind an older woman on her way home from a dance. It was very early in the morning and she was drunk, too, having put away a considerable quantity of beer. They were following her as a last hope; she had a reputation as a woman of capricious and unpredictable moods who sometimes sold her favors cheaply to young men. She walked heavily up the trail, humming to herself, elaborately pretending not to know that she was being followed; immediately upon climbing the ladder and entering her house she went into the kitchen area, squatted over a small hole in the floor, and began to piss down into the middle of that group of stunned youngsters who were gathered on the hard-packed earth beneath her, planning their next move. For a moment she was silent; then she began to hum again and laugh softly to herself. Two of the boys had flashlights which they now directed upwards toward that awesome double hole that held a double darkness like a black blazing sun, that was at the heart of all the painful yearning that had begun to twist them, that left them sweating and sleepless on the mats in their family's huts and on Saturdays drove them to wandering the trails like damned souls. Arcario's eyes were popping out of his head; another epiphany for a Cortez brother. He wasn't quite old enough to handle this as the rather ugly little joke it was intended to be, this coarse insolence that was intended to put them in their places: pissed on.

Amado was working in the hog pens where we had the mill set up to grind corn and where I went to prepare feed for the pigs and for Celso Corea's chickens. Now in the late afternoons after work Arcario would join us, waiting for Amado to finish up so that they could cross the river together. Maybe influenced by Amado, Arcario had also decided that in spite of my being both white and rich I was a kind of friendly presence in front of whom he could speak frankly. So for some days, highly diverted and plunged at times into my own private confusions, I listened to his discourse on "the pissing woman" and watched him in that short time begin to dominate the complications that had been brought about by the sudden awakening of his sexuality. Her identity was really never important to any of the participants — or to any of us who participated secondhand. She didn't represent any particular woman, but Woman, herself, in the roles of whore, temptress, shameless destroyer, bringer of wars and conflict, cunt, that horrifying hole into which man, helplessly drawn, pours out the pathetic offering of his potential. For Arcario, now and forever the veil of mystery and romance was lifted. It was the piss pouring out of that hole that knocked him out; it was the double function of that pearly mechanism that cut down and dissolved his fantasies. "Floods of piss," he said. "My God, it seemed to go on for hours, we kept looking up into that blackness, you could see everything, the lips of it and all the little knobs and dials, buttons and bows, and the thick brush of hair with the little drops of piss shining in it like jewels. And the piss pouring out, my God, ten gallons, twenty gallons, forty gallons, just like a horse, a stream as thick and twisted as a rope, an endless stream that splashed on the ground like a cloudburst, like a heavy downpour in the jungle pounding on the leaves, drumming, splashing all over us and wetting us up to the knees. And it was a miracle that it was only to the knees because I thought before she got through, maybe about noontime, we would all be swept away in that flood, swept down into the river and lost forever, carried out to sea."

"And then what happened?" Amado asked, panting, great drops of steaming sweat suddenly breaking out in beautiful symmetry all over his nose, as if he were being temporarily and painlessly tatooed for his rites of passage.

"Well, then she dropped a big board over the hole and went to bed and five minutes later we could hear her snoring."

"And then what happened?" Amado said finally.

"Well, nothing. We just stood there kind of dazed, staring at each other as though the whole house had fallen on us."

"And then?" Amado asked, beginning to laugh almost hysterically.

"And *then?* Nalga. We went back to the dance."

"You know, in a case like that and even if it *is* very bad for your lungs . . ." Amado began.

"Hermano, don't talk *pendejadas*," Arcario interrupted impatiently. "We were in another country."

He had seen something breathtakingly simple that, before then, had seemed so complicated; it slowly but forever crystallized his feelings about love and the limited extent to which man might safely wander into madness looking for it. He was like someone with a secret, as though he alone had been shown the very face of God, as though he alone now knew that God was not supposed to be worshiped but to be played with in a perpetual and joyous game. He was like me with my secret about death's beauty. For about ten days, like a drugged man, he contemplated his role in the sexual game. When he had it all clear in his mind he decided to move out boldly and dominate a simpler world, the world that was now stripped of sentimentality and illusion. On Saturday after we had paid off the men, he rushed across the river, bathed and changed his clothes, and came rushing back again with Chango, his best friend. They were both dressed in their Saturday clothes, bright colored shirts so starched they could have stood alone, striped flaring pants pressed razor sharp. Arcario's hair was oiled and perfumed and combed back and forth into a chaos of curls and bewildering geological phenomena. He got me alone because I was a soft touch beside Ramón and borrowed an extra 100 sucres. Chango, who was a year younger but more experienced in such things, had promised to take him to a little workingman's whorehouse that he knew. Arcario had promised to pay Chango's way too, a guide's fee for that first dizzying ascent.

"Get a good one," I told him. "Don't try to save money on some old whore with gonorrhea."

"Don't worry," Arcario said. "I'm going to go first class; I'm prepared to go as high as two dollars."

I didn't run into him again until late Monday when he came in from work. Coming down the road, he grinned broadly when he saw me and did a few swooningly lascivious dance steps in the mud.

"Apparently everything went O.K.," I said.

"O.K.?" he almost yelled. "Why didn't anybody ever *tell* me it was so wonderful. Wonderful? It was *magnificent*. It was just absolutely the best thing that's ever happened to me. My God, when I think of what I've been missing."

"They don't know it," I said, "but that's why little boys want to be big boys. And so now I suppose you'll be going back to Esmeraldas Saturday."

"Well, no," Arcario said. "As a matter of fact I've been thinking about getting married."

"To anybody in particular?"

"Well, yes, sort of, as a matter of fact, but I don't know her name. Listen, Martín, I was just coming down to look for you. Do me a great favor, will you? I want you to write a letter for me to this girl I met up the river a few months ago. I think I'm sort of stuck on her."

"With the typewriter?"

"Claro."

"Right this minute?"

"Claro."

We went over to the house, and I put a piece of paper in the machine with a flourish and waited for inspiration . . . Finally I asked, "What do you want to say? It's kind of hard to start when you don't know her name, especially since you're proposing marriage."

"Yes," Arcario said. "Well, start it, '*mi querida,* my dear.' "

I typed that and waited a few more minutes. " 'My dear,' " he said again and sat there frowning, thinking deeply and seriously, and then he said, shrugging his shoulders and looking helpless, " 'would you like to fuck me?' "

"Hombre!" I said.

"Well, help me; give me an idea; this is my first love letter."

"O.K. 'My dearest, my angel from heaven. The thought of you fills all my waking hours; at night I dream only of you and of your beauty.' "

"Simón!" Arcario cried, jumping up from his chair and dancing around the room. "Yes, yes, yes. Write that down just the way you said it."

I wrote it down just the way I had said it, at age fifty-seven a successful writer at last. And now, carried away and soaring, we finally got to the point, that he was about to build his own house and wanted her to come and live with him. It was probably the first love letter ever written from the coastal jungles that hadn't started out, "I send greetings to you and your family with the hope that all are in the best of health. All of us here are feeling fine. Having stated the above I now wish to state the following: . . ."

Arcario signed it, we put it into an airmail envelope, and he carefully folded it into his breast pocket, next to his heart. As he was getting ready to leave I asked, "Is she really the one you like?"

"Claro," he said. "At least, I think she's the easiest one to get. She's living up there with her aunt, and they don't get along too well; I think she'd like to leave. She's pretty, a good girl about twelve years old . . ."

"No, Arcario, you don't want a twelve-year-old girl. They're not ready yet for that kind of life, managing your house and cooking and washing and all. They're too innocent."

"She's not so innocent," Arcario said. "She already has one child."

So that was how Arcario got married. Ah, the power of the written word to set the heartstrings zinging.

As it turned out, he slept with the girl before he gave her the letter, which perhaps made its message redundant. And actually, it wasn't the girl to whom he had originally directed the letter who finally received it. It was Susana, his next-door neighbor, who got the letter. She may have it yet among her treasures, still unread, still in all likelihood unopened, since neither she nor anyone else in the family nor any of her neighbors can read a word.

In that same week that Chango's mother and father left the river for a week and Chango brought Dalmiro's Theresa across the river to stay with him as his private whore in the almost empty house, he mentioned to his best friend, Arcario, that his sister Susana was still in the house with him and that she had mentioned more than once that she was sort of taken with Arcario. Why didn't he come over in the evenings after supper and kind of hang around and love his sister up and see what happened? Disgraceful Chango, our local, limping, seventeen-year-old pimp, now pimping for his sister. For two nights Arcario loved her up with increasing élan, and on the third night she told him he could sleep there in the house if he wanted to, as long as he left before the first light, when the neighbors might catch him sneaking down the ladder. Susana was about a year older than Arcario and a tremendously big girl who outweighed him by at least sixty pounds. She was formidable, and perhaps, as it soon turned out, the only girl on the river who could have stood up to Arcario's ardor.

Arcario told me about it three days later. About ten o'clock one morning he came out of the field where I was running the disk up and down between the rows of coconuts. He wanted to explain that he hadn't been to work for three days because he had been sick. Well, yes, I believed him; he looked awful.

"What's wrong with you?"

He told me what was wrong with him, grinning like a fool. He had been on his honeymoon, he said, and things had sort of gotten out of control. Between nine and five A.M. he had done it to her eight times. He hadn't left the house at dawn as promised because, well, because to tell the truth he didn't think he could have climbed down the ladder without falling.

"Holy *shit*," I said. "Eight times? But why?"

"Well," Arcario said, "why *not*?

Transfixed with awe and love I studied Arcario Cortez as he

leaned against the tractor to keep from falling. His eyes were sunken and glassy, his long fingers trembled, he seemed newly emaciated, scourged, and rendered. Still, it was possible that he would live. And what heroic words had tumbled from his lips, made more beautiful by his black modesty. He was another Sir Edmund Hillary who — without ropes or tanks of oxygen or snacks of cheese or chocolate, without Sherpa guides or sponsorship from the National Geographic Society, all on his own with nothing but youthful grit — now stood alone on his solitary peak, every bit as exhausted and triumphant as Hillary himself. "Why not? She was there."

8

SANTO AND THE PEANUT PICKERS

FOR PERIODS of a few seconds, probably less than half a dozen times in all my adult life, a certain combination of light, sound, color, or scent will suddenly, magically, mesh with some part of my sleeping awareness. For apparently no reason I experience one of those fantastic Joycean epiphanies in which my senses expand and harmonize in an immense and enveloping reality. It is almost religious, almost sexual, and certainly mystical. Perhaps this vision, more common in more gifted people, forms the foundation of great art; it is like the flash of ecstasy that Dostoyevsky would experience just before an epileptic fit. For a moment one sees with the eyes of Van Gogh or understands with Blake that the whole universe exists in a blade of grass.

Late one evening bringing the tractor down the lane from disking weeds all day — the sky lemon-yellow and dotted with the first incredibly bright tropical stars — I felt an apprehension beginning to build like a promise. It was like an intimation of something overwhelming that was just about to happen and which I would be at the very center of. I was moving down to the last hill between pasture and plantings of young cacao trees, and the last of the light gave to the green and orange leaves of the chocolate a violent quality, so unreal, vibrating, and intense that I stopped the tractor. Now my eyes, which had begun to see everything, settled on a small nest almost hidden behind brightly glowing leaves. It was smaller than an orange, intricately constructed, and camouflaged with pieces of some white substance that looked like bark or lichen; it glistened and sparkled like a jewel under a beam of light, or more truly, like a jewel about to be dissolved into pure light by a laser beam. I don't know how I got off the tractor, but I was standing at the nest, staring at it in amazement, as a feeling of what I can only describe as grace swept up and crashed over me like an ocean breaker . . . and the moment slipped away as quickly as it had come. It had lasted less than ten seconds, but it was one of the most important events in my life. If I were more oriented toward religion I would probably have seen Christ's face among those leaves, and perhaps at this moment I would be writing a book about the glory of God.

The nest held two eggs, each the size of a pea, and a jeweled and glowing hummingbird, its throat made of rubies, its body made of greenish gold, sat in the upper branches of the tree and calmly watched me. That nest became very important for me then, and almost every day I would visit it, study the texture of its camouflaged exterior, check out the eggs, admire the neat and clever way the inside had been lined and woven with soft things — kapok, feathers, and hair. And I tried to use it as a catalyst to dive once more into that flooding, overflowing sensation of having been forgiven everything and of having stood for those few seconds, transfigured, as naked as those leaves, as honest as that sky, as profound as those stars, as close to the center of life as that nest and the watching, flaming bird.

The eggs hatched; a couple of times a week I would take Ramón's children out to the cacao planting and hold them up to the nest so that they could admire its tiny perfection. Their delight, their clear vision seemed to be an echo of what I had been allowed to glimpse. When some touring Peace Corps volunteers stopped by, I showed them as much of the farm as could be seen from the road and then took them to the nest; it became my major tourist attraction.

One afternoon at quitting time, driving down the lane with Ramón and Santo — one of our workers and an old friend from Rioverde — I stopped near the tree. "Come on," I said, "I want to show you something *fantástico*." Ramón and Santo stood before the nest, studying the birds, who by this time had begun to bloom like flowers, their fat nakedness enclosed in gaudy coats of mail. No one said anything, but as we turned to leave I caught

Ramón and Santo exchanging the most secret and complicated kind of glances: Santo's incessantly smiling face suddenly thoughtful and melancholy; Ramón's, disdainful, debauched, suppressing a ribald smile.

"What's so funny between you and Santo and the hummingbirds?" I asked Ramón at dinner.

"Why, nothing," Ramón said, but he looked at me with the admiration one gives a detective who has discovered something hidden beneath the surface of things.

"Oh, come on," I said. "All those funny looks? And then those giggles? It didn't mean *anything?*"

"No, nothing," Ramón said. "It's a secret between us, you understand? Something Santo told me in confidence; I'll tell you about it later."

"Some secret about hummingbirds, for God's sake?"

"Jesus," Ramón said, "you want to know *everything,* don't you?"

"Those are *my* hummingbirds," I said. "And I don't understand why they're so funny."

"O.K., O.K.," Ramón said. "Look, there is this belief in the jungle where we grew up together that if you eat the heart of a hummingbird it will so enflame you with passion that all your life you'll be, well, a special kind of macho — *arecho, listo.* You understand?"

I thought I understood, since the two words are among the most commonly used on the coast and in their sexual usage mean "aroused" or "horny." I laughed. "Do you believe it?"

"What? That after eating a hummingbird's heart a man could go through life with a perpetual erection, in a constant state of sexual frenzy?" And then just before he said, "No, of course, I don't believe it," his face grew thoughtful, and after a moment he said, laughing, "But in a manner of speaking that's a description of Santo, isn't it? Maybe there's something to it."

"Has Santo eaten the heart of a hummingbird?"

"When he was sixteen," Ramón said. "And, my God, it wasn't just one, it was two."

We ate for a while in stunned silence thinking of this terrible and powerful medicine, and then Ramón, the Latin macho, but only half serious, said, "Maybe when I was a baby someone cooked up one for me, too; that's the way I feel sometimes."

"Yes," I said, "maybe we've all eaten hummingbirds' hearts, but let an old man reassure you, *jovencito,* the effect wears off with time, the effect wears off with time."

"Ay, *caramba,*" Ramón said. "*Pobrecito.*"

When I stopped by to check out the nest a couple of days later, it was empty. Either the birds had grown up and flown away or something out there, a snake or a hawk had destroyed them. In a way I was glad they were gone, for they represented a kind of responsibility that I didn't know how to handle.

It wasn't until months later, when Santo had left the farm and gone back to Rioverde for a time, that Ramón felt free to tell me about him and about that most shameful and secret thing that can happen to a man. I was amazed that Santo had confessed a thing so personal to another man, for as he told me, my cheeks began to burn as I remembered that thirty years before, on my honeymoon, for Christ's sake, I had had the same problem, and I hadn't mentioned it to anyone but a doctor for at least ten years. But this revelation reopened for speculation the actual fate of those two young birds in whom I had been so interested. I'll never be able to prove it, but I'm convinced now that it was Santo who, the day that I revealed them hidden in the chocolate tree, sneaked back in the night, lifted them out of the nest, slashed open their breasts, and consumed their hearts.

If Jorge was destroyed by love, the arrow of love that pierced him was an almost accidental hit. Santo on the other hand lived in the front lines, where the arrows flew thickest. He rushed back and forth, boldly outlined against the sky, stripped to the skin, trying to get in the way of every arrow and yipping with joy when struck. Being in love, that was what life was all about, being in love. There was nothing else that mattered. How ridiculous he became finally, this clown of love who learned nothing as he grew older and who repeated his mistakes over and over, this last romantic, this man made foolish by women, this lovesick fool as moony-eyed at forty as at sixteen. At what age, one wonders, does innocence, that precious quality, the essence of youth, become stupidity?

Ramón and Santo had grown up together in Rioverde, and they were friends after a fashion; they had common memories. Santo was a few years older and, having been driven into extreme situations by passion, had a slightly wider experience of life's vices. I don't think he really liked Ramón much; his interests were so narrow and concentrated that he was incapable of friendship with a man. This may be one reason why, ultimately, Ramón liked Santo — he needed nothing from Ramón except a job.

Years before Santo came to the farm, when I was first learning Spanish in Rioverde, Ramón had spent months telling me stories about the people and the town. Some of the stories about Santo had been very funny, and they had always lived in my mind as precise descriptions of that very special relationship Santo had with his women.

This is one of the stories that I remember Ramón telling me: Santo and Crucelio were brothers and lived up the beach by the point where at low tide the women gathered from town to break oysters from the rocks and where the men caught lobsters in pools during the equinoctial tides when all the rocks around the point lay exposed and isolated in their little moats of water. There was someone named Sanchez, too — I don't remember who he was — and there was the mother and a couple of handsome sisters with their lovers. They all lived in the same house. It had one big room and a small kitchen with floors of split bamboo and was built almost on the beach, at the bottom of a steep hill where a ravine (full of gold nuggets some said) cut down out of the jungle and where, in the winter months, water ran. A couple of old broken canoes, supported above the ground by short stakes, sat in front of the house in the salt grass and were usually thinly filled with drying shrimp or salted fish during the long, dry summer months. At night the house was cooled by the offshore breeze that flowed down the hill like a river. All night long a little lamp made of a coffee can stuffed with a rag and filled with kerosene burned in the kitchen window. If one were fishing off the point one used that faintly flickering light and another lamp that burned in the house of Norco, a mile down the beach, to triangulate one's position in the world. (Norco's light was no sure thing like Santo's; he was a middle-aged alcoholic who precisely measured his catch each day and spent exactly 50 percent on aguardiente.

Ten fish or two fish, half the catch went to his wife — except, Ramón told me, if there was only one fish he might sometimes divide it into halves three or four times.)

Santo's house was so crowded with people that there were many days when there was very little to eat and no money at all to buy food. Poor people don't worry about tomorrow; all of life's problems can be squeezed into one day. Fishing was bad or the waves were too rough for their small canoes or a five-day fiesta arrived and everyone danced and drank to the last limits of their diminishing strength. Or children sickened and had to be rushed into Esmeraldas or to Florinda for injections of penicillin, or for iron, vitamins, or blood plasma. But on top of these normal crises that afflicted everyone in the town, there was another more serious, more destructive family flaw. There was no unity, no sense of family obligation. It wasn't only Santo who was the great lover in that house; they were all prisoners of the lusting passions, each of them so possessed by one lover that they had no emotion left for each other.

So when Santo and Crucelio, nineteen and twenty years old respectively, both fell in love at the same time and brought their women into the great family house, new sounds began to be superimposed over the night sounds and night rhythms in that quaking trembling house of lovers, over the squeals and sighs and the heavy breathings and the squeaking of the bamboo floor, the faint sound of tender whispers, wet smackings, delighted outraged giggles. The new sound was the sound of paper sacks being torn, ever so slowly, secretly, and crackers being snapped and quietly munched or the snapping sound of *cocada,* hard chunks of brown sugar and coconut, being broken into pieces beneath the covers. And at times the whole house would float on the cloudy vapors of fresh country cheese, as someone in bed broke a chunk into pieces, flooding the house with an aroma like some great epic fart. And now the loveless children, piled and abandoned in one corner of the house, were subjected to a second orgy, one they could understand, and they would whimper and complain with hunger, and the room would be filled with angry jealous conversations.

"Hey, hombre, what are you doing over there anyway, eating crackers?"

"Hell, no, brother, what's got into you?"

"Listen, don't shit me. I can smell, can't I? And what's that crackly noise. Hombre, you're eating *crackers,* and you're eating *cheese.*"

"Cheese? Now where would I get cheese? Brother, you're out of your mind. Ask Negra, here. Negra, are we eating crackers and cheese?"

"I swear to God, lover, we're not eating *anything.*"

"Negra, you're both lying. Your mouth's so full you can hardly talk. Well, O.K., O.K., if that's the way you want it, sneaking around, eating at night in front of your mother, your sisters. *Está bien, está bien.*"

"Oh, shit, brother, and weren't you both stuffing your mouths with cocada last night when you thought we were asleep?"

"*Mentira, mentira, mentira.*" Lies, lies, lies.

Last night, ready to write this down, I thought I would tell it first to Ramón who, ten years before, had told the story to me. I wanted to get all the names straight and have him fill in any details that I'd forgotten, and I wanted to offer him my conclusions — that love was not always glorious, but could also be selfish and diminishing. But when I had got this far, he interrupted me.

"You've got the whole thing wrong; I never told you a story like that about Santo."

"But what are you saying — that Santo didn't live in the house up there at the point with Crucelio and all that gang of people?"

"What I'm saying is that Santo never sneaked food into that house and ate it under the covers with Negra. It was Sanchez. And it was Crucelio and Julio Bone, the new man that Cornelia, Santo's mother, took up with."

"You're ruining all my work," I said.

"Well, I'm sorry," Ramón said, "but if you want to tell the truth about Santo you can say that he was super-romantic, that he was pussy-whipped, and that aside from Florinda he never really found a woman who was worthy of him. But not that he was selfish or sneaky. Not that he would eat food secretly in his own mother's house. His brother, Crucelio, yes; he was a shameless son of a bitch, *capaz de todo,* but not Santo."

"That's true," Ester said. She had been listening to my slightly addled version of Rioverde history and laughing about my vulgarities. "Santo was good; he was always a generous man; that's one reason why so many women liked him. Everytime he would come in from fishing on the sea he would fill a basket with the very best fish he'd caught and have one of the children on the beach deliver them around town to all the girls who had caught his attention. Of course, it wasn't just pure generosity either; he was investing in the future. He was the kind of man who wanted to be in love with all the women in the world. His instructions were very precise: two fish for Guma, three fish for Rosa, four fish for so-and-so, and twelve fish, including the pargo, for Florinda. He was generous but realistic, too, because almost every girl he invested fish in paid off eventually, and in the proper order."

"I never understood about Florinda," I said. "Santo was so handsome and charming and what? thirty-one, thirty-two years old? And yet he lived with Florinda for over a year, and she must have been over fifty-five."

"Yes," Ester said, "Florinda has always liked younger men. She may be old and fat and gray, but a young man always made her foolish. How she loved being *madrina* of the fútbol team, yelling and screaming during the games like a teenage cheerleader. But she is a good woman, a very strong woman. She was very good with Santo."

"Don't forget about the crumbs," Ramón said.

"What crumbs?"

"The crumbs that dropped in the beds in the darkness. And how the women would have to get up real early, while everyone was still asleep, and try to brush up all the little pieces of food that they'd been sleeping in all night, little bits of cheese and broken crackers and chunks of cocada. Cockroach bait." Ramón laughed and shook his head. "God, what a disgraceful family they were," he said. "They were a scandal in the town, those wild crazy *zambos* . . . How proud we were of them."

"Tell me about the hummingbirds' hearts," I said. "Did Santo cook them first?"

"No, he ate them raw. But, Martín, you're not being fair to Santo. It was never just Santo who was involved in that craziness; it was all the kids on the beach. Some of them went out with slingshots for weeks trying to kill a *kinde;* Santo tried for over a month. Not I; I was always *arecho* enough without any of that *brujeria*." His face grew soft in the candlelight as he sat there thinking of his childhood. Finally, he said, "Ester, go out in the kitchen and wash something, will you? I've got something to say unfit for the ears of a lady."

"Well, good. If I'm a lady now, I don't even want to hear it," Ester said, getting up to leave, "but speak up, speak up."

When we were alone Ramón said, "I just thought of something about Santo, about how he was, but it's shameful and nothing you could write about."

"Don't bet on that, Ramón. People like to be shocked."

"Well, actually, it's not shocking about Santo; it's about *haciendo la paja,* that vice of childhood, and now I'm not so sure I even want to tell you ... But, well, O.K. As you know, Santo was older than the gang of kids I ran around with. One day there were three or four of us hiding out in the grass hacienda la paja, and Santo caught us. He was maybe seventeen then and we were twelve, thirteen, and we ran away and hid from him, terribly ashamed. That same evening he came up to me where I was sitting on the beach alone watching the waves or the sun go down, or something, and he said, 'Listen, *chico,* let me teach you something about that thing that you were doing out in the grass.' 'What do you mean, hombre?' I said. 'I wasn't doing anything out in the grass, man. I don't believe in doing that sort of thing. What do you think, I'm some kind of *maricón?*' 'O.K., O.K.,' Santo said, 'my eyes deceived me, but listen, chico, doing it in a gang is pig stuff. Even a Brahma bull waits until it's dark. What you have to do is be alone in a nice place, in the shade someplace where it's pretty, and you have to think about the prettiest girl you know — how her eyes look at you, how her hands touch your face, how it is when your lips touch; and if you think hard and well and truly imagine how it is to be with her, it is a nice thing and nothing you have to be ashamed of. Out of your own head you can make it beautiful. Not pig stuff. Not gang stuff.' "

"But that was great of Santo," I said. "He was teaching you something very important, that sex is always involved with Woman."

"Yes, exactly," Ramón said. "And also that we weren't absolutely alone in the world with our depraved tastes ... I talked to the other kids about what he said, and it made sense, and you know what happened? In the afternoon, which was a sort of horny time for us, each kid would leave the beach and stand at the edge of the grass on the top of the bank and raise his hands up over his head like a boxer or stand at attention saluting and yell, "I dedicate this one to Gloria Estupiñan!' or 'I dedicate this one to Maria Charcopa!' And then he'd go off by himself."

"Until he grew up and made it really happen."

"Well, not really," Ramón said, laughing. "We didn't have much imagination, I guess. Just about everyone was dedicating one to Gloria Estupiñan. She was the prettiest girl in town and had shoes and brought a lunch to school, and we all figured we couldn't do better than do it with her. My God, she was the most dedicated-to little girl on the whole coast. Or I don't know, maybe she was just a scapegoat to protect the girls we really thought of and dreamed about. I don't know, maybe this little ten-year-old girl was like the town whore who had to receive our sexual dreams to protect the chastity of our friends' sisters. I mean you couldn't very well stand up on the bank and yell, 'I dedicate this one to Norma Avila!' if her brother was standing there listening to you, could you? That would end up in a fight or else the guy would jump up and dedicate one to *your* sister. You just couldn't go around dedicating with full freedom of choice; you couldn't make yourself vulnerable by revealing your most secret fantasies to the public ... Although some of the younger ones were too innocent to really know what they were doing or just how much they were really revealing — like little Ricardo, who always stood up there on the bank saluting like an insane admiral in the air force and yelling, 'I dedicate this one to my sister, Delia!' "

I have also apparently misinterpreted the second story about Santo that Ramón told me so many years ago, but I want to include it here anyway — as I remember it.

Between the time that he lived with Negra and Florinda, Santo spent some nine months or so with Rosa. He had his own shack on the beach now, still close to his mother's house, for he still fished with Crucelio. But he was separated from that mob of fornicating relations. In this new privacy he could develop and refine his finer feelings. The two of them always ate their meals in the same manner, compounded of ritual and emotion. Rosa would bring Santo his plate of food and then retire to the kitchen, where she ate in her proper place. But as a symbol of love and unity, Santo never ate more than half his food nor did Rosa eat more than half of hers. Midway in the meal Rosa would reappear and, with long hot tender looks, the plates would be exchanged, and Rosa would once more disappear into the kitchen to slick up that half of Santo's food that had been sweetened and consecrated by his love.

"Well," Ramón interrupted me, "it's amazing that you remember this story, but as usual you have it all wrong. It was not just Santo who ate like that; this is a rural custom that many of the people observe, since food or the lack of it is at the very center of their lives. But the point is not just pure romance. What the woman does is bring out a plate of food for the man; there is nothing special about it — all the best pieces of meat, most of the rice, and the plátano stay in their pots in the kitchen. The man eats just a bite or two, and then he calls his wife and offers her his food — *un hombre grande,* no? — as though he's offering her all the food in the house. She takes it, goes back into the kitchen and discovers with amazement that all the best pieces are still there, and this is what *he* eats. In some families there are terrible fights if this custom is not observed. Sometimes when Santo was angry, for instance, he would refuse to trade plates, a real sign of indignation and rejection, a real insult; Rosa would sulk for days."

"So, everybody does this? It wasn't just Santo?"

"Not everybody, but not just Santo either. Except that when one thinks of this sort of comical way of doing it one thinks of Santo because he gave the custom a kind of new meaning, a kind of style that grew out of his true emotion for the girl. He tried to make something pretty out of it."

Anyone who knew Santo would probably have insisted that his only true love affair had been with Florinda. It had begun when he was over thirty, and she was rushing toward her sixties. Those two ages, climactic and portentous of time's tyranny, held them together for a time in a sweet desperation as they both saw the doors of possibilities clicking shut. Each saw the other as some last chance at stability, each having been betrayed or disillusioned innumerable times before in that easy black *ambiente* of casual passion. They clung together against life and tried out of necessity and fear to build a romantic climate that would sustain them permanently. It didn't work, of course, but it worked for almost two years. When the romance was all gone, when they had milked the situation of every possibility and Santo, sane again, found himself with a gray-haired, rather fat, and jealous woman who was older and more possessive than his mother, he felt trapped and cheated. With Santo, love was everything, habit nothing. Wasn't this perhaps his greatest virtue, that he refused to accept and live with stale and exhausted emotions? And wasn't this perhaps his tragedy?

At the Easter fiesta he met a new girl who had come to visit relatives from the packing sheds at Kilometer 200. Before that she had worked as a maid in Guayaquil, and she talked with the loud, smart, clipped hipness of a Guayaca and pretended to be amazed by the plainness of the country girls and their simple dresses made of honest cotton. She stayed in Rioverde for a week, dancing every night and dazzling the men with an inexhaustible wardrobe of psychedelic Dacrons and the liberated manners of a cabaret singer. The women, threatened by her glamor and seeing themselves for what they were — plain, uninteresting, stupid, and poor — hated her. How they rejoiced, justified, when two days after she had left, two of the town's blades, burning and dripping, developed the unmistakable symptoms of gonorrhea.

There are no secrets in a small town for long, and there was no concealing this scandalous and hilarious development. Florinda was the town's self-appointed nurse and in fact almost lived off what she earned diagnosing and treating the minor cuts and fevers and grippes of the people too poor to travel to Esmeraldas to pay far more for the casual, intuitive, and identical diagnoses of the town's doctors. She might possibly have respected the men's secrets, but about this same time Santo refused to sleep in the same bed with her, and she discovered while washing his clothes that his undershorts were stained and polluted with the same infection.

Their romance had never been tranquil; it had demanded crises, convolutions, denunciations, reconciliations, and forgivenesses.

One could superimpose a certain meaning over life by making it dramatic and by injecting ritual into that deprived community mainly preoccupied with simple existence. Even on the farm, sixty miles away, we had heard of epic quarrels between those two desperate lovers — the door of Florinda's house barred, the windows shuttered, and Santo outside whispering through the cracks, begging to be forgiven and reinstated, or in a rage rattling the door on its hinges with threats of abandoning the town.

So this time, it was the last time, Florinda barred the door against him and sat there in the darkness waiting; this aging, tired woman, betrayed once more, rehearsing and polishing those furious words that flared in her head like red-hot sparks. She would never forgive him this time, that weak, unfaithful fool, infected by the embraces of a common whore. *Nunca, nunca jamás . . .* There were uncertain noises at the door, and she held her breath. Someone was trying to get in but no one spoke, and after a minute, silence . . . By ten o'clock Florinda, still waiting, might perhaps have been talked into some tentative forgiveness . . . At midnight she unbarred the door and stood for a time in the middle of that sandy deserted street, beginning to feel in that silent darkness a cold apprehension. There wasn't a sound in the whole town except for the pounding of the breakers on the high-tide beach and the glassy chunking of ocean rocks being moved and rolled in the waves.

Santo was in love again. That locked door had been a sign that he should follow his inclinations. He walked all night along the beach to Esmeraldas and by a stroke of luck met up with Ramón, who had come into town from the farm to buy supplies. Ramón loaned him the money to cure his gonorrhea and offered him a job. Santo said that he would seriously consider the job but that first he wanted to cure himself and then he must take off for Kilometer 200 to look for a certain wonderful girl who loved him and was waiting for him. Ramón was not to believe the jealous gossip that would soon be pouring out of the town — how he had become infected with a venereal disease, if that's what it was. It was impossible to imagine that that girl who had bathed each day in the sea, who had appeared each night in a crisp immaculate dress, who had moved with him slowly, tenderly in the slow panting rhythms of tangos, could have . . . No, it was unthinkable . . . No, she had never asked him for money, never. Except, well, just before she left she had borrowed a hundred sucres; it was just a loan.

A month later Santo came to work for us; he was emaciated and distraught. The girl? Well, she hadn't exactly been waiting for him as he'd expected, but he'd stayed there in her family's house — sleeping underneath it on sacks. But she couldn't stand being bossed around, she said; she got bored with his corny rural gallantries; she couldn't stand the nasal way he talked, as though his nose were clamped shut with a clothespin. She told him to piss off. He was absolutely through with women, he said. He was *absolutely* through with women. Now he had gonorrhea again, for Christ's sake. And that wasn't all, he told Ramón, beginning to shudder: he was covered with crab lice. "My God," he said, "I've even got them in my eyebrows."

Ramón, who was now the local *curandero,* another Florinda, to whom all the local people came for injections and medical advice, bought a quart or two of penicillin and a pound of DDT and began to cure Santo again. We sent a message addressed to Florinda out to Rioverde: Would she kindly pack Santo's clothes and entrust them to Pablo? He brought them back, contemptuously stuffed into a cardboard box. Santo moved into one of our shacks and cooked his meals with Jorge Avila, the carpenter. (Most of the buildings Jorge had built us a year or so before had collapsed, and we were replacing some of them. Apparently Ramón felt that Jorge was the only competent carpenter in Ecuador. He was the only one we used on the farm; sometimes, when we needed him for a week, we had to wait six months for him.)

A few months after Santo began to work with us, that Saturday afternoon arrived when the fútbol team from Rioverde marched down the hill led by Florinda, called up from limbo by Dalmiro's hired witch doctor. Blatant, bright eyed, laughing shrilly, as gay and nervous as the banners that fluttered at her sides, Florinda was in a fever, foolish as a drunkard, dancing on the lip of hysteria. She had been driven by love to come those sixty miles from Rioverde to laugh and dance in Santo's face, to show him that since the day he had walked out on her nothing but gaiety and mirth had filled her life. It was a long time later that we realized the real truth about that great gob of spit that she had directed at Dalmiro's feet; she hadn't been aiming for Dalmiro at all.

Santo was working in the outside fields when she arrived; he was unaware that she was on the farm until he came down to the store at noon to be paid. Someone must have told him then because he disappeared abruptly, not even waiting for his wages. He didn't put in a public appearance until Monday when everyone had left. How strange and insolent that he didn't make an effort to see his friends from Rioverde; he acted like he just didn't give a damn for anybody. But something funny happened during the game, Ester said, something that, while she watched, made goosebumps stand out on her arms. And it must have affected her deeply, for even as she told us about it tears welled up in her eyes.

"I was standing with Florinda during the game," Ester said. "I had never seen her so excited or so gay. She was like a young girl cheering on the Rioverde team, clapping and yelling and jumping around at every clever play.

"And then, sometime during the last part of the first half when everything was really exciting with the ball down in Male's end of the field and the goalkeeper diving and stretching like mad and everybody screaming, Florinda suddenly stopped jumping around and just stood there without moving, stood absolutely still in the middle of all that excitement. And I followed her eyes across the field. There was Santo. He had just stepped out of the jungle and was standing alone at the very edge of the field. He stood there staring at Florinda.

"It was a terrible moment because I felt like someone who opens a door on other people and sees something private that you're not supposed to see and don't even want to see, and I could feel the hair on my arms beginning to bristle and the chill of goosebumps. Maybe it was a minute, maybe it was less; it seemed like a much longer time — the two of them absolutely still, staring at one another across the field as though they were the only two people in the world. And it's funny that, remembering it, it seems to have happened in silence, as though the staring of those two was strong enough to blot out everything else. The feeling was so strong that it seemed like everyone should feel it, that everything ought to stop — the game, the screaming people, the clouds moving across the sky, and behind the clouds, that moving sun."

Telling us, her eyes were full of tears, and she sat there afterward, embarrassed; she wiped her eyes, laughed, and got up abruptly and went into the kitchen, and Ramón, who goes to pieces at a woman's tears, scowled and began to clear his throat, and grabbed a cigarette out of my package, a thing he hardly ever does. "You ought to write *novelas* for the radio," he called into the kitchen angrily.

"It's sad to see the end of something," Ester called back. She began to blow her nose.

Santo stayed with us for almost two years, left us for a year, and then came back again. Perhaps nothing illuminates his character in a kinder light than the fact that within a year he was completely absorbed and accepted into the community. This was a miracle considering the suspicious nature of our inbred group, where everyone was related at least three ways to everyone else and where in fact total familiarity had bred a strange and comical contempt among the inhabitants. In view of the fact that Santo's presence made of each married man a potential cuckold, his general popularity with everyone was a real tribute to his qualities.

How enchanting it was to watch Santo bloom and sparkle in the presence of a woman. He might come to work at seven with all the others and greet us politely but without enthusiasm, his face still sleepy and sullen, his voice abstracted. But let a woman appear about this time, walking down the hill with loaded baskets from the early morning Esmeraldas bus, and his whole manner would change. He was convulsed with an agitation of the spirit, an awakening and quickening of every sense. Looking at the dawn through Santo's eyes at this moment, one saw a newly created sun blazing in a sky the color of those celestial butterflies that flitted through the jungle shadows, the Morpho; one saw bright colored birds by the thousands rising skyward from the glistening trees, their throats bursting with ecstasy, and bands of paired angels descending from the clouds, hymning the glories of love and feeling each other up.

It was no simple sexual arousal. I could watch this in Antonio,

Víctor's nephew, who had come to work for us when he was about sixteen and whose whole body would become transformed in the presence of any young woman who appeared dressed in tight slacks or who walked past with swaying hips and a provocative smile. Antonio's neck would swell with pounding blood, his eyes would almost pop out of his head, tiny drops of sweat would suddenly appear on his forehead and his nose, the muscles in his jaw would clench spasmodically, his fingers would tremble, and he would have to bury one hand in his pocket to control and conceal the violent shameless swelling that threatened to betray him. Watching this reaction, which was so pure (dare I say straightforward?), I used to wonder if I were observing a future rapist.

Santo saw woman as holy, exquisite, mysterious, holding in her vulnerability and her endurance the secret meanings of life. For Santo woman was that other half of him with whom he needed to be joined in order to be whole. He wasn't alive and charming just for the good-looking girls with whom he thought he might have a chance to bed down. Any woman affected him to his depths; he sparkled and throbbed for them all, from the youngest preadolescent to the bent, trembling, toothless crones, the grayhaired half-blind widows dressed in their mourning black. During the peanut harvests we always put Santo out in the field with the forty or fifty women whose job was to pull the peanuts from their roots for sacking. Anyone else would have gone mad in that job. Not Santo. How he came to life in those days. And how he worked hard trying to be something just a little special to each one of them. At the end of the harvest he would be half dead with exhaustion, emotionally spent, and his face was as fulfilled and placid as though he had just returned from a two-week vacation in the world's largest whorehouse.

And the women? I don't know what they thought of Santo. He must have puzzled and confused them. For many of them he was probably the first man they had ever known who saw them as potentially glorious human beings, something more than chunks of meat to be seduced, buggered, dominated, and forgotten.

Out of that ragged and poverty-stricken mob of women who worked for us in the peanuts, a couple of them were named Rosa. It was those two Rosas, more than all the Marias, the Gumercindas, the Vertildas, who drove me in panic out of the fields when they were in possession.

Rosa Bone lived on the farm for about two years; her husband used to guard our plantings of pineapples. In his spare time he contracted special pineapple sales and at night hauled off enough fruit to supply Quinindé, a town of five thousand. One day, thank God, Rosa ran off with another man, leaving Bone with a couple of small children to care for. Slight, extremely unwashed, and uncombed, she was a rarity on the farm, a woman without black antecedents. When she was being paid by the hour to hoe peanuts, she would spend most of her time cooking up pots of weird local products in the field and selling hot-plate specials to the other workers. She had the disconcerting habit, when I arrived to reprimand her (it really wasn't a habit since I only approached her twice), of squatting at my feet and pissing while she argued with me. How in God's name can you hope to communicate with a pissing woman? Soul battered, boots spattered, speechless and sweating, I fled. Ramón, when I told him about it, was appalled at this high-sierran simplicity and refused to go near her.

There was another Rosa, the mother of Tomás and Chango, two kids well-trained in the ways of thievery by their more skillful parents. *This* Rosa's specialty, as far as I know, was stealing peanut sacks. We would start out in a peanut harvest with, oh, say, two hundred sacks and end up about a month later with six. At the end of each day she would waddle out of the field so swathed in sacks she had tucked into her bosom and into her bloomers that she could hardly move. In the mornings, still innocent, she was shapeless enough, but at night as she lurched homeward like an overloaded garbage barge, all of her human qualities disguised and exaggerated by peanut bags, she became transformed into a representation of pure feminine malevolence. Watermelon Slim, an old IWW organizer, an anarchist friend from other times in California, had always spoken of women as "piss tanks." I never saw those two roses without thinking fondly of old Slim, God rest his atheistic soul, and commending him for the precision of his language.

Deadly serious, I called this Rosa a major disaster area, a description she loved and which drove her into uncontrollable fits of high-pitched hysterical laughter, which she directed at me with both hands covering her face, her absolutely cold and appraising eyes studying my reactions through the spaces between her fingers. She was an enormous woman, about twice as gross as the Venus of Willendorf, with thick unbelievably intimidating haunches, the pillars of Hercules, 150 pounds to the haunch; an absolutely monumental and terrifying ass; great overflowing breasts like paired bursting sacks of cottage cheese. Is it possible that Neanderthal man might have worshiped at the feet of this ideal beauty, this redundance of generative capability? Perhaps. But to me she seemed simply to have been created for stealing sacks which she could absorb into her hidden cracks and crannies a dozen at a time. Some years, outraged by her blatant kleptomania, we would forbid her to set foot on the property, calling her to her face a thief and the disaster of the century, and she would shriek with laughter behind her hands, observing us coolly through her fingers with little, contemptuous pig eyes. But at the last harvest we felt sorry for her, she was so poor and so obscenely pregnant, so pregnant in fact that she was unable to walk with the other women that half mile to the field. We had to haul her to work in a wagon and haul her back at night. As we carted her in from the fields at night, jolted and jiggled like a mountain of Jello, wedged in among the peanut sacks, sweating and puffing, we decided that either she was at least eighteen-months pregnant or she had hidden beneath her skirts a basket full of pumpkins.

None of the other women ever came close to matching our Rosas in their capacity to shock and horrify; still, as a group, in their poverty and the simple unsentimental brutality of their perceptions, they were terrifying enough on their own account. We gave work to all the mothers, wives, grandmothers, and aunts of all the men who had ever worked for us. A good percentage were well past middle age. God knows they didn't earn much; we paid them by the pound, setting our price slightly higher than the price the women of Manabi received for the same work. But we were the first in the province who had ever raised peanuts for the market, the women were slow and clumsy, they never seemed to catch on to any of the tricks, and we raised the price again. We hoped that the more skillful and serious women would earn at least eighty cents a day; this would give them a certain dignity without humiliating the men who at that time were earning a dollar. The wages were important, of course, but perhaps not as important as we thought. More than anything the harvest was like a great tribal gathering, the social event of the season.

For all the time that they took possession of the outside fields with their cooking pots, their hordes of children, the little shelters of bamboo and branches that they constructed against the sun or the rain — during all that time it seemed to us that we were no longer owners of the land, no longer directing its destiny, that everything was now being decided by those Fates and Furies in their tattered dresses who crouched over the piles of peanuts or small cooking fires like witches, laughing together, gossiping, fighting inanely over trifles, claiming territory where no one was allowed to harvest, suckling their babes or swatting their children or sending them out along the secret jungle trails at the back of the peanut rows with sacks of stolen peanuts. I think if I had seen one of them, cackling, mount a broom and go sailing away over the trees I wouldn't have given her a second glance.

Ramón hated this month of harvest. He hated having on the property that mob of women who nodded and agreed with everything he arranged to bring about a degree of order and then simply kept on doing their own thing in their own inept way. Finally he threw up his hands in defeat and refused to go near them; he would appear only at five P.M. with the tractor and a wagon to haul Rosa and the harvested peanuts to the drying platforms, where we weighed and stored them (not Rosa, just the peanuts). He was grim-faced and abrupt with the women and later at dinner he was short-tempered with me, saying the same things over and over: that he couldn't work with women, that he lacked the character and the indelicacy to cuss them out as they deserved, that he was enraged by their incapacity to become more efficient with time, that if we couldn't mechanize the harvest, why did we keep planting those Goddamn peanuts every year?

I felt the same way only more so. After all, no one had ever pissed on Ramón — at least, not literally. I hardly ever went near the fields when the women were in control. From a distance the scene appeared to be from fourteenth-century Central Europe in its brutish evocation of serfdom and exploitation. As a child

I had never been able to believe those early American stories of how the Indians had turned their prisoners over to the squaws to be tortured and killed, but watching those squabbling older women, I began to believe the stories. After one harvest, when we gave the usual dance for everybody who lived near us — filling them up with roast pig and potato salad before filling them up with cane alcohol or muscatel — I was more convinced than ever that those old women, abandoned by their culture, were capable of any outrage. They came to the party with little pots hidden under their dresses and stole all the food — and then stole our pots. And after that they stole the plates and the knives and the forks and the glasses and the empty Coca-Cola bottles.

Late in the evening after the peanuts were weighed and the women had dispersed to their houses, after Rosa, puffing and blowing, shapeless beneath her day's harvest of stolen sacks, had lurched up the trail like some prehistoric monster disappearing to graze in the high pasture grass, I would take the tractor back up to the field and disk out the rows that had been harvested. Moving in behind their work was like moving over a battlefield stained with suffering and contention. The whole area was littered with scraps of paper, bits of torn material, broken bottles and gourds, still smoking campfires, collapsed lean-tos, great piles of stripped peanut plants. In the miasmic air, the stink of human shit. It was the custom of the women and more especially the children to gorge themselves on peanuts as they worked; their bodies screamed for protein. The first days of each harvest were the worst, notorious for the quantity and quality of the excrement that was produced, for everyone was half-sick with stomach cramps and diarrhea as they tried to satiate their hunger. All along the river the first week of each peanut harvest, the houses were full of wildly crapping kids. One year when we had peanuts near a planting of pineapples (and a watchman with a rifle to guard them), those extensive and almost interconnected puddles of diarrheic liquid were half mixed with human turds composed completely of crushed pineapples that looked as though they had been emptied from cans of Doles without any human mediation.

We are months from the last harvest, its scars have faded, the last six sacks of peanuts sit moldering on the guest-room bed, but remembering it now from this distance the scene is bathed in the cold, sour, sourceless light of a Bosch hell. And as I examine the memory, among the women there seem to be innumerable dust devils, mini-cyclones, moving witlessly with their cargoes of dust and dirt, sticks, dead leaves, and bits of torn paper, twirling, swirling in the dead air. Why do I see it like this so clearly in imagination when, if I ever saw a dust devil in those fields, it couldn't have been more than once? And why do I remember those ragged women as an undifferentiated mob divested of all its humanity when in actuality it was made up of many individuals whom I knew and liked? Roque's mother, Gumercinda; Cantante's noble-faced mother; Hipolita, the mother of Mercedes, who always embraced me when she came to the store; hard-working Mari, the failed whore; Gloria, Luceti, Daima, Vertilda, Susana; and dozens of enchanting children whom I meet each day on the road and try to identify out of their profligate anonymity; and two women who worked for a time one year, women of incredible beauty — one as tiny and tranquil, as finely made as a Chinese princess, the other in her late twenties as full-breasted as Elizabeth Taylor and with a face purer and more mysterious in its dark perfection. I suppose if we create mobs to serve our purposes then we must pay the price of being involved with and wounded by them.

9

THE WALKING WOUNDED

REMEMBERING SANTO when he worked for us, I see him as a wounded man, as a kind of convalescent slowly learning to use his limbs again: first as a man afraid to become deeply involved with love, and then as a man incapable of controlling his sexual machinery. But it is odd to remember Santo as a wounded man on the farm when we had so many truly crippled men on the payroll.

Dalmiro was one, of course. Alvarez was another. He, too, was from Rioverde, a man in his late twenties who, as a bystander, had been shot through the neck when a drunken kid tried to grab a revolver out of a *policia rural*'s holster at one of the Rioverde Saturday-night fiestas. For months Alvarez was almost completely paralyzed, and as time passed, the town, which at first had pledged to sustain him, was more and more caught up in its own problems. He was actually half dead with hunger when he sent a hysterical message to Ramón begging for money or work. We sent him enough money to eat for a couple of weeks and to come to the farm, and we promised to give him a job since that seemed to respect his dignity, just in case he still had dignity that needed respecting. We decided against simply sending him money, as it would have been impossibly complicated to get it to him each week, and also because without first seeing him we were incapable of visualizing Alvarez stripped of his joy, his capacity to bamboozle and con; we couldn't imagine a sad Alvarez, an Alvarez who wasn't talking loud and roaring with laughter and drinking booze straight out of the bottle with the boys.

When he came, one arm was beginning to atrophy, but we pretended not to notice. We kept him around the house for a couple of weeks, doing useless things, and then put him to work hoeing weeds with the other men, straining his capabilities to their limits. One of the things he had lost in those months when he had had to beg to stay alive was his self-confidence, but we gave that back to him by never letting him know that he wasn't expected to compete with anybody but himself. He had been a fisherman, an outboard motorman, a minor cog in the local lobster cartel, a buyer and seller of dried shrimp, a kind of con artist. When he arrived at the farm with a cripple's terror of the future, he had put all that behind him and he was thinking only of how he might somehow stock a little store in his house where he could sell soft drinks and cigarettes. When he left us after eight months (it was the longest time he had ever been away from the ocean), he was twenty pounds heavier and cautiously using his crippled arm, and he was talking about once more going out into the sea and fishing for pargo, those shining red snappers that schooled in the rocks off the Rioverde point.

Five years before he had been shot through the neck, Alvarez in his prime had had an encounter with a marlin. I wish I had spent more time on the sea and perfected my Spanish fishing vocabulary so that I could tell this story well. But like most fish stories this one would be believed by no one since its hero, the marlin, was probably twice as large as any marlin ever put into the literature and probably three times as large as any of those Atlantic marlin caught by old men off Cuba or by middle-aged executives from New York with rented 600-dollar reels, swivel chairs, hired gaff-boys, and gallons of chilled Tom Collins.

No one went looking for this fish. The fish had come into the shallow water off the point and had become cruelly enmeshed in one of Alvarez's lobster nets. Had it come in to die or been chased in by the sharks? No one knew, but there it was one morning, an absolutely incredible fish, longer than any of the canoes, endless and terrifying when one gazed down at his black length, motionless in the murky waters of the Humboldt Current.

For two days Alvarez and his brother Sanchez, each of them in his own canoe, tried to put ropes around that fish. They were timid and appalled by this monstrous creature who had swum into their lives with its promise of instant riches, and they were terrified at what they were attempting; they spoke in whispers. And in two days the fish acknowledged them only once; he rose to the surface slowly, his sword as long as a paddle, his eyes as big as plates, his back as black as death. He thrashed his tail once and sank again to the bottom, but in that moment he crushed one of the canoes and flung its occupant thirty feet out into the sea. Alvarez remembers, in the absolute silence that followed this scene, looking up and finding the canoe destroyed and his brother gone, and he screamed, "Ayee, poor my brother!" because for that second he thought he had been killed.

On the third day the whole village turned out with ropes and nets, but they were dazed by the size of the fish and as cautious as children, almost afraid to even look at it as it lay on the sand at the bottom of the sea among the rocks, trapped and patient, with the net closely wrapped around its body. Late that afternoon, almost at dark, the sharks came in.

The next morning they hauled the head out and Alvarez hacked it open with a machete and sliced through the armor and took out over one hundred pounds of meat. They say that a few days later they killed one of the sharks, though don't ask me how they did it or how they knew that it was one of the sharks that had killed the marlin, but they say that the shark was a pygmy compared to the marlin and that in its stomach they found the body of a full-grown horse. Nobody knows how it got there, but then nobody knows how that tiger got up on the slopes of Kilimanjaro either, do they?

There were a couple of other wounded men working on the farm with us during those resting months while Santo was recovering from love's low blows. They may not have been wounded when they came, but they were sure as hell wounded when they left.

One of them, whose name I have forgotten, wandered in off the highway, arriving as casually as though he had been blown in by a vagrant breeze. He was as black as Víctor, almost as strong, and when he smiled, which was almost all the time, he was as cheering to look at as a clown. There was only one trouble with him: he didn't know how to work. But we liked him, and when we fired him after a week, we offered him a contract clearing a hectárea or two of bananas at so much per hectárea. He accepted our offer and came to work about two days a week. He was new to this part of the country and had no friends in Male, but within a week, as though he had a nose as sensitive and far-reaching as a bloodhound's, he had scented out and settled down with three old maids who had been left several hundred acres of jungle about a mile up the river from us.

They were grotesque and rather frightening old ladies who dressed in very bright colors, wore bright bandanas of silk, and hid their faces as well as they could behind layers of chalk-colored powder, scarlet lipsticks, and dark glasses as large as paired butter plates. There was no hiding their predatory natures which, aside from their extreme states of physical disintegration, were really their most distinctive characteristics. They were loud and witty and obscene with any man that crossed their path, and when they walked up the lane through the middle of our farm to catch the Esmeraldas bus, chipper and stiff as crickets, I think all of us had to fight a first impulse to hide someplace, for they looked like nothing so much as a pack of hungry hunting animals. Their desperation and their need was so blatant, so naked, and their capacity to fulfill anyone's needs but their own so minimal that imagining being clasped to the breast of any one of them was like imagining being locked in the bony arms of death itself. Much later, when they began claiming all the land on the river and tearing down their neighbors' fences, insisting that their daddy had left them everything between Male and Mafua, we realized they were cracked. Then again, maybe they were just lonesome and kicking up a ruckus as an excuse to have the troops move in: better to have men on the farm with rifles aimed at you than no men at all. Desperation raised to the third power.

Within a week after our new contratista had moved in with the three harpies, they had offered him a 50 percent interest in all farm sales and three yearling heifer calves. "Why not?" he said, roaring with delight. They fed him real good; they washed and starched his clothes as stiff as cardboard; they treated him like a king. Eggs for breakfast every morning, by God, and great cups of chocolate, rich with milk and sugar to keep up a man's strength.

He'd been looking for something half as good as this all his life. He didn't know how long he could hold out, but he was playing hard to get; he would stop smiling for just a second and look worried and say he was going to hold out as long as he could.

And within another ten days he blew it all. He began to flirt with one of the younger girls in the village; maybe he did more than flirt — either I never did hear or I've forgotten the details. I don't know if the man who did it acted out of rage or if he was paid by three unknown parties, but we found Alvarez, one afternoon, lying behind the workers' cabins with his neck sliced at the back from ear to ear by a machete. He looked like a half-opened can of cranberry sauce. (It just don't hardly pay to be a stranger around these parts.) We hauled him off to the doctor and his assailant to the police, while both of them sat in the back of the pickup and talked about the incident calmly and objectively as though it had happened to someone else. I think both of them were sad and amazed to find themselves, on a day that had started out so sweetly, in such a complicated situation — though nothing much ever came of it. The machetero was an old friend of the *teniente político;* the victim was from another place. There was obviously no case, the teniente político said; he could vouch for the man's impeccable character, and if he had swung at so-and-so with a machete, so-and-so had doubtless had it coming to him.

The victim came back from the doctor late that same afternoon with fifty yards of adhesive tape wrapped around his neck, from which a half a bale of fluffy white cotton boiled — a black John the Baptist without religion, his head seemingly severed from his body and floating on cumulus clouds. He had learned nothing; he was as cool and folksy as though he were accustomed to having his head chopped off at weekly intervals. He greeted us with that same stupid and magnificent smile, the pure and radiant face of a man without guilt caught up in the tactile sensation of the moment. He was delighted to be walking, to be talking with friends in the just barely cool freshness of a lovely evening.

We suggested that for his own good he had better leave the area, and he agreed. He had blown it all, he said without remorse. He would have liked to stay one more night and jug that young broad, but he was half afraid that in the middle of the jugging his head might jiggle off; thinking of this possibility he roared with laughter. We didn't have time or enough light in the sky to measure his work in the bananas, and we let ourselves be cheated by a little and gave him a couple hundred sucres. The last we saw of him he was walking up the lane as smartly as he had come, heading for greener pastures and the big chance — old what's-his-name, with his head more or less accompanying him, nesting sweetly on a cotton platter, just possibly the most wounded man I had ever seen in my life, though this thought didn't occur to me for years.

Barry, another of our just barely walking wounded, hardly ever worked for us. He was about seventeen years old, a tall freckle-faced kid who scarcely seemed black, his skin was so light and his hair so red. His father was an independent farmer with enough cows and plátano to sell in the Esmeraldas market so that he never had to hire himself out as a day laborer. The whole family was miserably poor, but their independence had made them into models, the victims of everyone's envy. Barry had many sisters and no brothers, an ideal situation for a young male in a macho society. As the only heir he was worshiped by his parents, and his sisters cared for him as though he were San Pedro. I passed the shack where he lived one day and caught him as he was being pampered and patted; he had just come up from bathing in the river, and three of his sisters were fluttering around him — combing his hair, drying his back, cleaning his nails, bringing him stiffly ironed pants and shirt. There was something bored and satisfied in his look that indicated that this was the way it had always been, and I tended to see him as he saw himself, as something very special.

He was a quiet-talking kid who didn't move around much. He spent a lot of time reading or just gazing out over the river. I thought of him as a student or as someone who was figuring something out, and it occurred to me that he would probably become something that would delight his father — a bookkeeper, or the manager of a store in Guayaquil. He was somehow not a part of the wild local *ambiente,* removed from it not by arrogance but by delicacy. He came to us a few times looking for a week's work, perhaps before the Christmas or Easter fiestas, when everyone blossomed out in new shirts, pants, and shoes. He was impossibly incompetent, but we repressed our fury with him because somehow we felt that he was too finely made, this dreaming, abstracted prince. We would hire him on Monday and by Wednesday, unable to believe the shameless quality of his work, would pay him a week's wages and beg him to please, please, sweet kid, don't go away mad, just go away.

He came to my house one morning at five o'clock to tell me that his father was dying and to beg money for a doctor, but while telling me he suddenly burst into sobs and began pulling at his hair. We had very little money on the farm at that time, but stunned, my own eyes filling with tears, I emptied my pockets.

Two days later, far out in our banana plantings and by coincidence thinking of Barry's father and imagining him sweating in delirium in his hut, I caught a glimpse of him sneaking down a trail with a bunch of stolen bananas across his back. For years, of course, we had been fooled and lied to; a hundred people had come to us for money — their children or their wives or their mothers were dying — and later, like as not, we would discover that the money we had given them had been invested in bottles of aguardiente or a new fútbol or a down payment on a cheap transistor radio. I was always afraid to trust my suspicions and always did what was expected. Even Ramón, who thought of himself as being so tough and able to see into people's souls and who always started out by saying no, almost always ended up resentfully shelling out and feeling weak and foolish for having been so easily moved to pity.

Now we were angry with Barry for fooling us. He avoided us; he seemed puzzled by our anger at what to him had been such a wonderful joke and such a superb bit of acting. About three months later we stopped seeing him on the farm. We heard that he was sick and had taken to his bed. Now we heard that he was *muy grave* and that his terrified father had taken him to Esmeraldas. Three days later we heard that he was dead.

The deaths of young people, before they have scarcely begun to live, are probably the most shattering and obscene of life's mysteries. Barry's death, which had been pointless and unnecessary, convulsed the town. Everyone for a time became obsessed with his or her memory of his corpse, and his teenage friends were horrified because for nine days he refused to go away. Napo saw him at night on the trail, glowing greenly and beckoning. He came into Roldán's bed and straddled him, pinning his shoulders, trying to steal his breath, and staring into his eyes, and Roldán woke, choking and shrieking with terror. Arcario saw him late one night in the corner of the room where he slept; Barry was weeping, his arms raised in some awful posture of refusal and rage.

He had died of simple anemia, and he had been dying through the three years that we had known him. No wonder he had been so lazy, his face so quietly thoughtful and preoccupied, his skin so palely yellow and innocently freckled. No wonder he had let his sisters dry his back and tie his shoelaces; no wonder he lay in the shade reading a magazine while his friends wrestled or played volleyball. It's quite likely that we might have saved him with a few dollars' worth of iron pills. What *would* I have done if he had come to me again weeping and tearing at his hair and begging for help? Would I have believed him a second time, or would I have told him to go to hell? I was spared this test, which I might well have failed and which could have left me with a lifetime's guilt.

Lastly, there was Alejandro, perhaps more wounding than wounded, though the last time I saw him he was pretty bloody and his toenails had been scraped off from being dragged across the highway. He was the same Alejandro we had caught stealing plátano the first week we came to the farm — a big, immensely powerful black with the disturbing repellent face of a petty hood. He was about twenty years old and had a kind of built-in diffidence, a self-loathing that radiated from him. In my presence his eyes were ashamed and nervous, as though he thought that being white I had been given magic powers of divination to see into the secret intentions of his heart. He lived in the middle of the farm with Pedro Nazareno and his family, on a little piece of ground that almost cut our land in two, and for three years we never gave him work — probably because he never asked for it. There was no one who knew the farm like Alejandro; he had lived and prowled around on it all his life. And now Ramón, without my knowledge and in the most casual way, began giving Alejandro little jobs to do, sending him out into those parts of the jungle that only he knew to harvest bunches of cade for roof thatching or baskets of tangerines and avocados. I began to notice that Alejandro was hanging around the store more and more in the evenings and that Ramón, who was now in the full flowering of his ability to evaluate character, was finding Alejandro admirable and amusing. I warned Ramón against him because I was convinced that he thought of the farm as his own private preserve and that he had no honest feelings of friendship for Ramón. Someone had begun to rifle through the toolbox on the tractor every night. He had gotten away with all the wrenches and hammers and was now removing the bent nails and the broken bits of bolts that moldered and rusted in the grease at the bottom of the box. It was compulsive stealing — this was stuff without value — and I was sure that it was Alejandro though I had no proof except for the way he avoided my eyes on payday.

Ramón defended him. He had been meeting hippies on the road that year and giving them rides into town. Some of their qualities appalled him, but when I had explained the hippy philosophy as best I could he decided that there were many things about them that he liked. He agreed with me that their outrageous dress and their rather general disdain of personal cleanliness did not necessarily mirror an inner corruption. "I don't think Alejandro is a thief," Ramón said. "You know what I think? I think he's just a hippy; he's just trying to live his life. He came to me and asked for a chance and promised never to steal from us again."

Ramón gave Alejandro the job of cleaning the fence line along the southern boundary; he knew this territory well for he had already stolen and sold two of its four strands. A few days later Ramón asked him if he would like to make a trail into the banana planting along the highway so that we could more easily haul out a few bunches each week for a priest in Esmeraldas who was raising pigs. A month later he joined the crew of workers who hoed peanuts or harvested corn, and now almost every evening he would show up at the store just before dinner time, his sullen face would light up when he saw Ramón, and Ester would shove a plate of rice with meat or fish across the counter to him. After dinner

Ramón, Alejandro, Santo, and some of the other men would sit on the store benches until we turned the light plant off, listening to fútbol games from Guayaquil or playing *naipe* with a stack of incredibly beat up cards. About that time I was trying very hard to like anyone who was black, and I was feeling guilty because I couldn't. I couldn't like that guy. Maybe it was true, maybe I did have the magic power to look into his heart.

On Christmas Eve that year we had a party and invited Alejandro, Santo, Víctor, and a couple other workers to have dinner with us. We had lots of beer and whiskey or the evening might have been a disaster. I had wrapped a senile old turkey in banana leaves and dampened sacks and buried him in a hole full of hot rocks outside the kitchen door — the old Peace Corps volunteer still trying to teach new methods to the restless natives and still screwing everything up. Six hours later, when we dug him up at nine o'clock, he was still raw. Ester, brave on wine, weaved out into the kitchen and tried to cover our losses, and about midnight, squatting on the ground or sitting on the store benches, we had fried turkey, mashed potatoes drowned in curry-flavored gravy, and potato salad, thick with hard-boiled eggs. It was my weirdest Christmas, or could have been if I had been sober enough to make odious comparisons. That night I remember regretting that I didn't have the constitution for five or six daily shots of whiskey. Life through an alcoholic haze was so simple, sweet, and direct. I saw into everyone's soul; what lovely pure souls we all had.

Watching Alejandro rapaciously gnawing at the bones, both hands dripping with grease, his usually sullen face softened to ecstasy but half hidden behind chunks of meat, I began to like him a little for the joy and enthusiasm that flooded his face. The meat was as tough as old truck tires and just about as tasty, but it was probably the first time in his life he had ever had all the meat he could handle at one sitting. It was like watching that scene in *Nanook of the North* where that family of Eskimos sits down in an igloo and puts away four hundred pounds of whale blubber. Afterwards, his face shining with turkey fat, sitting around and belching like a geyser, Alejandro began calling Ramón *hermano* and *adu* (a street expression of the marijuaneros that means something like the army expression "asshole buddy"). It was all Peace on Earth,

Good Will toward Men, a strong, glowing hippy scene that warmed the heart. Christmas Eve was the high point of that friendship between Ramón and Alejandro.

The day of San Ramón arrived, Ramón's name day. I think it was in February or March, and I think Ramón intended to ignore it as he always did, until Alejandro, well after dark, came to the store and insisted that in honor of the day and of their deep and intimate friendship he wanted to buy Ramón a couple of beers in Luna's salón. It was one of the few times here that anyone had invited Ramón to do anything for which he wasn't expected to pay — double — and he was moved. He changed into a pretty shirt, clean pants pressed razor sharp, and knee-high rubber boots, and walked up the trail through the mud with Alejandro.

Earlier that afternoon I had been delivering corn in the pickup to one of our neighbors who raised chickens. At four o'clock, because it looked like rain, his majordomo had loaned me a heavy canvas tarp, and I had gone back to the farm with it for one last trip. It started to rain in torrents, I got the truck stuck by the loading platform where the corn was stored, and I left everything and went to the house to change into dry clothes.

Alejandro and Ramón and some of the local alcoholics had a beer together, and then Alejandro got up and excused himself. He said he felt embarrassed by Ramón's nice clothes and he wanted to go home, five minutes down the trail, and change into something more appropriate to the occasion. He was gone about forty-five minutes and came back dressed in the same clothes and sweating violently. They had another beer and at ten o'clock Ramón came back to the farm. I didn't know about this until later.

The next morning when we went to push the truck out of the mud we discovered that the tarp, worth about a hundred dollars, and the little hydraulic jack for changing tires had been stolen. Two days later someone broke into my house while we were eating dinner and stole . . . The truth is that I have been robbed so often that I don't remember what he stole. The typewriter? The radio? I think it was the typewriter. And for once I didn't suspect Alejandro. And for once Ramón didn't want to talk about the theft.

A day or two after the house had been ransacked I brought the subject up at lunch. "O.K., great psychologist, who do you think is doing this?"

"Please," Ramón said, holding up his hand like a Quito cop stopping traffic on Diez de Agosto, "I am thinking about this; I am investigating; I am gathering clues."

"But can we narrow it down to four or five possibles?"

"Please," Ramón said, "I'd rather not talk about it just quite yet if you don't mind. You don't mind do you?"

"Nope," I said. "When the captain commands, the sailor doesn't."

"I'm not the captain; I'm your humble servant," Ramón said. "And maybe we can talk about it tonight."

After we had eaten, Ramón tied the revolver in its holster around his waist, took his machete, and walked up the river trail, and I got back on the tractor and went up to the field and disked another ninety-million weeds. When I came back late in the afternoon, Ramón was sitting outside the store with some of the workers, and his eyes were glittering with hardness and excitement.

"O.K.," he said, motioning me into the house where we could talk alone, "now we can start talking. Your old partner is no idiot, is he?"

"Who did it?"

"Say it first," Ramón said, stalling.

"Say what?"

"Say, 'My partner, old Ramón, is no idiot.' "

"First tell me who did it, and then I'll say it . . . Oh, hell, O.K. Ramón, old partner, you are a *maravilla,* a real first class maravilla. Now tell me who did it."

"Alejandro. That son of a bitch Alejandro."

"Are you sure?"

"393 percent out of 100 percent sure."

"*Bueno,* tell me how you know."

First Ramón told me in detail about drinking beer on the night of San Ramón. Then he said, "I went up to his house after lunch today and he was sitting in Pedro's house with Heriberto and Carlos. I called up to him and asked him to come out, I wanted to talk to him. He climbed halfway down the ladder and then went back up and got his machete and came out again and we walked about fifty feet up the trail. I stopped and turned around. 'Why did you bring your machete?' I asked him. He thought that over and said, 'You have your machete; I thought maybe you wanted me to help you.' 'You haven't been to work for three days,' I said. 'No, I'm not feeling too good, a touch of fever.' 'Why did you leave Luna's the other night for almost an hour?' 'Like I said, I wanted to change my clothes.' 'But you didn't change your clothes.' 'No, they were still wet.' 'It took you an hour to find out your clothes were wet?' Alejandro shrugged his shoulders but didn't say anything. 'Why were you sweating so bad when you came back?' He smiled and said, 'Was I sweating? I guess I just sweat easy.' 'I notice that; you're beginning to sweat now, just like a horse.' 'Yeah, I told you I had a fever.' 'And you were panting a little, too, as I remember it now.' 'Yeah, I'm a panter and a sweater.' 'You know what I think, don't you?' 'Yes,' he said, 'but I didn't do it.' 'Didn't do what?' He lowered his eyes to my chest and blinked his eyes real fast about ten times and swallowed. 'I didn't steal that tarp or the jack.' 'Or the typewriter?' 'Or the typewriter.' 'Who said anything about a jack; we never mentioned the jack.' 'I heard you lost a jack; some of the guys must have mentioned it.' 'What guys?' 'Hell, shit, I don't remember; some of the guys.' 'We want that stuff back. Give it back. You're fired, and that's the end of it,' I told him. 'I'm innocent. I didn't do it,' he said. 'You did it, all right; it's written all over your face.' 'I can't help my face,' he said. 'I didn't do it.' 'Where's the tarp and the typewriter? We want them back and it won't go any further.' 'How can I give them back if I didn't take them? What proof have you got anyway? Going around accusing me, and I thought we were friends.' 'Friends?' I said, 'Shit you don't know what the word means.' 'All I got to say is, don't go around accusing innocent people when you got no proof,' he told me, and he turned around and started back to his house, and I yelled after him, 'Alejo, you've got one more chance to tell me, and then I denounce you to the policia.' 'Don't make me laugh,' he said. 'The rurál don't live who can take me in.'

"He did it, didn't he?" I said, because now I was sure he had done it, and now it was going to be ugly, but we had to be absolutely sure he had done it because it is a terrible thing here to turn a man over to the police. It's bad enough having a man put into jail, but it's really terrible when the man claims he is innocent and the police must work on him day after day to get a confession. If Alejandro was guilty I honestly didn't care what they did to him, but if it turned out later that he had been innocent, it would be something awful in our lives that we could never forget and that could wreck our lives here. I wasn't too interested in just the confession without actually seeing the stolen things brought in to the police. After three days with the police Alejandro would confess to anything; he would put his thumb print on any paper they put in front of him.

"He did it," Ramón said, "I say 732 percent out of a 100 percent he did it."

The next day Ramón drove in to Viche and put in a *denuncia* with the teniente político, and that same evening two rurales hitched a ride out as far as the farm and walked down the lane to the store. They waited on the benches until dark and then went up the trail, walking quietly with their revolvers loose in their holsters. They covered the door and the window of Alejandro's cabin and called him out. The place was empty; he had cleared out.

"Well, at least he's gone," I said.

"Sure," Ramón said. "He's gone to sell our stuff, and he'll be back as soon as he's blown all the money."

"Ramón, Ramón, are you absolutely sure it's him?"

"Yes, 876 percent out of 100," Ramón said. "Aren't you?"

"About 99.3," I said. "And I guess, without actually having seen him do it, that's about as sure as we can get."

Ramón was obsessed with the problem of Alejandro. He decided that the police were incapable of catching him and that, even if they really tried, he had too many friends on the river. Five minutes after the police started up the trail, Alejandro would know about it and leap out the back window into the jungle. "I'm going to have to take him in myself," Ramón said.

"If he comes back."

"Don't worry, he'll be back. He doesn't know who I am yet. That's one of the troubles on this farm; nobody knows who I am yet."

"He's big," I said. "For Christ's sake, be careful."

"It's too late to be careful," Ramón said, his face hard and serious. "This is one I have to win."

"You don't have to prove that you're *un hombre muy macho*," I said. "*No es bello morir por la patria.*"

"No," Ramón said, "it's not beautiful to die for anything. But sometimes you have to let people know who you are or they'll destroy you. It's either take that son of a whore in or sell the farm. Everybody on the river is waiting to see what we're going to do. Do you want to sell the farm?"

"I don't care that much. Do you want to sell the farm?"

"No," Ramón said. "Not out of cowardice."

We waited for two weeks and one Saturday afternoon Alejandro, dressed in new clothes and slightly drunk, walked down the lane past the store. Ramón watched him but didn't say anything. He was sullen and arrogant and didn't look at us as he passed. That night Ramón talked with some of the people from Male who said that Alejandro was now staying with his mother in Esmeraldas and that he would probably be going back to town on Sunday afternoon; he had just come out for one night and had invited all his friends to drink with him.

I came over from the pigpens late Sunday just as Alejandro, still a little drunk, still in the same new clothes which had now lost their newness, passed the store again, heading for the highway. Ramón was outside waiting for him.

"O.K., Alejo," Ramón called. "Your big moment has come; I'm taking you in to the police."

"Why, you little shit," Alejandro called back, "don't make me laugh. You're not taking me anyplace." He had a large butcher knife sticking out of his back pocket. He continued up the hill and disappeared in the grass. Ramón ran over to his house and came back with the revolver and a machete.

"You drive," he said. "Let me off just behind Alejandro when we get up to him, and then you drive like hell for Viche and bring back a rurál. I'll be waiting for you on the highway."

"Don't kill him," I said. "Not unless you have to."

"Don't worry. I've got this guy figured out; I'm not in any danger because he's got no guts. But you drive like hell, you hear?"

Alejandro was halfway to the highway, walking in the lane across the level ground where we planted our crops — coconuts on one side, new plantings of pineapple on the other. I slowed the pickup behind him and Ramón jumped out. Alejandro didn't turn around, but he took the butcher knife out of his back pocket and carried it in one hand. I drove like hell for Viche.

For about a hundred yards Ramón walked behind Alejandro up the lane. Neither of them spoke. It was just getting dark and they were walking directly into the last light that hung in the sky above the hills toward the sea. They were still about two hundred yards from the highway when Alejandro left the lane and cut across the field of coconuts that I had been steadily disking almost free of weeds. Ramón followed just behind him.

"Come on," Ramón said, "let's walk in the lane. I don't want any trouble with you. And remember, I've got a gun."

Alejandro snorted. "The trouble is I just happen to know that gun of yours is full of blanks."

"Don't be too sure about that," Ramón said. But it was true; the revolver held one bullet, and it was a blank.

"I'm sure enough," Alejandro said, and suddenly he began to run, running hard across the field of coconuts toward our neighbor's jungle a hundred yards away. Ramón ran behind him.

"You'd better stop or I'll shoot."

Alejandro kept running and Ramón without aiming fired off the gun and Alejandro kept running. Ramón rushed up behind him now and with all his strength swung the machete and struck the flat of the blade across Alejandro's shoulders. Alejandro screamed, spun around, his face wild, and brandished the butcher knife. He must have visualized some kind of confrontation where they would face each other, appraising the situation. But Ramón had been appraising the situation for two weeks, and he didn't hesitate now. He rushed in on Alejandro and brought the flat of the blade swinging down as hard as he could against Alejandro's arm. The knife fell out of his hand; his arm was almost paralyzed, and as he stooped for the knife Ramón brought the machete down three times, as hard as he could, across Alejandro's back. Each time the machete came down, Alejandro let out a sound that was half groan and half scream. Alejandro stayed there on his hands and knees, his head hanging down; he was panting and gasping for air. Ramón stood just behind him.

"You're right about one thing," he said. "You're sure an easy panter. Do you want to play some more?"

Alejandro shook his head slowly. Ramón let him rest for a couple of minutes and then said, "Let's go; let's go back to the lane." Alejandro started to get up and then suddenly sprinted off, trying to reach the jungle where he might have a chance to hide, and Ramón, running behind him and beside him as though he were driving a hog, kept swinging the machete as hard as he could across his back and shoulders; then he started in on his legs. Anyone within a quarter of a mile must have heard the brutal sound of that machete as it came slapping down again and again, as sharp and deadly sounding as pistol shots.

Ramón had maneuvered Alejandro almost back to the lane and almost to where the lane joined the highway. Between the lane and the coconuts was a long narrow line of high grass that I had been unable to disk down. When Alejandro got to the weeds he dropped down on his hands and knees and tried to crawl into them, like a badly wounded animal looking for a place to hide or die. It was quite dark now and Ramón could hardly see him, but he walked close behind him, prodding him from time to time to keep him moving in the right direction. About fifty feet from the highway, Alejandro stopped and stayed there in the grass on his hands and knees, panting and trying to breathe. Ramón, panting and sobbing, stood above him.

After a long minute, his voice breaking, Alejandro cried, "For the love of Christ, Ramón."

"For the love of Christ, *what?*"

"Don't take me in. Please."

"Come on," Ramón said, "we're almost to the road."

"Whatever you think happened," Alejandro said, beginning to weep, "I always did like you; I really liked you."

"Come on," Ramón said. "Get up and walk."

"No," Alejandro said, and Ramón swung the machete across his ass with all his strength, and Alejandro got up and walked.

At the edge of the highway, in the high weeds, Alejandro dropped into the grass. He stretched out on his stomach and wept.

"Come on," Ramón said, "let's go across the road."

"Listen, Ramón, I'll make a deal with you."

"No deals. Get up and walk across the road."

"I can't," Alejandro said.

"Get up and walk across the road," Ramón said. "Oh, you bastard, you son of a bitch, you easy-sweating cowardly son of a bitch. You *maricón de mierda*. Get up and walk across the road if you're a man."

"I can't," Alejandro said.

And maybe he couldn't.

Ramón grabbed him by one wrist and dragged him across the road on his stomach like a dead body, his feet dragging and rubbing and finally beginning to bleed on the rough asphalt. When I drove up about five minutes later with a policeman, Ramón was standing over the body. Motionless and half hidden in the weeds, it looked more like a pile of filthy clothes than anything human. Ramón's face in the headlights was expressionless but hard as granite, and all the muscles in his body were twitching and jumping uncontrollably. He kept yawning and trying to fill his lungs with air.

Along with the policeman I had picked up Heriberto Angulo, who was one of our friends and also a friend of Alejandro's. The four of us lifted Alejandro up and lay him in the back of the truck, and we drove back to Viche and the local jail. The next morning Alejandro was transferred to the big provincial jail in Esmeraldas; it was there that the interrogation, with the lengths of rubber hose and the barbed wire and the electric devices, would be carried out. Alejandro's suffering was about to begin.

10

VÍCTOR

YOUNG DIMA came from Rioverde to work for us. We liked him; he was an old friend from a simpler time when our roles had been more starkly defined, and he tried hard to earn his wages and seemed unaffected by the bad examples all around him. He was the youngest son in one of the more disreputable families on the beach in Rioverde, a calm, pleasant, reasonable kid who hauled water to the houses in the town or canoed people across the river for pennies. His brothers were disasters — brawling, bawling, blasphemous, thieving, hopelessly lazy, and yet, for all that, somehow engaging in their sober moments. Maybe Dima was too young yet to have taken on his family's qualities; he was only eighteen.

I hoped that Dima would stay with us permanently, and we gave him special jobs that would test his capacity and also teach him something about the new ways we were doing things. But after a few months he fell in love with one of the local girls, put her in the family way, and left us suddenly in one of those teenage panics over the realization of how his life must change if he allowed himself to accept the obligations of fatherhood. He joined the army and disappeared for two years into the *oriente,* where he was stationed on the Peruvian border on one of those nameless swift-flowing streams that come rushing into the Napo and the Amazon out of the Andes.

A week after he left us his brother Gregorio came from up the coast to replace him. Gregorio was an old friend, too, in a manner of speaking. He had devoted months of his life, when I was a volunteer, trying to talk me out of 400 sucres to buy a bed so that he could get married. I had spent dozens of evenings with him trying to explain that there was a little something more to marriage than simply owning a bed, and that if he moved into his family's house with his bride as he planned and had the only bed among the dozen or so of brothers, uncles, and cousins who also slept there, he just might with his incredibly high living standards be making a lot of relatives dangerously jealous. His mother, Gloria, ran one of the innumerable *salones* in Rioverde, and when business was bad and there was nothing to eat in the house she even did a little whoring at the grocery store. Gregorio's bed seemed to me like a very complicated addition to that establishment; while I didn't mention my thoughts aloud, I figured that if Gloria was driven by hunger to engage in extra screwing while there were at least eight able-bodied men in the house, well, let her do it in a simple and straightforward manner like everybody else in town — on the floor.

It was three years later. He had never been able to save the sixteen dollars that a bed and mattress cost, but now with money coming in every Saturday that old fantasy began to live in his mind again. He had brought a woman with him — not the older one-eyed widow about whom he had used to speak, laughing and giggling about her in shame and with a kind of defeated humility as though in his heart he felt that she was as good as he deserved. Instead he brought with him a tiny, quite beautiful girl who may have been as young as twelve. She had an Indian face that was proud and reserved, and she always dressed with such care and in such crisply starched dresses that one had the impression she had just changed after bathing. I liked to watch the way she managed her household; she cooked and washed and worked in the yard with the competence and skill that comes with thirty years of experience.

Gregorio was, like almost everyone from Rioverde, a good worker. And four months after he came to the farm he had realized two of life's impossible dreams: Ramón bought him a bed and a 600-sucre two-band radio, to be paid for in painless weekly deductions from his wages. When the bed came he spent an entire weekend lying on it, smoking filter cigarettes, his face frozen in the near idiot's grin of someone who finally owns something finer than anyone else. In the moment when he first stretched out, the idea had burst in his brain that what gave dignity to a man was the things he owned; he was seeing himself now as essentially finer than any of the other workers on the farm. A lifetime's philosophy was crumbling as he saw himself with possessions, his fingers grasping at the first rungs of middle-class respectability. I walked by his cabin a half a dozen times that weekend, and when he saw me coming he would frantically spin the radio dial looking for the one or two Christ-oriented English-speaking stations that blared out their incessant and repetitive propaganda for salvation; his eyes were alight with incredulity at owning an English-speaking radio.

But basically Gregorio was a flawed man, a stupid country lout. Dima was the only apple in that family barrel who had come out whole. The six dollars a week that he was earning was more than he could handle. He paid for the bed and the radio — we saw to that — and by the time they were paid for he was bored with them. He was even slightly resentful that we had deducted two dollars from his wages every week, the *ricos* robbing a *pobre* and restricting his movements; the four dollars that were left him scarcely paid for his food. He was growing bored with his woman, too. God, he just lay around the house all the time like a middle-aged family man too broke to join his friends on Saturdays as they drank and danced. When he had paid his debt to us he went back to his bachelor ways with real zest, trying to make up for all the drinking he had lost out on. I watched the girl with a growing unease as she washed clothes or pots in the little winter stream that ran past the cabins, a dirty jungle stream that the cattle drank from and polluted with their droppings. She was pregnant now, and sometimes one of her eyes was blackened or her lips were cut; Gregorio on Saturday night was macho and stupid like his father and pushed around the only person who wouldn't fight back. Beating up your woman is, of course, one of the normal manifestations of a passionate nature. Ramón, who has never struck his wife, thinks it is because he never really loved her properly. The disintegrating relationship between Gregorio and his woman was typical of this area, and it was happening with such rapidity that I could see it now as something inevitable, the death of love in satiety. Up until this time I had always pitied the local women with their common-law mates. I had assumed that they were madly eager to legitimize their relationships in legal marriage. I had thought that they were forced into transient housekeeping because of the man's reluctance to place himself under the law and the stern eye of God. Not at all, I now realized. The woman is even more terrified than the man of being shackled into an imprisoning situation and of finding, after those first flaming ecstatic months of passion have cooled to barely glowing coals, that she is stuck with a drunkard, a lout, a fool, or someone too lazy to work.

Out of a kind of luck that he didn't at all deserve, Gregorio had found a girl of beauty, charm, and character; he now proceeded to blow his chances with her and destroy his happiness. Like his older brothers, he had always been a complete fool when he drank, and he must have been profoundly unsure of his manhood since he so insisted on painting himself in all the macho colors. What had obscured his true character in Rioverde had been his poverty; he had never had the money to fulfill himself, to dance before the world in all his potential foolishness. We began to anticipate episodes, but we hardly thought that in Male, among strangers and without the reassurance of his drunken brothers, he would dare to leap on tables at such frequent intervals to proclaim his virility and his willingness to prove it in hand to hand combat. But now almost every week we began to hear stories about his *imprudencias*. His wife sat alone in the cabin on weekends. Nothing had really happened yet. He was undersized, delicately boned, permanently stunted in childhood, both physically and mentally, from malnutrition; no one felt seriously threatened by him yet or inclined to take his challenges seriously, but it seemed as though the time were coming when he could no longer be ignored. What was sadder was our conviction that out of some irrationality he was desperately seeking a situation where everyone would finally have to reckon with him. He was a man with a bed and a radio (and now a cigarette lighter), and yet people continued to treat him as though they didn't really like him very much. How wonderful to be at the center of attention for a change, if only for five minutes — even if to reach that goal one found oneself finally in a pool of familiar blood, flat on the floor of a jungle salón with a smashed-in face or a slashed arm from a furiously swung machete.

Ramón, who had never particularly liked him and who will forever carry Gregorio's teeth marks on his stomach from some distant teenage Saturday night brawl in Rioverde, began to talk about firing him. "He's going to get himself killed if he stays around here; let's send him back to the sticks."

"Talk to him first," I said. "Talk to him hard; scare a little sense into him. He still works fairly well, and I feel sorry for his wife."

"I've talked to him a dozen times," Ramón said. "You can't teach those stupid country Mendozas anything; they've got heads like *guayacán*."

It was only a few days later that Ramón fired him, and under conditions so stark and pure that even Gregorio understood why he had to go. We had been harvesting corn that week, one man to a row, walking down the rows with baskets and piling up the unshucked ears in mounds at the edge of the disked ground. Three or four times a day I would disk down the harvested corn rows behind the men so that they didn't have to haul their baskets more than a few feet. In the afternoons, if it didn't rain, I would go out with a couple of men and shell out the corn into sacks with a small tractor-driven sheller, the only one in the province.

Harvesting corn was the best work on the farm. Except for the chaff that gradually worked into one's sores and set the arms to itching, it was clean and untiring work. Unlike working in the peanuts, where the pace of one's work was relentlessly open to view, harvesting corn was almost secret. It was easy to crouch down unobserved in the eight-foot-high rows and smoke a cigarette or tranquilly work one's way through a five-pound hand of bananas. Best of all it was community work. The idea of working in groups is one of the few African traits that doesn't seem to have become lost in the transplanting. When we wanted to punish someone for being lazy or crafty, we would take him out of a group and put him off to work by himself; alone he is like a drooping blossom ripped from the vine. This is a puzzling contradiction, for if the Ecuadorian black is anything he is an anarchist.

In the corn harvest, six or eight men always worked together, moving together across the field, setting their pace to the slowest picker. No one dared to be outstanding and to earn the title of kiss-ass to the owners. There was always much talk and laughter, a kind of party feeling, men kidding one another, men screaming with delight at some outrageous joke, someone getting started on an interminable monologue about a snake so long that it took fifteen minutes to slide across the trail or a whore so destroyed by love that she wouldn't take money but offered instead to support the teller for life and furnish him with nothing but the finest silk shirts or a drunken friend with a machete who stood up to six Manabitas in a jungle dance hall. At about half-hour intervals someone would have to relieve himself and he would come back from the heavy jungle growth at the edge of the field with bunches of bananas or a hatful of oranges. It averaged out, during the corn harvest, that each worker had about three bowel movements a day between 7 A.M. and 2 P.M. when they quit for the day, and on a certain Monday when a certain tree of tangerines was ripe, eight men had a simultaneous urge to defecate. Poor constipated men. It took them each precisely an hour and a half.

Except when I was impatient with the men and moved in with them to set a faster pace, I usually worked a little apart. I didn't like to be a damper on their obscene humor — or the butt of it. But I liked to be close enough to hear them, not that I completely understood their jive and all its scatalogical subtleties, but it felt good to be enveloped in the music that they made.

The day that we fired Gregorio I wasn't even listening. I didn't hear anything this time, just a sudden jolting silence. I looked across at the men through the rows. A frozen tableau. Everyone had stopped working and talking and they were all staring at Gregorio and Víctor in a kind of incredulous expectancy. After half a minute Víctor said something, and I couldn't hear that either, and there was another long period when no one moved; then Gregorio laughed weakly with a funny, sick look on his face, and now, no one talking, the men once more began to move up the corn rows; one of the younger kids working by himself began to sing a sad and lonely love song: *Maldito cabaret / Donde gasté / Los años de mi vida . . .* Something had destroyed the unity of that crew as effectively as a spray of machine-gun fire.

At two o'clock when we went back to the house to eat, Gregorio came in behind us, smiling foolishly. Ramón paid him off. "For

God's sake, go back to the sticks where you belong. Go get killed in Rioverde."

"It was just a joke," Gregorio said. "No offense meant."

"Funny joke, Goya. No, *vaya, vaya, vaya con dios*. Today."

Gregorio left and I said, "Well? What's this all about? Tell me."

"You couldn't hear from where you were? It was just incredible. For no reason at all Gregario, who hadn't said a word all morning, suddenly calls across to Víctor so everybody can hear, "Hey Víctor, you old pile of shit, how about letting me fuck your wife?"

"Oh, my God," I said. "He's crazy."

"Yes," Ramón said, "a real stupid animal. You know what he was really saying? 'I spit in your face, Víctor; let's fight to the death; I'm ready to die.' And Víctor was magnificent; I've never been so proud of him. You should have seen him, his face drained, his hands clenched into fists, grinding his teeth together, trembling. And after a minute he called back so everyone could hear, smiling, but with his voice trembling with rage, 'Why, sure, Goya, let's make a trade; you fuck my wife, and I'll fuck your whore mother.' "

Gregorio left the farm but for the next six weeks we saw him almost every Sunday. His wife, using her pregnancy as an excuse, went back to her mother's house in Rocafuerte. Gregorio got a job with the Texaco outfit and moved into the bachelor's bunkhouse at the campsite just a couple of miles down the road from us. He worked as a machetero cleaning out the right-of-way for the pipeline that would pass just behind our farm. Afraid of being robbed, he had left his mattress and his radio with us, and on Sundays he would sadly sit on the store bench polishing his radio with a rag and listening to the Guayaquil fútbol games. He was alone now. He hated working for Texaco, where he had lost his dignity, where he was just one more ant among hundreds just like him, and after a few weeks he quit his job and went back to Rioverde.

Some months later we heard that Gregorio's child had been born, had died of tetanus, the seven-day sickness, and that his wife had refused to return to him. I imagine he is back on the beach again, his radio pawned or broken and his mattress long since thrown into the weeds. I remember him in his youth in Rioverde when he longed to be married, when he stood alone at midnight in the town's single sandy road and screamed, cursing life and his bad luck, beating the ground with his fists, eating dirt, and weeping. I guess he is back there now still doing the same things.

From the moment out in the corn field when Víctor defeated Gregorio with a few well-chosen words, he became for me the real superstar of the farm. I had thought that only Dorothy Parker knew how to slice people up with her tongue. Víctor had been with us almost from the beginning, and I had scarcely noticed him as a person — or, at least, as a person with superstar qualities. Once you began to observe Víctor he grew on you like . . . like a brain tumor? For a year I had thought of him as a pretty stupid type; he had done some outrageous and dishonest things that made me urge Ramón to fire him, but Ramón had made excuses for him. They just didn't make blacks like Víctor anymore, Ramón insisted. Well, they certainly didn't make them as *black,* anyway.

Víctor had lived on the river where I was a Peace Corps volunteer, but so far upriver that I don't remember having seen him those few times when he might have come down out of the jungle to buy salt or kerosene or to dance for three days running at the town's fiestas. But from the first moment that I saw him at the farm there had been something familiar about his face that troubled me. One day, seven years before, riding out to Rioverde on the truck that connected us with the provincial capital, I had sat across from a young Negro who was so incredibly ugly that I could hardly believe it. With the camera hidden in my lap I had taken a couple of secret pictures of him as proof that we weren't necessarily made in the image of God. Everything about that guy was gigantic, somehow monstrous — his nose, his neck, his teeth, his shoulders, his feet. He was like a coal black Primo Carnera with every separate part of him blown up to monumental proportions and with everything off scale so that nothing really fit with anything else. His fingers were too big for his hands, his hands too big for his tremendous arms, his head too big for his body, his nose too large and crude on that large crude face. The pictures I took of him turned out in time and he was identified as Adolfo; he was coming from somewhere to live for a time in

Rioverde, and he moved in with Santo up the beach a mile past Ramón's house and went out every day into the ocean to dip up shrimp. I started to get friendly with him until Ramón told me that he was stealing lengths of bamboo from a new house that Ramón was building. This put him on my list, I decided I didn't like him, and I didn't talk to him anymore.

Now, seven years later, Víctor came to work for us. He was about twenty years old, big and solid, so black that in certain lights you could hardly see him; at a distance out in the field he was invisible, a pair of ragged pants floating above the weeds. At night under a harsh direct light or in full sunshine he stood revealed in shadows and highlights, and at certain times he seemed to be lit from within by blue and purple lights. He was extremely handsome, but where had I seen him before? He had been with us for a month when his mother, his twin sister, and one of his brothers came for a six-month visit. His brother was Adolfo, that monstrous fellow from another time. If you stood the two brothers side by side they had a quite identical look, except that while in Adolfo every feature was gross and brutalized, a subtle refinement of those same features had turned Víctor into a black peasant god, all rural strength and vigor, health, and simple uncomplicated good humor. Now, side by side, they were both beautiful — Adolfo stood revealed in Víctor as the culmination of his own potential. Adolfo was all extras — electrically operated windows, tons of chrome, twin gold-plated exhausts. Víctor was the economy model with everything pared away to essences, a Negro by Brancusi. Pondering this enigma I decided that what made them both agreeable to look at was that their physical characteristics exactly mirrored their own inner qualities. They were harmonious; they were exactly what they seemed to be. Their souls were not hidden in their bodies but existed outside them in plain view.

I think no one who ever worked for us on the farm was ever quite so primitive and basic as those two, but to describe them thus is to split hairs. All our workers were exclusively jungle educated. Not 10 percent of them could read or write; most of them had never been out of the province; trips to Quito or Guayaquil were culminating events in life — one or two day trips they dreamed of making before they died. The rest of the world could be described in about fifty words: New York, Miami, Al Capone, Europe, Brazil, Pelé, Cali, Cassius Clay, Kennedy, Peru, Colombia, un machete "Collins." But where was Europe in relation to New York, and which country was larger? Our workers with names like Stalin, Hitler, or Kennedy were as unaware of the leaders for whom they were named as their fathers with the names of Socrates, Copernico, Aristotle, or Platón. Ramón's father had somewhere heard of Columbus but thought he was one of the first presidents of Colombia.

Víctor and Adolfo existed on another deeper and purer level of innocence; they had not one drop of curiosity about Europe or the world soccer matches or the wars in Israel, Lebanon, Vietnam, Argentina, or Ireland. They believed that Hercules could kill lions with his bare hands and that a man could turn into a vampire at midnight, because they had actually seen these things with their own eyes at the movies. They had seen a cowboy with a six-shooter kill thirteen men without reloading; it was strange but it had to be true, and since it was confusing they preferred not to think about such things. They set about mastering their own world. They moved through the jungle with all the assurance of animals, and the complete sophistication and toughness with which they confronted their world made the other workers seem timid and uncertain by comparison. Everyone but Víctor and Adolfo, for instance (and I put myself at the head of this group), was deathly afraid of snakes. Cleaning out a tangle of weeds someone would fling his machete into the air screaming *culebra,* and the workers would freeze in alarm, their eyes rolling, or they would bound out of the brush like stampeding buffaloes — except for Víctor, who would run into the weeds and come out a moment later with a dead but writhing snake balanced on his machete to receive the extra ten sucres we offered for every poisonous variety. With the offering of this bounty, our farm, just as in the case of Folke Anderson, no longer contained nonpoisonous snakes; even the lovely eight-foot boas got their names changed from *noopa* to *mata caballo,* "horse killer." And one mad hustling black who was with us for a couple of weeks used to bring in six-inch earthworms all beat up and mangled as though they had been struggling for hours on almost equal terms with their captor, who would squat with his trophies outside the store and argue with me until at times I was almost 2 percent convinced that they weren't just night crawlers but actually cousins to the coral.

There is another cause for uncontrolled terror and hysteria on the farm — wasps. There are many kinds, most of them are lethal, and some of them inject a venom so powerful that being stung by three or four at one time is like having a major heart attack. Some of the wasps don't sting, they dive-bomb you and flee, but whatever the type we knock from the branches the reaction is always the same. Watching the workers shrieking and scattering, ragged shirt-tails flying, arms waving because one of them has slashed a hidden nest, I was confronted in an amused way with doubts about their basic heterosexuality. In this almost effeminate hysteria, did not some small aspect of the black soul stand revealed? With the simple unashamed honesty with which they admitted their terror of an insect, the mask of machismo behind which they normally hid themselves was ripped for a moment from their faces. I felt closer to them observing the honesty of their reactions. In contemplating this girlish delicacy I lost a little more of my vague fear of the Negro, the fear that is engendered by differences; it is a subconscious feeling of the black's potential for implacable destruction. "Though I'm black I'm still delicate," is a common saying here when I ask someone to do something that seems to indicate that I am ignoring his humanity. Watching my shrieking workers flee I felt that I better understood James Baldwin's remark, "We are not an heroic people." Well, we're not either, just a little more hypocritical.

By their reactions, Víctor and Adolfo didn't do much to encourage these new insights. While everyone else was running, they, already perhaps having been stung a time or two, would keep on stolidly swinging their machetes. I have seen Víctor gently pluck a wasp's nest from a tree branch and hold it in his hand. This either showed contempt for pain or a profound understanding of that particular nest. If any other of the workers had been stung he would have tried to quit for the day, complaining of fever and dizziness, symptoms that disappeared after five minutes.

Víctor had just recently separated from one woman and married a second. His first woman had left him when they moved out of the jungle to Esmeraldas; she walked city streets, dazzled; she talked to friends and then decided she could do better as a whore. Víctor spent his second honeymoon in the same shack that Ramón and Ester had stayed in for a time when we first got here. Víctor was our third hog man, and his job was to wash down the pens, grind corn, feed and water the different lots, and do for the babies just about anything that they needed done to them. In California I had taken care of 1200 pigs alone with less trouble than Víctor now had with our modest little bunch of 50. Washing shit out of pens was not exactly Víctor's idea of the good life; he couldn't understand why we got so angry if a few pigs had to wait three or four hours to drink water. He didn't like being a slave to a bunch of pigs who ate better than he did. Working under a roof all day was like being in jail, it was too different from wandering free in the jungle. Besides he had special and, we hoped, temporary problems. Being so newly married he had carnal appetites that needed to be satisfied at unbelievably short intervals. His capacity for steady and uninterrupted lovemaking filled us with awe; it was stupefying, and of such a supernatural character that the thought was put into my head that we were indeed in the presence of a black god. Still, awestruck as we were, there was something grossly irritating about the thought of Víctor over there in the shack, conscientiously screwing himself to death while the pigs squealed in their pens for a glass of cool water.

Adolfo and Víctor had grown up on an isolated stretch of river thirty miles from a store or a light plant or even the rumor of a civilizing decadence. They were part of an inexhaustibly large family (the mother had worked her way through four husbands) that lived off the jungle. They hunted with dogs for the meat they ate; they fished with nets, hooks, and spears. The fruits and vegetables that made up their diet were gathered over a ten-mile-square area — plátano, bananas, *chantaduras, caimitos,* oranges, avocados, chocolate, squash, corn, and beans — everything that either grew wild or was raised by their neighbors. Out in that wilderness the idea that they were stealing or trespassing never entered their minds — or if it did to the extent that they concealed their thefts, they lived without the slightest feeling of guilt about it. This was a common way of life for many of the poorer, and not so poor,

people of coastal Ecuador. Their basic confusion about ownership
and private property was one of the main characteristics that they
brought to the farm. Within three days Víctor had walked every
trail on the property (and both our neighbors' property as well)
and had pinpointed every tree and bush that would serve his purpose. He had catalogued 500 acres; he knew which trees were
ready to harvest and when he might reasonably return to harvest
the rest. Within the first week he had harvested a hundred abandoned coffee plants growing forgotten in the shade of the Luna
pasture. It was pure theft, but we tried not to react like dogs in
the manger; after all he was harvesting coffee that we had no
intention of harvesting ourselves. But he didn't know that. We
felt that it would have been nice if he had asked permission, and
nicer still if he had harvested our coffee in his off hours. We resented paying wages to a man for robbing us and taking certain
rights of possession while the pigs began to droop and sicken. I
was trying very hard, about this time, to view life through the eyes
of the opposition. I wanted to understand how it was to be black
and poor. Whatever little insights I achieved seemed to nourish
my propensity for self-loathing. It is not always necessarily pleasant to be white and rich, standing on top of the pile, the king of
the mountain. I felt like the president of a large company who
had earned his job only because his father owned 51 percent of
the stock. Maybe Víctor wasn't stealing after all. We were already prejudiced in his favor by his charming ways, so now we
tried to admire his enterprise. He had ambitions to better himself
and to augment the somewhat less than generous wages that we
paid. Wasn't this maybe the man we had been looking for, someone we could actually help, someone like Ramón with the urges
and energies and the intelligence to dominate his poverty?

We were disabused of this conception of him when he spent
the first money that he earned. Or no, rather we were once more
reminded of how impossibly difficult and foolhardy it is to think
about implanting one's values in another. We had pegged him
correctly, he did want to move out of poverty, but he wanted to
move away from his idea of it, not mine. He was twenty years
old, strongly made, obsessed with his own beauty and his sexual
magnetism. Moving out of poverty simply meant that he would

have the money to adorn himself to magnificence and to transform all those lonely, deprived adolescent fantasies into blinding reality. He took the first money that we paid him, plus the sale of fifty pounds of coffee beans, and had the best dentist in Esmeraldas cap two of his perfect teeth with gold. Now when he smiled at you, a thing he did with more frequency, it was like being slapped across the face. A gold-plated cross on a heavy gold chain; cheap dollar rings in the shape of a number four die, the numbers represented by colored gems of cut glass; a massive slave bracelet in silver with the name Marlboro incised across it; a four-pound wrist watch that perpetually indicated twelve minutes past quitting time — as the weeks passed he gradually acquired these things plus shimmering flaring hippy pants and Dacron shirts in pure bright colors. It occurs to me as I write this that he must have been stealing ten times more than we ever realized.

Ramón was bowled over by this new, opulent African chieftain look. But weren't we all; we felt shabby and disreputable beside this gorgeous kid. On Saturdays when the men came to the store at noon to be paid, Ramón always dropped his very abrupt and serious manner and gave way to his admiration of Víctor when he sauntered in. "My God," Ramón would cry, "look what's coming. They just don't make them like this anymore. Have you ever seen anyone so *black?* Ay, *negro, negro.*" And he would lean across the table with its piles of sucre bills and grab Víctor's arm or rub his back or pat his ass. Disgusting. Víctor, smiling shyly, would lower his eyes like a young concubine about to be sold on the block for a record-breaking price; he bowed his head with modest complacency, accepting this admiration that he knew was so well deserved.

After he had been paid off and before the next man entered, petulant with all this excessive adoration I would say to Ramón, "Look, I realize you're madly in love with this guy, but do you realize that yesterday between eleven and six he didn't show up even once to check on the pigs?"

"I'll talk to him about that," Ramón would say.

"He's still harvesting coffee," I might say; or "I hear he's packing off sacks of pineapples"; or "Did you see that great pile of oranges in front of Víctor's house?"; or "I caught Víctor in the cacao with his hat full of chocolate beans."

"Yes, I talked to him about that; it's all settled. He's promised not to steal anymore."

"But I hear he's stealing all of Pastór's plátano."

"Yes, I also heard that. As a matter of fact Pastór is desperate to sell his farm to us."

"I talked to Pastór too," I said. "He claims that between Víctor and the people we sold lots to on the river he doesn't have a chance; they're cleaning him out. When he's cutting weeds on one end of the farm, they're packing off plátano on the other end. Now, seriously Ramón, don't you think we'd better get rid of Víctor?"

"I'll talk to him again. He's very *simpático,* that Negro, don't you agree?"

But how could I deny that Víctor was simpático? Everyone up and down the river agreed with us that he was just about the neatest thing that had happened here since the 1958 earthquake. He had only two flaws, this almost perfect man — sustained and repetitive work bored him, and he was a goddamn thief. Were these flaws or simply coastal characteristics developed to the highest power? We took him out of the hog pens and put him to work in the fields.

We had a back-type motor-driven sprayer that we used almost constantly during our summer war with the bugs. Our biggest problem was the *cogollero,* a kind of army worm that didn't march but had set up permanent bivouacs in the corn and the peanuts; it also liked young newly planted coconuts. The poisons we used were strong and dangerous, our water supply, the river, was a half mile from the fields; it was a real hassle hauling tanks of water and trying to teach the workers how to handle these deadly poisons. We spent days teaching the necessity of using a face mask and of bathing and changing clothes after work, but in spite of all our preaching no one could work with these spray materials for any length of time without developing headaches, dizziness, purple spots, and debility. Many of the workers were terrified of the sprays and would even stagger out of the field moaning softly after having used weed killers instead of insecticides; their diet of rice and plátanos kept them in a constant weakened condition at the edge of malnutrition. Most of the men came to work at seven in the morning having eaten nothing more nourishing for breakfast than a plate of boiled plátanos and a cup of hot river water well-laced with amoebas, six teaspoons of sugar, and a shard of cinnamon. They had no resistance against these poisons, real or imagined.

But not tough Víctor, stainless steel and gold. Here he comes day after day, striding down the peanut rows, almost obscured in a drifting mist of deadly vapors through which almost all we can see is the dull gleam of teeth. He has seen us 200 yards away and has begun to smile; when he catches us watching him he fumbles in a pants pocket, pulls out the face mask and holds it up an inch or two from his mouth. Or if he has left the mask at home he breathes through his hat or a shirt tail. We wait for him at the edge of the field at the fifty-gallon tank, from which he dips his spray material, to rebuke him furiously for his carelessness. He is embarrassed to be caught committing suicide, but he appreciates our concern, and he bows his head, smiles patiently, and promises to use the mask. And he plunges his arms up to the elbows in the tank to wash away the sweat. My God, Víctor, *don't*. Why doesn't he drop dead, or at least stagger about a bit? Aghast, feeling almost as though we are losing our minds, we explain again how poison is absorbed through the skin and again make him promise to bathe and change his clothes. The next day when Víctor comes to work he is dressed in the same clothes, which stink of Aldrin, Fosferno, and DDT.

He must have been a walking death trap for bugs in his chemically treated rags, but the bugs didn't seem to mind. At many times during the year Víctor had the curious power of attracting butterflies; sometimes for hours he would be at the center of a swirling cloud of bright yellow wings as he moved down the coconut rows macheteing grass or hoeing grass out of the peanuts or the beans. I tended to romanticize this power, wanting to think that it indicated some profound and mysterious affinity with nature in this very natural man, but I had to reject this idea when I, too, but to a lesser degree, found myself on certain days surrounded by thousands of butterflies that followed me as I moved across the fields or gathered on my hands and shirt as I sat smoking in some sunny clearing.

Víctor liked the job of spraying. In almost three years he was only poisoned once: spraying tobacco against those great-horned three-inch worms (the same ones that love tomatoes), he apparently bathed in the fifty-gallon tank and broke out in dozens of purple snakelike welts. He was cured with three days rest and a visit to a quack doctor in Esmeraldas who charged him (us) 600 sucres for a bottle of lotion for allergies, a free sample that had been sent by a drug company. What Víctor liked about this work was its built-in irregularities; many times the little gasoline motor broke down, many times he finished up a field by ten o'clock. After spraying he was supposed to bathe, and we gave him the rest of the day off to do this. This gave him extra hours to prowl through the wilder parts of the farm and even to move past the familiar property lines into new territory. He was harvesting mostly avocados, plátanos, oranges, chocolate, pineapples, and bananas. Cacao, after years of depressed prices, was rising from twelve to fifty dollars a sack, and our new plantings, just beginning to bear fruit, were so full of possibilities that Víctor even began planning out a night schedule. Reports began to reach us of rows of lanterns and flashlights moving down the chocolate and pineapple rows. We hired our first night watchman, Washington, who the first day on duty was guarding my house when the second typewriter was stolen. We were afraid to put Víctor to cleaning or pruning cacao; he couldn't resist filling his hat and his pockets and small baskets with the beans. In fact toward the end of our relationship we were afraid to put him to work anyplace on the farm where he couldn't plainly be seen from the road.

Insatiable Víctor, turning all our crops into silk shirts and golden gee-gaws. He tried to do it alone but found himself falling behind. He sent word again to his mother, his sister, and to Adolfo; they came and began to organize the harvests. Later others were invited in; more brothers, cousins, aunts, half-cousins, grandmothers — all of them more like Adolfo than Víctor, all of them oversized, heavy-limbed, awkward country bumpkin types. One got the impression that God had spent all his artistry and patience in constructing Víctor to perfection and then, bored, had wandered off leaving the rest of the tribe half completed with all their bumps and lumps and bulges. One day Ramón, threading his way through the piles of drying produce outside Víctor's house, counted sixteen weird faces in the windows of that two-room shack, and in an explosion of outrage gave Víctor twenty-four hours to clear the premises, which he did. Twenty-four hours after that it began slowly and secretly to fill again with the same people or slight variations on the same people, creatures from the Black Lagoon, I called them. From time to time we gave Adolfo work; for a month or so we suffered along with Segundo, the oldest brother. During the peanut harvests we put aunts, sisters, and grandmothers out in the field; the best worker in that whole family was Víctor's mother, as rough as a bear, with feet as large and square as barges. Working for us interrupted her schedule; she made much more stealing and, because of her age, didn't feel she could handle two jobs. What a ruthless and innocent family they were, and how stupid we were, bedazzled by Víctor, to let ourselves only half believe what was really going on for over two years.

When Víctor came out of the Río Verde jungles at nineteen, he made the change from hunter to hired man with a minimum of trouble. Adolfo on the other hand never completely understood this new, more civilized life. He didn't have Víctor's blind impulse to settle down with a woman and found a family; he was a drifter, a nomad, like the wild *cauchero* across the river who sleeps each night in a different camp. Adolfo could never figure out the complications of working for someone as an employee. He could never understand our insistence that he begin work at seven and keep at it until two. How could he go to work at seven if there was nothing in the house to eat for breakfast and he had first to roam the trails looking for something to cook? How could he promise on Monday that he would come to work on Tuesday when he couldn't possibly look into the future and know what kind of a mood he might be in? Maybe on Tuesday he would feel like hunting with his dogs or flirting with one of the river girls. Maybe he would have a fever. Maybe he would wake up in a pensive mood with the undeniable impulse to lie around the house staring at the ceiling or plinkity-plunkiting on his four-dollar guitar. Even if he came to work at seven it didn't mean that he could always finish out the day. A group of interesting-looking people might walk down the road, men and women bright and gay in party clothes; Adolfo would drop everything and chase after them.

If it was a fútbol team heading up the river for Male or Mafua or Delicias, chances are that Adolfo would decide to join them. Digging out a stump he might dislodge a *juanta* or an armadillo, and off he would run behind his dinner. Burning brush, his eyes watering from the smoke, he would remember that out there in the coolness of the jungle there was a certain avocado tree now ready to harvest, and he would drop his tools where he stood, grab up his machete, and walk the secret trails.

One payday I discovered a terrible thing about Adolfo, and I told Ramón about it. "All the men were sitting on the benches waiting to be paid — telling jokes, horsing around — and Mercedes in fun pretended to swing at Adolfo with his machete. Instead of trying to protect himself he got this childish look of terror on his face and hunched over with both arms wrapped around his head; he began to groan and whimper like a whipped dog."

"I thought I told you about that," Ramón said. "When they were little kids on the river their father would come home drunk late at night and beat his children on the head with clubs as they lay sleeping. I don't know that it affected Víctor very much, but Adolfo has never gotten over it. Who would ever marry Adolfo now? At night it is really sad; no one outside his family likes to sleep in the same house with him. All night long he talks in his sleep, croons, and cries; or with his hands empty of anything, he will think he is playing his guitar and move his fingers over the strings, singing; and he does this all night long for hours at a time — talking, singing, crying, making music on his guitar, plinkity plinkity plunk, plinkity plunk. One night when we were kids in Rioverde, I got drunk and was afraid to go home and slept in Crucelio's house. Adolfo was there, and drunk as I was it got under my skin something awful. It is bad not to feel safe at night. You have to mock him and laugh at him or else cry with pity."

When Víctor had been with us for a little over a year, he came to us and said that he wanted to stay with us forever and that he wanted his own land where he could build a house and plant plátano to sell. His first child by his second woman had died at birth from tetanus, but he was expecting another and wanted more room. Because we liked him and thought he had style, and because we admired his ambition, we wanted to help him. At this point his thievery was only vague rumor, and we liked him so much that we preferred not to believe his jealous co-workers, who probably resented his special place on the farm. We gave him ten acres on the highway and raw planks for the floor of his house; we told him to dig up the guayacán corner posts of the cattle shed that had collapsed and use them in his new building. He built the walls of split bamboo and the roof of cade, and the whole thing couldn't have cost him more than five dollars if that, since, come to think of it, he probably stole the nails out of our bodega. For two months he worked in the afternoons with his family. He cleaned a part of his plot and put in plátano that he stole from Pastór and young pineapples that he stole from us. We didn't mind; we wanted all our neighbors to steal the pineapple plants left over from the harvest, feeling that if they had their own plantings perhaps they wouldn't be so compulsively driven to raid our fields at night.

But why had Víctor built his house so big? I wondered without asking, afraid to confront the gruesome possibility that he needed more floor space for more relatives. It couldn't be that, the place was enormous, there was space in the new house for thirty more cousins, for prides of lumpish uncles. He cut down all the high grass along the highway and painted the outside front wall in blocks and stripes of red and green. Someone painted strange indecipherable letters across the door, running all the words, if they were words, together. When everything was done he came to us with his new plans. What he had just figured out, he said, was that if he had a salón with music, Pepsi, beer, and aguardiente he could make an extra week's wages every Saturday night. Ramón agreed. We made a down payment on a 400-dollar phonograph and guaranteed Víctor's honesty for the monthly payments he was pledged to make. We loaned him money to buy a pile of phonograph records, tawdry country music from rural Colombia, cases of hard liquor and cheap colas, packages of hard mints, a couple dozen glasses. Saturday afternoon Ramón hauled everything out from Esmeraldas for a grand opening night.

And Sunday morning Ramón in a rage cut off Víctor's credit when he came to the house to report that the salón had been

destroyed and that he had lost, as close as he could figure, something like a thousand sucres, about forty dollars. What he really
needed now, he said, was a little more money. He couldn't read
or write, he could scarcely make change, he had trusted everyone
who asked for it with unlimited credit. His family had helped
him serve drinks; by midnight they were drunker than the customers and pocketing what little money came in. Opening night was
closing night.

With everything practically free, the waiters as drunk as the
patrons, and Víctor in a daze of happiness off in a dark corner
admiring his phonograph, a weird anarchy began to grow among
the people; the air became electric with possibility. It was the same
old crowd with one new face: a tall slim girl from Quinindé
dressed in very tight Levis and a tight white shirt that threatened
to rip into pieces under the pressure of her small, tight, pointed
breasts; her face was royal, sullen, challenging, disdainful of this
drunken group of country louts. When the usual fights started
about 2 A.M. everyone but Víctor got involved. No one in that
smoky room had ever felt so joyfully vicious and savage; when the
fighting was over, everyone gulping in air, some of them probably
feeling really alive for the first time, they couldn't stop. Screaming with joy they broke all the glasses and the bottles and the
benches and then smashed the tables and then kicked holes in the
bamboo walls. It was one of those truly great parties that is
talked about for years, true creative violence raised to new levels
beyond the sound barrier.

For two weeks we ignored Víctor and left him to simmer in the
stew of his own debacle; he hoed weeds alone in the young pineapples, shunning his companions. He was depressed and confused
by that violence, which had seemed to be directed at him; he was
a man who liked order and wanted things to be pretty and deco-
rous. Jesus, his own friends. Jesus, his own *relatives*. And there
was something else that itched and burned in his heart; it was that
new girl, but maybe he didn't know that yet. On Saturdays he
sat alone in one dark corner of his house, his only solace the
cheap quick music and a slow-beating languorous tango that he
began to play over and over. He didn't light candles or open the
door; he had nothing to sell. His wife sulked, neglected, in the

other smaller room where the two of them slept on a woven mat; his mother and sister circled around him at a distance, studying his face with alarm, darting in from time to time with special plates of little somethings prettily deep-fried in rancid grease. Finally, wanting to bask once more in the radiance of his golden smile, we took pity on him and offered to finance him very modestly once more, if he would do exactly as we said. Víctor agreed, his face alight. We had to save him if we could; the first phonograph payment was coming due.

We spent three nights trying to teach him the first ten numbers and how to write them on a piece of paper. Not much progress there. Now with piles of corn and beans in different colors we showed him how to subtract and make change: if Maria has three oranges and Gloria has five oranges and Víctor steals two oranges (a stern firm smile at this point) . . . And Víctor, carefully moving beans back and forth across the counter and murmuring "*Soy hombre pobre pero honrado,*" gives an answer like a question. We are heartened; the answers are clever but intuitive. By Friday we realized that it would take more time than we would ever have to transform plain homespun Víctor into the local J. P. Morgan. We confronted him with plan B. His wife, who had had three years of schooling, would wait on the tables (if he had any tables) and collect the money. This was to be done immediately after each drink was served. A good round dozen relatives were to be asked to leave at once. He could keep his mother, his twin sister, and his nephew Antonio, who was working for us. Víctor was to build a strong cage of hardwood in which he would sit with his phonograph and records, his bottles of hooch, his cigarettes and candies, and his box of small cash carefully piled toward the center; the cage was to be padlocked; there was to be no credit; if a man arrived with his tongue dragging on the ground and begged for a life-giving drink, there was to be no credit. O.K.? . . . O.K.

The second opening was a success but not an easy one. We had loaned him money for only six bottles of "painkiller," and he had to send Antonio the two miles into Viche at least three times to restock the salón. The following Saturday things went a little better; Víctor loved sitting in his cage surrounded by his things and the growing pile of sucres. It would have been a perfect scene if someone hadn't broken a bottle over Antonio's head.

Hard-headed, seventeen-year-old Antonio, sweet and generous, imprudent and lazy. We remember him kindly, that lanky brawler; in all the time he worked for us I don't think he stole much of anything and, being Víctor's nephew, this rather put him in a class by himself. He had one bad trait that may end up killing him. He felt impelled at the most inappropriate times to open up his big mouth and say big insensitive things that impelled almost everyone else to take a swing at him. When he called some man's mother a whore, why couldn't the man realize that he really didn't mean it? He didn't know the man's mother; hell, he scarcely knew the man. Antonio had tremendous family feet that stumbled over each other as he swung his uncoordinated arms like helicopter blades in the heat of battle. He never won a fight, and he never learned to keep his big country mouth shut. About twice a month he came to work on Mondays with a split lip or a bit of his ear chewed off or his cheek gashed by ringed knuckles. In the year and a half that he helped his uncle Víctor in the salón business, he must have had bottles broken over his head at least three times.

Víctor's business prospered but his style of living didn't seem to change much. He made regular phonograph payments and invested his surplus in pants and shirts. Apparently that's all he wanted, for after a good weekend he would disappear for a day or two, not bothering to tell us that he wouldn't be coming to work. We began to get a little bored with Víctor.

We had bought Pastór's farm by this time, twenty-five acres of barely planted ground that cut through the middle of our property. With real delight we infuriated our neighbors by cutting down all the plátano there, which they had been accustomed to stealing. What were we trying to do, starve everyone to death? We promised to pay Pastór as soon as we could, and with the down payment he opened up a little salón on the river. Of the twelve houses in Male, five of them were salóns and the other seven did a languid business in cheap cigarettes, rice, sugar, and penny mints. This is a trait of the poor, this incestuous compulsion to do an identical business with one's closest neighbors. Everyone takes in everyone else's washing. What a stink of poverty the tattered, sweat-soaked five-sucre bills take on as they pass and repass back and forth, back and forth. On payday, when we returned from the bank with enormous piles of small-denomination bills worth twenty cents a piece and stacked them on the table, the whole room for a time would hold a faint sickening odor like a memory of vomit.

The *salones* had an average life of about a month; it took the owner that long to drink up his capital. Only one salón at a time has a chance of success — the one with the loudest phonograph. Pastór didn't last a month. In three weeks he drank up all his profits and his stock. It almost killed him; his liver stopped working, his eyes and his skin turned yellow, he wasted away before our eyes. He was bored, he said, with running a salón; he offered to sell his business establishment and his good will to Víctor. Víctor, believing with all of us that the people on the river were slightly more genteel than the highway crowd, was interested; he was looking for a more civilized clientele. He took over Pastór's great open shed, which was still only half-roofed in leaves of cade. On Saturdays he packed his phonograph off to one of his two establishments. It looked like a real triumph was just around the corner, for his phonograph was stereophonic and unbelievably powerful.

For about eight months there was music on all sides — one Saturday blessedly filtered by trees and distance, the next Saturday carried to us on the river's current, blatant and vulgar, spooking sleep with idiot dreams that interpreted those banal rhythms. Each month, by prodding or by taking it out of his wages, we squeezed the phonograph payments out of Víctor. Each month he put up a little more resistance, his excuses were more heart-rendingly piteous, more insanely inventive. When he was within two months of being free and clear, the music stopped, and Víctor's night spots remained closed for months on end. It was about this time that Ramón first began seriously to listen to the rumors of his stealing and to give credence to the magnitude of his thefts. Not only had Víctor lost interest in his dance halls, he had also lost interest in working for us. He began taking whole weeks off, and not even his wife could tell us where he was. By Ramón's reckoning his income and his expenses couldn't possibly be balancing out. He still dressed in new clothes, bought fish and meat from the traveling vendor, and had even begun to send his wife to Esmeraldas on the weekends while he headed up the road in the other direction toward Quinindé; our slow, low-flying jet-setter was spending half his salary on bus tickets. He was buying and selling plátano, he said. He was getting his wife settled in town to have her third child, he said.

Víctor had changed, we seldom saw him, and we felt vaguely but foolishly deprived now that the farm was no longer the sun around which he turned. Ramón and I had felt like really great guys for having helped him to be something more than just a sweating machetero. Was Víctor going to blow it all? Was he going to be yet another proof of our bad judgment? He was in another orbit now, circling some black, mysterious, as yet undetected star. His face was sad and disoriented, not sullen yet but strange and troubling. One got the impression that it was a real burden for him to talk to us and that in fact while talking to us he had to suppress yawns of boredom. This struck us as strange even while we realized that we were suppressing the same yawns and for the same reason; we had no common future together. In the totality of our life here — as its quality steadily deteriorated in the ridiculous complexities of dealing with the other workers, of planting and harvesting strange mildewing crops, of scrabbling for money to pay our workers every week and the other debts, which each month spread like a cancer and at times threatened to close us down — Víctor played a minor role. What set him apart from the others was simply that we had elected to climb up on the stage and join him in the action. When I thought about what was happening to him, which I didn't do very often, I realized a couple of rather cynical things (someone wiser or more cynical might have said that I was finally beginning to mature). One thing: whatever happened or might happen to him, he was more important to us than we were to him, not as a human being but as a symbol of our capacity to work with black people. And two: in any situation he had a greater capacity to disappoint us than to give us any kind of satisfaction. He had standards that we couldn't accept; he had flaws that we couldn't forgive. The problem on both sides was a certain incapacity to love, on my part an incapacity that had stained my whole life, on his the simple inability to leap the cultural gap that would enable him to see Ramón and me as human beings, not simply as things to plunder. Cautiously we began to leave the stage for a quieter vantage place where we could watch him act out his own destiny.

Víctor didn't know how to lie, or at least how to tell consistent intermeshing lies; his babblings to Ramón and to me were wildly contradictory. Why was he such a blundering amateur now when he had conned us so brilliantly before? Why had he closed his *salones*? Well, the phonograph broke down, and trying to fix it he had ripped out all the wiring by mistake. Frankly, it cost more money to repair than he had, and well, frankly, he was bored with serving cane alcohol to stupified zambos and having his house full of people all day Sunday, asleep all over the floor, too drunk to go home, lying in their own vomit or pissing in their pants as they slept. The records were all scatched and warped; they were out of style besides. His wife was fed up with the country; she acted like she didn't even love him anymore, as surly and complaining as an old hunting dog.

This was Víctor's story, and it sounded reasonable. Ramón didn't believe a word of it. When I reported this conversation to him he said, "Oh, bullshit" — using up in one blazing moment 50 percent of his English vocabulary, old Ramón our hawk-eyed psychologist. "Don't you think I went down that very same road when I was Víctor's age? The phonograph on credit, the bottles on credit, sitting up all night waiting to sell a few drinks to a bunch of drunks, the whole house finally smelling of vomit. And the stupid bickering, the arguments, everyone shoving, drunk as animals, and the shameless women fucking underneath your house in the dirt for ten sucres. Let me tell you one thing, Martín. *Óyeme bien.* If you are making money at this, You Do Not Get Bored. I am talking about poor people about whom you know very little."

"Yeah, but I'm learning," I said. "At the rate we're going I'll soon be an expert."

But this wasn't true. Poverty was something that I understood less and less. For eight years in Ecuador I had been obsessively preoccupied with the subject. After four years, when I thought I knew it all, I had even written a book about it. I had read as much of the literature on development as I could understand, and much more that I couldn't make heads or tails of, solemn tomes by solemn sober-suited professors who gathered their statistics in the libraries. Almost all my friends were either extremely poor or they were serious students of poverty: Peace Corps volunteers and staff members, AID officials, OAS officials, missionaries as interested in saving bodies as in saving souls. For almost ten years practically all my conversations in Spanish and in English had circled around this subject and worried it to death. Every year I was more confused about its causes and its cures; there seemed to be hundreds of causes and possibly no cures at all. At times gagging on this *ambiente* into which I had chosen to submerge myself, choking and retching on the poverty that was all around me, I had felt like a peeping Tom, a degenerate voyeur, and I began to question the basic morality of any middle-class westerner presuming to move into a deprived culture to judge it or to try to change it. Thinking about the early ethnic arrogance I had displayed as a Peace Corps volunteer made my blood run cold.

Poverty was still an obscenity, but now I was so closely involved with it, so emotionally dominated by its squalor, that it had turned as mysterious and shapeless as a night killer. Still . . . Still, at times I wondered if this condition was even relevant in man's passage from birth to death. The unhappiest man I ever knew was my father, who died and left the bulk of an almost two-million-dollar estate to the humane society; the happiest people I had ever known were these ragged wretches on the river. If now some wild God should suddenly appear and say, "Choose between being your father or Arcario Cortez," in a flash my skin would turn black and my clothes to rags. How could I bear the alternative? What I am trying to say, if anything, is simply that I feel that the inevitable relationship of wealth and unhappiness does not exist among the poor; there is no real link between poverty and unhappiness.

The shape, the quality, the causes of poverty all evaded me. What made it? How much of poverty was due to the exploitation of the rich, those blood-sucking maniacs, shameless in their insatiability? How much poverty was necessary for national political reasons? How much was due to economic colonialism or world banking policy? How much was due to ignorance or to malnutrition, the father of stupidity? How much to the cultural imperatives? How much of poverty is simply a self-inflicted wound, freely chosen for whatever reason? It had been years since I had recited one of my vapid truisms, that perhaps there were only two real sins: to commit murder and to be poor. How could I have ever said a thing like that to a credulous peasantry, believing as I did that being rich was also a sin? But if I truly believed this, why was I breaking my ass trying to be rich? Pondering this I decided that there was no sin in *trying* to be rich, only in being rich. In the same vein, then, being poor is no sin if you are trying *not* to be poor. And what about that decent poverty that Ramón and I claimed to have freely chosen as a guiding principal? We were still practicing it, though with a little less enthusiasm; we could seldom describe our poverty as decent. What we were learning was that it costs a hell of a lot to live in decent poverty.

And Víctor, who now seemed to be living a pointless and crumbling existence, what was he proving about poverty? That even when it wasn't inevitable and could be conquered, it *was* inevitable and unconquerable? What was happening to Víctor?

"What's happening to Víctor?" I asked.

"I don't know yet," Ramón said. "And that's a very strange thing because usually I can look into a man's eyes — especially with someone like Víctor who grew up like I did — and tell exactly what he's thinking. My idea is this: for some reason he wants us to fire him. He must think that's the only way to get his severance pay. Also I think he wants to get rid of his wife, and she won't leave him unless he buys her a house in Esmeraldas."

"He doesn't want to leave his wife. He wants to open up a little fruit market in town, is what he says. He would buy out here and she would sell. Why don't we loan him the 3000 sucres that he needs?" By some strange accident we happened to have a little money on hand that week.

"Go ahead if you want to," Ramón said. "He doesn't want to buy out here, he wants to steal out here. As for me, I have other plans. First, I'm going to repossess the phonograph, and then, if that's what he wants, I'm going to fire him."

"He's been here for years; if you're going to fire him you'd better have 6000 sucres around to pay him off."

"Not if I can catch him stealing," Ramón said. "Not if he doesn't want to go to jail."

I went outside and sat on one of the store benches, and after a while Víctor strolled down the hill, surrounded by a few dozen bored butterflies that he had met up with at the little pools of water where the high grass and the caña brava shaded the road.

"Ramón says you're bored on the farm and don't want to work for us anymore," I said when he sat down beside me.

"But, *amigo,* how could I not want to work here," Víctor said without much feeling.

"But you haven't worked all week. How does a poor man live without working?"

"Like an animal," Víctor said. "Ah, life, what a tangle it is. It's not true that I don't want to keep working here, but now I'm all mixed up thinking about how to get some money to buy a little house in town for my wife; we need another little something to make ends meet."

"So if we loaned you the money? That's what you want, isn't it?"

"Ah, but if you loaned me the money we could really better our situation; there wouldn't be any more desperate thoughts about not working here."

"Víctor, look at me." He raised his head, it was so heavy and so hard to do, and our eyes locked. "Are you stealing from us? Everyone says you are stealing from us, and not just a little bit."

What an exhausted look he gave me before he dropped his eyes in shame, the guilt and the necessity clearly painted across his face. And now, with his eyes studying those great stealing hands that lay in his lap like sleeping animals, he mumbled in a voice so low that I could hardly hear him, "Lies . . . the people . . . talking against me . . . *puro maldad* . . . Why? . . . *Pobre pero honrado . . . humilde y leal.*"

I went into the store, got the money, counted out thirty 100-sucre bills, and gave them to him. We were both so depressed we didn't even try to speak; everything between us heavy, dead, ponderous; everything was behind us now, all the play acting, the concern for him that I could never quite manage to honestly feel, the friendship for me that had been part of his role. He stayed another polite five minutes and left. An hour later he had sent his wife and children to live permanently in town, and that evening he went to Quinindé and brought back with him that long-legged, pointy-titted girl with whom, almost a year before, while his salón was being ripped to pieces, he had fallen hopelessly in love. Immediately everything became clear: those innumerable bus trips to the south, his surly, unhappy wife, his abandoned dance halls, his sad abstracted preoccupations. The poor bastard had lost his mind; he had fallen in love again. He didn't come to work on Monday, nor on Tuesday or Wednesday.

On Friday Ramón repossessed the phonograph. He would have it repaired and sell it to Jerdardo. Jerdardo is one of our new steady workers and, at the age of thirty-five, is beginning to realize that he can't possibly get through the week on the wages we are paying him. He is earning almost two dollars a day, top wages now that everything has doubled, but he has seven children, and one of them, the oldest, has already been seduced, made pregnant, and deserted at the age of fourteen. Jerdardo wants to open up a little salón underneath his house, with music, aguardiente, and sweet cheap wine for the women. The complicating truth is that Jerdardo is just a hair's breadth short of being an alcoholic; he has mixed motives. But who wouldn't be a drunk with seven children at his age and all the probabilities of having seven more?

"I doubt it," Ramón said, "but maybe he can make a go of it."

"Include me out," I told him coldly. "I wash my hands of Male's nightspots."

Jerdardo's wife worked in a salón once; she knew the ropes, how to collect for the drinks without infuriating the customers. I don't know too much about Jerdardo's wife; I have seldom seen her since the day we caught her stealing peanuts at harvest time and publicly humiliated her — at least we hoped so. I remember her as a hag, with an Indian face brutalized by childbearing and deprivation, long tangled hair as coarse as a horse's mane, a dirty dress, a gaping toothless mouth. She appeared to be more of an alcoholic than her husband and years older than this slightly crippled man who had worn her out. To embrace her in the night, to bring forth children from her, strikes me as an act of courage or depravity.

And what of Víctor? We still felt a vague academic interest in the plunging trajectory of his luck, especially since, while we saw him plunging to disaster, he no doubt saw himself being borne aloft to the gates of paradise on the ecstasies of love. How was he solving the gut problems of existence? Now he had two women who were depending on him. "What's Víctor doing?" we asked his nephew Antonio. But Antonio, who worshiped his uncle, was thrown into confusion by the question and began to babble disconnected things that not even Ramón could understand; but they aroused his deepest suspicions. I saw Víctor a few more times but mostly at a distance. He never came back to work. He was enslaved and dominated by love; all the harsh realities of his poverty had faded away for a time. He was too crazy, too happy to think about anything as boring as work. Working on the tractor one evening at sunset I saw him walking up the road; he had both arms around his girl. He was in a daze of happiness as though he couldn't believe his luck, his face bent into hers as he drank her beauty. For a moment I could see her face through Víctor's eyes: beautiful, all her sullen arrogance melted into submissive adoration. They were made for each other. Watching them I was inclined to forgive Víctor almost everything. Until . . .

There had been hurricanes in Panama, Guatemala, Honduras; all the banana plantings had been destroyed. Suddenly bananas began to boom in Ecuador. Buyers with big eager smiles and driving new Land-Rovers stopped every day at the farm and begged us to rejuvenate our abandoned acres. Without, of course, putting anything in writing they guaranteed us instant and immense wealth. We fell for their line and sent crews of men into our jungle to clean out the weeds and to fell the fast-growing second-growth timber. Hooray. We were going to make 4000 dollars a month extra. And now, moving in behind the macheteros to check their work, we discovered that all the barbed wire in the fence along the highway had been stolen. The next day, quietly investigating, softly interrogating Antonio, Ramón found out that Víctor was selling rolls of second-hand barbed wire to our neighbor across the road. Marco, *pobre pero honrado,* trembling before Ramón's contempt, insisted he didn't know that the wire had been stolen; Víctor had said it belonged to a brother. Marco, perhaps dipping into thievery for the first time, was terrified at being apprehended so quickly and at being so clearly an accomplice.

So now after almost four years we were finally in agreement that Víctor had to go. It wasn't just a question of firing him; hell, he wasn't even working for us. We had to get him off our land, and not just that; we wanted him so far away from the farm, so many miles up the road that he would never make it back to rob us of our harvests. Ramón drove out to Víctor's house and called him out into the road. In a ten-minute monologue he detailed the whole history of Víctor's ingratitude and threatened him with a year in jail if he didn't pack his things and leave. I don't know what Víctor's plans were, but they didn't include leaving the house that we had helped him build and the hectárea of plátano that he had planted on our land. Of course, his plans had never included the possibility that we would face him with the proof of his thefts. I guess what he really wanted was to go on living in the house and to go on stealing. He was mute and trembling before Ramón's insults. But he didn't leave. He had no place to go except to his wife in Esmeraldas, and that didn't seem very practical, women being the way they are about other women. He held on.

While we waited another week, his nephew Antonio continued to work for us. I had never seen him so quiet, so depressed, and so dedicated to his job. It was Antonio who had told Ramón about his uncle's business in barbed wire — poor Antonio, who had scarcely known what he was saying, tricked by Ramón and his clever questions. He had thought he was protecting Víctor, and now feeling like a traitor he was torn into pieces by remorse. At first we treated him with special kindness, that same embarrassed consideration that one shows to the families of condemned criminals. Later Ramón's attitude hardened; he was terribly frustrated that he had been unable to frighten Víctor off the farm, and his anger spread to Antonio. He had probably known for months about his uncle's true character; by being loyal to him he had automatically been disloyal to us. One afternoon as four or five of us squatted in the shade outside the store, getting a sack of peanuts prettied up to sell, Ramón began to harass the boy.

"Tell me how it feels, Antonio. I don't mean how it feels to know that your uncle is a lousy thief — you've always known that, haven't you? I mean, how is it to know that now *everybody* knows it, that your uncle is a shameless *ratero*."

"Don Ramón, lay off," Antonio cried in a trembling voice, all the veins in his head and neck beginning to swell terribly with blood and the whites of his eyes turning red. "Don't talk that way about my uncle; he's not a thief; he's my uncle Víctor."

"The worst kind of a thief," Ramón said in a loud voice. "A Judas. He says he is your friend, that he likes you, and all the time behind your back he is robbing you. There are lots of stinking thieves who won't do that."

"Lay off, lay off," Antonio cried. He stood up and faced Ramón with his fists clenched and the tears beginning to well up in his eyes.

"Let me talk the truth on my own farm," Ramón said. He got up, too, and faced Antonio and smiled at him with cold anger. "Let me say it again, *joven,* because I'm talking the truth, as hard as it may be for you to hear. Listen well, *joven.* I've got a message for your uncle Víctor, that cheating, robbing, lying, lazy son of a bitch, a message from me, Ramón Prado, that he pack his shit and get the hell off this farm if he doesn't want to go to jail. And if you think I'm lying, you don't have to work here either."

For the first time in his life Antonio, who had never flinched a second before charging into combat and defeat, held back. It made me very proud. He was only seventeen, but he realized that he was facing something that he couldn't handle. In his heart he knew that Ramón was telling the truth; in his heart he was still dominated by the strongest family loyalties. Víctor was just about all he had. He stood there glaring and blinking at Ramón, his man's head trembling on his delicate childish neck as though the weight of all his thoughts and confusions was heavier than he could bear. He turned away from us finally, hid his face in his hands, and began to sob like a child. "I don't want to work on this lousy farm. My uncle Víctor is a good man; he's my uncle. I won't ever work on this lousy farm again."

Later when I was alone in my house, much later, in bed unable to sleep, thinking bleakly about this incredibly ugly confrontation, its true meaning suddenly exploded in my face; I understood what I had seen. In my imagination, both of them, Ramón and Antonio, stood before me with their naked hearts in their trembling hands. Antonio loved Víctor; Ramón, too, had loved that man. And Víctor had humiliated them both with his betrayal; he had made them suffer. What could they do but scream with pain and outrage. He had wounded them and shaken the already feeble foundations of that timid faith that allowed them to work together; he had destroyed some part of the code that gave meaning to their lives.

The farm is only fifteen or twenty miles from the equator, so close in fact that I can never remember whether we cross it going north to Esmeraldas or south to Quinindé. We are at the very heart of that band of deep tropics where life began, a band that slices broadly across the middle of the earth and over which hangs the dead and exhausted offal of the polar storms. At sea this area is referred to as the doldrums. No winds blow, only stagnant eddies that fade like dying sighs among the jungle leaves. There are no violent changes in the weather. If it began to rain at midnight yesterday, there is about an 80 percent chance that I will wake at twelve o'clock tonight and hear the rain coming a mile away, across the fields, or drumming louder on the banana plants. Clouds hang over the low hills for months at a time, and the faces that we see in the clouds seem to be almost as permanent as those faces disguised as trees across the river. God help us when it starts to rain. If I remember the year correctly, it was early in 1970 that the last terrifying rain began; it finally stopped in January of 1973, that month when normally the winter rains are scheduled to begin. It didn't rain for six months. There are no weather stations in the province; a meteorologist would lose his mind down here poring over his data, trying to find a pattern.

The night before Víctor's last day on the farm, the ponderous exhausted cycle of the seasons began to turn. All night long tremendously towering cumulus clouds, glowing ominously silver in the moonlight, moved in sluggishly from the ocean and formed a ring around the houses where we tried to sleep. And all night long we were bombarded by the almost continuous rolls of thunder. The hills across the river were steadily illuminated in the cold, static, electric-green light that seemed to freeze still further the eternally frozen chaos of waiting trees.

So Ramón couldn't sleep. The night before, Compás, our cowboy's son, had reported that Víctor was talking wildly out on the road. He wasn't going to leave, we had no right to kick him off the farm after he had planted so much of it with plátano; the house was his; the plátano was his; he would go to the law if necessary. Ramón, in bed, flinching no doubt from those crashes of thunder, lay there all night thinking about Víctor, thinking about Víctor and building up a head of steam. I came over to the kitchen from my house at about six, just in time to see Ramón driving off in the pickup with a macho spinning of wheels and flying gravel. The empty holster of his revolver lay on the table.

So Ramón is up there on the road, thunder and lightning crashing and flashing around him. It is the last moment, the death of the gods, all those Wagnerian chords getting ready to resolve themselves at last. Or so I saw it. Not Ramón. He was marching to another music — banks of guitars backing up a nasal Frankie Lane, the drumming of horses' hooves on wooden bridges, and a thousand snarling smoking pistols. This was the last reel, the shootout, the white hats versus the black hats. *A la muerte.*

"Víctor," Ramón bawled, standing at the edge of the highway and yelling across a ditch of water and clumps of high grass that almost hid the house. His arms were folded across his chest with the revolver prominently displayed. Víctor, half asleep, struggling into a shirt, came to the door, saw Ramón facing him just out of pistol range, and quietly disappeared into the house again. "Did you tell Compás you've decided to stay on the farm?"

"My God, no, Ramón," Víctor yelled back through the closed door. "That's all lies, I swear, pure lies, *la maldad de la gente.*"

"Five hours," Ramón yelled. "You're off this farm in five hours, you understand, or you and Marco go to jail. I swear this on my mother's honor."

"*Bueno, bueno.* No problem, Ramón; there's absolutely no problem. Just give us a little while to get our things together."

"Until noon, *hombre,* and I swear I'm not fooling."

There was a long pause, a whole minute of nothing but pure thunder, and then Víctor, opening the door a crack and sticking his head out, asked, "*Amigo* Ramón, can you loan me fifty sucres for bus fare?"

"Well, holy shit," Ramón cried. "You just robbed us of eight thousand sucres in barbed wire, and now you want fifty sucres more?"

"Oh, now Ramón, it wasn't eight thousand sucres," Víctor said in a hurt and chiding voice. "It was a loan of closer to one thousand avocados. *Por la necesidad,* Ramoncito, *por la necesidad.*"

Without answering, Ramón turned and got into the pickup, and Víctor, standing in the doorway but ready to leap for cover, called again to Ramón, "But where am I going to go?"

"*Vaya a la mierda,*" Ramón advised him, driving off. Go to hell.

Until eleven o'clock that morning Víctor and Antonio sweated outside in their planting of plátano; they cut down every plant. By noon they were gone.

"But weren't you afraid?" I asked Ramón when he was telling me about it over coffee. "Weren't you afraid of losing your temper and taking a pot shot at him if he stood up to you?"

And Ramón thought for a moment and decided to confess and told me, smiling, "Well, yes, as a matter of fact, I was, and that's why before I drove up there I filled the revolver with blanks. Like in the movies. They don't use real bullets in the movies, do they?"

Sometimes at night when everything is quiet, after we have eaten, perhaps even eaten well, and turned off the news programs, after we have said as much to each other about the next day's work as we are likely to say, while Ester is putting the children to bed in their house and I am thinking about getting up and going to mine, I may look up through the candlelight across the table and catch Ramón staring at me. He has a way, when he is tired, of turning off his mind, and his face becomes as empty and tranquil as the face of a resting animal. At first I resented this long, rude, unblinking stare that seemed aimed at stripping me to the heart of my secret intentions or that plumbed me to my depths, as if Ramón were sitting there thinking with disappointment, "Is that *all?* Is that *all?*" I would stare back aggressively, trying to make him back off or blink or look at something else. It never worked, he wasn't really looking at me; my face was simply a convenient target for concentrating, no more than a catalyst for attitudes that he would in his own good time bring up from his depths, feelings about life that had nothing to do with conscious thought. And so on this night perhaps a week after Víctor had left the farm, I looked up to find myself impaled on that vacant meditative stare like a bug on a pin. I sat there smoking and staring back at him from time to time. He was very far away someplace. Just before I got up to go to bed I stared at him again and noticed a curious thing: the whites of his eyes had suddenly flushed red like the eyes of Antonio just before he began to cry. Something sad was about to come bubbling up. He came swimming up to consciousness, caught me looking at him, smiled, blinked his eyes, sighed heavily, passed a hand across his face, and sighed again, almost groaning.

"My God," he said, "I just realized that aside from you there is not one person in all this damned world that I trust anymore."

"Have people changed so much, so fast?"

"No, but something has changed. I can see through the masks that people wear now; their faces are beginning to seem terrible to me, like the hungry faces of wild animals."

"What shows is the way they see you now. You're the one who has changed. Now you've got something that they want. You got out of the cage, and they can hardly see you for all those piles of red meat that you could toss to them if you wanted."

"What cage?"

"*La jaula que se llama 'pobre,*'" I said. The cage called "poor."

It had been a week since the thunder had begun to boom and roll in all the hills around us, and in all that time it had scarcely ever completely stopped. Tonight it was giving a performance to the east, toward Rioverde, and we sat there, both of us intensely depressed now, listening to that distant rumbling in back of the farthest hills.

"Yes, you're right," Ramón said. "It was money that separated us from everyone, wasn't it? Right from the beginning. Remember when you first came back joking about how you were going to buy back your childhood and live out your own adventure story? And now you want to leave the farm, you say, and all you're really going to do is try to buy another fairy tale."

"Well, maybe," I said. "Then again, maybe I can make it simpler. You know those three days while we waited for Alejandro to confess, they really got me to thinking; they were the worst three days of my life. My God, my God, what if he had been innocent?"

"Well, he wasn't," Ramón said, "but I know what you mean. But tell me, how else could we have done it?"

"I don't know, but I will never be placed in that position again. Never. But Ramón, why don't you tell me the truth? You would like to run this place by yourself, wouldn't you?"

This was something we had been talking about for some days, and Ramón sat staring at me gravely. "Well," he said finally, "don't you think it's true that eventually every son wants to be free of his father? Or maybe he just wants to show off and prove that he is *capaz,* that he can do it on his own?"

"Oh, you bastard," I cried, really hurt. "I'm not your goddamn father."

"Oh, yes, you are," Ramón said sadly. "You're my father, my brother, and my son, my best friend and my partner; you're something overpowering here in my heart that I can't get rid of, and maybe being partners is what has made it all so complicated."

"Well, that's one thing we can't change, can we." I said. "Here or there I'm still half-owner of the property."

"Look," Ramón said, "leaving the farm is *your* idea, not mine. I think the way you want to leave is stupid; I think it just might kill you. All I'm saying is that if you *do* decide to leave, it is really a compliment to me. I mean that by trusting me to protect your interests you are doing me the greatest honor. And that's the part I like, that I can pay you back for what you've done for me. Do you think it has been easy for me all these years to have been so long the victim of your generosity?"

"Oh, man," I said, "now that's putting it very nicely. But if it has been so hard for you, doesn't that prove I'm not your father?"

"Oh, I don't know," Ramón said. "Maybe just the opposite. Did I tell you that Plinio decided to divide up his cows among the children? He must be feeling very sick; he wanted us all to have our inheritance. He told me last week in town that he had a cow for me. Poor my father, fourteen cows and twenty children. I guess I should have felt honored, but I turned him down as nicely as I could. Though I guess there is no nice way to deny a father his rights."

"You should have been a little kinder," I said. "You should have accepted the cow. Maybe with our hundred cows he thinks that you were sneering at him."

"How can you be kind and honest at the same time?" Ramón asked. "I just don't have that thing in my heart for him." He clenched his fist and sadly beat two times at his chest.

We sat for awhile in silence and the thunder boomed away to the east. "Listen to it," I said. "Old Víctor's right in the middle of it tonight."

"Good," Ramón said in a hard voice. "May a bolt hit him right in the ass." He was silent again for a minute and then burst out, "Oh, Martín, he *hurt* me . . . And you, you liked him, too, didn't you?"

"Yes," I said, "and God help me, I still do."

"And may the friendship give you much pleasure," Ramón said, violently shaking his head. "No, no. No more whore friendships. I want no more friendships. As soon as you start to like someone here he senses it like a whore wondering how much she can get out of you. No, Martín, when you leave there are going to be some changes. I want to run this farm like a business, like everybody else here runs a farm. No more free chickens, no more loans to help people get drunk, no more free land, no more two-hundred-dollar parties with hired bands and free drinks and all the roast pig you can eat. Look, a man comes for a job, he gets hired; in three months he gets fired. Next man, please. Thank you very much and goodbye. Everything fair but firm; everything like the law says."

I didn't say anything.

"Go on, keep breaking your own heart if you want to. Not me. I'm through with those deceptions. It's all lies, play acting. I am degraded when they glance first at my pockets instead of my face, like whores studying the bulge in my crotch to see if I am a well-made man or if I'm ready to do business. It's all what you call 'bullshit.' "

I still didn't say anything, and Ramón, smiling, said, "My English isn't bad, no? Don't I talk just like a gringo?"

"You sure do," I said, "and you're getting pretty eloquent in castellano, too."

"Martín, we were never smart enough to invent a whole new way of running a farm. Do you remember that great hacienda up the coast from Paraíso, near the border, where they sell a boatload of coconuts every week? Do you know what they do there to control the stealing?"

"Yes," I said, because I knew.

"Every year they shoot a couple of thieves right out of the trees with rifles. And it's not just there, you know."

I was looking out through the coconuts to where distant flashes of lightning were reflecting on the clouds. "Jesus, it's black out tonight," I said.

"Yes, but what do you think?"

"That there must be a better way. Killing a man over a coconut seems a little extreme. How about aiming for their legs? How about shooting their butts full of salt?"

"Ah, but now honor is involved. Even the most disgraceful kind of thief feels insulted at getting shot at — especially if you hit him. Now he has to prove that he is a man. And he hides out there in the weeds at night and waits until he can take a shot at you so that he can respect himself again. And listen, Martín, I hope you understand — it's not just one coconut; it's the whole damn crop. There are about a hundred people who live around here, and they don't want to rob the coconuts; all they want to do is pick one or two a day. What it adds up to is the whole *cocal*."

I didn't say anything, and Ramón continued after a minute, "It's not really that I don't want friends, but what can you do here on the river?"

"There is this very famous poem in my country," I said. "Some people think it's the greatest poem, and what the last lines say is that it is better to die surrounded by friends that you have bought and paid for than to die alone."

"Ay, *caramba*," Ramón said, "that's not poetry, that's the final knockout punch, the death blow. That's what I like about the gringos. But how can they be so tough?"

"Not many gringos talk that tough," I said. "So save your money and buy a couple of gringos. Provide, provide. You know why you like gringos? You feel safe with them because you don't have one single thing that they want to take away from you."

"And vice versa," Ramón said. "You know, that's why I always liked Santo. He never tried to con me. He never pretended . . . I just thought of something. His nickname in Rioverde was 'Mister.' Maybe that's because he was honest and didn't pretend with anybody, a real gringo. With your own kind, with gringos, you can relax and enjoy one another without being suspicious."

"And all these people on the river that are beginning to frighten us so — aren't they your own people?"

"But you said it," Ramón cried. "Of course they're not my people. I got out of that cage, and it's sad and lonesome out here, but I swear to God I'll never get back in."

"And so now you're going to start shooting them out of the trees?"

"Listen," Ramón said. "There's a war on; turn on the radio; it's not just here in Male. It's the whole world, there's a terrible war going on all over the whole world. And we're right in the middle of it. You know who the enemy is? It's all those fucking Víctors and those fucking Alejandros, those idiot Dalmiros, those stupid screwed up Jorges. They all want what is not theirs; they want what is mine. And I'm not saying they're wrong; I'm just saying I have another job to do, to take care of my family, to take care of you, to educate my children . . . Oh, Martín, I haven't forgotten." And now suddenly the tears simply gushed from his eyes and he could hardly speak. "It is awful — awful — awful — to be poor, to have nothing. It turns people into wild animals, into beasts of prey . . . Will I have to start shooting them out of the trees? Oh, *Christ,* how do I know? You're the one who keeps saying that ten thousand people starve to death every day; you're the one who keeps quoting the experts who say that in three years there'll be a hundred million people starving to death every year . . . Is this *possible?* And is it possible that this is general knowledge and that nobody is doing something about it?"

I couldn't take any more; this was all just too much. I rushed over to the door, swung it wide, and playing the clown, bawled into the darkness as loud as I could, "*Socorro, socorro.*" Help. Help. And Ramón, smiling now, said "O.K., O.K., but don't; you'll frighten the children."

"I'm going to bed," I said, but instead I sat down again and listened to the thunder, softened almost to music by distance, over to the east in Rioverde, where Víctor had gone back to live. It was nice to think that the thunder had followed him, and I hoped he was right in the middle of it muttering terrified African charms with wide rolling eyes. I found myself staring at Ramón; how he had changed since I first knew him, how hard and sad and stubborn his face. I thought of those two ultimate sins, the two unforgivable sins against life: to murder and to be poor. Poor Ramón. It looked like he was moving toward that awful moment when he would have to commit the first one to get saved from committing the second. I got up and went to the door. "Loan me your flashlight, will you, Ramón? The weeds are so high since Dalmiro left I can hardly get over to the house."

While he was looking for it, on a sudden impulse I leaned out into the darkness and yelled again. "Help. Help." But this time I didn't yell it very loud. And this time I wasn't fooling.

Part Three

Firmly clutching his knife, which he perhaps would not know how to wield, Dahlmann went out into the plain.

Jorge Luis Borges, "The South"

11

FULL MOON ON THE RIVER

Two YEARS after I ran head on into two banana trucks in an Andean pass and, in the face of Ramón's dominating insistence, chose like a coward not to die, and four years after we bought the farm and I began to believe that, while I didn't especially like what we were doing to the people or what they were doing to us, I could still manage to live with it in some minimal degree of acceptance, the whole pattern and tempo of those disasters to which we were witness so accelerated for a period of about four weeks that after it was all over both of us had been permanently changed.

I felt as dazed and victimized as I had felt at the age of nine when, taking a bath one evening, or rather, being given a bath, I had for the first time in my life taken the name of the Lord in vain. I sat there in the tub, frozen with amazement, while every woman in the household — the cook, the maid, my nurse, and my stepmother — appeared in the bathroom even before the echoes of my blasphemy had died and began to slap my face. They weren't hard slaps but they came with machine-gun rapidity and went on for what seemed an endless time, and I remember thinking that their sound was identical to the sound of a stick stuck into the spokes of a whirling bicycle wheel. When it was all over, sitting there belly-button deep in soapy water that had begun to cool, staring back bleakly into those outraged fanatic faces, having lost in one moment all my power over these women, which up until that time I had used with all the disdain of a little prince, I made what I still feel was the only appropriate comment: "Well, holy Jesus *Christ*." Things would never be quite the same again.

That month on the farm began with faint portents, the slow

distant ominous roll of drums from off-stage, but before it was over, audience and orchestra were all mixed up together in a howling screeching cacophony, and we were playing the kind of music that if we had only written it down might not have been inappropriate for a movie version of Velikovsky's *Worlds in Collision*.

We were harvesting corn that month out of a twenty-five acre field along the highway and across our private lane from the coconuts. It was the same field where a couple of years before we had caught Esmundo stealing my machete. We would never plant or harvest corn on the farm again, but perhaps at that time we didn't quite know it yet. That afternoon as I was disking down a harvested part of the field along the road, Ramón drove up the lane in the pickup, parked, and walked out across the field to where our paths would cross. When I stopped he motioned to me to kill the engine, and when I yelled that I couldn't because I didn't trust the battery, he yelled back that I'd better get off the tractor then and we would walk away from it a little bit where we could talk. "I have some bad news for you," he said.

"What's wrong?" I asked, imagining all kinds of things and glancing down toward the river for signs of smoke that would indicate that the farm buildings had just burned down.

Ramón didn't answer me until we had left the noise of the tractor and he had squatted down in the dirt and with a nod of his head invited me to squat beside him. "I just heard it on the radio," he said, and it seemed to me that his voice broke just a little. "I'm sorry, Martín. Stravinsky's dead. I thought you ought to know, because I know how much you liked him."

I disked later than usual that day, until long after the sun had set and the hills no longer stood out against a lighter sky. I wanted to be alone to examine my feelings, just as I had tried to be alone that day in the army when Franklin Roosevelt died and later when Kennedy was brought down. I had been touched by Ramón's taking the trouble to drive out and tell me something that to him was of no importance but, because he knew I loved Stravinsky, had choked up his voice with sadness for me; he had tried to take a part of my sadness on himself. I was doubly touched by this sensitivity of Ramón's because after almost eight years together it had begun to seem that whatever concern he had for me had become highly stylized and mainly manifested itself in a constant and unthinking harping about my lack of character due to the number of cigarettes I smoked each day. Ramón smoked about four; I smoked about forty.

But Stravinsky's death did not put me to thinking about Ramón; it was much more than that. The whole quality of the day had changed in that moment when Ramón announced his news. The clouds suddenly seemed heavier, closer to the hills, blacker; that darkness that crept across the earth seemed now charged with portents; it was the end of an era; we had lost someone irreplaceable. I didn't like that feeling of being further unanchored from my past, I felt that I had already gone as far as I could reasonably be expected to go. How odd it suddenly felt to be disking down weeds in a jungle clearing in Ecuador, six- or seven-thousand miles from that place where at fifteen years of age I had first been electrified by hearing *Le Sacre,* where I had first been subjected to the power of art and where, by a curious arrangement of circumstances that I have long forgotten and never even begun to understand, I immediately substituted for my wavering belief in God and my more wavering belief in the sanctity of family life, a belief in art. Is this what comes of slapping little boys in the bath tub?

Our own more personal tribulations began the next day. I was out in the same fields, this time having connected the tractor-driven corn sheller, and Víctor, Washington, our other yellow-colored Manabitan night watchman, and young Antonio were helping me, tossing ears of corn into the machine from the piles we had made earlier in the day. So Víctor is back in the story? Yes. I am backtracking now. We still didn't know that Víctor had just begun to take down our outside fences to sell to Marco; it was a month off yet, that morning when Ramón with his revolver full of blanks would run Víctor off the property; he was still our friend that afternoon. So we were all out there husking corn when above the noise of the tractor we heard a woman scream and scream and scream. Across the field, at the edge of the highway, one of Washington's innumerable young sons ran out through the wall of grass and began yelling and waving at us. I turned off the tractor and we all listened to that screaming, which went on and on; it was not so much a call for help as a statement of some final repudiation. "My God," Washington said, "it's the old lady," and he ran off with the other two behind him. I sat there on the tractor alone and angry because I wanted to shell corn that until now had been too damp to run through the machine, and I was frustrated by a typical situation where all the help, jazzed up and looking for some excitement, had simply run off and left me there. It was going to rain; I started up the tractor and worked by myself; whatever that crazy woman was screaming about had nothing to do with me.

Just before dark Víctor and Antonio strolled back; there was still a ton of corn unshelled and it was beginning to drizzle. Why all those screams? A banana truck had run off the road and killed one of our neighbors, an old man whom I don't remember ever having seen, a sort of disgraceful old man, Ramón told me later, who was usually about half drunk whenever he was seen in public. Washington's wife, leaning out the window of the upstairs room, had seen the truck as it hit him. The truck had taken out thirty feet of fence in front of the house and had come to rest in a little ditch where Celso Corea's lane ran off into the jungle. The driver and his helper had leaped out of the cab and disappeared in the weeds. We filled the pickup from the remaining piles of corn and hauled it into a bodega underneath Washington's house; there was still a crowd of people there when I drove up, most of them gathered around something torn and crumpled in the weeds. I didn't go over to look; I was more interested in watching the people, my neighbors, as they stripped the truck cab of its jacks and tools, a long piece of heavy chain, a bundle of something that looked like clothes. An old woman had found a piece of rubber tubing and some old buckets and cans and was syphoning the diesel out of the tank. All of these prizes would later be offered to us at very special prices. Víctor, who had picked up his brothers Adolfo and Segundo when he went running out of the field, had been among the first to arrive on the scene, and they had already collected the windshield wipers, a coil of rope, and a long length of chain that had been wrapped around the front bumper.

There was something special about that crowd that, when I realized what it was, made my scalp tingle. I had never seen half of them in all the years that I had lived among them; they appeared to have materialized out of screams and splattered blood as though their only function along the road was to crouch patiently in hiding until they could take advantage of their good luck. I watched them with growing dismay, an incredulous outrage, these people without resources, these people who didn't have a dollar's worth of food in their houses, who in fact didn't even have anything but a pile of rotting leaves and strips of bamboo that they could call a house — corrupted by their poverty into some final degradation, changed into vampires and grave robbers.

At the sound of any crash, that deserted highway — lined on both sides by almost impenetrable walls of grass behind which it was impossible to make out the huts in which people lived — would suddenly come alive with swarms of running figures, in tattered clothing, attracted by the sound of death. Toward the end of that week it was these ghouls, the living more than the dead, who struck me as being deformed and destroyed, who filled me with dread and loathing. I wonder if they were the same ones who two years before had stripped the jacket from my unconscious body as I lay blinded in my own little pool of blood. Perhaps not; that spot was 150 miles away. Were their ears that sharp? Were their senses so finely attuned that they were waiting there at 10,000 feet, hidden among the rocks and the millions of dwarfed yellow orchids that clung to the cliff faces in that place of almost perpetual fog?

The next day a six-year-old child was killed by a hit and run driver less than a quarter of a mile from the farm. In spite of the piteous pleadings of my workers I refused to go near the place, but as I crossed the highway with another load of corn I saw toward Viche that bright moving spot of color glowing on the road against the green of the jungle. It pinpointed the spot where the girl had died. It was the same swarm of people who, from a distance and in the brightness of their dresses and colored shirts, seemed engaged in some kind of festive celebration.

Nor did I see the next two bodies, Wednesday's and Friday's contributions. One of them had been run down at the other end of the farm near Niki Padovani's pastures. I remember no details; at the dinner table we very carefully did not talk about highway deaths; we were all getting paranoid and found our situation so ominous with presentiments that we had begun to believe that talking about a death today would result in a new one tomorrow. On an even guiltier level I felt some force pushing me into the arena, some higher law that was insisting that I leave the audience and become involved with the local suffering. I remember thinking that the dying would go on until I stopped resisting and stood before one of the dead, contemplating its deadness. All of these thoughts crystallized the next day when one of our neighbors, one of the Charcopas, got off the bus in front of Washington's house, passed in front of it, and walked into the path of another passing bus. Washington's wife, standing in the window, was being ground rather fine, and it was said that her screams could be heard almost to Viche, two miles away.

Segundo, Víctor's oldest brother, the fifth and last victim of the series, died on the sixth day; we were all there to see it. The corn in the bodega had begun to heat, and I had taken the corn sheller and the tractor across the road to Washington's house so that we could shell out the corn and spread it in the sun to dry. I think that just Ramón and I had gone out there, with the idea of doing it alone because it was Saturday afternoon, we had paid off everyone, and we figured that all the workers would be buying groceries in Viche or Esmeraldas or bathing in the river and putting on their fancy clothes for the weekend orgies. But by half-past four when we were finishing up, we had collected a crowd, mostly children and travelers waiting for the bus, but even some of the workers like Víctor and his nephew Antonio; they were endlessly fascinated with this modern machine into which you could throw husked ears and out of which poured a more or less steady stream of more or less golden kernels.

Later I would remember having seen Segundo as he stepped off the road and walked over to the house and began yelling something to Washington's wife, who stood in the window on the second floor. He was wearing a pair of great white shoes; Segundo was the kind of a guy who gave you the feeling that once you had taken account of his clothes you had plumbed him to the depth of his soul. He was staying in Víctor's house because his wife had, in a final summing up of his qualities, described him as a perfect example of hopeless bumdom and asked him to get permanently lost. She was right; we had fired him two weeks before, but his last act was an act of honor. He owed Washington's wife two sucres for some clothes that she had washed, and he had come to pay her. A minute or two later, the corn all shelled, I climbed up on the tractor to turn off the machine, and as its whining died into silence there was the sudden chilling sound of a speeding car hitting a body, a sound that, even if you have never heard it before, is immediately and fully recognizable: a kind of awful thump, the rending of crumpling torn metal, a shattering windshield, tires screaming on asphalt.

I spun around to see the body of Segundo soaring through the air above the wall of grass that lined the road and hid the car; he was perfectly relaxed, perfectly at rest, and as he floated through the air in an unbelievably protracted arc, he looked like nothing so much as some mildly clever TV advertisement for air travel or a Sealy Posturpedic mattress — a faintly smiling man, lounging back on a little cloud of bliss and being magically and painlessly transported from here to there in a flash of time. It was an impression made more real by the brutal clearness with which I now observed his face; I had really never noticed it until this moment as he died; he had a second-class face with the pouty lips and the conceited, self-indulgent expression of a César Romero, and with the same wavy, dramatically silvering hair. As he floated through the air, not a single lock was out of place, but how strange, those great white shoes that he had been wearing a moment before were gone from his feet. In that second when I felt nothing but amazement, and in fact very little of that since it had happened so quickly, a whole series of complicated and contradictory feelings began to build. It wasn't until later that I realized that for perhaps the first time in almost eight years I was seeing something with my own eyes, that I was reacting to something that hadn't been filtered through Ramón's Latin sensibilities. I was on my own. What I felt erupting out of me was absolute rage, a rage so overpowering that for a short time I lost all control.

While Washington's wife began her hysterical screaming from the upstairs window, beating with her fists against the window frames, while Ramón and Víctor, paralyzed, stood staring at one another and cursing, while all the people, the ghouls, began appearing out of the grass to join the crowd (I seem to remember them suddenly appearing on their hands and knees as though they were coming out of holes in the ground), I turned my back to the road and sat on the tractor, hammering the steering wheel with my fists and bawling over and over, "Stupid fucking niggers, stupid fucking niggers" — screaming a word that I had almost succeeded in eliminating from even my most secret thoughts. I had known the moment that I heard Segundo's body being smashed that it was all his fault, that in the most careless and criminal way, without looking right or left, fully absorbed in how magnificent he must appear to everyone in his Saturday clothes, he had wandered out into the middle of the road like a fool and killed himself. And almost at the same time I realized that all those others who had died that week had done it in exactly the same way. Was it possible that I was finally confronting one of those ultimate secrets of the black soul: that they were a people who could be beguiled by nothing but trivialities, that they were a people so cool that they couldn't give a damn about anything, not even their own lives? Imagining this fool bedazzled and absorbed in the contemplation of his gorgeous feet so enraged me that I wanted to rush over and kick blindly at his lifeless body.

By the time Washington's wife and I had stopped our screaming, by the time I had climbed down off the tractor and walked the thirty feet over to Segundo's body, the car that had hit him was disappearing down the road. The driver and a companion had run over, looked briefly at Segundo in the grass, run back to the car, and sped away. Half a dozen people had recognized the owner of the car, and wind rushing through his shattered windshield had disgorged hundreds of papers with his name printed on them; they moved slowly across the road with the afternoon breeze, and some of the children had already begun collecting them for whatever value they might have. He was a responsible businessman from Esmeraldas from one of the good families; at one time we had bought chicken feed from him. We stood before Segundo; his body was unmarked except for one small, deep triangular cut, like a dagger wound, from which oozed a drop or two of dark, almost black blood. He was very tastefully arranged for family viewing. He lay on his back in the grass in a perfect position for a long sleep, his face peaceful, still faintly smiling, his eyes closed, his hands at his sides with the palms down and pressed against the grass in some final farewell. His heart was still beating in his chest, but as I watched him, as I stood staring at this fluttering heart, this terrified idiot heart, which now found itself deserted in the body it had nourished for so long, it tremblingly slowed, hesitated, beat wildly, and suddenly stopped.

Young Antonio, his nephew, began to sob; in that crowd of people he was the only one from whom tears poured. He walked around in circles, pulling at his hair and sobbing. Víctor walked back and forth across the road, staring toward Viche where the car had disappeared, and from time to time cursed loudly. Ramón was motionless and thoughtful. Segundo's mother and sister came running up from the house where they lived; they had been expecting the thrill of another death and perhaps a little plunder, but they stopped short and groaned together at what they saw. Segundo's brother Adolfo crouched at his feet and stared at his body with dazed, expressionless eyes — Adolfo, that great hulking misshapen man with his enormous monster's hands fighting with each other. We didn't know until the next day that he was having a crisis of conscience. He had been invited with Segundo to a dance ten miles down the road and had been dreaming about it all week. Unless he could be very strong his brother's death was going to wreck all his weekend plans. Someone, some older woman, knelt by his side and whispered in Adolfo's ear. He ran off and returned almost immediately with a bedspread and his guitar; he had ripped the spread from a clothesline and it was still damp. The women laid it over Segundo but left his head uncovered, as though he were being tucked in for the night or as though, until someone in authority had spoken, he could not be regarded as dead, only resting.

I staggered back to the house where we had parked the pickup. Washington and his wife were standing in an upstairs window; he was awkwardly patting her head, and she was wailing with terror, saying over and over again in a loud wild voice, "Let's get out of this house; I don't want to live here anymore; I want to go home; I don't want to stay in this house anymore; let's go someplace else; I don't want to stay here anymore." I knew exactly how she felt; her home was in Manabi and now she was a prisoner in the heart of enemy country. A furious and bitter thought flared like a match in my head as I listened to her, a pang of jealousy as she used the word *home*. She had something, some last resort, some final refuge that I didn't have anymore. I had burned all my bridges; this fucking madhouse was my only home, and it hadn't yet occurred to me that I might leave this place without having some destination in mind. I had not begun to think about the alternatives to continuing on the farm, but a kind of panic was building in me, an impulse to start running, as my mind in little irrational starts and rushes sought, if not some destination, at least some temporary hiding place. But I held on and didn't start running wildly; I thought of the *Boy Scout Handbook* and its counsels about fighting hysteria when lost in the woods.

About ten people crowded into the pickup — Adolfo with his guitar, Antonio, red-eyed and still sobbing from time to time, a few awestruck kids dumb with excitement; Ramón and Víctor sat in front with me. We drove to Viche to inform the police and the *teniente político,* who by law had to arrive, inspect the body, and declare it officially dead before it could be moved. "Well," I said, "nice, no? It's been a damn nice week, no?"

"Stupid damned zambos," Ramón said furiously, as though he had caught my own rage and was reacting identically with me. "Víctor, excuse me, but that was really stupid; that brother of yours committed suicide."

"Son of a *bitch,*" Víctor said for the tenth time, shaking his head as though he had been slugged.

"The real son of a bitch is that son of a bitch who killed him and ran off," I said. "Oh, Jesus, Ramón, how I hate your country; how I hate your country."

"Yes," Ramón said, sarcastically, "everything is different in your country, isn't it? They don't run away up there, do they? Now listen to me very well and I will tell you again. If you ever have the bad luck to hit and kill someone I hope you'll have the good sense to run and hide just like he did."

"Even if it's not my fault?"

"There's no such thing in Ecuador," Ramón said. "When someone dies it's always someone's fault. Someone has to pay. Especially when they think you have money."

"Don Ramón, help me," Víctor said. "See that they pay *us* and not the *rurales*."

"Don't worry," Ramón said, "I'll help; I'm tired of seeing black bodies on the road and black blood running in the grass. It's an insult to my race."

"What's a dead Ecuadorian worth these days?" I asked, sarcastically.

"Oh, about fifteen thousand sucres, I imagine," Ramón said. "Isn't that what your friend Chino paid? But I think Negroes are going for about half that, and a real dumb one like Segundo, a real black one like Segundo, well, who knows? Maybe the real black ones aren't worth much of anything."

"Let's try for nine thousand sucres," Víctor said. "With nine thousand sucres I could buy a little store in Esmeraldas and even stock it with products." Nine thousand sucres was worth about three hundred and sixty dollars.

"What about his wife?" I asked. "Aren't you forgetting about her?"

"Didn't she kick him out of the house not even two months ago?" Víctor said. "That bitch, she doesn't deserve anything."

"He's not even cold yet," I said. "Jesus."

"Don't hassle Víctor," Ramón said. "When are you going to realize that poor people don't think like you do?"

"I realize it," I said. "And it's driving me crazy."

"Son of a *bitch*," Víctor said. "With *seven* thousand sucres I could buy a little store and fill it up with products."

We got to Viche; all the police where gone somewhere, but the teniente político was sitting in his office. He was a really corrupt man, a little aging drunkard from Manabi who had been put into his job by an equally corrupt colonel in the military junta that had recently taken over the government. He had only been in his job about three months, but he had filled the local jail with poor people whom he fined to the absolute limits of their ability to pay, and he had done something unheard of around here: he had thrown a woman into jail for telling him the truth about himself. Now he told us that he was sick and tired of coming up to our farm to look at dead bodies and that he had anticipated none of this unpleasantness when he had agreed to serve as the supreme

law of the town. "In one week I've certified four bodies in front
of your property and nobody has paid me a cent yet. Was he one
of your workers? Who wishes to respond for this new cadaver?"

I watched Ramón's face thicken with rage. A year before he
would have controlled himself, but now he knew his power; Ramón had recently been appointed by the governor of the province
to the post of inspector general of Male; it was a beautiful title
that meant only that he could make arrests and issue warnings to
drunks; more importantly he had impressed himself on all the
leading figures in Esmeraldas, the businessmen and the politicians.
Ramón also knew something about the teniente político that none
of us knew yet, that he was about to be thrown out of office. A
few days before, Ramón had picked up and driven into town one
of the local policia rurales, who was going in, he said, to complain
to the governor that the teniente político was absolutely shameless
and corrupt and to state that he demanded to be transferred out
of town. If not, he promised to kill the teniente político as a public
service. Three days after Segundo's death the teniente político
was hauled out of town in disgrace and ordered to leave the province permanently.

We stood before this man who staggered and swaggered on the
steps just outside his office, dressed in a filthy shirt and laceless
sneakers, his lizard's face set in a cold grin full of power and
greed.

"My dear Don Ramón," he asked again, "who wishes to respond
for this latest cadaver? I don't see how I can fulfill my many
obligations here for much less than 300 sucres."

Ramón stepped over to him, grabbed him by one arm, and
squeezed it with all his strength. In a very low voice, almost
whispering into one ear and smiling evilly he said, "My dear teniente político, get your ass into that car. *Now.* You understand?
What we want is permission to take a dead body out of the road,
and we want it *now.*"

The teniente's face flushed with anger until he looked at Ramón,
then he went white and, beginning to tremble, he allowed himself
to be led down the steps and into the pickup. Just as we backed
around to return, the local open-air bus came streaking down the
long hill into town, heading for Esmeraldas; Adolfo with his guitar
jumped out of the pickup, flagged down the bus and leaped into

it. He had decided to be strong. Tonight he would dance. We headed back for the farm, the teniente político sitting between us in the front seat. No one spoke; we had opened the little front windows on each side of the car so that the wind streamed into the cab against the drunken stink of our passenger. Ramón's jaws slowly relaxed in their clenching and unclenching; the teniente, with violently trembling fingers, unsuccessfully kept trying to light a cigarette. About half way back Ramón began to laugh, and he leaned forward and began talking across the teniente's body.

"Martín, you know what I'm thinking of? That story you told me about the man who jumped out of a ninetieth-floor window and, when he passed the tenth floor and someone yelled and asked him how he was, said, 'So far, just fine.' "

We both laughed and the teniente tried to smile and said, "Don Ramón, what made you think of that? I don't understand."

"Ah, my dear teniente," Ramón said, smiling into his face and putting one arm warmly across his shoulders, "you will, you will."

I left the truck with Ramón, left the little crowd of people who were still gathered around Segundo, and walked alone down the long lane to the river and the store. It was almost dark and I could hear the rain moving closer as it beat and crashed and rumbled on the leaves in the jungle, moving erratically across the hills like a herd of monstrous animals hopelessly lost but driven by the wind. It had the good clean sound of the only kind of power that I could any longer endure, and I hoped that before I reached the store I would be caught in a cloudburst and drenched by it. I wanted to be drowned in downpours of rain, but the power was in the noise, and when the rain finally came it was only a light but steady drizzle. Ester was beginning to fix something for us to eat when I got there; she had just returned from the road where she had been sent by someone's child who had begged for some medicine to tranquilize Washington's wife, who it seemed was losing control, who couldn't stop shuddering and weeping. Ester had run into the garden, cut a little handful of lemoncillo grass, grabbed the children, and headed up the hill. She had come back alone, leaving the children with that crowd on the road as though she felt that the contemplation of death was a basic part of their education.

The two of us were alone on the farm; there was no one to

help me start the light plant, but it seemed appropriate that our customs should be shattered, that we should eat in darkness and that the diesel motor should remain silent. Over an hour later, long after dark, Ramón drove down the road. He went into the kitchen, and as I sat alone in the other room I listened to the murmur of his voice and hers — it seemed as though they were consciously excluding me from the conversation. We ate in silence. Even the children, who had returned to the house with Ramón, were drugged and still, as if studying the body of Segundo or seeing him finally wrapped in a sheet and carried to Víctor's house had exhausted them. As soon as they had eaten they curled up on the couch and fell asleep. The body of Segundo floating through the air kept filling my vision, repeating itself like some idiot fragment of music that one can't erase from one's mind, that one keeps humming over and over. "Well," I said finally, "I guess I'll go to bed; the end of another great day."

"Yes," Ramón said, "let's all go to bed. My God, I'm tired. I don't think I've got the strength to pack the kids over to the house. And tomorrow is another hell of a day. Víctor's absolutely useless; I'll have to take him in and buy the coffin and arrange with the cemetery and everything. We might as well close the farm down for a week, because for the next nine days it's pure fiesta — drums and singing and aguardiente."

"Maybe we ought to buy coffins by the gross," I said. "Maybe we could get a special discount for quantity buying."

"I met the lawyer," Ramón said. "Man, didn't he get out here in a hurry. He was waiting in Viche when I took the son of a bitch of a teniente back. He gave Víctor 3000 sucres, and he's promised to pay 3000 more. I guess that's about as good as we can do."

"Watch yourself with that damned teniente político," I said. "You might just end up in jail again with your insolence."

"Oh, *him*," Ramón said. "Don't worry about him; he's just falling past the third floor."

"Tell Martín what Segundo said," Ester said as I stood in the doorway ready to leave.

"That's just the old women talking," Ramón said. "How can they invent those tales so fast? I don't believe any of it."

"Tell me."

"Did you see him when he came to the house and paid Washington's wife the two sucres that he owed her? Now the women are saying that he gave her the money and said, 'Here, I'd better pay this debt just in case; you never know around here when you're going to get killed.' "

"No, I don't believe that either," I said. "People who don't know they're going to die don't go around making up famous last words."

"No, no," Ramón said. "Those weren't his last words, not according to Celso's wife. She was standing with Segundo, waiting for the bus, and here comes the car going about a hundred kilometers an hour down the road, and Segundo yelled, '*mata* Gancho, *mata* Gancho, let's see if you will kill me too,' and he took one step out into the road just as the car came by."

We stood staring at one another in that flickering candlelight, and I could feel the goose flesh on my arms and the strength running out of my legs.

"Mata Gancho?" I said, finally. "I don't understand."

"Remember the old man who was killed on Monday? That was his nickname, Gancho, Hook, because he used to hide along the trails in the bananeros and jump out on the women when he was drunk and try to wrestle them down."

"And mata Gancho?"

"Segundo was yelling, 'Killer of Gancho, killer of Gancho.' I don't think you understand how all these deaths have affected everyone. There is terror out there on the road now. The people would like to waylay one of those fast moving cars rushing through their country and smash it into rubble with their bare fists. You know, up until about eight years ago no one here had ever seen a car; they are just now beginning to realize that it is a dangerous weapon."

"Tell him everything," Ester said. "Tell him about the boy."

"Oh, Jesus," Ramón said, "not now. Tomorrow."

"No, tell me now."

Ramón stared at me. "Didn't you smell anything at lunch today?"

I shook my head.

"Well, there was a body floating in the river, caught in the grass where we get our water. A boy, about fourteen. That's all."

"So we have two dead bodies on the farm," I said.

"No," Ramón said. "At least as far as I know, just Segundo. Ester took a stick and pushed the boy out into the current, and he went on his way."

"Ah."

A couple of months before, driving back to the farm one night from Esmeraldas, Ramón and I had passed a body lying in the road. When I began to stop, Ramón swung one leg over the gearshift and jammed his foot on the throttle. "Just keep going," he said.

"But there's a body in the road."

"Just keep going," Ramón said. "They put you in jail here for reporting dead bodies. Just leave him there, *tranquilo*."

"And what if he's not dead and needs help?"

"We don't involve ourselves in such things," Ramón said. "This is Ecuador, and you mind your own business."

"What a stupid country," I said.

"What a stupid gringo," Ramón said. "*Piensa mejor*. If the man is dead, what good can we do him? If he's not dead, maybe he is drunk. If he is not drunk, maybe he is the bait in a trap, and as you are bending over him a couple of other men will step out of the weeds and club you to death."

"And if he is injured and dying and needs help?"

"Then God have mercy on his soul," Ramón said. "I tell you with complete security that I am right: no one tonight that passes that man is going to stop. Unless, of course, some stupid gringo like yourself comes along without someone like me with him to take care of him."

I began to remember another night when Ramón and I had sat for two hours on this same road in a downpour, without a jack to change a flat tire, and had been helped finally by the new bishop of Esmeraldas. Suddenly a new flash of remembrance flared in my head like current newly flowing along newly connected wires, and I was remembering something forgotten until this moment, something that until this moment I had never known. How amazing.

"It was gringos who picked me up on the road that day when I hit the two banana trucks. I just now remembered. My God, I remember a woman's voice, someone leaning over me like an angel trying to wipe the blood out of my eyes, a voice talking to me in English with a German accent. It was such a sweet voice, like my grandmother's. Yes, I was lying in the back of a Land-Rover."

Ramón didn't say anything.

"It was gringos who picked me up," I said again, feeling glad and bitter and accusing. "I wonder how many of your countrymen drove by me before the gringos came along. Not counting the ones, of course, who stopped just long enough to steal something out of the wreck."

Ramón didn't say anything.

I lit a candle in my house and sat by the big windows that in the daytime looked out over the river. It was still raining, a little harder now, and water falling through a dozen places in the rotting thatched roof dripped onto the floor, on my books, my desk, the bed. I had piled what I could under sheets of plastic so that the dear little termites would not wet themselves as they cleaned up the last of my things. The house looked as though I were preparing to vacate it for an extended time. It had become almost impossible lately to find a place in the room where I could sleep without being rained on, and this was a point of great resentment and constant conflict between Ramón and me: in more than a year, in spite of constant promises, he had been unable or unwilling to bring out a man from Rioverde who understood the almost forgotten art of weaving a new dry roof of cade. Ramón, Ecuadorian to his roots, had decided that thatch in this wet climate rotted out too fast, but that since I refused to agree to replace my roof with sheets of tin — and where would we find the money to put me inside a thundering tin drum where for nine months out of every year I would be subjected to that dreadful and maddening cacaphony? — I should be allowed to rot and steam in my own stubbornness until I came to my senses.

In the darkness the river was invisible, but even above the drumming of the rain on the leaves outside I could hear directly across from us the clear rushing menace of a little intermittent stream that tumbled out of a canyon behind Roque's house. It was never the highway that had worried me; it was always the river that had seemed to hold in its constant flow, as it slid past the farm like a moving sheet of glass, the future promise of disaster. In the flood times when overnight it rose over its banks and stood three feet deep in the store and the kitchen, it roared and howled, and as the boulders in the stream bed were swept down in the current they rattled and clunked together with a threatening, almost human voice. For days at a time the river was choked with trash: roots, leaves, and whole trees, some of them ninety feet long; the bodies of bloated cattle and pigs upon some of which vultures rode with ragged outspread wings as they fought to keep possession of these rolling corpses bobbing and twisting on their way to the sea; empty canoes; the roofs of houses; islands of reject balsa chunks from the higher balsa mills; islands of water hyacinth ripped from the quiet lagoons of low water. A year before this awful month a newly arrived Peace Corps volunteer had drowned upstream from us, and in the week it took to find him, a dozen volunteers in motor canoes probing up and down the river had discovered four other bodies bobbing tranquilly in the water and caught in branches. Three of them had been black, two of them had been murdered. The river of Emeralds. To me at times it was not a river at all but just a gigantic sewer, draining all of the jungle country between Esmeraldas and Quito, including Quito's sewage. With such a harvest of carrion, who could doubt the truth of the country people's tales of an enormous fish, the mera, who slept at the bottom of the river and who from time to time rose to the surface and swallowed a swimming man whole. It was a joke that the mera preferred whites to blacks and found Germans to be tastiest of all. One day they said the mera had gulped down two German sailors as they swam beside their banana boat. Was there a mera sleeping out there in the channel, below the houses, waiting for one of us to make a slip? I wasn't sure enough that there wasn't to not mention the possibility to friends who came for a visit and a swim, and I was constantly screaming at Ester when I found Martita and Ramoncito swimming unattended among the rows of tied up canoes.

By nine o'clock it had stopped raining; by half-past nine the clouds had parted and a wide strip of sky appeared, as though the sky had split open like an overripe melon to reveal its seeds, the stars. A full moon now rode above the hills, splashing the river and the trees with silver lights and black shadows, stabbing the people with its rays of madness and delirium. Was it the moon that brought out the worst in everyone that night, the night that Segundo died, the night when so many curious things happened as we finally slept? Surely, if there had been no moon, one would have to be invented to account for the irrationalities that erupted up and down the river. I went to bed thinking that I would be unable to sleep, and to drug myself I gave in to an impulse that had been growing — a desire to balance my books, to itemize the pros and cons of my situation as Robinson Crusoe had once done. If anything would put me to sleep, the compiling of lists should do it. "I am cast up and abandoned in a wild and savage place." It was the only thing that occurred to me, and as I debated whether this belonged in the pro column or the con column I was swept under into an exhausted sleep.

Around midnight, as nearly as reconstruction is possible but without attempting to put events in their proper order, the following things happened:

Arcario for the first and only time in his life took a great swing at his Susana and knocked that enormous girl flat on her enormous ass.

Cantante, across the river with Arcario but in his own shack 500 yards upstream, drove his fist into one of Cira's eyes. She was one of the two women he was living with, the really serious one.

On this side of the river, Pastór with one wild drunken blow knocked out two of his wife's teeth outside Carlos Angulo's salón, in front of twelve witnesses.

Jorge Cortez, a mile upstream on Bone's farm, in a rage with his wife's infidelities, clipped Adelina on the chin and knocked her unconscious. Four days later, under a waning half-moon, he would murder her with two machete blows — one that almost severed her arm, one high across the back as she tried to run from him.

This was Dalmiro's last night on the Esmeraldas River. Sometime after midnight he was directed by the moon's rays to commit himself to dignity and justice. He had been helping Esmundo make charcoal across the river ever since he had left our farm in disgrace six months before. The terms of his peonage he now decided were unjust. He crept to Esmundo's bedroom from the kitchen, where he slept on empty charcoal sacks, and from the doorway aimed a great flood of piss at sleeping Esmundo and his sleeping wife.

And now tonight, as the whole fabric of life on the river un-raveled in the face of the people's inability to contain their pas-sions, even placid Santo, who no longer had any passion at all, was to be subjected to the final humiliation that symbolized the end of his maturity and the beginning of his old age. From this night on it would all be downhill. If it was Santo who some months before had plucked out and eaten the hearts of my young hummingbirds, tonight he would learn that those hearts were no great aphrodisiacs. Coming back from Víctor's house, where he had gone earlier to leave candles and to sit with the bereaved family, he had stopped off at Carlos Angulo's salón to listen for awhile to a happier music and to observe with fascination Pastór as he rolled and crawled and wept in the dirt after having struck his wife. Carlos Angulo had left the area some months before with a crew of younger men to saw wood planks in the jungled hills outside of Quinindé in a clearing called El Diablo. His wife, Elena, was managing the business at home, and she was doing a much better job than Carlos had ever done because she only drank when invited to by one of the customers, who was expected to pay. She was half drunk when Santo arrived sometime after mid-night; she had begun talking openly about her intentions to get herself a man, and several men with ulterior motives had been buying her shots of aguardiente with cola chasers. She was a hu-man being, too, she said. Carlos had no right to leave her for months at a time, whoring his money away in Quinindé. Don't think she hadn't heard all about it. Didn't she have needs just like anybody else? The moment she saw Santo standing in the door of her salón, what may have been no more than the angry yap-ping of a big mouth, turned into desire and the determination to betray her husband. The brilliance of the moon behind Santo was almost frightening. As soon as he had seated himself at one of the tables, she brought him a bottle and a shot glass and sat down beside him. "Do you remember what you told me six months ago, that you would like to have me?"

"But, of course," Santo said bravely. He had been slightly drunk when he had spoken those ardent words, and now sober and soberly melancholy from visiting Víctor's house he found the prospect less exciting than drunk Elena. Besides that and more importantly he had been having so much trouble with his sexual machinery that he had scarcely had the nerve for the last six months to speak warmly to a woman, let alone think of sleeping with her. But now Elena's hands caressed his leg beneath the table and he felt a glad reassuring stirring.

"Walk down the trail when you've finished your drink, and wait for me by the coconuts of Mercedes."

"When?"

"Now," Elena said. "This very second; give me ten minutes."

She joined him in five minutes. He scarcely had time to tramp down a little nest of grass a few feet off the trail in a deep pool of shadow in the blazing moonlight that almost gave color to the leaves and the yellowing ranconcha roofs of the houses. She groaned when she saw him and pulled him down beside her and her need was so great that Santo was violently aroused to his full manhood. After months of terrible self-doubt he was flooded with relief. That damn traitor with its own life, its own capricious laws, was perhaps finally ready to cooperate. Praise God and hurray. But no, things were not going to be simple for Santo anymore. Poor romantic Santo, who had always found perfection and soul-stabbing beauty in women and in the idea of their sweet yielding, whose passion had always blinded him until it was too late to know the truth that they were human, not divine, was now aware of Elena's sour drunken breath and the funky smell of her unwashed body. And so now at the moment of penetration when by rights it should have been clear sailing, he realized with horror that he was being betrayed again. "Oh, my God," Santo groaned.

"But don't stop now," Elena cried. "Move. Move."

Santo moved, moved desperately, moved until the sweat poured off him.

"Put your hand here," Santo begged. "Touch me here."

"Oh, my God," Elena groaned, "what are you trying to do to me?"

They moved and pressed and slid and sweated, Santo feigning a passion that had turned to pure horror. "Grab me," Santo begged, "touch me here."

"Ay, it's dead, it's dead," Elena cried. "What's wrong with you? Are you the kind of man who doesn't like women?"

"Elena, Elena, for God's sake, help me. Bend down; kiss me here."

"*Degenerado,*" Elena cried, pushing him away. "Roll away, let me up. I've got to get back. And you, you, why don't you go and find yourself a man?"

Santo sat by himself for a long time in that little circle of darkness in the damp grass. Just below him, but hidden, the river sucked and murmured as it rolled away to the north, and it seemed to give off a kind of phosphorescent glow from the moonlight that hung over the river like a mist. He had chosen a bad spot, and now he could feel a hundred pinpoint ticks crawling over his arms and legs, but somehow he didn't have the strength to move. He sat there studying the strange light that hung over the river as the ticks crawled over a body for which he no longer had any affection or respect.

What a terrible and curious night. What else might have happened that we never heard about? Why, for instance, were there only *four* wife beatings after five highway deaths, four wife beatings between those deaths and the drownings of five brothers two days later when their canoe overturned? We were clearly involved in disasters that happened in series of five. Who might have been the other woman who was struck and kept her mouth closed about it? It was typical of our hick-town *ambiente* that by noon the next day all of these things that the participants would rather have not discussed, that they would have preferred to keep secret, were general knowledge up and down the river. Wife beating is more or less common, and there are almost never any consequences, but these strange midnight blows that might very well have taken place at the same instant were not ordinary; they held a malevolent power and the consequences were long lasting and, in the case of

Pastór, final. Pastór's woman would never return to him, and from this moment on, those who knew him would begin to comment on his eccentric behavior; until that night I had been the only one who had ever been convinced that the man was insane. After that night everybody knew it. Cira refused to speak to Cantante for months. Adelina died. Susana went to Guayaquil and got a job as a maid, and if Arcario had not written her a begging letter she may well have decided to stay forever.

The next morning while we ate breakfast, Cira came to the store and said that she would cook for us. This was good news. Cira in fact was about the only woman around that we would have wanted to prepare our food, and we had been trying to hire her for a month without success. The time had almost arrived when Ester and the children would be leaving us for nine months of every year. Martita was six years old and Ramón, wild to educate his children, had arranged to put her in a private Catholic girl's school in Esmeraldas; Ramoncito, nicknamed Moncho, the cleverest, most enchanting kid ever born, would now begin a three-year sentence in kindergarten; we looked forward to their going with real dismay, unable to imagine the emptiness they would leave behind, for they were the real light, the real delight of the farm. How we mourned them when they left us with only the memory of their innocence, their sticky hands, their ardent kisses, their tears and laughter, the bed wetting, the mattress burning, their honesty. Ah, well . . .

We said nothing to Cira about her blackened eye and she offered no explanation until she got Ester alone. As we talked in the store (Cira had immediately taken over and began furiously sweeping all the rooms and raising a choking cloud of dust), Pastór's woman, her mouth swollen, marched out of the grass with a wooden suitcase and headed up the road toward the buses, and a few minutes later Arcario's Susana, with all her clothes thrown into a plastic fertilizer sack, climbed panting up the bank from the river like a younger but still formidable version of her overwhelming mother, Rosa, and scowling, head down as though she were plowing air, disappeared up the road.

Dalmiro's life was also permanently changed, though probably less than anybody else's — unless there is some basic difference between half starving in Male and half starving in Rioverde. At lunchtime he staggered, half falling, into the dining room, where Ramón and I were eating bowls of soup. He seemed not to have changed much in the six months since we had seen him last, but his clothes had almost disintegrated, and his black skin had been permanently stained with charcoal. He had come, he said, to say goodbye to his cuñado; he was going back to Rioverde; things had not turned out too well across the river. He went into a long sputtering harangue against Esmundo which I couldn't understand. Six months making charcoal . . . living like an animal . . . except for the rags on his back he had no clothes . . . I tried to catch Ramón's eye, but he was bent over his soup and eating very seriously; he took no part in the conversation and in fact seemed to be unaware that a conversation was taking place. He was still angry with Dalmiro and perhaps by not looking at him he hoped not to be moved by pity.

"Have we any money?" I whispered to Ramón, who still without looking at either of us pulled out two 100-sucre bills and laid them on the table. "Do you have another?" Ramón shook his head. "Do you have an old pair of pants, a shirt?" Without a word, his face carefully set in no expression at all, Ramón got up from the table, went over to his house, and came back with some almost new clothes; he laid them on the table with the money and left the house without finishing his meal.

When Dalmiro had gone I stayed in the house, not knowing what to do and not wanting to do much of anything. I hated Sundays, when everyone sat around without moving, brought low by their hangovers and bored to the point of desperation; now we were going to have eight days of Sundays in a row while the dead were buried and mourned. This was a different kind of Sunday, heavy and muted, with something permanently gray about it, as though a fabric of depression was being spread over us from horizon to horizon. It was a fabric through which we could still see but which filtered out everything that was comic or slapstick and ridiculous. But worse, the day was menacing, dangerous. I felt as though something was robbing us of the power to direct our lives, but the feeling was vague; I had no earlier experience to help me. And it wasn't until over a year later, when an earthquake, 8.5 on the Richter scale, visited the farm for a few seconds, that I began to understand what had happened to us during that month when the true quality of life began to reveal itself, or if not that, when we were forced to re-examine and crystallize our feelings about the quality of this life that we had made for ourselves.

(The house where I slept had begun to twist and tremble, to dance and shake and howl as nails popped from the tin roof, the plates and bowls shattered on the floor, and the swaying timbers, brought back to momentary life and the memory of ancient winds, creaked and bent and cracked. In Esmeraldas, twenty-five miles away, all the public buildings, the municipal hall, the schools, and the officers club, everything built with the corruption of public funds had been destroyed. Cement lampposts snapped off at their bases; the dead were buried beneath collapsing walls; padlocked doors burst open and the contents of stores vomited themselves out into the street — oranges and potatoes mixed with burst open sacks of flour and oatmeal and broken bottles of cooking oil, kerosene, Pepsi and beer. The main theater in town was showing *Earthquake* that night, and the townspeople, none of them particularly sensitive critics, all agreed that only Hollywood could have made something so blatantly boring and dishonest. It had taken only ten seconds to make excellent critics of the lot. Ah yes, this is how it was, I thought, as that year-old memory of a bad month lived in my mind and I connected this helpless chaotic time with that earlier time when we lived in the growing certainty that life was really much too much to handle and that we could be sure of almost nothing. How that bucking, whipping house purged my confusions.)

I was still sitting at the table when Ramón came back. He had driven to Víctor's house for a few minutes to check out the wake, in which he was now so personally involved that he must have felt like a stage director checking the attendance of a minor but well-organized spectacle. I could hear him outside talking with someone. He came to the door and peered into the room where I sat and said accusingly, "Well, he's still out there. Dalmiro, your cuñado. He's out there crying."

I got up and looked out. Dalmiro in his rags was squatting with his back against the trunk of a coconut palm with a fist jammed into each eye like a little boy.

"He's crying for *you*," Ramón said. "He's crying because he'll never see you again. He's not crying for *me;* he doesn't even *like* me who tried to help him, who brought him here, who bought clothes for him, who listened to him while he talked and talked and talked about that damned old cow of his. He's crying for *you* who hardly ever even spoke to him except to say good morning, you who never even touched that cracked old man."

"How could I talk to him?" I asked angrily. "Shit, I can't understand him."

"You know what I mean," Ramón said. "It's like with the kids; you don't wash their clothes or sit up with them when they're sick or get involved with their temper tantrums. You just sit in that chair and they rush in and climb all over you and plaster you with kisses, and when they begin to get on your nerves you go over to your house. You sit on that tractor and wave to people a mile away, or you sit over in your house as though you were in another world, or you tell me, 'Go get some of your old clothes and give them to Dalmiro.' "

"The farm pays for your clothes and mine. What the hell difference does it make?"

"Because they're *my* clothes. You know what I'm talking about. You sit there eating your soup and you send me out to give my clothes away to the man who called my mother a whore."

"What's got into you?" I cried. "Moon rays? I didn't *send* you anyplace. I *asked* you if you had some clothes you could give Dalmiro. And I didn't mean you had to give him your best clothes, either."

"Yes," Ramón said. "You would have given him some of your old rags torn ten ways up the crotch."

"So that's why you gave him your best clothes. To humiliate *me.*"

Ramón shrugged and turned his back to me; he stared out at Dalmiro. "He said to tell you he would never forget you," Ramón said bitterly. "He said to tell you the years here were the best years of his life, that here he had been the happiest. Remember that old mattress you gave him when he slept in the chicken house, the one Ramoncito used to pee in, the one Martita set on fire, all torn and the stuffing coming out? He said to thank you again for that, that for a while he had never slept so well."

"He couldn't possibly mean that," I said helplessly. I felt my cheeks burning as though someone had just struck me across the face. "He's just saying that to humiliate *you*. It's you he really likes and wants to hurt."

"Maybe. Maybe it's partly that, but doesn't it do something to you here in your heart to know that you were so well thought of by someone you regarded as vomit?"

"I have never regarded Dalmiro as vomit," I cried, beginning to tremble. "What are you trying to say?"

"You know what I'm talking about," Ramón said. "I've been trying to run this farm the way I think you'd want it run. And for some reason you come out looking like some little prince, and I come out with my hands all covered with shit and people saying I'm a bad man, that I have no heart."

"What makes you think you're running the farm the way I want it run? What makes you think I want you *running* the farm? Ever since the wreck you've taken over everything; you can't imagine a partnership as anything but some kind of a struggle for domination. So run the farm; I'm too old to fight with you about something that each day interests me less and less. Run it right into the ground if you want to, but don't get mad if I don't do anything but disk with the tractor. That's all you've left me to do. You've become arrogant," I cried. "You've lost your style. You're getting middle class. There are ways to fire a man so that he thinks he's been promoted. Then there's *your* way."

"I'll let you haul the next thief off to jail with your big mouth," Ramón said. "Instead of half beating him to death with a machete I'll let him think he's been promoted with your stylish approach. Was that one of the jobs I took away from you? Ah, little prince, you have never *touched* a poor man."

When Ramón is angry he begins to smile and whistle; now smiling desperately, he began to whistle some tuneless little something through his teeth as he stared at me, studying my face as though I were a clown. That crack about never having touched a poor man enraged me for some reason. A week before, Ramón had called me away from a group of workers to tell me at great length how disgusting he found my habit of bumming drags off the cigarettes of some of the workers. "My God," he had said, "how can you take a cigarette out of Quevedo's mouth and put it in your mouth. That man could have anything."

So now, beginning to smile myself, I remained silent for a moment as I tried to think of the cruelest thing I could say to him. When I had left the Peace Corps to go back to the United States, Ramón had broken down as we waited for the bus in Santo Domingo, and it was those tears for me (when had anybody ever cried for me?) that had made me feel responsible and that had made me promise on my honor to come back. I imagined, and now I hoped, that he remembered that terrible farewell with embarrassment and that he regarded his loss of control as having been unmanly, for he had never mentioned it.

"What do you mean *touch?*" I said. "If you'll remember I once held the poorest man in Rioverde in my arms while he cried like a baby."

Ramón, grinning like a fool, whistling up a storm, said insolently, "Well, it brought you back, didn't it? You're *here,* aren't you?"

"Now what does that mean?" I asked, beginning to laugh. "That you were just acting, that it was all just an act like Barry pulled on me?"

Ramón, whistling little tuneless notes, stared at me without answering, and I stared back, mocking him, smiling widely and whistling the march from Prokofiev's *Love for Three Oranges.* To an outsider watching us we might have appeared as two old music-loving friends passing a Sunday afternoon; if Ester had seen us in this moment she might well have felt a stab of fear; we had both of us been caught up in the local madness and were on the point of exchanging blows.

I went over to my house and sulked. I had never been so bored and had never seen so clearly that there were no solutions to the problems of the farm. God, how bored I was with the farm. The adventure had gone out of it; we had cleared the land, ripped out its great trees, fenced and tamed it into pastures, plantings of coconuts, squared fields of pineapple, cacao, and oranges. Now the last mysterious stronghold, the center of the farm, was almost cleared of everything but the old banana plantings that we were in the process of rejuvenating. We had cut away the mystery with the trees. The place was finished, the job done; all that remained now was the day to day drudgery of farming. There was nothing left to plan, to anticipate, to be surprised by. But farm what? At this very moment we had twenty-five acres of cleared land and could think of absolutely nothing to plant on it. All of our impulses to farm had been more or less frustrated, our hopes brought crashing down. We had tried to raise chickens only to find that much of the time the country had no chicken concentrate; we had raised pigs that nobody wanted to buy; we had planted corn (sometimes three times in a month, trying to get a stand) and had ended up spending more on insecticides than the value of the harvested crop; we had raised a new variety of beans from Brazil, Caraota, the most delicious beans in the country, but no one, especially the Negroes, would buy them because they were black and if eaten would probably make them have blacker children; our plantings of sesame had rotted on the stalk shortly before harvest; our modest twenty-five acre fields of peanuts had glutted the market. Selling peanuts in Quito, arguing with the *comerciantes* over the price, had been ultimately so unpleasant and degrading that we had resolved to plant no more peanuts ever, *nunca jamás*. And damn those shameless whining peanut buyers to hell. Soybeans? The extension service urged us to plant soybeans; everybody wants soybeans. We planted soybeans and *nobody* wanted soybeans; nobody but the extension people even knew what they were. Pineapples? Pineapples did well and we had a market in Esmeraldas that bought our entire output, but Evans in Santo Domingo, who had large plantings, could have dumped his surplus in our market and wiped us out at any moment — not that our loss would have been a tremendous one; our field was small and the local people were stealing at least half of what we raised.

Driven into the corner by the fading of our expectations, we had now pinned all our hopes on cattle, coconuts, and bananas. In other words our situation was serious. Foot-and-mouth disease was rampant in the country, and we had already suffered an outbreak of the disease in its most benign form. In order to spare us heart attacks the veterinarian had called it by another name, but we weren't fooled by this little Latin trick of disguising reality;

a whore is a whore, not a lady of the night, and we had the *aftosa* infection on our farm. We also had things without names. During one four-month period ten cows, one after the other, miscarried. We were only slightly reassured, after testing our herd again, to know that it was not brucellosis. What was it then, for God's sake? Nobody knew. Perhaps the chute was too narrow, perhaps there were poisonous weeds in the pastures, perhaps it was simply God's will. We listened with growing apprehension to the horror stories of our neighbors who had lost whole herds of animals from unknown tropical diseases, and then one day, God passed on and live calves started to be born again.

Something awful was beginning to happen in the coconuts, nobody knew what. It was a new plague from Florida or Panama that was already wiping out hundreds of thousands of trees along the coast. Now it moved inland; the palm fronds yellowed, drooped and broke, turned black. The government coconut experts, confused and helpless, began to suggest the old-time remedies — sheep dip mixed with salt or buckets of ashes. A couple of their old-time helpers suggested voodoo chants and the sacrifice of chickens. I thought we would get at least equally good results by sacrificing a couple of coconut experts, slitting their throats and hanging them in the trees, but no one thought this was very funny except Ramón, who had a fine distrust of anyone who called himself an expert — *ingenieros de mesa* he called them, "table engineers," know-it-alls who sat at the table with pencils and doodled things on sheets of paper.

Just as we began to realize that we were rushing toward insolvency and that it would be unreasonable to expect any of our projects to yield a profit that would feed us, the hurricanes and the earthquakes of the early seventies devastated the banana republics of the Caribbean, and about twenty minutes later, funny little Chinamen in droopy Panama hats and vaguely disreputable Americans with flushed faces and soft fat asses and steely-eyed Ecuadorians with pencil-thin mustaches began stopping at the farm and slapping our backs. They had been talking out on the road with Ramón and they knew more about the farm than I did. Hadn't I heard? There was going to be a new banana boom, prices would soar to unheard-of levels. The banana boats were already on the way. But we have no bananas, I told them. But of course you do, they said. We've been out through your jungle with your partner. All you have to do is cut down the second-growth trees, replant a few little spots, and you'll have over a hundred acres of the best bananas in the country. No, I said. Four thousand dollars a month, they said. Bullshit, I said. Maybe five thousand dollars a month, they said. I'll talk it over with Ramón, I said.

I fought as long as I could but not very hard. We were being pushed through the only door still open; it was our only chance, and it seemed petty to raise obstacles against this foolish gold-plated insanity if I could come up with no alternative. God help us, we were left with the bananas. Ramón, blazing with his famous enthusiasms about things of which he is still innocent and ignorant, was convinced that the bananas would save us. Too many great fortunes had been made in the past for bananas to be anything but the quick and miraculous way to the solution of all our problems.

"Name one great fortune," I said.

"Salas," Ramón answered immediately.

"Salas has eight thousand acres," I said. "If he cleared a dollar an acre you could call that a great fortune down here."

"Don't be cynical," Ramón said. "We'll either make it big or go down with a great crash."

"I don't want to go down with a great crash," I said.

We sold some cows, and instead of paying the bank Ramón hired a crew of axmen and we spent eight thousand dollars clearing weeds and felling trees; we cut roads through the farm in parallel lines and hauled in gravel to the muddy spots with a new trailer; we built a packing shed with a cement tank for washing the fruit and a cement floor to protect the boxed fruit from stains and dampness; we signed up in the government's banana program and some time later government airplanes began flying over the farm at two-week intervals and dumping great quantities of oil and chemicals in long smoky lines. The only thing that matched Ramón's excitement during this time was my own depression; watching the rape of the farm I felt like a man who has just agreed to sell his sister to the white slavers. Bananas. Never in our bleakest moments of facing up to agricultural reality had I ever thought that we would sink so low. We were about to become pawns in one of the international export traps that have so thoroughly enslaved the continent and kept it poor; we were about to join that indentured and doomed group of gamblers made up of diamond, rubber, tagua, gold, and oil hunters, the hunters of leopard skins for the New York furriers, the growers of coffee and chocolate — all of us tossed and whipped by the boom and bust nature of the free enterprise system controlled by our rapacious northern neighbors. We were about to become the most despicable element of a filthy business, growers of bananas, the very end and bottom of the totem pole, the latrine orderlies of the banana business, the ones who paid for everything, who planted, weeded, harvested, hauled, packed, and delivered the end product to the boats, who paid for the hauling, the harvesting, the boxes, the airplanes, who even paid the inspectors who threw out half a load of fruit to prove their power or their displeasure because in addition to paying their wages you hadn't realized the necessity of also stuffing a couple of 100-sucre bills into their back pockets as a little extra. How I dreaded this new situation about which I knew almost nothing and about which I knew too much; I felt like a man reading a second-rate mystery who reads the last pages first and now has no reason to wade through all that intervening crap since he now not only knows who pulled the trigger but also that he himself was the victim. The charm and excitement of the race are in thinking, until the last moment, that you have a chance to win; even though I was Hemingway's child I still found the pleasures of going down to defeat with style and grace to be highly overrated. I had always admired those hogs who screamed and shrieked beneath the butcher's knife, who did not go gently into that last good night.

With the glut of fruit, how quickly those fawning, back-slapping banana buyers who had promised and at times even supplied modest support would change into scowling insolent wretches who dumped your fruit into the sea or who left it rotting in the bananeros. The buyers' aim, of course, was to fill the boats as quickly and as cheaply as they could; for this reason they would tie up twice as many growers as they needed so that, when they had twice as much fruit as they could use, they could pick and choose from the glut and lower the price on what they finally took. If you were not a Quito lawyer or a politician with the power to threaten, if you were too dumb to know whom to bribe, you had about as much chance as a lamb surrounded by wolves.

Well, I had been convinced for over a year that it was impossible to be a successful farmer in Ecuador; being a flexible type I had tailored my expectations. As long as we could pay our bills, as long as we remained solvent enough to stay on the farm, the pleasure of playing with the land would be its own reward. If I couldn't be a farmer I would be an artist. I wouldn't hang plastic sheets off cliffs in Australia in the name of art or dig half-mile ditches across English fields or pile tons of rocks in haphazard patterns on museum floors until the beams cracked or plant mushrooms at the top of Mexican volcanoes. No, I would be the greatest artist of all that crazy bunch. I would cut square miles of beauty through the jungle, I would lay the ordering hand of man over that squirming proliferation of chaos. What excited me now about this land was its tranquil beauty as it lay exposed and naked to the light of the sun, its perimeters razor sharp, starkly delineated by the walls of jungle on our neighbors' land. When we had come here you couldn't see thirty feet ahead of you. Now from the road the place was open, squared away, as pure and forthright as a blank sheet of paper; you could gaze down for a mile over the tabled fields as they sank gently toward the river. What I really loved now was a great field the day before planting as it lay at sunset, darkly rich, with not a single weed, not a single plant to mar its perfection. After that everything was anticlimax, frustration, heartbreak. I was as impotent as Santo or, if potent enough to impregnate the land, capable only of producing diseased monstrosities. I realized now that my only pleasures in farming would be the pleasures of foreplay. But what was I going to do now? We had turned the heart of the farm over to the banana company; I had run out of land to foreplay with.

God, what a dismal Sunday. It was as dismal, as painful as any of those times in life when one is forced to peel off the brilliant colors of one's illusions to confront the gray reality and feel with resentment and fear that great changes are about to be forced on one. At the age of fifty-nine, having invested everything in the boat that is to carry one to a final destination, one is terrified to suddenly notice that the hull is rotten and that the water is pouring in.

How odd that all those random deaths and all that random violence, events that scarcely touched us, were having such a tremendous power to shake us up. Lying on my back and studying the disintegrating roof of my house and a cluster of bats who clung together at the highest peak, I seemed to find in this restricted and senseless view of rural squalor the symbols for the end of a journey I had been impelled to make, that naive journey into the heart of poverty, where I had hoped and expected to find order and meaning in my life. I was achieving all of the trappings of poverty without gaining any of the insights about it that I had been looking for. I had found no special meaning in life. I had become poor, or no, I was going through all the motions of being poor without fooling anyone, least of all myself. No one on the river felt impelled to reveal some feeling of mutuality or kinship because of my stained and moldy clothes or the rotting away of my possessions or the contemplation of this house, which was rapidly becoming uninhabitable. Nor by repudiating my possessions had I achieved any feeling of kinship myself. What I admired most (and envied and resented for the destructiveness that went along with it) was a poor man's — perhaps a black poor man's — capacity to grab at the fleeting delight of the present moment, to clutch at "now" and with the senses transform it into joy. None of that capacity had rubbed off on me. But more importantly I did not feel like a poor man, nor could I ever. I had been given too much. I was not cut off from the world's culture, and unlike a poor man I had no feeling of being isolated from the human stream. How can one feel poor who has stood before the paintings of Cezanne, Bonnard, Van Gogh, or Breughel, who has read Tolstoi, Montaigne, Proust, and Conrad, who has listened to Poulenc, Stravinsky, Bartók, and Beethoven? Still, if I couldn't feel poor, I didn't feel rich either, and perhaps this was part of the problem. By rejecting wealth and turning away from the use of power, by failing to define myself in terms that poor people could understand, I had sowed confusion in everyone's mind. If I didn't know who I was, how could anyone

else on the river see me as anything but a grotesque, an eccentric
fool whose only purpose was to be plundered?

I was an old man now with an old man's narrow wisdom; I had
become an old man in one split second as I tried to drive a pickup
through a two-foot space between two banana trucks. What wisdom I had gained was not very much, simply the crystallization of
my feelings about money and power into the kind of dogma that I
could lean on to get me through whatever years remained. It was
depressing now to realize, along with everything else that had begun to undermine the foundations of my life, that those few qualities that I admired in myself and that in my secret thoughts
allowed me to feel superior to many of my friends who scrabbled
their lives away in mediocre passions unworthy of them, were the
very qualities that marked me here as a fool and a weakling. Even
Ramón no longer took me very seriously; he had long since
dropped his pretense that decent poverty was a decent goal and
had begun to regard me as an obstacle to the kind of life he
dreamed of having. It was a mockery of life to treat it like a game
and to kill yourself with work when the final objective is to end up
decently poor. To hell with that. When the bananas paid off he
wanted a Mercedes-Benz and preferably with a chauffeur. What
he needed right now was a telephone in the house in Esmeraldas
so that he could be in instant touch with the banana company in
Guayaquil; it was humiliating to be the only grower of bananas
without a telephone. He could hardly wait for school to start so
that he could move his children out of the jungle into the decency
of paved streets, theaters, stoplights, and crowds of people who
went about fully clothed. He didn't want his children playing with
these naked savages with their lice and their ringworms and their
swollen worm-infested bellies. They didn't come to the house to
play, Ramón insisted, but only to raid the kitchen and steal his
children's toys. In Esmeraldas they could at least play with the
children of respectable people and begin to learn good middle-class
manners. Later he would send them to the American high school
in Quito and later still to the United States, where they would learn
to speak English without accents and would graduate from the
university as doctors or engineers. Ramón had already selected
the spot on the wall beneath his wedding picture where those two

sheepskins would hang, marvelous jewels in their crowns of glory, ornate golden script on heavy mottled paper. Those children would be so highly educated when they came back to Ecuador to serve their country in positions of honor that it would probably be impossible for them not to sneer a little at their former friends.

"Yes," I said, "if they ever come back. And they'll sneer at you too; you and their mother with your third grade educations."

"Maybe," Ramón said. Maybe that was the price you had to pay to put your children at the top of the heap, and he would rather lose them that way than to have to throw them out as smokers of marijuana or as petty thieves. "Do you realize," and his face flashed with joy as he realized it himself, "that it is just remotely possible that one day Moncho could be the president of the republic. Think about that, the first black president of Ecuador."

"Would you wish that on your son?" I asked. "Why don't you let Moncho decide if he wants to be a politican?"

"Do you want to be president of the *republica?*" Ramón asked, bending down to his son, who was half listening to us and smiling at being the object of so much attention.

"I want to drive the tractor," Moncho said. "Ar*um,* ar*um,* bar*um.*"

"You *see,*" I said.

Until I realized that it was none of my business and that my ideas were a great confusion to Ramón, what bitter arguments we had had about the education of his children. Like all people without children I knew exactly how they should be raised — or at least how they shouldn't be raised. I smarted with pain when, being stubborn and assertive, they got their fannies whacked by parents who had lost patience with their little shows of independence. How I loved them and wished for the power to guide their lives. In my willingness, you could almost say my neurotic passion, to live a deprived life and to postpone every gratification by spending everything on the clearing of more land, was I not earning the right to claim the children as my own? Was it a self-delusion that I was doing it all for them? I would leave them hundreds of acres of pasture and a great herd of pure-bred Brahma cows. They could work the land or sell it. Of course, I hoped that they would want to be farmers and dreamed even that they would want to be artists; to me these were the only two things in life to which one might honorably sacrifice oneself. But what they became was unimportant as long as they stayed loving, stayed strong and unafraid, and got from life everything that they deserved. It was irrelevant whether Moncho ended up as the president of Ecuador or a forty-dollar-a-month cowboy, whether Martita became a movie star or a poor man's wife, so long as they arrived at their destinations under their own steam.

But, of course, they weren't my children and the only rights I had to guide their lives were the rights I wrested from Ramón, and he who was repelled by my philosophy wasn't about to listen to my half-baked theories. He had no intentions of sacrificing his life to end up with a couple of grinning but poverty-stricken zambos who walked about barefoot and with their broken-zippered pants gaping. After one particularly brutal quarrel — I think it was over whether or not the children should have overcoats or ponchos (*"Ponchos? Ponchos,* for Christ's sake?" said Ramón. "You mean like the *Indians* wear?") — Ramón accused me of wanting to humiliate his children and deprive them of a decent education. Stunned by this insult, which was like a pail of water dashed into my face, appalled by the abyss that had opened between us by this stupid confusion between overcoats and education, I could only stare balefully at Ramón with disbelief. It was months before I ünderstood Ramón's terror of my ideas; he saw them as a threat against what was now his main purpose in life, the raising up of his children to the highest positions he was capable of imagining for them. It was months before I could speak freely to him about his children without revealing the resentment of an old man who has been robbed of his treasures and who, by being deprived of them, has at the same time been denied some great all-encompassing reason to keep on struggling. I felt for a time that, not only was I traveling to my final destination in a rotten-hulled boat, but by some trickery that left me sour and embittered I had even been robbed of the dignity of a final destination.

Now, as I lay on my back that Sunday afternoon staring at the ceiling and thinking of those children that I had let go of — those children, as perfect and as vulnerable as flowers, who must soon be molded into weird unnatural shapes, not only by the insensitive educational system of a poverty-oriented land, but also by the fanatic ambitions of their father — I suddenly remembered something dreadful that had happened a few months before, something that I had almost succeeded in forgetting, and now I realized that it hadn't been this week's senseless deaths one after another that had triggered my paranoia; it had begun much earlier. Two German tourists in a Volkswagen camper had wandered into the farm one afternoon: a mother and her almost thirty-year-old son. They were curious, lost people, obsessive travelers who had been wandering for years, and it seemed to me after I had talked to them for five minutes that what they were searching for so desperately was the particular pair of scissors with which they could cut the umbilical cord that still bound them together. I was drawn to the woman, who was being ground down and exhausted by her travels and whose face in its suffering was beginning to resemble the wonderful spare face of Isak Dinesen — all eyes and bone structure, all spirituality and death. We went over to my house to talk and little Moncho followed us; he wanted to listen to us make amusing and meaningless sounds in English. As we talked, Moncho grew drowsy in my lap and finally slept.

Late in the afternoon we left the house, and I warned my new friends to be careful on the steps, which were beginning to rot away. As I followed them with Moncho, still sleeping in my arms, his head draped over my shoulder, the top step suddenly burst apart, and Moncho and I went plunging through the staircase to the ground ten feet below. It was shock enough to find myself on the ground with my back practically broken, humiliated in front of strangers by my rotting house and having to pretend that nothing had happened, that I always came down the steps that way. But the real shock was in the meaning of the fall: this little boy for whom I had so much love and for whose safety I would gladly have given my own life could have been killed even as I held him in my sheltering arms. When in his whole life had he ever been safer? All my tender feelings immediately transformed into raging ones, I limped over to the dining room and began screaming at Ramón — but in a whisper so that only he would hear — tears of fury bursting from my eyes.

"Every day for over a year you have promised to get my house fixed; now see what your lies have done. Do you want to kill me? I guess if I am stupid enough to let you try I can't complain, but how dare you put your son's life in danger with your lies. Oh, Ramón, you liar, you lover of mañana, you country lout who puts off everything, who can't make a decent plan, whose word has no value. You *liar,* no?"

For once Ramón did not answer; he trembled and paled before this anger of mine that he had never seen before and grabbed up his son, who now, held in safer arms, gradually stopped weeping and slept again. It was too late now, but why had it never occurred to me until this moment that I might have dominated Ramón with fear and honest anger and ended up more in control of a disintegrating situation? I could still not plainly see the future, but now I knew that it wasn't going to be the future I had been planning, and perhaps one of its components from now on would be the growing isolation and loneliness of old age, as I withdrew from a life over which I was having less and less power. The next morning the carpenter replaced all the steps in my house and all the steps in all the other houses, but nothing happened to the roof; there seemed to be no connection between the two things.

I had had another illumination that never left me. As I lay crumpled and humbled beneath the staircase I felt a terrible guilt for my arrogance in thinking that I could have acted as a buffer between those two children and the obscene and senseless terrors of life. What a blow it was to realize that I was incapable of sparing them from a single tear, a single wail of terror, and to realize at the same time that no one, no one in the whole world, could spare them anything.

Well, well, well. What a day. I was being drenched in a kind of reality different from the rain of yesterday that I had longed to be drowned and cleansed in. I had come over to the house to sleep, not to construct a Robinson Crusoe list of self-pitying bitchings built around the fact that I was finally facing the fact that I had grown old. I would think no more but would cheer myself up by reading something light and gay, something frothy like Kafka or Camus. And I noted with bitter satisfaction as part of the local conspiracy that as soon as I picked up a book and tried to read a few pages heavy black clouds immediately gathered over the farm, so that inside the house it became almost like night. It began to rain — but naturally only over *us*. Across the river, a hundred yards away, the dry hills flamed in the last rays of sunlight; children shrieking like parrots splashed naked in the water below Gumercinda's house or ran round and round the drying clothes that lay along the grassy banks, patches of pure color like grace notes. Someone, it looked like Arcario, sat atop a great boulder at the edge of the river, motionless and abstracted, his chin cupped in his hands. Yes, he was too sad looking to be anyone but Arcario, who was now a bachelor again and would probably eat tonight in his mother's house.

Upstream — a few hundred yards past the last hill, where all the poor people had their farms — lay a great flat area of jungle and abandoned bananas, a tremendous farm deserted for thirty years. It had been taken over by the bank against an unpaid debt when the banana market had crashed, an event that coincided with the owner and his wife simultaneously discovering the pleasures of imported Scotch whiskey. He had lost the farm and hanged himself. The bank had put the land up for public auction at ten-year intervals, but no one had ever bid on it. For years one of the bank inspectors and several of the local people had been urging us to buy the property, but talking it over, Ramón and I had decided that it would be sheer insanity to extend ourselves, even if, as the banker hinted, we could have bought it all for less than five dollars an acre. We had over four hundred acres that we couldn't manage properly; what would we do with another seven hundred acres across the river, where during the rainy months it would be impossible or dangerously rash to cross over? Still, this evening as I stood in a dark and dripping house, deafened by the rain drumming on the big leaves outside, that glowing land across the river bathed in sunlight struck me as pure and poignant, reminding me of a more innocent time when we had thought to find simplicity and essentiality on our farm. Maybe it was over there, that quality I missed so desperately; though how odd that, if I really believed this, in four years I had never once crossed the river to walk back into the mystery of those seldom used trails, to test the vibrations of the land and to appraise firsthand the kind of challenge it might present. The farm was called Tierra Nueva, the New Land, but even as I stood studying it in the rain, enjoying the sound of its name, which promised another more uncomplicated beginning, the illusion of its uniqueness burst as the rain clouds surged across the river, darkening the land, and then blotting it out in sheets of slanting rain. The sun went out; Gumercinda in a flash gathered up the clothes, the children shrieking ran for shelter, and Arcario leaped off his rock, jumped into a canoe, and pushed out into the current. How stupid to think that things were different over there and that its isolation by a band of muddy water might have preserved it from contamination.

It rained hard all night, but perhaps not as hard on the farm as at Tiaune, a little gathering of grass huts some fifteen miles to the north toward Esmeraldas, where during the early hours of the night a flooding creek washed out the bridge across the highway and isolated the capital of the province for a couple of days. The thief who stole our chickens that night, while Ramón and Ester were the guests of honor at Segundo's wake and while I slept in the booming drum of my dripping house, did not know, of course, that all traffic had stopped and that none of the buses could get through. He had tied all our chickens, about fifty pounds of them, into two bunches by their legs, had hauled them up to the highway, tossed them into the high grass five feet from that flattened out spot where Segundo had died, and then crouched under the big leaves of a banana, where he smoked half a pack of cigarettes waiting for the bus that never came. We reconstructed his movements late the next afternoon when someone discovered the chickens and told us where they were. We scarcely wondered who the thief had been, the list of possibilities was so enormous now; we knew only that it hadn't been Víctor, who had the perfect alibi of his dead brother, or Alejandro, who a few weeks before had been sentenced to nine months in prison when he finally confessed to having stolen the canvas, the jack, and the typewriter and had even given the police the names of the people to whom he had sold the stuff.

Several of the chickens were dead when we brought them back to the store; they had smothered in those piles where they lay without water for eighteen hours. Anita, our enormous pet chicken, was still alive but just barely. We put out food and water and sat on the store benches, full of rage and hatred for the people, watching our poor flock as it staggered in the dust, eyes bloodshot, beaks gaping, feathers broken and askew, legs swollen and bloody, collapsing — a tattered band of survivors from a pogrom. They would never lay again. Anita, unable to walk, ate and drank resentfully from our hands, her eyes malevolent and unforgiving, her great heart broken. She died that night in her old box, where we had put her, and I found her in the morning with her head sunk on her breast but somehow still looking proud and regal, a memory of old memories, of a foolish time now tainted. One feels like a fool for giving one's heart to a chicken; one feels like a monster when one grieves more for a chicken than for dead Segundo.

Earlier that day while everyone in the area was attending the funeral of his choice, I stood on the bank of the river on our deserted farm and watched a large canoe with an outboard motor as it appeared upstream, drifting down and circling, circling in the current as though the motorista were drunk or feeling playful, wanting to write great curling figures over the water. A man in the bow, holding a long pole, leaned out over the edge, staring intently down into the water. Directly in front of me he suddenly shrieked and ran back through the canoe, clutching at something, something *clothed*. And now, the motor dead, the two men leaned into the river together and hauled and wrestled with their awful burden as the canoe silently drifted past the farm and disappeared around the first bend. Had I really seen this? Had it really happened? When Ramón came back from burying Segundo, he told me that six brothers in a canoe overloaded with bananas had overturned that morning a mile to the south of us; five of the brothers had drowned; the last male member of the family had been that shrieking man with the pole. That terrible tableau to which I had been the only witness became more and more obscene to me as time passed. Except for that short conversation with Ramón, I never heard this tragedy mentioned again by anyone. It was as if five leaves from a tree had fallen into the current and drifted away into oblivion. And later, out of a growing confusion, it seemed to me that since I alone had been witness to that man who had lost his brothers and since I alone had been pierced by his demented cry, out of some human decency I should now carry a burden, the memory of his loss, dragging up from time to time the sound of his piercing shriek as it echoed out over the water and lost itself in diminishing echoes among the unfeeling trees. It was a cry that was as much a curse flung into the face of God as anything I ever heard, or if it was not that at the time, it became so more and more as I listened to it, remembering, letting the cry become more my own, more my own accusation. Would that poor and suffering black man ever have the courage to face God with this crime? In case he didn't, he had a witness; I would speak for him.

Late that afternoon (I had escaped once more to the house, and once more, but this time emptied of all thought, I lay on the cot, staring at the bats) the helicopters began flying back and forth across the far end of the farm. There were two or three of them and they flew very low and slow, most of the time hidden behind the trees, passing back and forth over a long line that stretched between the two low hills that delineated our own horizon. Their great blades, beating the air, disturbed the quiet of the jungle with that queer, empty, arrogant, idiotic sound that helicopters make, the sound of Vietnam, agribusiness, and fat-cat oil executives. For a month we had read in the papers that the Texaco pipeline was completed and that very soon the oil would begin to flow to the seaport of Esmeraldas. Ecuador was about to become the second largest producer of petroleum in South America, and a great ceremony in town was being prepared, in which little flasks of oil would be presented to the local leaders and other flasks of more precious stuff would be consumed by the gallons. Today Texaco had filled up the line and was testing it for leaks; we had heard that one of the helicopters carried special electronic equipment for detecting any pipe joints that had been badly welded. Perhaps this was true, more likely it was an invention of the press. At any rate the helicopters missed a tiny hair crack in the line about a hundred yards from the south corner of our property. From the first day, though of course we didn't hear about this until a little later, a small but growing pool of oil appeared behind a bamboo country school out in the middle of one of Padovani's pastures, about fifty feet from the Viche River. At first only the little kids knew about the leak; then it became one of those blessings for the country people, who could now use free oil to start their fires of charcoal instead of buying expensive kerosene. I watched the helicopters for half an hour and then noticed that Arcario, beating his way through weeds, was approaching the house.

"*¿Puedo?*" Arcario called through the door at the top of the stairs.

"Ah, Cassius Clay, the great battler. Yes, come on in."

He was dressed to travel, in clean pressed pants and a wildly flowered shirt that I had never seen before, aflame in all the hottest colors. Now he owned three shirts, and for a year this new gorgeous production would appear only on Saturdays, then little by little, as it tore and faded, it would begin to replace his tattered working shirts.

"Two favors, Martín; don't turn me down, I beg you."

"O.K.," I said. "One is money; what's the other?"

"That you write a letter for me now. I want to take it in to Esmeraldas and send it on down with Occidental."

"To Susanna?"

"*Claro.*"

"Why did you hit her?" I asked. "Don't you realize she could kill you with one blow if she ever fought back?" Arcario, smiling inscrutably, said nothing. "Why did you hit her?" I asked again. "Why are you such a disgraceful animal?"

"She was believing some lies about me," Arcario said. "*Pendejadas.*"

"What lies? What pendejadas?"

"Absolutely nothing," Arcario said. "*Inventos de la gente.*" Inventions of the people. "That I was messing around with another woman, with the woman of Ortiz to be precise. Pure lies, pure inventions."

My God, yes. I had heard that story and only half listening had even heard that it was Arcario who had run off for a time with Ortiz's woman, a woman much younger than Ortiz but much older than Arcario. We had been occupied that week with other things closer to home and more depressing than the sexual confusion across the river. Arcario had been gone for a week, I knew that much, for he was supposed to have been working for us as a contratista, cleaning pastures, and had failed to show up. He had been back on the river for about four days, and it was just four days ago that Señor Ortiz had packed a little airline bag full of one-pound packages of table salt and walked off into the jungle with the intention of killing himself. We had heard that he had eaten two pounds of salt before he left his house, braving the raging sarcasms of his wife, who had just returned from Esmeraldas, and the horrified cries of two friends and his hired cowboy, all of them aghast at this sad dramatic madness. Had he eaten the other six pounds of salt? No one knew; no one even knew what to feel about this cuckolded neighbor of ours whose will to live had been destroyed. It was too bad; it was awful, but eating eight pounds of *salt?* People talked about it with solemn faces and then broke down into delighted laughter. Well, we heard he was back on the farm again, still alive, as pale as a ghost but already beginning to make a bitter and tentative peace with the woman who had betrayed him.

"But isn't the story true?"

Arcario shook his head. "Inventos, inventos."

He was wearing the evidence that would give him away, but it took me a minute to put the two things together, and we stood there staring at one another, Arcario probing my gullibility with his eyes while things clicked together in my head. I knew he had had no money the week before, for I had been unable to give him the *anticipo* for his work that he had asked for. And now he was wearing a brand new twelve-dollar shirt. Of course. I was turning into a psychologist as profoundly competent as Ramón, who could sniff out crimes from the unlikely new shoes on someone's feet or the unexpected smells of pork steaks frying in an unlikely hut.

"That's quite a shirt you're wearing, *adu.* About the wildest one I ever saw."

"Yes, isn't it cool?" Arcario said, holding out his arms and examining the swirling shimmering designs with admiration.

"But don't you feel a little ashamed to be whoring for new clothes?"

"Ah, Martín, don't speak so crudely. It wasn't that way at all. I asked her for nothing until she offered it."

I went over to the typewriter, put a sheet of paper into the machine, and asked, "O.K., what do you want to say?"

"This," Arcario answered immediately, having been composing

this letter for the last twenty-four hours. "Hurry up back; I've been bitten by a machaca.* Signed, Arcario Cortez."

We both laughed, delighted with his smartness. "What a sly toad," I said, and wrote, "My dearest love: Forgive me. I am truly sorry. I have been an animal. It is you I love, only you. Hurry back, I beg you; I have just been bitten by a machaca." "Sign here," I said and he did, a five-minute job. I wrote Susana's name on the outside of an envelope, which Arcario would send by bus to the busline office in Guayaquil. Arcario was now the second Ecuadorian I had met in eight years who had apologized for something that he had done. No matter that he didn't know it or that if he had been able to read he would not have agreed to send a note so lacking in the macho virtues. "And now that other thing. How much money do you want?"

"One bill," Arcario said, which doubly translated means four dollars.

As he stood in the door, ready to leave, glowing in his shirt like that outside sunset and made more radiant yet by the good feel of money in his hand, I glanced across the river at the great trees on the spine of the hill, the late sun shining on their frozen branches; they were waiting for me, I suddenly realized. "Now it's my turn for a favor," I said. "Take me across the river tomorrow in your canoe. Up to Tierra Nueva. I want to walk back into that land."

"Claro," Arcario said. "Encantado. I'll be coming back from Esmeraldas on the first bus in the morning. Is six o'clock too early?"

"No, that's perfect. Now one more thing, Arcario. Stay on your toes for a while, you hear. Think about being ambushed; old men don't like to have young men screwing their wives."

He fumbled beneath his shirt and drew out from his belt a short, battered kitchen knife and flashed it back and forth before my face, smiling but trying to look tough. "Nobody molests Arcario Cortez," he said.

"He's not a poor man," I said. "He's not going to kill you with

---

* A flying insect known as the *chuchora machacu* in the Amazon basin, but called the *machaca* in coastal Ecuador. Its fatal sting is legendary, but now a cure has been found: sexual intercourse within twenty-four hours. This would seem to be hard on priests, nuns, and children, though I have heard that priests may save their lives by coupling with nuns (and vice versa) in this most menacing situation.

a knife. If he doesn't shoot you himself he'll hire a Manabita for 500 sucres to slice your head off."

"*¿Qué va?*" Arcario snorted. "With those two great dogs of mine that sleep underneath the house?" He owned two of the skinniest, most pathetic-looking dogs that I had ever seen.

"What a macho whore," I said. "Run along and mail your letter; I'll see you in the morning."

He turned to leave, hesitated, and faced me again. "Look, Martín, this is just between the two of us; it is a very delicate thing. What happened is not her fault or mine, and I am in no danger from Ortiz. He knows where the blame lies and that he drove her to it. It has been years since he has been able to do anything with her."

After Arcario had left and I sat there thinking about the infinite capacity of people to complicate their lives, two down-to-earth thoughts occurred to me: What would Ortiz do if he were bit by a machaca? What would have happened to his wife's sanity if she had fallen in love with Santo instead of Arcario?

On Bone's farm, about a mile upstream, Jorge Cortez murdered his wife that night sometime after midnight. By six o'clock the next morning when Arcario walked down the long lane from the bus and waited for me on a bench in front of the store, the horrifying news was just beginning to spread with mysterious swiftness up and down the river, but by some intricate chain of coincidences he met no one who had yet heard about his brother. As we crossed the river, we had no idea that Jorge had crossed it three hours before and that he was watching us from where he lay hidden in the tall grass behind his mother's hut, his hair, his shirt, his pants, caked with drying blood.

We left the canoe on a little beach where the Male creek enters the river, and Arcario led me upstream along the river trail and then off at a ninety-degree angle along a smaller, more overgrown trail that cut away from the river toward the mountains. We walked through an old pasture that was heavily overgrown with caña brava and second-growth acacias, the same pasture where Jorge's cows had been macheted by his jealous neighbors who now claimed possession of the grass. We came to an old abandoned banana plantation that stretched long and narrow between the Male creek and the high trees of the Esterilla farm, which formed the southern boundary. The plantation was shaded with the fast-growing pulpy trees that have no value as wood: *mambla, ceibo,* rubber, *higua.* All of the valuable trees had been stolen. A long steep hill on the other side of the creek ran the length of the farm, boiling over with enormous trees, and all along that hillside we could hear dozens of pairs of *guacos,* male and female, screaming at each other and filling the morning air with their idiotic squabblings. "Do you know what they're saying?" Arcario asked me. "Listen, the female is saying, '*trabaja, trabaja, trabaja* — work, work, work — and the macho is saying, *¿Para qué? ¿Para qué? ¿Para qué?* — What for? What for? What for?' " I listened, laughing; that was exactly what they were saying, those great black and white Esmeraldas birds as large as hawks, so accurately reflecting the deepest feelings of the people.

We walked back through the old abandoned farm for almost an hour, almost without speaking. From time to time I asked for and was immediately given the names of strange trees or plants, with which, by the hundreds, Arcario was intimately acquainted. Once he stopped and said, "This is what I like to do more than anything; walking these trails really makes me feel good. Why don't you give me a job just walking out in the jungle? Up there ahead of us, on the Mafua creek, is where I was born and grew up with my brothers, where everything was quiet and the river was full of fish. My mother still spends half her time out there, planting tobacco and *avas* or trapping fish."

We reached the end of the bananas and stood at the edge of a great area of virgin forest. Enormous black-trunked trees stood closely together, and it was so dark and shaded that the brush was sparse, and in spots the black soil showed. We stood there peering into the gloom, making a conscious decision to go into it, as if we were deciding to dive off the twenty-foot board into icy water.

"Do you want to go on?" Arcario asked, and at this instant, from a sunny spot thirty feet ahead of us that glowed like flames, Arcario's youngest brother, Amado, the Beloved, slowly and tentatively rose up from behind a clump of weeds. Shading his eyes he peered at us.

"Are you alone?" he called softly.

"What's happening?" Arcario called.

"Keep it quiet," Amado said, "get over here fast."

Behind him, his mother and Jorge's young sons rose up from the weeds where they had been hiding and faced us. "It's Ortiz," I said. "He's after your ass."

Crouching down, Arcario raced through the grass and I watched him talking to his mother and to Amado; their faces were expressionless but tense with the effort to control their fear. Their eyes held a certain glazed, stupid quality that they transmitted to Arcario as he listened. All that morning I had been casually conscious that we were in Ortiz's territory, that we were back there someplace, perhaps very close to the very spot where he had gone with his salt to kill himself. It wasn't very likely that he had seen us crossing the river, but now I was half convinced that he was out there with a gun and the hot desire to take a shot at Arcario. Arcario turned to me and called, "Get down; hide yourself. There are two men out here with guns who want to kill my mother."

Squatting in the weeds I strained to hear and understand the low mumble of their voices. Even when they were talking directly at me, loud and clear, I could scarcely understand their jungle lingo. Now I understood nothing. Except that we probably weren't hiding from Ortiz. I had walked into some foolish domestic situation where apparently my life was in danger or, if not that, where I might be obliged to be witness to a murder. In a most unlikely place and at a most unlikely time, I was becoming involved with those people across the river who had always lived in my mind as free, placid, and uncomplicated and whose only preoccupation would have been (I thought) their sophisticated partnership with the jungle. In less than an hour on this other side of the river, where I had come to experience or appraise the wild honest freedom of this peaceful, enormous, and almost empty land that had been sleeping before my eyes for years, its blemishes smoothed away by the width of the river, I found myself, my mind blown by its improbability, hiding in the weeds so as not to get shot at.

Arcario was standing over me with his family lined up behind him. "Come on," he said. "We have to cross the creek and go back on another trail. Don't worry, they won't be waiting there. I'll explain as we go." The little kids with their enormous dazed eyes stood close against the legs of their grandmother, as though they would have liked to hide beneath her skirt. Arcario's mother, with her punched in face and flaring nostrils, gave me a pathetic smile, her attention wandering. She was probably much more devastated by the realization that two of her sons were now murderers than by any thought that she was being hunted. Moving as quickly as we could, we cut down off the path and began macheteing our way through the old banana planting, through a tangle of vines and brush. We stumbled and clawed our way down a small cliff overgrown with vines and expensive hothouse exotics, a sheer face dripping with water and black, glistening, loosely set rocks and long exposed roots that tore free as we clung to them, trying to let ourselves down. We walked through the creek for a hundred yards or so, sometimes jumping from rock to rock, sometimes wading through pools waist deep. Except for some of the earliest Tarzan movies, I had never seen a jungle stream more beautiful or more cleverly arranged to give a rebirth to my earliest fantasies about life on the equator; all of this was given a terrific reality by the fact that I was being guided away from danger by my trusty black companion, Arcario. A wild toucan, one of the few I had ever seen, its great Manabitan beak breaking the air before it, dove across the narrow strip of sky above us. Sweating and panting we finally climbed out of the gorge into a flat area and entered a grove of trees that shaded the ground, and a few hundred feet from the creek we came to an abandoned trail that appeared and disappeared as we moved along it. We stopped for a minute and Arcario began to explain.

Adelina was dead. About three o'clock in the morning, the old woman who had been asked to stay in his mother's house to take care of the chickens was awakened by Jorge. She lit a candle and opened the door to him and stood there speechless with horror. His clothes were soaked in blood. And his face — there was something wrong with his face. It was like looking into a pool of night. He had come looking for Arcario, who had gone to Esmeraldas. Two of Adelina's uncles had resolved to avenge her murder by killing Jorge's mother; Jorge sent the old woman running up the river trail to find Amado and send him out to the Mafua lean-to to find his mother and his children and bring them in. That was about all we knew out there on the Tierra Nueva farm that morning as we hurried out of its shaded menace and confusion. Arcario brought us all back to the river, took me across to the farm, and crossed back again to manage the family councils; he was now, at twenty-two, the head of the family. Later that same day we heard that more than once his mother had been viewed through gunsights, but that finally the two furious men had begun to talk together; they had decided that to kill that old woman in her innocence would be truly evil. They had decided to spare her.

The rest of Jorge's story came down to us little by little as time passed. Like a man slashing weeds, Jorge had brought down his wife; he had cut her down with two machete strokes and stood over her with his rage dying as her blood ran away. Her last act was contemptuous; she had cursed him with her eyes and put him in her power. As he watched her he knew that he could not escape but would be pulled back by that last dying look, which pierced and enslaved him. He had tried to run, cutting up through our plantings of bananas to the highway with the idea of catching a bus to Esmeraldas, where he might cross the river at the ocean and escape up the beach to Tumaco in Colombia. Maybe he was already thinking of how he could find his brother, José, who was also wanted for murder and hiding in another country. But when the bus came and stopped for him his feet had refused to move. He was literally paralyzed by the power of Adelina's curse. Not that he would have been allowed to enter the bus if he had been able to, for the driver's assistant was screaming, "Go; go; go," even before the bus had fully stopped, and he was hysterically trying to close the door against the tall, blood-drenched Negro who had stepped out of the woods and stood there with staring eyes, with one arm raised over his head, like something out of a nightmare.

Jorge went back to his cabin and hid outside it and watched the crowds of people as they began to gather, some with flashlights, some with candles or lamps made out of coffee cans — all this moving light focused on the hut, growing brighter as time passed, as more and more people arrived, and the growing sound of their cries and curses filled the night. Jorge was powerless to leave, he lay there in the brush, exhausted, half dead, the light going out of his eyes, his brain going numb. He was held by the feeling now that somehow he had been moved into the very center of all that light and sound, the wildly waving flashlight beams and the wail-

ings of the women and Adelina's relations out of their minds with
rage, cursing and screaming and beating the ground. It was as
though he were watching his own death; he began to cry.
Abruptly, as though he were being switched off, he fell asleep.
When he awoke a few minutes later, two of Adelina's uncles had
arrived from downstream; they carried rifles and stood together in
the darkness with other members of the family, about fifteen feet
from Jorge. They were all talking of what must be done. They
couldn't kill Jorge for he was probably miles away by this time;
killing Arcario or Amado would probably start a feud that would
wipe out both families. A woman had died; why couldn't another
woman pay? They would kill Jorge's mother. Someone, one of
the women, knew for a fact that she had left her house on the
river and had gone back into the jungle for a few days, to her little
farm on the Mafua creek, with two of her grandsons. Jorge lay
there and listened to them discuss the merits of killing his mother
and his two sons, and after a long time he heard them decide that
the death of his mother would be sufficient to wipe out the stain on
their honor. When it was all worked out, bottles of aguardiente
were passed around and Adelina's uncles squatted in the dirt outside the house, drinking and cursing and spitting. At first dawn
they would cross the river and walk back to the Mafua farm.

So Jorge had to move again. It was the hardest thing he had
ever done — pushing himself up from the ground, getting to his
feet, quietly, quietly, moving away from the house and cutting back
through the bushes and down to the river. He walked along the
shore until he found an unchained canoe and stole it and floated
down the river, slowly crossing it by paddling with his hands. On
the beach below Arcario's house he almost began to cry again.
Arcario's canoe was gone, Arcario and Susana were gone, the shack
was empty. He climbed further up the hill to his mother's hut and
sent the terrified old woman who finally opened the door to him
running up the river trail to find Amado and send him to the Mafua
lean-to to warn his mother and his children and bring them in.

For years we had been drinking the river water, hauling it up in
buckets to the kitchen, where very gradually that coffee-colored
sludge would lose its burden of silt and become transparent. In
the mornings there would be a half inch of muck at the bottom of

the bucket, but the water would seem to be as clear and pure as
rain water. Boiling the water also seemed to precipitate out those
impurities that made one reluctant to regard it as water at all but
rather as some ominous soup for nourishing all the tropical diseases that ravaged the people and set the drums to booming for
the dead children. In the week of quiet days that followed
Adelina's death, made quieter and duller for me by an attack of
what was probably malaria, I scarcely left my house, and in a kind
of benign delirium the idea of our life here on the river became
entangled in a dreamlike way with that murky river water that
clarified itself with tranquility. I could never make the comparison work, and as I dozed I struggled with this analogy of trying to
see our life here as the clear water that became polluted and murky
with the violent agitation of our passions. Lying in bed, gently
sweating, I tried more accurately to identify the filth that darkened
the water. Of what did it consist? Was it in our actions, in our
minds? Or was it something sprinkled over the lenses of our
ethnic spectacles that made us see evil in the natural processes? I
never did succeed in threading my way through this labyrinth and
lost interest in doing so when Ramón finally brought me the pills
that would cure me. Still, one little thought (perhaps the one that
made confusion out of all the rest) stayed in my mind: the water
dipped from the river was no more deadly to drink than the same
water the morning after, when its impurities had settled out. It
was life itself that one died from.

We had a whole week of quiet days, during which many things
came to an end and many things came to a new beginning. We
shut down the farm and buried all the dead and even celebrated
novenas for most of them. Jorge decided to give himself up to the
police. He wanted to by-pass the local *rurales* in Viche, where the
possibility existed that he might be treated capriciously or sadisti-
cally, and so he waited until one night when he could sneak
through the town on the darkened bus without being seen and
when one of his brothers could go with him to Esmeraldas to turn
him over in a dignified, almost ritualistic way. Susana came back
to Arcario from Guayaquil, leaving the same night that she received his note, as soon as she had found someone who could read
it to her. Cantante came to the house where Cira was now cooking

for us; he was distraught with worry and looking for the sympathy
that Cira had always given him. His other woman was sick and
hemorrhaging. When he told her, Cira looked deep into his eyes
with the total rejection of a feigned loathing and said, "And do you
think I give a good horseshit?" and left him on the outside porch,
his mouth gaping with astonishment. A new respect was born that
afternoon but a reconciliation was still months away.

It was Pastór who disintegrated before our eyes. It came into his
mind that there was something shameful in his wife's having left
him and that by having done so she had exposed some secret flaw
of his to the general public. Now when he was sober he became
shy and solitary, and we began to hear reports that, when anyone
passed on the trail that ran past his front door, he would begin
talking in an intimate voice to prove that he was not alone but, on
the contrary, passionately engaged. "No, no, my love," he would
say softly, "don't cry. Of course I love you, my sweet. Dry your
eyes, my dear one. Here, let me kiss away the tears." His amused
or confused or incredulous neighbor having moved a little further
down the trail, Pastór's voice would rise. "Ah, my darling, that's
the way. Give me a smile, doll. Here, eat this cracker; open your
mouth; I've spread it with a bit of your favorite cheese." And
now yelling, wanting to be heard, peering through the cracks in
the wall at his departing neighbor, "I will buy you dresses. I will
buy you shoes, my bird, my love, my little doll." And then a final
shriek. "I will buy you two blue pots!"

What a tumble that poor man took. When we first came here
he was almost a community leader, in friendly competition with
Mercedes in trying to bring a little order to the village. He was the
manager of the fútbol team and a landowner who had no need to
work for daily wages. At the end he was the village's buffoon, a
humbled drunkard who ate and slept in anybody's house, accepting kindness like a homeless dog. He tried desperately for a time
to reconstruct his life but always blew it with a foolish lie or a petty
theft or some monumental binge at the most inappropriate moment. It was a month or two after the ending of this story that he
began to exhibit himself on Saturday nights in the salones up and
down the river. Later he would end up unconscious. Or he would
stumble down to the river's edge and sing heartbreaking love songs
in a voice completely unlike him, a voice of incredible purity and

sweetness. Male, this ribald little village, half corrupted by its easy access to the sophistications of Esmeraldas or Guayaquil, was more amused than shocked by Pastór when he would unbutton his trousers and slap his virile member on the table, among the candles, the playing cards, and the little spilled pools of aguardiente, and invite his neighbors to inspect and certify his manhood. "There she is, ladies and gentlemen," he would shout. "Who says I'm not a man? Ten inches, by God. I'm not trying to fool anyone. If anyone can better me, let him step up." In Male the people laughed or laughed it off. In Rioverde, where the Male fútbol team had gone to play a return match, the rigid country people with their decent sense of propriety were simply appalled at this unspeakable grossness. Late the next afternoon after the Sunday game, when Male invited Rioverde to set a date for a rematch on the farm, they declined with dignity. Rioverde would have no truck with perverts. Pastór was obviously no Catholic; he was probably even a Mason.

The great psychologist Ramón Prado, who could find the hidden truth in the flicker of an eyelid, reconstructed the beginning of that final day. Why should I disbelieve him or even doubt an explanation so drenched in probability? His version was certainly more logical than the first official reaction of the government, which deployed squads of specially trained parachutists and elite, guerrilla ranger-types all around the farm that afternoon, all of them carrying submachine guns and beating the bushes for subversive terrorists.

"All those little kids are out there behind the school," Ramón said. "They're just fooling around, waiting for the teacher to ring her bell. That little pool of oil is as big as this table now, five feet across and maybe a foot deep in the middle where the gas in the pipeline bubbles up. All the mothers have sent their children to school with little buckets or gourds to dip up the oil and bring it home, and now one of the kids, thinking of that fire they make in the morning, wraps some dead banana leaves around a stick, makes a torch, and lights it. He waves it around chasing his friends; they shriek with delight and begin to make their own torches. And then one of them, re-dipping his still-burning torch into the pool of oil, sets the whole thing ablaze where the gas bubbles up like farts in the water, and God knows how long it burns like that before it all heats up and the fire hits the line and the whole damn thing explodes and splits wide open."

So I was in my house that morning about nine o'clock, fully dressed for the first time in perhaps a week but feeling cured of whatever fever I had had, standing by the big windows on the river side, moodily staring down into those chocolate eddies, when a low devouring roar began behind the house and behind the little hill. Peering out through the trees, I could see that to the south, west, and east, the sky was absolutely black and roiling with what looked like a long line of encircling atomic clouds, a tremendous line of boiling clouds shooting upwards with terrific speed, in black, violently agitated columns. Except for that blackness it looked exactly like the final shot of *Dr. Strangelove*.

It never occurred to me that the Texaco pipeline had blown up and that fifty-thousand barrels of oil were now pouring into the Viche creek and almost encircling the farm. From our river, below the last hill, it was impossible to see that three-mile-long stretch of creek full of oil, sending up a solid row of one-hundred-foot-high flames just behind the trees that bordered Celso's farm or meandered at the edge of Padovani's pastures. All I could see from the house was that absolutely intimidating line of clouds, which instantly convinced me that we were about to be engulfed in some great natural catastrophe. I had dropped hundreds of tons of bombs on Berlin, set Orly ablaze, ripped up the secret factories of V-2 bombs at Peenemünde, or tried to. I had led hundreds of planes one day over Posen, where, because I was pissing in my pants with terror, we had missed the Messerschmidt plant and hit the marshalling yards instead. It was full that day with a thousand freight cars loaded with German munitions, and I was one of the few soldiers in the war who had ever been decorated for hitting the wrong target. I, who had participated in some of the greatest violences of the twentieth century could not now imagine what I saw exploding before my eyes. We were about to be torn asunder in some elemental whirlwind, some final judgment of chaos and destruction, annihilated in a wall of boiling vengeance from out of which at any moment the figure of a raging God could be expected to emerge. *Oh, daddy, daddy, you bastard, why were you never fair?*

I rushed over to the store and Ester, who was standing in the road outside it, staring up the hill, turned to me in confusion and cried, "For the love of God, what is it?"

"It's a hurricane," I said. "What else? Where are the children? Find them. Put them in the store underneath the counter. Cover them with blankets. Where's Ramón?"

"He went to Esmeraldas early this morning."

"Find the children," I yelled again and ran up the hill, curiously calm, curiously elated, toward that inevitable death behind the little hill. At least we would all be going together. On a more spiteful level I felt as though I had won something, or if not won, at least driven my opponent into such a rage that he had now ended the game by sweeping the board clean and tipping the pieces into my lap. One thing was obvious; it was all over. How crazy. There was an element of comfort in running toward those black boiling clouds and knowing that finally everything was being taken out of our hands. How crazy. How funny. It was like that afternoon on the Andes road when I lay in my blood and felt the springs and cables going slack, the tension running out, life dissolving into eternity.

From the top of the first hill, the ring of flames shooting up behind the trees across the horizon was clearly visible. The crackling roar of the fire, the crashing of branches, the dirty crankcase smell of burned oil now falling all around like rain — everything was suddenly clear. We were not the doomed and noble players brought low by hubris in some divine drama. We were nothing more than the clowns in an ugly farce financed by the Texaco Oil Company, now making an ecological statement, an immediately forgotten headline in Quito's *El Comercio*. It was almost a letdown, a disappointment, which nevertheless I immediately adjusted to.

I walked further up the lane to the middle of the coconuts and sat down by the road with my back against a coconut palm where I could observe the spectacle. It occurred to me that a grandiose and dramatic death for me was simply going to be out of the question; I would be killed like one of Graham Greene's characters who died in Naples when a pig fell on him from the third story of a tenement house and whose mourning friends, when they heard the details, were convulsed by fits of uncontrollable laughter. I sat there waiting for Ramón, pleasantly drowsy.

And now, really, honest to God, like the last three minutes of a Fellini movie, the whole chaotic morning turned into delightful and graceful clownishness. Here they came, the people of Male prancing up the road to see the woods ablaze and to savor this newest disaster with all their senses. Behind Mercedes, the town leader, Uldarico, Pastór, Santo; the two brothers, Demetrio and Julián; the last of the Cortez brothers, Arcario and Amado. From out of the woods to join the crowd — Víctor, Adolfo, young Antonio. They had been out there stealing something, and in a few days we would know that it was the barbed-wire fences. Pedro Lamilla and his son Ysidro, with his incredibly wide, corn-fed, idiot smile. But they were *all* smiling and their perfect teeth shone in their black faces, and their bodies gave off sparks as though each were a generator whose function was to produce life, joy, and excitement. Shirt tails flying, their ragged work pants ripped from hip to ankle or patched with scarlet or electric-blue flowered fabrics robbed from the women's shirts. And the women, with their hard sulky faces but screeching with delight, walked in the shadows of the men, separate. Their hair, cut as short as a boy's, was as hard as a helmet made of rowed screws, and behind their smiles, deep in their eyes, there was some ultimate cynicism, as though they were saying, "Ah, you men, and now you have set the woods on fire, now you have fucked everything up again. But don't worry, we will pick up after you, we will put everything back where it belongs." Elsa, Lidia, Maria, Fulvia, Lurdi — Lurdi, incredibly beautiful, with the deep tranquil eyes of a Madonna and the slow knowing smile of a whore. Dici, Erlinda, Mari, Susanna, and, panting behind the rest, the great garbage barge Rosa. Almost all of them were packing babies, and around them — like little planets circling a galaxy of suns — the children. Little Vernaldo, limping Byron with a sliver in his foot, Mario, Carlito, Lolita, Panchita, Mártire, Dário.

Here they came, the tiger pack, the beautiful teenage dudes, the still-yawning late sleepers with their vacant, unflawed faces upon which life had so far left but one message: "I burn." The slim loungers, the lanky brawlers, high stepping, magnificent, aping the smart, cool hipness of the Guayaquil marijuaneros. Donald, Tomás,

Stalin, Alfredo, Marco, Pepe, and Lucho. The ghost of dead Barry danced with them alongside crooked Chango, whose crooked smile seemed innocent now with the excitement of the moment.

Here came the workers, their machetes cradled in their arms; held thus, there was no menace in those curving knives. They smiled and winked wickedly at me as they passed, sure that they could quit early on a day like today when the woods blazed and the sun was going out and it looked like maybe the world was coming to an end. If it didn't, we would pay them for the good intentions they had shown in coming to work. Chila, Quevedo — the supermacho with the cheap, purple tatoos across his chest almost invisible against his black skin. José Artiaga, Hermán, Adolfo — the *cuco,* the spook, a horribly ugly man with great, square, yellow teeth and a smile of pure evil. He was the sweetest, most helplessly incompetent man in the province. Where had he ever found that wicked mask?

"Come on, hombre, get up off your ass; come with us," they called.

"No," I answered, "I am observing American progress; I am studying good old Yankee know-how. Look at those clouds; they're up to twenty thousand feet; look how they're turning white on top. That's ice, man. Texaco has brought ice to Esmeraldas. *Viva el progreso. Viva, viva.*"

"Oh, man, don't talk crazy. Come with us."

I shook my head and waved them on. I could not go with them; I had come to a decision, and I must wait here by the road to tell Ramón. Until this moment I had never felt so manipulated, so like a character in a vaguely surrealist comedy that was now obviously coming to an end. In that instant on the tractor when I had swung around to see Segundo's dying body floating through the air, seeing it with my own eyes instead of Ramón's, I had begun to know that I must leave this place. I had loused things up again. By playing a passive role, by choosing to remain uninvolved, I had inevitably become the most superfluous element in the rush and passion of this wild, jungle life. Ramón, who in a few weeks would with tears of exasperation in his eyes accuse me of never having touched a poor man, would see into the very heart of my dilemma, and because I had thought it a secret I would tremble with rage at his words.

But wouldn't part of my anger have grown out of that feeling that it was Ramón's as much as my own — what? — timidity, fear, laziness, superficiality that had separated me from much that I didn't want to be separated from? I had come with every intention of living here until I died. How could I have chosen to live a second-hand life with my emotions filtered through another sensibility? Goddamnit, I was not some white voyeur who got his kicks from peering through the leaves at the writhing bodies of poor, ignorant, and suffering blacks.

I was leaning against a coconut palm out in the middle of our farm, watching the black upward-rushing clouds and the white ice clouds forming at their summits while I denied to myself that my motives for being here were base. And as I thought it my whole body began to heave and tremble, and I could feel something that was both guilty and joyous beginning to build in my chest, some-thing that could only come out as a great cry. I lifted my hands and coolly watched their violent trembling.

It was Ramón who out of love had tried to protect me from the dangers, the humiliations, and the ugliness; he had stood between me and these things. It was Ramón who out of love had said, "Don't go in there . . . Don't talk to Orestes; he wants to screw you . . . Let me handle this; go in the house . . . Keep your eyes straight ahead and keep going . . . Step on the gas." It was Ramón who had done my dirty work, who had beaten down Alejandro with a machete and almost killed him, who had cleared the farm of his father and his brothers, who had tossed Dalmiro out into the weeds like a broken bird because he was pissing on a dance floor upon which I was dancing at the time. He had guarded what he thought was my dignity and my honor. In a sense it was Ramón's growing aliena-tion from his own people that had set me apart. He didn't *want* me to dirty my hands by touching a poor man.

Suddenly, and now the tears began gushing from my eyes, I re-membered a midnight many years before when I had been called to Ramón's shack on the beach at Rioverde. He and Ester were dy-ing of malaria, and I spent an hour in that tiny room where they lay huddled together on a shelf of split bamboo with everything they owned piled around them. Walking back down the beach through the high-tide breakers, wet to my waist, I had begun to

shriek and sob. Part of that grief had been simple rage against God
and the criminally idiot way he had arranged the world; part was
the terror of contemplating their deaths; and part was an absolute
self-loathing. I had discovered in the midst of my rage and fear a
throbbing joy. I noticed the light of the candle as it wavered against
the wall, how it left the faces of my friends in darkness; I noticed
the stink of the blankets and how their arms glistened with sweat; I
listened to the breakers shuddering on the beach and the sound of
the wind in the palms. I made a list of the things that they had piled
around them in the bed to guard: a pair of pants, a half-pint jar of
watermelon seeds, a rusty flit-gun, a pail of ground corn, an incredibly scruffy plaster-of-Paris dog, chipped and peeling. As I
stood there contemplating these awful things, plunged into despair,
that joy that set me trembling had come, and the whole shack began to blaze with grandeur and with meaning. Another part of me,
entirely separate, a part I had always hated, was delighted with the
drama of this moment and the transmutation of life into art; even
as I stood there I had begun to search for the words that would describe their deaths. I would write it down. I wanted to share my
terror. And now, once again, I was being filled with that same delight. I shook and sobbed with joy as suddenly my whole life here
began to form a pattern closely interwoven with all those running
figures who had passed along the road. I began to see the lives of
the people as long, long melodic lines, a hundred songs woven together — tragic, stupid, ribald, wickedly funny.

Everyone had passed, and I sat alone in the middle of the farm,
thinking of the incredible Male opera with the new certainty that I
must write about it. It was quiet except for the distant sound of the
burning jungle. But now, bawling like a foghorn, her eyes rolling
in dismay, some half-digested somethings — pillowcases, brassieres,
or underwear — hanging from her mouth, Ramona, our pet cow.
She had come running behind the people, looking for companionship and feeling deserted and troubled beneath an ominous sky from
which ashes, bits of burned grass, and the charred remains of leaves
had begun to fall mixed with the scum of burned oil that would turn
the river into a rainbowed, gunmetal oil slick. Ramona was a community animal who wandered free, up and down the river, and it
had been some time since I had seen her. We had been worried

about her because she seemed to loathe animals and identified only with people. But apparently she had learned that she was a cow; she was pregnant. She bleated and kicked her hind legs in the air with pleasure when she saw me, came galloping up to gore me with love, and I fled before her, around and around among the coconuts, until she grew bored with the game. She lay down in the shade and I lay down beside her, using her great gurgling stomach as a head-rest. We were waiting for Ramón.

We were resting in the center of a U-shaped area, almost completely encircled by flames. But there was still an opening toward the river. I couldn't see the river, which lay below the lip of the hill, but the long line of great trees that formed one boundary of the Tierra Neuva property glistened in the sunlight under a patch of clear blue sky. For a week I had been thinking of that land and of the creek we had fled down, just ahead of those furious men with guns, and of that long, wild hillside alive with the calls of birds. The remembering was all mixed up and confused, because of that malarial fever, with those memories out of my youth when I had been charged and changed by reading *Treasure Island* or *Green Hell* or *Typee* or *Lord Jim,* when I had been, like old Bill Swanson, undone by the lure of the tropics. Well, on one level it was suddenly all clear.

I must leave this farm to Ramón and let him run it in his own exuberant and improvisatory way. He must have his chance to live free of my domination. And vice versa. I had subverted my own impulses for too long, but now I was going to see things through my own eyes. Ramón was no longer going to be the hero of my life; I was going to be the hero of my own life at last. I would buy those seven hundred acres across the river and build a little house on it. I wanted to work the land and dominate the trees and clean out a long rectangle that would lie clean and grassy in the sun from the river to the mountains. I wanted to begin again with the jungle and examine it with more patience; perhaps, after all, it would have something to tell me. I felt that if I went out alone and stood alone in the menace of the trees and gave myself over to the leaves I might, for a moment at least, be moved with awe or terror. And I wanted to begin again with the people. They had something that they were wild to share with me; I had only realized it in that moment when I observed my trembling hands and knew that I was happy and that that joy had grown out of a sudden visualization of the lives of the people as a complex but flowing musical line, as something beautiful and heart-breaking that I must try to put down on paper — and share. It would end on the day that the pipeline exploded and the rivers ran with fire and the people went dancing up the road.

I was tired of waiting for Ramón, and I wanted to go running behind the people and stand with them at the edge of the flames. I could imagine what they would say. "Oh, man, isn't this awful? Christ, man, this is heavy stuff. Life. Christ, man, life, isn't it just shit? Isn't it all just a great pile of shit?" And with their eyes, their faces, their skin, their feet, they would be saying, "Oh, Christ, man, what a gas. Isn't it wonderful; isn't life wonderful?" And with their waving arms they would embrace it all: the trees, the flames, the river, the clouds, sunshine and wind.

Ramona turned her head, observed me gravely with her enormous eyes, and belched in my face. And at that moment, driving down the hill through the smoke, Ramón appeared. When he saw me, his face broke into a great smile, and he laughed and yelled at me, pointing back to the towering black clouds that by now had completely obscured the sun, "Hombre, hermano, and *now* what the hell have you gone and done?"

Tierra Nueva
Esmeraldas
25 November 1976

o well-disposed light
o fresh source of light
those who invented neither gunpowder nor compass
those who tamed neither steam nor electricity
those who explored neither sea nor sky
but without whom the earth would not be the earth
We the hump growing more benign
as more and more the earth abandons its own
we the silo
storing to ripen
all of the earth that belongs most to the earth
my negritude is not a stone
nor deafness flung out against the clamour of the day
my negritude is not a white speck of dead water
on the dead eye of the earth
my negritude is neither tower nor cathedral

it plunges into the red flesh of the soil
it plunges into the blazing flesh of the sky
my negritude riddles with holes
the dense affliction of its worthy patience.

Heia for the royal Kailcedrate!
Heia for those who have never invented anything
those who never explored anything
those who never tamed anything

those who give themselves up to the essence of all things
ignorant of surfaces but struck by the movement of all
    things
free of the desire to tame but familiar with the play of the
    world

AIMÉ CÉSAIRE, *Return to My Native Land*